THE CRITICAL LIFE
OF TONI MORRISON

Literary Criticism in Perspective

Brian Yothers, Series Editor
(University of Texas at El Paso)

About Literary Criticism in Perspective

Books in the series *Literary Criticism in Perspective* trace literary scholarship and criticism on major and neglected writers alike, or on a single major work, a group of writers, a literary school or movement. In so doing the authors—authorities on the topic in question who are also well versed in the principles and history of literary criticism—address a readership consisting of scholars, students of literature at the graduate and undergraduate level, and the general reader. One of the primary purposes of the series is to illuminate the nature of literary criticism itself, to gauge the influence of social and historic currents on aesthetic judgments once thought objective and normative.

SUSAN NEAL MAYBERRY

THE CRITICAL LIFE OF TONI MORRISON

CAMDEN HOUSE
Rochester, New York

Copyright © 2021 Susan Neal Mayberry

All Rights Reserved. Except as permitted under current legislation, no part of this work may be photocopied, stored in a retrieval system, published, performed in public, adapted, broadcast, transmitted, recorded, or reproduced in any form or by any means, without the prior permission of the copyright owner.

First published 2021 by Camden House
Reprinted in paperback 2025

Camden House is an imprint of Boydell & Brewer Inc.
668 Mt. Hope Avenue, Rochester, NY 14620, USA
and of Boydell & Brewer Limited
PO Box 9, Woodbridge, Suffolk IP12 3DF, UK
www.boydellandbrewer.com

Our Authorised Representative for product safety in the EU is Easy Access System Europe - Mustamäe tee 50, 10621 Tallinn, Estonia, gpsr.requests@easproject.com

ISBN-13: 978-1-57113-934-4 (hardcover); 978-1-64014-213-8 (paperback)

Cover Image: Toni Morrison, courtesy of the photographer, Timothy Greenfield-Sanders. All rights reserved.

Library of Congress Cataloging-in-Publication Data

Names: Mayberry, Susan Neal, 1951– author.
Title: The critical life of Toni Morrison / Susan Neal Mayberry.
Description: Rochester, New York : Camden House, 2021. | Series: Literary criticism in perspective | Includes bibliographical references and index.
Identifiers: LCCN 2021004181 (print) | LCCN 2021004182 (ebook) |
    ISBN 9781571139344 (hardback) | ISBN 9781800102118 (ebook) |
    ISBN 9781800102125 (epub)
Subjects: LCSH: Morrison, Toni--Criticism and interpretation.
Classification: LCC PS3563.O8749 Z763 2021 (print) | LCC PS3563.O8749 (ebook) | DDC 813/.54--dc23
LC record available at https://lccn.loc.gov/2021004181
LC ebook record available at https://lccn.loc.gov/2021004182

For Tom, my dearly Beloved

CONTENTS

Acknowledgments		ix
Introduction		1
1:	*The Bluest Eye* (1970)	7
2:	*Sula* (1973)	47
3:	*Song of Solomon* (1977)	71
4:	*Tar Baby* (1981)	93
5:	*Beloved* (1987)	113
6:	*Jazz* (1992)	143
7:	*Paradise* (1997)	159
8:	*Love* (2003)	183
9:	*A Mercy* (2008); *Home* (2012); *God Help the Child* (2015)	199
Coda		237
Works Cited		241
Index		291

ACKNOWLEDGMENTS

Writing represents a journey in liberating, companionably solitary confinement. Nobody, however, can do the time alone. Writing, as Toni Morrison puts it, is a "craft that appears solitary but needs another for its completion." My five-year stint in solitary was eased considerably by bread and wine from a number of astonishingly considerate others. Lib Hayes proved a mainstay of ideas and emotional support. Keith Byerman and Andrea O'Reilly mustered the enthusiasm. The consummate professionals associated with Camden House, notably Jane Best, Sue Martin, Steven Moore, and Jim Walker, provided sound editorial, design, and indexing advice. Timothy Greenfield-Sanders, Morrison's go-to photographer, who documented her life in *The Pieces I Am*, graciously allowed me the book cover art. Undergirded by such fellowship, writing evolved for me into an adventure as well as a trip, an experience of self-discovery segueing into the origins of others. I took refreshment along the way from the passion and honesty of students in my Morrison seminars. I owe much to the unflagging service of the staff at Alfred University's Herrick Memorial Library, especially Ellen Bahr and John Hosford; to the generous support from AU administrators, particularly Provost Beth Ann Dobie; and to the Margaret and Barbara Hagar Professorship in the Humanities for the release time associated with its endowment. I might not have made it home were it not for loyalty from and laughter at my Whoodle, Rosalind o'th' Green, who sat regally by my side in her un-endowed and under-stuffed chair.

I continue to appreciate the spirit of Toni Morrison, friend of my mind. I marvel at the unfailing generosity of my children Neal McDowell, Caroline McDowell, and John Moorhead, who tolerated my absentminded presence with general good humor. Most of all, I thank my husband, Tom McDowell, who encouraged and believed in me because he wanted to. This book is for all of you—those whom I have the sheer good fortune to miss long before they leave me. I am well aware, though, that the real gift comes from those who have shared with me the closed yet wide-open space which allowed me room to write.

INTRODUCTION

If there were better criticism, there would be better books.
—"The Language Must Not Sweat," 1981

Toni Morrison's literary critical life, as well as her critical literary life, began in earnest when she was in her late thirties. A single parent of two sons still in diapers, she moved to Syracuse, New York, a city where she knew no one. Working a day job as a senior editor at Random House's textbook subsidiary L. W. Singer Publishing, she wrote fiction at night to fend off loneliness and to create stories about people like her—stories that she wanted to read but had never seen in print. Having stated more than once that she had originally intended to be a "reader," not a writer, she turned a short story drafted for a local women writers' support group into a disturbing novel initially filed by the Library of Congress as "adolescent fiction," read in and then banned from various public schools. *The Bluest Eye* elicited absolutely no recognition from the Modern Language Association until five years after its 1970 copyright and nearly two years after *Sula*'s publication in 1973.

Morrison's agonizingly slow critical start appears to rest upon three major cruxes: a culture in which ideologies of whiteness were founded on "an American Africanism—a fabricated brew of darkness, otherness, alarm, and desire that is uniquely American" (*Playing in the Dark* 38); the ongoing absence of a criticism that would locate writers like Morrison specifically as African American; and Morrison's troublingly complex novels deliberately designed to unsettle readers. *The Critical Life of Toni Morrison* reveals, however, that her steady and steely efforts to overcome what may now seem surprising hurdles—Morrison was, after all, helping to lay the groundwork for a dramatic shift in the reviewing establishment's attitude toward African American writers—allowed this multitalented artist and savvy businesswoman to catapult herself into a career—first as editor and then as writer—that literally changed the direction of American literature and criticism, elevated Morrison to the pantheon of "public intellectuals," and gained her almost cult-like personal adulation. Those fiercely determined aspects of a self-made black female wordsmith ultimately drew enough public attention to dominate television talk-show host Oprah Winfrey's Book Club and coalesce/culminate in a popular film documentary produced and directed by a white male shortly before Morrison's death in August 2019 (see Greenfield-Sanders's *The Pieces I Am*).

Her life is connected to the "critical" in more ways than one. Morrison single-handedly inspired necessary but difficult discussions about America's vexing cultural conditions. Moreover, she stimulated a postmodern critical apparatus that transformed literary criticism and situated her oeuvre at the center of contemporary theory. As Nancy J. Peterson puts it, "the rise of Morrison to national recognition has been motivated not only by the substantial, magnificent body of work she has produced but also by a consequential rethinking of what we mean by the term 'American,' a rethinking of the relationship between Anglo-American and African-American culture, of the relevance of race to all areas of culture and aesthetics, society and politics" (2).

In *The Source of Self-Regard*, her final publication before her death, Morrison attributes her initial unresponsiveness to the late 1980s debates about literary canon formation to her attempt to avoid "another toreador's red cape designed to provoke and thereby trick a force from knowing its own power." She opted to "focus on how to create nonracist, yet race-specific literature within an already race-inflected language for readers who have been forced to deal with the assumptions of racial hierarchy"—to write "as though there were nothing to prove or disprove, as though an unraced world already existed." Accepting herself as "an already and always raced writer," knowing full well that no one has ever lived in a world where race does not matter, she nonetheless tried not to "transcend race, nor to aspire to some fraudulent 'universalism'—a code word that had come to mean 'nonblack,'" but rather to "claim the liberty of [her] own imagination." In essence, despite African American art having come to represent "explications of pathology" and/or "restorative balms to rashes of racism," Morrison insisted on writing "outside the white gaze, not against it but in a space where [she] could postulate the humanity writers were always being asked to enunciate" (198–99).

In an effort not to produce literature that became "another houseboy, opening doors for guests to enter a party to which it had not been invited," Morrison originally remained silent about her responsibility as social healer along with her role as African American literary theorist. Ultimately, however, because the problem of what constitutes African American literature lay not only at the center of her self-conflict, but at the heart of her writing, she believed herself "forced" to participate in the development of African American criticism and pedagogy. Because she would need to clarify what makes her an African American writer, "other than melanin and subject matter," in order to participate in said critical discourse, she "entered the debate not as an artist only, nor as an academic only, but as both," supposing that her "dual position could help expand and deepen the arguments about the validity, necessity, and direction of African American scholarship" (*Self-Regard* 201–3).

INTRODUCTION 3

Resisting its re-segregation into African American studies, Morrison wanted African American literature and criticism to become, like the "so-called race problem," a thing apart that sits past and present at the heart of the nation. In other words, because both her life and her work are so caught up in and reflective of the development of American culture prior to and during her lifetime, she wanted her critical life to encompass not only her work and the critical reactions to it but also her own critical responses to her own work in the ongoing and increasingly uncertain "fight for the privilege of intellectual freedom" (*Self-Regard* 201–4).

* * *

Morrison's creative and critical texts are widely acknowledged to be challenging, complex, subtle, beautifully evocative, and exceptionally difficult for many readers. Ironically, reasons for creating *The Critical Life of Toni Morrison* are exceptionally simple. Toni Morrison is the most important American novelist since William Faulkner and the most important American woman writer since Emily Dickinson. Her influence as a writer, critic, teacher, editor, and public intellectual is profound, for she has effectively changed the face of literature and literary criticism not only in the United States, but worldwide.

Morrison performs brilliantly in many genres—fiction, of course (eleven novels, and two published short stories), but also drama/staged performances; poetry; nonfiction essays and books on historical, social, and political issues; and critical essays on the work of others and on her own work, such as her introductions to other writers' texts, her forewords and her one afterword to her own novels, and her literary critical essays, such as "Home," "Rootedness: The Ancestor as Foundation," and her stunning Nobel Prize Lecture. The three essays that comprise *Playing in the Dark: Whiteness and the Literary Imagination*—Morrison's singular effort to generate a literary critical methodology that recognizes and embraces rather than ignores or remains willfully blind to the African American presence in American literature—have literally transformed America's attitude toward American letters. For an African American woman—in fact, for an American woman—to achieve such literary prominence in the United States and around the globe is unprecedented. The story of Morrison's achievement in making a home for herself—and for other African Americans and women—in the stony bedrock of "white male" American literature is the subject of *The Critical Life of Toni Morrison*.

To date, the *MLA International Bibliography* lists 2,736 responses to Morrison's works, of which 393 are dissertation abstracts. Despite such eagerness from reviewers and scholars to critique Morrison's oeuvre, particularly in the twenty-eight years since she received her Nobel Prize award, *The Critical Life of Toni Morrison* is the first history of Morrison's critical reception to be published. Just as the Library of Congress originally mislabeled *The Bluest Eye* as "Adolescent Fiction," the *MLA Bibliography* has occasionally filed articles, books, and book chapters on Morrison's contributions under misleading or misinformed headings and/or key words. This volume attempts to address those errors. *The Critical Life* is structured according to the chronology of her novels, with references to and summaries of criticism on her short stories, plays, essays, speeches, and meditations included where appropriate. Each chapter first allows Morrison to tell her personal tale of that book's history, either by way of her Vintage edition forewords (only the Plume paperback of *The Bluest Eye* provides an afterword) or the lack thereof since something else will suffice. The chapter then describes the history of each novel's initial critical reception, its defining critical moments, and its second-wave criticism, which categorizes major critical approaches stimulated by it and includes chronological summaries of prominent journal and book articles.

The Critical Life of Toni Morrison is, finally, as much a cultural history of the United States as a literary critical reception history of an American writer. America's preliminary response to this African American writer, from probable disdain to a certain failure to see, reveals America's uncertainties, fears, prejudices, and blind spots with respect to the race, class, and gender tensions that continue to disrupt its core and cause it nightmares. Responding to a wake-up call from Morrison's respected colleagues, America saw its way to awarding her third novel, *Song of Solomon* (1977), the 1978 National Book Critics Circle Award for Fiction and a 1988 Pulitzer Prize for *Beloved* (1987); two-thirds of the way through her great trilogy on the African American experience (*Beloved*, *Jazz*, *Paradise*), the world via the Swedish Academy selected this African American writer in 1993 as the first black woman of any nationality to win the Nobel Prize in Literature. America's more recent reactions to this African American writer—looking past her writerly weaknesses, refusing to criticize, elevating her to rock-star status even as her last books suggest the wearing-down of an octogenarian's creative energy—may ironically conceal behind political-correctness some of the same uncertainty, fear, prejudice, and blindness as those first rejoinders.

Did Morrison's critical life come full circle, then? We'll let her have the last word. In a speech composed on the very cusp of the twenty-first century, "How Can Values Be Taught at the University" (2000), delivered at Princeton University's Center for Human Values, Morrison doffs her writer/critic's robes to don the professor's gown. Answering whether institutions of higher learning should teach values by urging the university not to confuse values with "religiosity" or dogma, she proposes that we honor its value-laden history by virtue of its community leading by example: "How do we treat each other? The members of our own profession? How do we respond to professional and political cunning, to raw and ruthless ambition, to the plight of those outside our walls? What are we personally willing to sacrifice, give up for the public good? What gestures of reparation are we personally willing to make? What risky, unfashionable research are we willing to undertake?" She concludes her comments by insisting: "If the university does not take seriously and rigorously its role as guardian of wider civic freedoms, as interrogator of more and more complex ethical problems, as servant and preserver of deeper democratic practices, then some other regime or ménage of regimes will do it for us, in spite of us, and without us" (*What Moves at the Margin* 196–97).

INTRODUCTION

Morrison's critical life acknowledges betrayal yet embraces the possibility of treating love as unmotivated respect. Her legacy may be summed up in a filmed statement she makes to journalist Bill Moyers: "We are here, and we have to do something nurturing that we respect before we go. We must. It is more interesting, more complicated, more intellectually demanding and more morally demanding to love somebody, to take care of somebody, to make one other person feel good.... It's so uninteresting to live without [love].... There's no risk involved. And that [risk] just seems to make life not just livable, but a gallant, gallant event" ("Toni Morrison: A Writer's Work"). Like her dead character Love in her novel *Love,* Toni Morrison still sits somewhere perched atop a tombstone humming such harmonies to us.

CHAPTER ONE

THE BLUEST EYE
(1 9 7 0)

The Bluest Eye's Critical History as Told by Toni Morrison

The history of Toni Morrison's literary critical reception had best begin with a story.[1] As the 1988–89 Distinguished Professor in Syracuse University's Jeanette K. Watson Distinguished Professor Lecture Series, Morrison gave three public lectures at SU about the African American influence on American literature, and three informal talks about selected novels. During the question-and-answer hour of her seminar on *The Bluest Eye*, Morrison was asked if, in retrospect, she might have been aware of the Persephone archetype on some level, either consciously or unconsciously, while writing her first novel in the late 1960s. After all, *The Bluest Eye* does—like the myth—feature a girl/"maiden" overpowered and raped by a father/father figure who "loved" her but whose seed brought not life but death: the death of Pecola's unborn baby; Pecola's own "living death" in the underworld of insanity; and the unheard-of absence of all the marigolds in narrator Claudia's world, including the marigolds whose seeds she and her sister

---

1   Credit for this story, for connections between the Persephone archetype and *The Bluest Eye*, for analysis of Morrison's decision to write an afterword instead of a foreword to her first novel, and for ways in which said afterword allows Morrison to address her own critical history goes to Elizabeth T. Hayes. Retired Professor of English at LeMoyne College in Syracuse, New York, Dr. Hayes attended Morrison's SU lectures. She is the author of "'Like Seeing You Buried': Persephone in *The Bluest Eye, Their Eyes Were Watching God*, and *The Color Purple*," a chapter in *Images of Persephone: Feminist Readings in Western Literature* (1994), likewise edited by Hayes.

Frieda had planted in an imitative-magic fertility ritual meant to assure the safe birth of Pecola's baby.

Having been attending politely to all the usual Q&A demands, the author's demeanor abruptly darkened as she noted that others had pointed out to her parallels between the Persephone archetype and *The Bluest Eye*. She replied sternly that she had never intentionally rewritten an existing narrative; that was simply not the way she worked. Lightening up to laugh that she had earned a classics minor in college and thus was "not unfamiliar" with the Persephone myth, she ultimately conceded that while she had not been consciously using said archetype in *The Bluest Eye*, the story may be there, on some level (SU, Oct. 5, 1988).

* * *

In 1994, Penguin Random House published a Plume paperback edition of *The Bluest Eye*, the original in a series of what became Vintage Random House editions of Morrison's earliest eight novels, each with a foreword—or, in the case of *The Bluest Eye*, an afterword—written by the author, analyzing the historical, social, and/or personal events that inspired the novel. Though Morrison never explained why *The Bluest Eye* is the only one of her first eight novels with an afterword instead of a foreword, we can say something about why.

The Bluest Eye's afterword begins with a story told in the first person:

> We had just started elementary school. She said she wanted blue eyes. I looked around to picture her with them and was violently repelled by what I imagined she would look like. . . . Astonished by the desecration she proposed, I "got mad" at her. . . . [This] was the first time I knew . . . [that] beauty was not simply something to behold; it was something one could *do*. (209)

The Bluest Eye is Morrison's "effort to say . . . something about why"—why her elementary school friend felt "racial self-loathing" and why many years later Morrison herself is "still wondering about how one learns that." The "Black is Beautiful" movement in the 1960s made her question "why, although reviled by others, could this beauty not be taken for granted within the [black] community?" Realizing that "the assertion of racial beauty" is a reaction "against the damaging internalization of assumptions of immutable inferiority originating in an outside [white] gaze," Morrison sets out to explore in *The Bluest Eye* "how something as grotesque as the demonization of an entire race could take root inside the most delicate member of society: a child; the most vulnerable member: a female" (afterword 209–10).

If, unlike Claudia and Frieda's poor but supportive family, Pecola's family is "crippled and crippling," Morrison notes in the afterword that all young girls share "some aspects of [Pecola's] woundability." To examine "the social and domestic aggression that could cause a child to literally fall apart," Morrison stages "a series of rejections" for Pecola, many of them "routine," such as the child's teachers never calling on her in class, or the white store owner's reluctance to touch her black hand to take the money for her candy purchase. Other rejections are "exceptional" (afterword 210–11)—such as "pretty, milk-brown" Geraldine in her "pretty gold-and-green house" taking one look at dark-skinned Pecola in "the dirty torn dress . . . the plaits sticking out on her head . . . the muddy shoes" held together with chewing gum, and saying to the child, "You nasty little black bitch. Get out of my house" (*BE* 92). The "monstrous" (afterword 211) rejections Pecola suffers are those committed by her family: her father Cholly rapes her; her mother Pauline refuses to believe Pecola's report that Cholly is the rapist despite the evidence literally right before her eyes; and when Pecola's pregnancy becomes obvious, her mother gives her such a beating that "she lucky to be alive," according to neighborhood women who enthusiastically punish their own children but are shocked by the severity of the thrashing Pauline gives her daughter (*BE* 189).

As Morrison states in the afterword, her challenge in writing her first novel was to create language capable of "holding the despising glance while sabotaging it." She wanted to "hit the raw nerve of racial self-contempt, expose it, then soothe it . . . with language that replicated the agency [she] discovered in [her] first experience of beauty" when her childhood friend's confession of praying for blue eyes stuns and horrifies her. Because that confession was "so racially infused . . ., [her] struggle was for writing that was indisputably black." Admitting with a touch of humor, "I don't yet know quite what that is," Morrison adds: "but neither that nor the attempts to disqualify an effort to find out keep me from trying to pursue it" (211).

Her dismissal of attempts to disable those efforts to craft indisputably black writing is a small but no doubt satisfying dig at the reviewers of *The Bluest Eye* and *Sula* in the 1970s, most of them male or white or both, who downplayed her novels not only for their subject matter—the lives of black girls and women—but for the paucity, or in some critics' narrow view, the absence of white characters in her books, warning in so many words that Morrison would never amount to much as a novelist unless she could create believable white characters. As the Nobel Laureate in Literature in 1993, the year she wrote *The Bluest Eye*'s afterword, Morrison clearly had amounted to immensely more than "much," especially because she had continued to write about black girls and women, black boys and men—and white people, too.

In the second section of *The Bluest Eye* afterword, Morrison describes her tactics for "grounding [her] work in race-specific yet race-free prose. Prose free of racial hierarchy and triumphalism" (211). With the exception of the first paragraph and the final two paragraphs, four of the six-and-a-half pages of the afterword are taken word-for-word from, and comprise the entirety of, *The Bluest Eye* section of "Unspeakable Things Unspoken: The Afro-American Presence in American Literature," Morrison's October 1988 Tanner Lecture in Human Values at the University of Michigan—an examination of race in American literature, including her critical readings of the opening sections of her own first five novels.

According to "Unspeakable Things," interestingly enough, the first sentence of *The Bluest Eye* is not "Here is the house" (3), the sentence we read on the first page of the novel, but rather the first sentence of the italicized section on the third page: "*Quiet as it's kept, there were no marigolds in the fall of 1941*" (5). Only once in the afterword does Morrison even mention the Dick and Jane primer text that opens her novel: "The shattered world I built (to complement what is happening to Pecola), its pieces held together by seasons in child time and commenting at every turn on the incompatible and barren white-family primer, does not in its present form handle effectively the silence at its center: the void that is Pecola's 'unbeing'" (214–15). On the other hand, Morrison discusses at length in the afterword the strengths and significance of her phrase "Quiet as it's kept," the first words in the italicized prologue section of *The Bluest Eye* that appears to be a second preface following the three versions of "Here is the house."

"Quiet as it's kept" appealed to Morrison for several reasons. It is a familiar expression from her childhood, with a "'back fence' connotation": black women conversing conspiratorially—gossiping, telling anecdotes, sharing neighborhood news, exchanging secrets. In addition, "the words [themselves] are conspiratorial," and "the conspiracy is both held and withheld, exposed and sustained," which—given the "political climate," that is, "the great social upheaval in the lives of black people" in 1965–69, the years Morrison spent writing *The Bluest Eye*—mirror what the writing and publishing of the book felt like to her: "the public exposure of a private confidence" (afterword 212).

Morrison particularly values the "speakerly" quality of "Quiet as it's kept"—"how it speaks and bespeaks a particular world and its ambiance" and also suggests that a "thrilling revelation" will be imparted to the listener, creating an instant "intimacy . . . between the reader and the page" that it "seemed crucial" to Morrison to achieve. She does not want the reader to have time to put up defenses or try to maintain distance from the story because, in her words, "I know (and the reader does not—he or she has to wait for the second sentence) that this is a terrible story about things one would rather not know anything about" (afterword 212–13).

The "Big Secret" paragraph that follows is the longest in the afterword: fifty-six lines of text, nearly two full pages, more than twice as long as the next-longest paragraph and four-to-fifteen times longer than any other paragraph in the afterword. Morrison, a stylist of the first order, is clearly signaling this to be the key paragraph in *The Bluest Eye*'s afterword.

She begins with a pair of rhetorical questions: "What, then, is the Big Secret about to be shared? The thing we (reader and I) are 'in' on?" The second rhetorical question and the series of answers that follow are all sentence fragments: "A botanical aberration. Pollution, perhaps. A skip, perhaps, in the natural order of things . . . an autumn, a fall without marigolds. Bright, common, strong and sturdy marigolds. When? In 1941." Summing up and underlining the vital information in the sentence fragments, Morrison returns to full sentences:

> In the temperate zone where there is a season known as "fall" during which one expects marigolds to be at their peak, in the months before the beginning of U.S. participation in World War II, something grim is about to be divulged. The next

sentence will make clear that . . . a child . . . mimicking the adult black women on the porch or in the backyard [says] . . ., "We thought it was because Pecola was having her father's baby that the marigolds did not grow. . . ." (afterword 213)

To the child speaker, no marigolds growing anywhere in town that fall is the shocking event to be reported, while the "illicit, traumatic, incomprehensible sex coming to its dreaded fruition" is just that—incomprehensible—so the child's focus turns to the phenomenon of no marigolds. Morrison thought that "could-be victims of rape" narrating the story would be a "novelty" and would also give young black girls a voice they had never had when she was growing up and still did not have in the late 1960s when she was writing the novel. The opening sentence of the novel, then, "provides the stroke that announces something more than a secret shared, but a silence broken, a void filled, an unspeakable thing spoken at last. And it draws the connection between [what the 'outside world' would call] a minor destabilization in seasonal flora and the insignificant destruction of a black girl"—though for Claudia, both are monumental events that she and her sister spend years "trying to fathom, and cannot." Thus, as Morrison notes, "the book can be seen to open with its close: a speculation on the disruption of 'nature' as being a social disruption with tragic individual consequences in which the reader, as part of the population of the text, is implicated" (afterword 213–14).

Two problems in the novel Morrison was unable to fix to her satisfaction. The first is that "the shattered world [she] built (to complement what is happening to Pecola), its pieces held together by seasons . . . does not . . . handle effectively the silence at its center: the void that is Pecola's 'unbeing.' It should have had a shape—like the emptiness left by a boom or a cry." The second problem stems from her inability to create throughout the novel the same "feminine subtext" achieved in the opening sentence with "Quiet as it's kept," the phrase that immediately brings to mind "women gossiping, eager and aghast." Nonetheless, she is pleased that she was able to connect "Cholly's 'rape' by the whitemen to his own [rape] of his daughter" by "subverting the language to a feminine mode," especially because rendering Cholly's "'rape' by the whitemen" "'passive'" and thus "'feminized'" makes it "more accurately repellent when deprived of the male 'glamor of shame' rape is (or once was) routinely given" (afterword 214–15).

What Morrison attempts in *The Bluest Eye* through her "choices of language (speakerly, aural, colloquial), [her] reliance for full comprehension on codes embedded in black culture, [her] effort to effect immediate co-conspiracy and intimacy (without any distancing, explanatory fabric), as well as [her] attempt to shape a silence while breaking it are attempts to transfigure the complexity and wealth of Black American culture into a language worthy of the culture." Even so, as she completed the afterword in November 1993 (when she was no doubt also crafting her Nobel Prize acceptance speech), Morrison notes that "hearing 'civilized' languages debase humans, watching cultural exorcisms debase literature, seeing oneself preserved in the amber of disqualifying metaphors" make her narrative project "as difficult today as it was thirty years ago" (afterword 215–16).

Morrison adds to the afterword a dignified but pointed coda aimed primarily at white male reviewers commenting on the novel's release in 1970: "With very few exceptions, the initial publication of *The Bluest Eye* was like Pecola's life: dismissed, trivialized, misread. And it has taken twenty-five years to gain for her the respectful publication this edition is" (216). If Morrison sounds angry, even bitter, about the early critical reception of her first book, her reaction is not unjustifiable.

* * *

Two final questions about Morrison's telling/not telling of *The Bluest Eye*'s critical history coalesce. First, why did Morrison choose to write an afterword for *The Bluest Eye* instead of a foreword? Second, was Morrison's creation of a Persephone narrative in the novel perhaps more intentional than she was willing to admit? Did she in fact create a 1940s black American Persephone in *The Bluest Eye* to explore the 1960s African American community's perceived need for a "Black is Beautiful" slogan?

We can glean the answer to the "afterword-rather-than-foreword" question from the text of the afterword itself. No assembly is needed, however, if we, again, consult the first paragraph of Morrison's *The Bluest Eye* section in "Unspeakable Things Unspoken"—the only paragraph of "Unspeakable Things" that does not appear in *The Bluest Eye* afterword. Requiring her beginning sentence, "Quiet as it's kept, there were no marigolds in the fall of 1941," to employ "simple, uncomplicated ... ordinary, everyday words," she demands that this simplicity be "not simple-minded, but devious, even loaded," for Morrison wants no theatrical staging of any kind at the beginning of *The Bluest Eye*: "So important to me was this unstaging, that in this first novel I summarized the whole of the book on the first page. (In the first edition, it was printed in its entirety on the [book] jacket)" ("Unspeakable" 20). A foreword would ruin for new readers Morrison's careful, deliberate unstaging of the unspeakable event reported in the meticulously crafted first sentence of *The Bluest Eye*, while an afterword would allow all the first-time readers of the novel after 1993, when the newly written afterword was added, to feel the full effects of Morrison's deliberately unstaged, crucially important, meticulously crafted first sentence. Thus, *The Bluest Eye* became the only one of Morrison's novels with an afterword.

The second question—was Morrison aware of the Persephone archetype on any level, consciously or unconsciously, as she wrote *The Bluest Eye*?—elicited from the author the equivalent of a firm "no" in answer to the "conscious awareness" query. Conversely, Morrison's answer to the question of her possible unconscious awareness of the Persephone archetype while writing the novel was the equivalent of a soft "no" with a hint of a question mark at the end. She revealed that she was "not unfamiliar" with the Persephone archetype, a perfectly phrased simultaneous non-confirmation/non-denial—precisely the response one would expect from a master wordsmith with no interest in confirming or denying. We should remember, too, that this particular archetypal story of a "resurrection/fertility deity" who dies and then returns to life in the spring, heralding a renewal of life for the earth and its people, has been "not unfamiliar" to human beings around the globe for thousands of years—and with good reason: this story anthropomorphically "explains" the seasons, a crucial fact of life on planet Earth. It also demonstrates one of the most powerful beneficent binding forces in any society—and a consistent Morrisonian concern—mother love.

The text of *The Bluest Eye* may address Morrison's possible unconscious channeling of the Persephone myth. While Morrison is particularly proud of the "speakerly" quality of the novel's opening phrase "*Quiet as it's kept*," also noteworthy is the main clause of the sentence, which discloses the secret quietly kept: "*there were no marigolds in the fall of 1941.*" Claudia and Frieda attribute the failure of their flowers to Claudia's incorrect placement of seeds they had been selling to buy a bicycle, opting instead to plant them near Pecola's apartment (*BE* 5). Despite the girls' efforts to save their friend and her baby through sacrifice and spell, Claudia reports in the third sentence of the novel that the seeds sowed by the sisters "*were not the only ones that did not sprout in the fall of 1941; nobody's did. Not even the* [white people's] *gardens fronting the lake showed marigolds that year*" (*BE* 5). Both siblings blame Claudia for burying their seeds "*too far down in the earth*," and "*for years*" Claudia shoulders this guilt. As an adult, though, she understands her childhood trauma differently:

> *The earth itself might have been unyielding. We had dropped our seeds in our own little plot of black dirt, just as Pecola's father had dropped his seeds in his own plot of black dirt. Our innocence and faith were no more productive than his lust or despair. What is clear now is that of all that hope, fear, lust, love, and grief, nothing remains but Pecola* [suffering the death-in-life of the insane] *and the unyielding earth.* (BE 5–6)

The "unyielding earth" is also the *deus ex machina* of the Persephone myth. When Zeus refuses Demeter's pleas to order the god of the underworld to release her daughter, the Maiden of Springtime, whom Hades has kidnapped and carried off to the underworld to rape and crown Queen of the Dead, the angry goddess goes on strike, refusing to let anything grow on earth until her beloved has been returned to her. Living things across the wintery landscape starve and die, but not until the male gods miss the animal and grain sacrifices made to them by people on earth does Zeus finally order Hades to release Persephone. With Persephone's return from "death" in the underworld to the land of the living, Demeter resumes her duties as goddess of the harvest, and life returns to normal.

The italicized "*Quiet as its kept*" entry into *The Bluest Eye* is not the only Persephone-myth echo in the novel, however. The two-page "Big Secret" paragraph—the central paragraph of the afterword—clearly connects the novel to the Persephone archetype, for the Big Secret, kept quiet until Claudia divulges it, is an unprecedented "botanical aberration.... A skip, perhaps, in the natural order of things" (afterword 213). Pecola's tragedy is that she has no natural Demeter-mother willing to sacrifice everything to save her daughter from the rapacious arms of figurative death.

Morrison returns once again to this botanical abnormality so fraught with human significance in the novel's three-page coda praised by reviewers, scholars, and readers alike. Whenever the adult Claudia sees her irreparably damaged childhood friend Pecola, whom she and her sister had tried but failed to help, she reflects: "how I did *not* plant the [marigold] seeds too deeply, how it was the fault of the earth, the land, of our town [that the seeds did not grow]. I even think now that the land of the entire country was hostile to marigolds that year" (*BE* 206).

Hence years after the tragic events of fall 1941, Claudia's speculations about the singular absence of marigolds from her town that year is extended to the absence of marigolds in "the land of the entire country" (*BE* 206). As Morrison underscores in the afterword, she is not merely writing about land hostile to a certain flower in 1941, but about a nation actively, dangerously hostile to people with dark skin for four hundred years and counting, as well as relentlessly threatening to women, especially black women. In the poignant final paragraph of the book, Claudia states her conviction as follows:

> This soil [the United States] is bad for certain kinds of flowers. Certain seeds it will not nurture, certain fruit it will not bear, and when the land kills of its own volition, we acquiesce and say the victim had no right to live. We are wrong, of course, but it doesn't matter. It's too late . . . it's much, much, much too late. (206)

This two-and-a-half page conclusion is one of the most moving passages in Morrison's oeuvre. Whether her application of the Persephone myth was conscious or unconscious, Morrison wields the archetype as a critique of American racism brilliantly—and beautifully—in this her first novel.

Most surprising, however, is that she never places *The Bluest Eye* in the category most appropriate to the novel: Morrisonian fiction that employs "Western mythology . . . to show that . . . something [is] askew" (Brown 461). In a 1995 interview with Cecil Brown, Morrison explains that when she uses Greco-Roman "Western" mythology in her novels, she is signaling that "something [is] wrong; [the characters] are outside of their history . . . pulling from another place that's not going to feed them"—like Milkman nervously thinking of Hansel and Gretel as he enters the decaying mansion where Circe lives with a pack of half-wild dogs, or Hagar referring to the three beds she and her mother and Pilate sleep in as Goldilocks's beds (461). Morrison tells Brown: "I tend to use everything from African or Afro-American sources. The flying [in *Song of Solomon*] is not about Icarus; it's about the African flying myth. . . . [In my novels, the] people who are connected to the Afro-American tradition or the African tradition are generally the ones who are [on] the wholesome track," and by extension, those connected with Greco-Roman mythology are on the [unwholesome]/wrong track (461).

The "white gaze" has been an immensely unwholesome trajectory in America, destructive to the gazers (unbeknownst to most of them) but especially destructive to those on the receiving end of this debilitating stare. In *The Bluest Eye*, the many echoes of the Persephone myth—one of the preeminent archetypes in Western mythology—unquestionably signal that "something has gone wrong" in Pecola's life, as well as in the lives of all the black, brown, and high-yellow people in *The Bluest Eye*, not to mention all the people of color in the Western world (Brown 461).

Why then does Morrison fail to identify *The Bluest Eye* as one of her novels that "use[s] ... Western mythology ... to show that something has gone wrong" (Brown 461)? One probable reason is that when admiring readers began pointing out the similarities between Pecola and Persephone, Morrison was already seething about reviews that "dismissed, trivialized, and misread" her just-published first novel (afterword 216). Even if she had recognized that she had inadvertently used elements of the Persephone archetype in *The Bluest Eye*, she likely would not have admitted it, especially since she was not subscribing to racism or sexism but rather using the archetypal elements to trenchantly critique the "white-gaze" racism and to a lesser extent the sexism that destroy Pecola in the novel. These unwitting "white-gaze" racist comments and "male-gaze" sexist comments from even the most complimentary reviewers of *The Bluest Eye* not only set Morrison's teeth on edge but set her on her lifelong path of critiquing "white-gaze" critics of not only African American literature but of the entirety of American literature by way of her extraordinary fiction and her insightful criticism.

The Bluest Eye's Initial Critical Reception History

Morrison's critical reception history officially opened between the publication of her first novel in 1970 and the appearance of *Sula* in 1973.[2] Immediate reaction to her first five novels provides the subject of Leroy Staggers's 1989 doctoral dissertation, "The Critical Reception of Toni Morrison: 1970 to 1989." Staggers divides reviewer responses into three broad categories: those arising from a Euro-American tradition, those arising from an Afro-American tradition, and those arising from feminists drawn from both groups. According to Staggers, each of these categories incorporates beliefs and values that transcend literary judgments. Euro-American critics, for example, typically focus on traditional literary elements such as tone, style, and narrative techniques, while Afro-American reviewers add the implications of cultural context and social message to textual analysis. To distinguish between American literature generally associated with a European heritage and American writers with an African heritage, Staggers quotes Bernard Bell:

---

2 Elizabeth T. Hayes provided examinations of *The Bluest Eye*'s initial critical reception and defining critical moment.

> The network of understandings that defines black American culture and informs black American consciousness has evolved from the unique pattern of experiences of black people in North America.... These experiences—of Africa, the transatlantic or Middle Passage, slavery, Southern plantation tradition, emancipation, Reconstruction, post-Reconstruction, Northern migration, urbanization, and racism—have produced a residue of shared memories and frames of reference for Black Americans. (5-6)

The Bluest Eye's first review appeared in *Kirkus Reviews* (Aug. 1970), a bimonthly American trade publication for libraries and booksellers with 150-word reports of new books. Alice Woff adroitly marshals her limited words, judiciously quoting and paraphrasing Morrison's text to capture the essence of Pecola's tragic life, concluding with the assessment that the novel is "[a] skillful understated tribute to the fall of a sparrow for whose small tragedy there was no watching eye" (Oct. 1, 1970). When Editor Woff reprints her August review in October, however, she alters its header from "Fiction" to "Adult Books Suggested for Young Adult Consideration."³ Applauding Morrison for her adept characterization and authentic dialogue, the November 1970 issue of *Library Journal* likewise recommends the novel to young adults, case workers, and public libraries. As Staggers wryly puts it: "the word was out to those in the book publishing and book trading businesses that this was a book that would sell, as well as a book that has a message. What the message is and what it signifies would be left for others to write about" (18). Staggers also aptly describes the initial critical evaluations of the quality of *The Bluest Eye* as "tentative," attributing this uncertainty to its position as Morrison's first novel. However, the fact that Morrison was a black female writing a book about young black girls while the critics reviewing the book were mostly male, white, or both no doubt more significantly influenced the tenor of the book's criticism than its preliminary placement in her oeuvre.

A case in point is Haskel Frankel's November 1970 response in the highly respected *New York Times Book Review*, his every compliment preceded or followed by a gratuitous swipe. Acknowledging that Morrison "reveals herself, when she shucks the fuzziness born of flights of poetic imagery, as a writer of considerable power and tenderness ...," Frankel nevertheless determines that "Miss Morrison has gotten lost in her construction." His misconstruction of *The Bluest Eye* becomes obvious when he criticizes the author for "yield[ing] center stage to Frieda and Claudia—who aside from knowing [Pecola] ... serve little purpose beyond distraction"; he also considers Pecola's visit to Soaphead Church to ask for blue eyes Morrison's "most telling statement on the tragic effect of race prejudice on children" but then adds that "the scene occurs ... far too late [in the novel] to achieve the impact it [could] have had" (Gates 3). Apparently, Frankel missed

---

  3   This is the same book about an eleven-year-old rape and incest victim—which will later be banned from schools for graphic sexual content—that the US Library of Congress initially labeled "Adolescent Fiction."

Pecola praying for a blue-eyed beauty that would shame her parents into nuclear-family bonding as she witnesses Pauline and Cholly's naked fight with fists and iron skillets.

Frankel's praise that Morrison is "someone who can cast back to the living, bleeding heart of childhood and capture it on paper," and that "given a scene that demands a writer's best, Miss Morrison responds with control and talent" is followed by mocking comments on three phrases he didn't understand. Nonetheless, after tallying the book's "flaws and virtues," Frankel "found [himself] still in favor of *The Bluest Eye*," a grudging remark surprisingly offset by his closing: "There are many novelists willing to report the ugliness of the world as ugly. The writer who can reveal the beauty and the hope beneath the surface is a writer to seek out and to encourage" (Gates 3–4).

Two weeks later, the *New York Times* daily newspaper followed with a review by revered literary and cultural critic John Leonard. Providing the highest praise yet on Morrison, Leonard writes that her prose is so good that "the novel becomes poetry," adding that "*The Bluest Eye* is also history, sociology, folklore, nightmare and music" (46). In another short but laudatory November 1970 response, Raymond Sokolov notes for *Newsweek* that much black writing is designed to be "forensic" in tone so as to "speak across ethnic and political gaps" to "persuade or frighten whites into action" and to "cajole or exhort other blacks into solidarity and revolution." On the contrary, he continues, Morrison's tone in *The Bluest Eye*, while not without political consciousness, is "private" and "conversational." Sokolov appreciates that Morrison expresses her consciousness "in a novel instead of a harangue," that she tells you like it is without constantly telling you that she's telling you and that you'd best pay attention (96).

Poet and advertising executive L. E. Sissman enthusiastically reviewed *The Bluest Eye* for the *New Yorker* (Jan. 23, 1971), noting that Morrison "writes ... affectingly and often in the freshest, simplest, most striking prose ... in carrying the reader through this short and tragic story." He fails to remove his condescending white-male blinders, however, when he describes Morrison's characters—Cholly's "life of appalling oppression and dislocation" (Cholly was raised by a loving great-aunt in a tight-knit though poor black community until he was twelve. His early life with his wife and children in Lorain, Ohio, was contented); Pauline's "life of unbearable misery" (Pauline spent sixteen hours a day happily housekeeping for the wealthy white family who had given her the nickname she had always longed for); "Frieda and Claudia, whose life is only marginally less hopeless than the Breedloves"—a statement that even a casual reader of the novel would dispute (Gates 4–5).

Sissman's white-male bias becomes most evident when he quotes the bulk of Pauline's first-person account of going to the movies with her hair fixed like Jean Harlow's, where she loses a front tooth when she bites into her candy and settles down into a depression. Sissman concludes: "Here again we see, as the overriding motif of this book, the desirability of whiteness, or, as the next-best thing, the imitation of whiteness; as a corollary, blackness is perceived as ugliness, a perception that must surely have given rise in later years to the overcompensatory counterstatement 'Black is Beautiful'" (Gates 5). Quite the reverse, Claudia tries to save Pecola's baby because she values the baby's "black eyes, the flared nose, kissing-thick lips, and the living, breathing silk of black skin" (*BE* 190). Morrison reemphasizes in the afterword that "the extremity of Pecola's case stemmed largely from a crippled and crippling family—unlike the average black family and unlike the narrator's" (210).

Sissman goes on to list some minor flaws, chief of which is Morrison's "placing the story in a frame of the bland white words of a . . . school reader," which Sissman considers "an unnecessary and unsubtle irony" but which many 1970s white readers considered a wake-up call. Nevertheless, he finally dismisses said flaws: "None of this matters . . . beside [Morrison's] real and greatly promising achievement: to write truly (and sometimes very beautifully) of every generation of blacks—the young, their parents, their rural grandparents—in this country thirty years ago, and, I'm afraid, today" (Gates 5).

While Staggers speculates that the absence of detailed textual analysis in the original reviews resulted from *BE*'s "outcry against racism," which "induces guilt for Euro-Americans," he stresses that responses appearing in publications intended for African Americans not only accentuated Morrison's message and its implications as they highlighted her style and talent but revealed empathetic readers (22). He offers four 1971 reviews to illustrate.

Her pronoun use identifying her racial sympathies, Sharyn Skeeter comments in a monthly publication that targets African American women: "We can 'feel' the characters and their situations." One of the first to recommend *BE* to black readers, this *Essence* review, unlike similar Euro-American responses, notes that the Breedloves' tragedy results from "direct, as well as subtle racism" (59). Staggers observes that *Essence* readers would feel vindicated rather than guilty about the reference to racism. *Black World* critic Liz Gant speaks familiarly of Morrison as "Sister Toni." Although Staggers defines *Black World*'s readers as fewer in number than those of the more popular *Essence* magazine, they have "a higher level of education and a deeper understanding of racial problems." Just as Gant is also "unabashedly direct in using pronouns such as 'we,' 'us' and 'ourselves,'" she, too, underscores the novel's racial issues (Staggers 23). In her review of the novel in *Freedomways*, actor and activist Ruby Dee says simply: "My heart hurts." Clarifying that her reaction includes a wide-ranging lament for African American heritage, Dee maintains that Morrison's characters "are the kind of people that all black people know of—or are—to varying degrees" (319). Even more broadly, a *College Language Association Journal* review (Dec. 1971) extends its investigation into character, structural, and thematic elements beyond racism.[4]

---

4 The College Language Association (CLA), founded in 1937 by a group of black scholars and educators, is an organization of college teachers of English and foreign languages that serves the professional interests of its members and their collegiate communities.

The Bluest Eye's Defining Critical Moment

On December 30, 1973, the *New York Times Book Review* printed Sara Blackburn's review of *Sula*, the earliest critique of Morrison's second novel to appear in that apogee of book review publications. To net this coveted assignment, Blackburn devotes the two opening paragraphs of her assessment of *Sula* to a "take-back" of her former praise for *The Bluest Eye*, admiration no doubt rejected by the *Book Review* editor in favor of Haskel Frankel's patronizing critique of the novel.

Blackburn subsequently claims that Morrison's first novel attracted undue attention from the publishing industry and was received indiscriminately by middle-class feminists: "socially conscious readers—including myself—were so pleased to see a new writer of Morrison's obvious talent that we tended to celebrate the book and ignore its flaws" (3). More irritating to Morrison, as she reveals in the 2019 documentary *The Pieces I Am*, Blackburn insists that Morrison boxed herself in by concentrating on her own black community without including white characters: "Toni Morrison is far too talented to remain only a marvelous reporter of the black side of provincial American life" (3).

Blackburn's brief reappraisal of *The Bluest Eye* was the first note of Morrison's supposed "narrowness" (3) to be released by the *New York Times Book Review*; it was also the first review Blackburn had placed in a prestigious publication. Blackburn's byline identifies her as a short-story writer and critic—that is, a fiction writer trying to support herself, a token woman in the 1970s male world of journalism. She likely viewed her 1970 submission of *The Bluest Eye*'s laudatory review as a mistake to be learned from. When she landed the review of *Sula* three years later, she submitted a mixed response that also included what amounted to an apology for her ostensibly overly enthusiastic reaction to *The Bluest Eye*.

Blackburn's frustration with Morrison's refusal to transcend what Blackburn considers the "limiting classification 'black woman writer' and take her place among the most serious, important and talented American novelists now working" (3) drew the ire of other African American authors such as Clarence Major and Alice Walker. In letters to the *New York Times* editor (Jan. 20, 1974), Majors allows that Blackburn reveals "a typical white attitude toward untypical black writing," protests that "for a long time white readers and critics have tried to dictate what black writing should be," and suggests that "Blackburn's problem is she wants Morrison to be other than what she is. This is not the business of a book reviewer or critic." Walker is less tactful: "As I read over Ms. Blackburn's review I began to discern why, as a reviewer, she seems so utterly untrustworthy: it is because she, like only too many reviewers before her, is incapable apparently of experiencing black fiction as art but must read it instead as sociology" (26).

Not long after publishing her more discriminating review of both novels, Blackburn was hired as a book review editor for the *New York Times*, a position she held until her death in 2002, while Morrison continued to write provocative books about race relations before and after receiving a Nobel Prize for literature about people of many colors. While Morrison may have been incensed at Blackburn's retraction, that review and *The Bluest Eye* itself have become symbols of white readers' "white-gaze" misunderstanding of Morrison's fictional project, a defining moment in the professional evolution of two powerful women—and in the critical reception history of *The Bluest Eye*.

The Bluest Eye Criticism[5]

The *MLA International Bibliography* identifies 242 citations issued on *The Bluest Eye* between 1979 and 2019. Of these, 143 are published in academic journals (113 peer-reviewed), and a notable 69 (29 percent) appear as book chapters. MLA lists 25 dissertation/thesis abstracts during this period; 5 monographs have emerged on the novel, 3 after the turn of the century.[6] If professional scholarly attention comes primarily from US sources (172), criticism on *The Bluest Eye*, remarkably enough, drew attention from 45 foreign publications (21 percent) in venues sponsored by Australia (1); Brazil (1); Canada (1); China (2); Denmark (1); France (5); Germany (1); Hungary (1); India (6); Ireland (1); Italy (1); Japan (3); Korea (3); Lithuania (1); The Netherlands (1); Nigeria (1); Norway (1); Poland (2); Romania (2); Spain (7); Turkey (1), and the United Kingdom (2).

Twentieth-century BE criticism produced 22 articles from multicultural journals: *Black American Literature Forum* (4), which in 1992 became the *African American Review* (5);[7] *College Language Association Journal* (6); *MELUS* (2); *SAGE* (2); *Callaloo* (1); *Ethnic Studies* (1); and *Minority Voices* (1). Unlike first responses on *BE*, most of the twenty-first-century American criticism extended to the broader academic publishing community with only eight articles appearing in multicultural journals: *African American Review* (3); *Griot* (2), *MELUS* (2), and *Callaloo* (1).[8] Journal and book articles, presented in chronological order, stem

---

5   Because *BE* reconsidered as *God Help the Child* has, as Faulkner's Dilsey puts it, "seed de beginnin, en now ... de endin" of an era, in this chapter I will separate *BE* criticism into twentieth- and twenty-first-century responses, which encapsulate to some extent Morrison's continuing cultural impact. Only *Beloved* (with 890 citations) and *Song of Solomon* (with 265 citations) have elicited more MLA notice than *BE*.

6   One book considers *The Bluest Eye*, *Sula*, and Kingston's *The Woman Warrior* as female bildungsromane (Feng 1997); one studies survival in Silko, Morrison, and Roth (Rand 1999); one includes *The Bluest Eye* in a comparison of Faulkner and Morrison (Schreiber 2001); one examines Morrison's language in *The Bluest Eye* and *Beloved* (Simpson 2007); and one incorporates *The Bluest Eye* and *Beloved* among studies of narrative beginnings in twentieth-century feminist fiction (Romagnolo 2015).

7   The official publication of the Modern Language Association's Division on Black American Literature and Culture, *African American Review* (*AAR*) has featured prominent African American writers and cultural critics, including Amiri Baraka, Cyrus Cassells, Rita Dove, Charles Johnson, Toni Morrison, Ishmael Reed; Trudier Harris, Arnold Rampersad, and Hortense Spillers.

8   Taking twentieth- and twenty-first-century criticism together, 17 percent appeared in journals with a multicultural focus.

primarily from archetypal; intertextual; feminist/womanist; psychoanalytic; ecocritical; structuralist; African American/postcolonial; and new historical/cultural theoretical approaches. Quite a few scholars use *The Bluest Eye* to experiment with pedagogical or reader-response strategies.

The Bluest Eye and Archetypal Criticism

Given that Morrison has described her work as a concerted effort to disrupt Western mythology with African American story, archetypal critics took eager notice of her first novel. If Norris Clark begins the discussion of "flying black" as Morrison uses it in *BE*, *Sula*, and *Song of Solomon*, Grace Hovet and Barbara Lounsberry enhance Clark's 1980 conclusions with a seminal essay on the same three novels about the special associations of flying with freedom, with raising oneself, with the transcendence of growth—and as a symbol of thought, imagination, and sexual potency—in the African American community (1983). After they introduce the legend of the "flying Africans who rose up from the slave fields and flew back to Africa," Hovet and Lounsberry point out that "Afro-American writers often make distinctions among kinds of birds and kinds of flight." These critics delineate the characters in *BE*, *Sula*, and *Song of Solomon* as falling into three kinds of fliers: "(1) the 'nesting birds' who never dare to fly; (2) the daring but dangerous fliers whose flights often lead to 'the fall,' isolation, madness, or death; and (3) soaring, whole fliers with a sense of both identity and community . . ." (120–21).

Three scholars note Morrison's adaptation of Greek myths in *BE*. Madonne Miner observes in 1985 that the author's sense of déjà vu with the places she depicts in the novel results not only from her skill at recreating a black neighborhood in Lorain, Ohio, in 1941, but from her use of a sequence of rape, madness, and silence "originally manifest in mythic accounts of Philomela and Persephone." This confluence of events "provides Morrison with an ancient archetype from which to structure her very contemporary account of a young black woman" (176). Elizabeth Hayes adds in 1994 that "Morrison deconstructs [both] the traditional reading of the [Persephone] myth, particularly its implied valorization of social codes that permit and even sanction . . . destructive domination of women," and its presentation of "Persephone's abduction and rape . . . as natural events, approved and ordained by the masculine higher powers, to insure the continuation of life on earth." Hayes contends that in *The Bluest Eye*, Morrison presents "Pecola's sexual initiation graphically as . . . the brutal rape of a helpless child of eleven by her own drunken father," resulting in Pecola's "complete [and permanent] loss of self . . . and the sterility of the earth" represented by the shocking absence of marigolds in the fall of 1941 (192).

Centering her argument on *Sula*, Michele Pessoni claims in 1995 that Morrison's novels broadly "lend themselves well to interpretation by current feminist archetypal theory." *BE*, Pessoni asserts, provides an example of what Karla Holloway calls "Demeter denied"; Morrison transforms the original story "in order to depict and condemn a modern society where the myth has gone awry, a society in which patriarchal consciousness destroys these sacred [mother/daughter] bonds by destroying the human capacity to feel." Pecola Breedlove is "the unwilling and unready Persephone forced to descend into a benumbing abyss of silence and madness." Like Miner, however, Pessoni maintains that Claudia MacTeer, left behind to tell the story, begins to feel "the stirrings of a Demetrian anger, which, though painful, promises resurrection and a necessary 'coming back to life'" (439–41).

All these feminist archetypal critics agree that if the early American literary canon exhibits writers despairing of "the loss of some intangible force that might restore meaning to a world decaying into wasteland decade by decade," subsequent writers like Morrison "began to explore the possibility of discovering divinity and meaning from within, of reconnecting to the feminine archetype buried deep within the human psyche in order to resurrect a way of seeing and feeling that offers the promise of healing and life to an ailing world." For Morrison "the deity resurfacing from some collective unconscious yearning is more than just the repressed virgin of Christianity. She is the spirit of the Great Goddess, the archetypal feminine virgin/mother/crone who can provide what traditional patriarchal institutions have failed to provide: reverence for all forms of life" (Pessoni 439–40).

The Bluest Eye and Intertextual Criticism

Although preliminary scholarly response to Morrison's first novel unsurprisingly hit hard on African American and feminist/womanist concerns, also unsurprising given the unfamiliar name recognition of a newly published novelist, the greatest number of critics turned to *BE*'s intersections with already known texts.[9] Twentieth-century intertextual criticism can be categorized into articles that emphasize themes followed by those that juxtapose Morrison with other individual writers or, more broadly, with multiple international writers, women writers, or African American writers.

Initiating the discussion in 1982 by examining the "grotesque within the grotesque" in *BE* (American obsession with whiteness) and Gayle Jones's *Eva's Man* (American fixation on sexual dominance), Keith Byerman believes the novels "show the particular appropriateness of the grotesque in black literature that is also social criticism" (447). Comparing the ways in which violent fights between their parents affect a brother and sister in Stephen Crane's *Maggie* and *BE*, Rosalie Baum concludes that, while in both cases "alcoholism plays an important role in the lives of the parents and thus of the children," in both cases alcoholism is nonetheless "shown to be much more *caused* than causing" (91). After he explains that *BE* is "an unusually effective exploration of racism in twentieth-century America in part

---

9   Responding to the limitations of second-wave feminism with regard to the history and experiences of black women and other marginalized groups, Alice Walker coined the term "womanist."

because of the place it gives to central legacies of Western civilization," Thomas Fick posits that Morrison turns to Eliot's *The Waste Land* and Plato's "Allegory of the Cave" in Book VII of *The Republic* to provide specific thematic and structural elements in her novel, and more importantly, to illustrate "the close relationship between intellectual traditions and particular economic and social conditions" (10). Marilyn Atlas's consideration of literacy in America leads her to read slave narratives alongside *BE*.

Three twentieth-century intertextual scholars analyze *BE*'s expressions of motherhood. Gloria Wade-Gayles looks at mother/daughter relationships in the fiction of Dorothy West, Paule Marshall, and Morrison. Marie Umeh compares two contemporary black women writers, Nigerian Buchi Emecheta and African American Toni Morrison, to show that they pose "interesting alternatives to the traditional, stereotyped images of the black woman as mother, drawn largely by black men" (31). Jeanine Casler speculates about reasons for the rejection of the maternal, presenting a study of monstrous motherhood across cultures.

Favored individual writers who stimulate comparison with *BE* are William Faulkner, Ralph Ellison, and Maxine Hong Kingston. After an African American woman in his 1996 Faulkner and Morrison class [mis]interprets his use of the terms "Standard English" and "Black English" as racially denigrating, William Dahill-Baue opts to investigate black dialect in *The Sound and the Fury* and *BE*. Theresa Towner examines black matters from the perspective of Flannery O'Connor's affectionate term for Faulkner—"the Dixie Limited"—specifically comparing *BE* with *As I Lay Dying* (see Kolmerten 1997). In this same collection, Keith Byerman focuses on black daughters in *Absalom, Absalom!* and *BE*.

John Duvall and Robert Young liken *BE* to *Invisible Man*. Duvall contends in 1997 that Soaphead Church's letter to God directly echoes Ellison's novel. Moreover, "with its oblique reference to the necessity of an authorial self-fashioning distinct from that generated by a birth name, [it] encodes many of the issues of identity that Morrison clearly struggled with" regarding her renaming of herself, and also in her novels, where naming and authentic racial identity are central. Duvall goes so far as to argue that Morrison's covert address to Ralph Ellison "indicates the scope of her writerly aspiration, which even with her first novel seems to be to supplant Ellison as a cultural authority on the African-American experience" (251). Focusing on African American subjectivity, Young follows up with the similarities of the Invisible Man's invisibility and Pecola's request for blue eyes. Wen-ching Ho and Chang-fang Chen trace Morrison's affinities with Kingston, Ho concentrating on the search for a female self in *BE* and *The Woman Warrior* and Chen using Bakhtinian strategies to address these ethnic writers.

Five scholars notice *BE*'s connections with other individual texts or writers. Paula Bennett takes the mother's part in a study of incest and maternal deprivation in *BE* and Woolf's *To the Lighthouse*; Sharon Gravett views *BE* as an inverted *Walden*; Kimberly Drake observes how rape leads to silence and resignation on the part of the victim in *BE* and Wright's *Native Son*; Aribert Schroeder tracks

Morrison's variations on Chester Himes's *Third Generation*; and Cheryl Malcolm looks at father/daughter seduction in *BE* and Latina playwright Milcha Sanchez-Scott's *Roosters*.

Additional twentieth-century intertextual scholarship on *BE* can be catalogued according to three headings: Morrison's associations with international writers; with multiple women writers; and with various African American writers. Two critics treat Morrison together with Nigerian literature. Lita Hooper takes a black feminist approach to *BE* and Nigerian author Emecheta Buchi's *The Bride Price*; Thelma Ravell-Pinto's book chapter considers these novelists' attitudes toward beauty and comparative aesthetics. Highlighting novels that attempt to speak for traumatized children, Laurie Vickroy illustrates how *BE* and Marguerite Duras's *The Vice-Consul* "bear witness to the psychic damage that results from living in a colonized situation" (Abstract). Daniel Candel Bormann discerns how *BE* and Mikhail Bakhtin's *Rabelais and His World* treat the material bodily principle.

Three scholars note Morrison's affinity with several other women writers. Michelle Schiavonne ponders images of marginalized cultures portrayed in *BE*, Paule Marshall's *Brown Girl, Brownstones*, and Louise Erdrich's *Love Medicine*. Grounding her argument in contemporary theological and psychological feminist theory, which determines that women, unlike men, locate epiphany in ordinary interpersonal experience rather than in the unique solitary quest, Kristina Groover allows that the experiences of domestic practice, storytelling, and participation in community create sacredness by effecting positive transformation. She interfaces Sarah Orne Jewett's *The Country of the Pointed Firs* with numerous twentieth-century texts, including *BE*. In an inaugural study of "the Girl" and the complexities of female coming-of-age at the end of the millennium, Gina Hausknecht proposes the individual stories of girlhood as told by Jane Campion, Angela Carter, Kathy Acker, and Morrison as counter-narratives to a corporately produced cultural ideology and canonical authority. Aleksandra Izgarjan includes three African American texts, Baldwin's *Go Tell It on the Mountain*, Walker's *The Color Purple*, and *BE*, in her study of the "untranslatability" of African American Vernacular English.

Twenty-first-century *BE* intertextuality reconnects first with Faulkner, the initial comparisons made in a Japanese publication: Hisae Tanaka notes the racial consciousness present in *The Bluest Eye* as well as "That Evening Sun," *Light in August*, and *Absalom, Absalom!* Observing the interactions between sex, race, and power, George Potter weighs in on scenes of forced domination in *BE* and *Light in August*. In another foreign, this time Irish, publication, Mary Grace Elliott considers the schisms of motherhood in *BE* and *As I Lay Dying*. Taking a similar trauma studies approach, Evelyn Schreiber's monograph focuses more broadly on the oeuvres of both writers as she analyzes ways in which their subversive voices disrupt how others become eroticized. Françoise Buisson's contribution to a book on Faulkner and Morrison scrutinizes their respective quests for beauty in *The Sound and the Fury* and *BE*.

Two books include chapters that link *BE* with other revelations about incest. Stating that some black writers may have felt compelled to "tone down" the horror of incest, Lynn Scott explains as she quotes Elizabeth Wilson on the domestic propaganda sanctioned by the white middle class: "Incest does not take place in the white middle-class family; it is a vice of class and racial others who lack the rationality necessary to control their impulses. Suspicions that others engage in incestuous practices have long been part of the arsenal of moral prejudice that has been used to justify the social and political hegemony of the white middle class" (38). Scott argues, however, that not only does James Baldwin tackle the issue head-on in *Just above My Head*, but that he and Morrison in *The Bluest Eye* make symbolic and ideological uses of incest stories, representing incest in a manner that contributes to "a significant shift in the discourse of incest and the incest taboo in the past thirty years." Both writers "explore how a discourse of incest obscures other 'tabooed' subjects that are, in fact, more 'unspeakable' than incest" (84). For Morrison, that subject is racial self-loathing.

Monica Michlin proposes that *Push* forwards the study of incest Morrison began in *BE*. Michlin reads Sapphire's 1996 novel, made into the 2009 Academy-award-winning film *Precious*, as "a talking book that *signifies* upon previous African American novels revolving around the three major themes of invisibility, literacy and incest within the black family." After she underscores the "oralized narrative" of Precious's recollections of trauma and the "empathetic reading contract" her voice establishes, Michlin illustrates how Precious's "journey into literacy" equates to a contemporary neo-slave narrative and how Sapphire's portrayal of self-empowerment and rebirth via delivering the story pays tribute to yet also critiques *BE* and Alice Walker's *The Color Purple* (Abstract).

Vernita Burrell looks to *BE* and Baldwin's "Sonny's Blues" to urge an open dialogue between the literary and the ethical, which takes care to address the unique style, content, or purpose of the narrative while simultaneously "searching for and accepting the ethical messages contained within its aesthetic beauty" (3). James Saunders addresses the broader ethics of *BE* and Shirley Jackson's "The Tooth" via a narrow thematic approach. Even as these texts scrutinize a tiny part of the body, perhaps the body part least likely to provide any significant insights about the human condition, Saunders illustrates how the consequence of this inconsequential loss renders two women "driven to the depths of emotional destruction" (204). Philip Goldstein zooms out again to evaluate the modernist fiction of Morrison and Ralph Ellison as lying somewhere in between the Black Arts Movement and Communism.

Morrison's work still draws comparisons to the Bible and Shakespeare. In Shirley Stave's 2006 collection on Morrison and the Bible, Rebecca Degler tracks the importance of ritual or alternate religions in *BE*. Six years later, Chris Roark maintains that though Morrison famously rejects comparisons with Western authors, *BE* mentions Ophelia in a way that suggests parallels between Shakespeare's victim and Pecola Breedlove. Juxtaposing song, as a form of collective information-sharing that heals the individual, with what Roark calls an isolating "soliloquy sense of self," Morrison references *Hamlet* to critique Western tragedy. In so doing, she writes against the limitations of Shakespearean drama, the novel as her own artistic medium, and, by extension, readers who "selectively appropriate[e] African American culture when they pursue traces of *Hamlet* in *The Bluest Eye*. Vernacular African American culture, in particular the blues, emerges as a powerful alternative to the alienation imposed by Hamlet's "'soliloquy sense' of the self" (Abstract).

Twenty-first-century intertextual criticism naturally connects *BE* to increasingly abundant texts written by other females of color. Juxtaposing *BE* with *The Color Purple* and Lorraine Hansberry's play *A Raisin in the Sun*, José Martins discusses how black women keep contact with both black and white worlds; Pecola Breedlove, for example, strives to assimilate. Part of a book-project attempt to recast American literary history since the genesis of the European concept of a New World, Cheryl Wall embraces the enticing changes in the air as effected by the work of Maya Angelou, Morrison, and Alice Walker. Between the 1970s, when Morrison published her first novel, and the 1990s, when she was awarded the Nobel Prize in Literature, "she and her black female contemporaries had remade the American literary landscape" (968). After Tim Peoples describes political storytelling as too often "didactic where it should be transcendent, argumentative where it should be exploratory," he concludes that *BE* and *Their Eyes Were Watching God* avoid these pitfalls as each author develops "a distinct ethos of storytelling that arises from conflict with the political and artistic situation she finds herself in" (177–78). If Morrison does not always solve the problem of integrating past and present suffering, for example, she invites readers to meditate on the issues via her art.

Shalene Vasquez laments the scarce comparisons between lauded African American female writers like Morrison and the most critically and commercially successful female Caribbean writer, Jamaica Kincaid. Building on recent efforts to locate Morrison in transnational spaces, Vasquez provides a close reading of ways in which "a foundational 'Caribbean' work," *Annie John*, "implicitly expands on Morrison's representations of female autonomy and visual culture" in *BE* (Abstract). Nancy Backes contributes a book chapter on the desperate adolescent "Other" in novels by Paule Marshall, Morrison, and Jamaican American author Michelle Cliff. As she argues that Morrison's novel and that of another Caribbean (Haitian) writer, Edwidge Danticat, depict females as commodities in a male-driven society, Michelle Hunt determines that *BE* and *Breath, Eyes, Memory* ultimately encourage women to defy dominant standards of beauty and sexuality by supporting each other.

The Bluest Eye and Feminist/Womanist Criticism

Also unwaveringly popular with *BE* critics has been a feminist/black feminist theoretical approach. Twentieth-century concerns include black female identity;

mother/daughter, father/daughter relationships; barriers to self-acceptance such as family roadblocks, violence, and white women; and body politics. Noting that even Morrison states she is always writing about love or its absence, Jane Bakerman emphasizes that Morrison's female characters especially seek a sense of self-worth. If the traditional initiation rite, that is, the individual's search for genuine values, is painful but enlightening, Bakerman continues, "Morrison's early works explore the results for black women when the values are real and powerful but designed primarily for middle-class whites." With these values known by black women to be useless, even damaging, Morrison merges her "basic theme with the initiation motif, and the initiation experiences, trying and painful as they are, fail" (541–42).

After she presents statistics confirming that "'Whites Only' could have been stamped on almost every literature series for high school students circulated before 1965" (435), Ruth Rosenberg turns in 1987 to the tough love that barely cushions the lives of *BE*'s black girls: "The girls' guilty self-recriminations form the prologue and the epilogue, for it has not occurred to them that the earth itself might have been 'unyielding.' It is this 'hard ground' that the novel explores—a world that permits the foreclosure of childhood, that imposes a premature adulthood." Rosenberg confirms her arguments with research by sociologist Joyce A. Ladner, who "calls the pubescent black girl 'emotionally precocious' because she has either vicarious or personal experiences of violence" and must develop early on the coping skills needed to survive (441–42).

Whereas Robert Sargent adds a chapter on self-identity in *BE* and *Sula* to a book about black women writers keeping the faith, H. H. Gowda discusses the feminine black voice in Morrison's first novels while Lizabeth Rand concentrates on female discourse in *BE*. Rajyashree Khushu-Lahiri comments on the connections between matrilineage and migrancy in *BE*. Contributing to a black feminist anthology published in 2000, Renita Weems encapsulates the words often used as validation for ignoring artists like Morrison: shallow, emotional, unstructured, reactionary, just too painful: "That she is a woman makes her work marginal. That she is Black makes it minor. That she is both makes it alien. But these criticisms have not stopped the flow of her ink." Weems's essay points out that as a black female artist who insists on portraying the tragic as well as the fortunate of her lot, Morrison joins those responding to "Who will revere the black woman?" with "the black woman artist will revere the black woman" (94).

Twentieth-century feminist scholars also focus on the mother/daughter, father/daughter relationships in *BE*. In an essay which confirms that *BE* exemplifies the need for mothers to maintain a strong authentic self so that they may foster the same in their daughters, Joyce Pettis explains that Pauline fails to nurture her daughter because she herself has lived as an unnurtured child. These neglected mothers "carry their own guilt and self-hatred over to their daughter's experiences" (224). Andrea O'Reilly argues that Morrison "articulates a fully developed theory of African American mothering which is central to her larger political and philosophical stance on black womanhood in America." After O'Reilly outlines that theory of mothering, she delineates "how initiation into motherhood and perspectives on maternity in *BE* and *Tar Baby* enact and represent Morrison's maternal philosophy" (83).

Vanessa Dickerson hones in on the figure of the naked father when she turns to father/daughter interactions. Comparing the scene where Claudia and Frieda become aware of their unclothed father checking on them during the night as he makes his way back to bed from the bathroom with Cholly's drunken, naked sprawls and ultimate rape of Pecola, Dickerson finds the "magic, the miracle of Morrison's novel" to be "the survival, if not the transcendence, of a black father like MacTeer who, in spite of the stress of being a black man in a white paternalistic culture, is able to foster in his children a feeling of security and a good sense of self. The saddest reality in the novel is the naked father like Cholly who, distressed unto madness by his total segregation from purportedly godly ideals of manhood and fatherhood, raises children who cannot see, and so deny the value and beauty of their selves and wish for the bluest eye" (123).

Various barriers to acceptance, self and otherwise, also worry feminist critics. Michael Awkward considers Morrison's use of central female characters to be a refiguring and re-directing of the African American literary canon. He contends that many works by black male writers represented literary "roadblocks" to female "artistic self-hood" and that Morrison's efforts to avoid the white gaze in *BE* authenticates black and female experience. as it "created canonical space for several of the black female novels that followed it and revised the 'overwhelmingly male disposition of the Afro-American literary canon'" (McKay 1988, 8). In a 1990 collection of essays on women and violence in literature, Karla Alwes examines violence done to black women in *BE*. Françoise Burgess posits that *BE* reveals black women's nemesis to be the white woman: "The white woman has all the assets in hand by virtue of her birth and her race. How can we be surprised by the black woman's animosity towards her and her determination to demolish the idol with clay feet? In the eyes of the black woman, the white woman, far from being an admirable creature, only benefits from an unjustifiable situation" (Abstract).

A number of twentieth-century critics concentrate on body politics in *BE*. Jane Somerville affirms that idealized beauty results in the denial of love; Malin Walther confirms that one of Morrison's missions is to revise these standards of beauty. Alluding to Luce Irigaray's concept of the "male gaze," Walther argues that "feminist application of this theory has focused on the entrapment of white female characters in the gaze," presupposing a "universal" standard of feminine beauty. Morrison, however, "forces a reconsideration of the framework feminists use to discuss the specular system and female beauty" as she "explores the visual system upon which definitions of beauty are based, identifies the racial underpinnings of visual beauty, and reorients the gender-based construction of the gaze"; her efforts have moved to "redefine beauty out of the specular system and into a racial authenticity" (775). Anne Cheng relates "how the politics surrounding the discourse of beauty at the intersection (that is, the active collusion, rather than mere parallel) between race and gender may have displaced or misrecognized the experience of beauty" (191).

Jane Kuenz underscores the body politics embodied within *BE*'s three madams: "The novel's unhappy convergence of history, naming, and bodies—delineated so subtly and variously elsewhere—is, in these three, signified most simply and most crudely by their bodies and their names: Poland, China, the Maginot Line. With these characters, Morrison literalizes the novel's overall conflation of black female bodies as the sites of fascist invasions of one kind or another, as the terrain on which is mapped the encroachment and colonization of African American experiences, particularly those of its women, by a seemingly hegemonic white culture." Morrison "rewrites the specific bodies and histories of the black Americans whose positive images and stories have been eradicated by commodity culture" by "shifting the novel's perspective and point of view, a narrative tactic that enables her, in the process, to represent black female subjectivity as a layered, shifting, and complex reality" (421).

Twenty-first-century feminist criticism on *BE* also accents the black female body. Vanessa Dickerson continues to be concerned: "For white men a site of political empowerment; for black males a source of being, love, and shame; for white women a source of, among other things, freedom and aestheticization—the body of the black female matters deeply" (2001, 195). Nonetheless, for all that it provides, Dickerson cautions, this body is neither saved nor precious nor privileged, and its problematic recovery cannot occur in isolation, but rather in cooperation.

Elisabeth Mermann-Jozwiak weighs in on body politics in *BE*. Observing that the bodies of Morrison's female characters are somehow marked, Mermann-Jozwiak contends that the marks "signal their differences and allow them to be interpreted and contested by their communities and by readers alike." Specifically, this scholar considers Pecola's body, dominated by discourses of power manufactured by a white supremacist society, and *BE*'s ensuing "ideological critiques of discursive constructions of the body" (189). Sarah Sherman gauges *The Bluest Eye* body as caught between religious and consumer-cultural concerns. Focusing on two prison memoirs as well as Morrison's rape narrative, Laura Doyle looks at the violation of and resistance from bodies in and outside prison to "describe bodily resistance as it operates within the pressures of sexuality, race, and nation" (184). Linden Peach studies Morrison's exploration, mainly with the women in her fiction, "of the stigmatization of body difference other than skin color and of how this process of shaming is countered by a performative view of body identity" (274).

Some twenty-first-century feminists concentrate on issues of female beauty and desire. Julia Emberley reads the representation of fashion in *BE* as an example of how women writers adopt what she calls "transactional reading" (a "way of reading objects in everyday life in order to negotiate their meanings and values for subjective and aesthetic experience"), which establishes "an implied readership with those who share an understanding of the complexities of fashion and its various meanings in everyday life." Both elucidating and transforming the alienation that ensues from advanced capitalist commodity states, this communication process reveals that one value of the "literary" lies in "its encounters with everyday materialities of desire, change, and signification" (Abstract). Two book chapters identify Morrison's revisions of racialized attitudes toward beauty. Althea Tait demonstrates that racialized body aesthetics are not only informed by the constructs of both gender and race but serve as a tool of social control in consumer cultures. Aleksandra Izgarjan points to the destructive impact that the ideal of white female beauty, disseminated via mass media, has had on the African American community: by imposing images of breathtaking white beauty, the white community metaphorically suffocates its African American counterpart by breaking it physically and psychologically.

Other contemporary feminists employ *BE* to deliberate on social justice. Jeannette Riley, Kathleen Torrens, and Susan Krumholz include Morrison among those authors who envision "a world that does not devalue and separate people, a world connected to ideals of justice grounded in the interrelationships of words and deeds." As they propose "a new way of seeing and interacting with the world around us, recognizing our individual responsibilities for creating better communities, questioning government actions, and seeking, above all, a society that sustains people regardless of gender, race, class, ethnicity, sexuality, or access to resources," these current writers also articulate "a feminist vision of justice—one which asserts that interdependence, responsibility, respect for and relationship with the environment, and an ethics of care are the foundation for a more reasoned and reasonable practice of justice" (Abstract).

Four scholars specify the social justice ramifications of rape and prostitution. In a feminist reading of rape narratives, Tessa Roynon emphasizes Morrison's subversive effort to re-theorize sexual violence. As she displays "a consistent commitment to forging new and emancipatory ways of representing sexual violence," fiction like *BE* demystifies the rapist (38). Susmita Roye joins Payel Pal and Gurumurthy Neelakantan in bringing Morrison's prostitutes into the oppositional fold. Pal and Neelakantan advocate that *BE*'s revisionism not only includes the socioeconomic struggles of black prostitutes in capitalist America but also "interrogates the black community's double standards in censuring the prostitutes on the one hand and turning a blind eye to the pedophiliac excesses of those in power on the other" (4–5). Referring to Gurleen Grewal's 1998 description of the anticonventional females in Morrison's novels who "embody a positive, oppositional space" because the "body/bawdy imagery characterizing these women is radically opposed to bourgeois norms" (37), Roye clarifies in 2012 that Morrison is not recommending Chinas, Polands, and Miss Maries as role models, but is "hinting by highlighting their resistive attitude that a certain amount of opposition to oppression is possible. Morrison's whores are interrupted girls who have grown into resilient women" (223–24).

A number of recent feminists respond to Morrison's confession that the compulsion to fill in the literary vacuum of black female experience, the urge "to find a 'person,' a 'female,' a 'black' like herself in literature" sculpted her into a writer (Roye 212). Ágnes Surányi, P. V. Annie Gladys, Edwinsingh Jeyachandra, Monika Singh, Khamsa Quasim, Mazhar Hayat, and Uzma Asmat showcase BE as depicting African American female experience from childhood to womanhood, including the celebration of African American women's resistance and resilience as mothers. Roye adds to the conversation about un-displayed underdog presences. Appreciating Susan Mayberry's effort to dispel a "one-sided view" of Morrison's war against absence by including the black boys (*Can't I Love What I Criticize? The Masculine and Morrison* 2007), Roye nonetheless believes that in BE "black boyhood/manhood mostly runs as an undercurrent to shape and present black girlhood/womanhood" (213).

Roye also concludes that Morrison's "world of fiction is often black but never bleak. If the disturbed girlhoods of her disrupted girls express her anger, then brave endeavors by some of these girls to survive their amputation constitute not only a message of hope but also an agenda for action. Morrison's remonstration is expressed through both 'interruption' of her disrupted girls and their courageous leap beyond it" (225). Aytemis Depci and Bülent Tanritanir analyze the triple oppression of women in BE, and Lee Insoo turns to theorist Julia Kristeva to consider its narrative battle over the meaning of menstruation.

Finally, feminist/womanist approaches embrace narrative openings and unclosed endings. As she fills the void of books on narrative beginnings, particularly from a feminist perspective, Catherine Romagnolo also provides in 2015 a critical awareness of how "social identity plays a role in the strategic use and critical interpretation of narrative beginnings" and how beginnings become subversive when they disrupt "the reinscription of hierarchically gendered and racialized conceptions of authorship and agency" (Abstract). Romagnolo includes BE among novels by twentieth-century American writers who "have seized the power to disrupt conventional structures of authority and undermine historical master narratives of marriage, motherhood, U.S. nationhood, race, and citizenship" (Abstract).

Gema Ortega examines Claudia MacTeer's dialogic escape (2018). If the character of Pecola has drawn more attention, it is Claudia's voice that inaugurated in Morrison's work "the use of hybridity as a narrative strategy that granted her subsequent heroines the power to subvert the authority of gender and racial master narratives." Claiming that Morrison conceives of hybridity in line with Bakhtinian "inner speech," Ortega contrasts Pecola, who has internalized the authoritative word, with Claudia's crossbred voice. In her story of heroic self-actualization despite adversity, Claudia becomes "the first in a long line of Morrison's heroines to create herself as the narrative develops, emerging as an empowered character through and because of the process of negotiating others' voices into an independent narrative of self that resists and escapes silencing and victimization" (126–27).

The Bluest Eye and Psychoanalytic Criticism

Interestingly enough, given the psychic contortions of characters like Pecola, Pauline, Cholly, and Soaphead Church, along with what Morrison designates as an entire community in trauma, twentieth-century criticism on *BE* contains few psychoanalytical studies. The first such analysis appeared in 1993 in the *Indian Journal of American Studies*. Harihar Kulkarni explains the novel as presenting "black persons who become grotesque by embracing the generationally inherited white culture and its value structure as their own" (1). Katherine Gilbert is up next to talk about ways in which characters internalize pain as coping mechanisms. Aeju Kim notes the psychological effects of migration.

Four scholars delineate the trauma in black American communities. Reemphasizing the African adage that "it takes a village to raise a child," Leester Thomas contends that if a child feels out of place or evicted from home, that child can be traumatized for life. He judges *BE* to illustrate poignantly how rejection of self by the family itself and by others ravages the psyche of African Americans since it is "tantamount to placing one outdoors and consequently destroys one's chances of gaining dignity and achieving self-realization" (Abstract). Mark Ledbetter sifts through and assesses the victims in the novel. In a collection that explores the role of shame as an important affect in the complex psychodynamics of literary and philosophical works (1999), Brooks Bouson defines *BE* as a "complicated shame drama and trauma narrative." If Morrison "seems intent on using her fiction to gain temporary narrative mastery over the shame-laden traumas she describes," she also writes books that emotionally involve her readers as they demand participatory reading (207). Centering his study on the "semiotic spaces of whiteness," George Yancy asserts that although interrogating whiteness is central to *BE*, Morrison "avoids any slippage into white display." He goes on to affirm that by allowing readers to "feel Pecola's mind and body torn asunder by whiteness," Morrison enables us to come to terms with "the heteronomous nature" of Pecola's "psychologically fissured identity" (299–301).

Twenty-first-century criticism on *BE* also continues to produce limited psychoanalytic studies. MLA specifically cites one article or book chapter which stresses respectively family systems therapy, neuropsychology, Lacanian psychology, melancholy, trauma, and psychosociology. Identifying himself as a middle-class white male, Jerome Bump claims nonetheless to identify with the family dynamics of *BE*. He challenges the belief that "black families are more dysfunctional than white families" and that authors like Morrison "are making the problem worse" as he confirms that the contemporary definition of a functional family is shifting in "the direction already taken by the black family, toward a structure of relations transcending blood kin which can include gays and lesbians." Bump insists that by expanding the concept of the "family romance" to the "family dance," and honing in on what he calls the reader's "orphan feeling," family systems therapy becomes particularly qualified to "define family dynamics that are more specific and yet more applicable to a wider variety of literary works" (151).

Naomi Rokonitz turns to the women's kitchen-table talk overheard by the children in *BE*. She argues that Claudia's "heightened empathy," and the "concomitant sensation of participation in observed action, constitute a powerful epistemological tool that is facilitated by the biological architecture of all human beings who are not disabled by neurological impairment." As Claudia exercises her receptivity, she is able to overcome the linguistic barrier between herself and the adults and discover "truth in timbre." Accumulating her knowledge base in fragments, relying heavily on embodied understanding, she learns to "'read' gesture, expression, eye movement, body odor: to feel the ambience and cadence of a conversation through attunement to its physical and emotional thrust," acquiring a perceptiveness that "enables her in later life to articulate, with subtlety, sensitivity and captivating poetry, the constellation of events that lead to the tragedy recounted in *BE*" (385–86).

Yang Ding and Xiangguo Kong take a Lacanian tack on the novel. Because the prohibition of an "Other" by a white-dominated society allows the Breedloves no opportunity to establish their ideal ego, they remain split in the permanent contradiction of the Mirror Stage. Kathleen Marks considers the evolution of melancholy from *BE*'s unyielding earth. As she explores the underexplored contributions to discourses about the definitions of melancholy, Marks determines that the novel reveals "a fruitful melancholic stance as well as a destructive one," or in Morrison's terms, "there are both vincible and 'invincible' melancholies. One leads to perception and insight, while the other leads ultimately to self-directed anger" (177).

Two twenty-first-century studies deal with trauma from different perspectives. Manuela López Ramírez underscores "Morrison's especially dramatic depiction of the destruction of the female teenager's self and her struggle for psychic wholeness in a hostile world. The adolescent's fragile identity embodies, better than any other, the terrible ordeal that the marginal self has to cope with to become a true human being outside the Western discourse" (75). Combining Marxism with a psychoanalytic point of view, Reza Hassan Khan and Shafiqur Rahman propose that *BE* depicts a community in which a racist ideology is internalized, where the sufferers of racial abuse "both endure and resist in a complex inverse interrelationship between the two actions." This psychosocial approach both examines "the politics of postmodern consumer culture of capitalism in a racist community" and traces "the sadomasochist attitude of the characters in this framework of internalized racism in the African-American community" (Abstract).

The Bluest Eye and Ecocriticism

Also interesting, given the fairly recent nod to ecocritical theory, two notable twentieth-century scholars adopt that approach with *BE*. The second article listed by MLA, in fact, contains Barbara Christian's observations about the significance of and connections between community and nature in the novel. For Christian, few contemporary novelists exhibit such an interest in the meaning of nature, much less in the relationship between the characters' belief system and their view of nature: "The interpretation of nature is central not only to her characters' attempts to understand themselves but also to the fables Morrison weaves, the way she tells her tales" (65). Another well-known African American scholar, bell hooks, contributes a chapter to a 1999 multicultural anthology that urges Americans to become more in touch with the earth. Explaining that Native American and African people shared from the beginning "a respect for the life-giving forces of nature" and that the vast majority of twentieth-century black Americans lived on Southern farms, hooks laments that little work has been done on the "great migration" of black people from the agrarian South to the industrialized North. She maintains that *BE* fictively documents the way such a move "wounded the psyches of black folk": "Estranged from a natural world where there was time for silence and contemplation, one of the 'displaced' black folks" [Pauline] "loses her capacity to experience the sensual world around her when she leaves southern soil to live in a northern city" (364–65).

The Bluest Eye and Narratology/Structuralist Criticism

BE drew four notices from twentieth-century structuralist critics. Donald Gibson designates Morrison's novel in 1989 as a counter-narrative to nineteenth-century French diplomat and ethnologist Count Authur de Gobineau's "Essay on the Inequality of the Races." For Gibson, Morrison need not have read Gobineau's racist treatise to react to him, "for his legacy is not only in his text but in western civilization's air. Her novel calls into question the mode of his thought and the whole authoritarian, politically reactionary system of beliefs about the nature of reality on which his and like thought is based" (19). Linda Dittmar approaches Morrison as a "readerly" writer in Barthes's sense that "her self-reflexive narration refracts and defers meanings. In part it also concerns political issues—notably racial and sexual. Ultimately, Morrison's writing demands "a double-reading which recognizes, at once, her place within the history of Western narrative in general and her place within a specifically Afro-American tradition" (137–38).

Claiming that Morrison "both dis-articulates African American experience from its place in a system of negative associations in the cultural imaginary of what she terms the American 'Africanist' discourse" and "re-articulates the concept of black American experience around the diversity, not the homogeneity, of its historical forms," Abdellatif Khayati elaborates via the cultural politics of difference and "in the act of [Morrison's] narrative writing, which participates not only in an historical struggle among subaltern communities but also in forging a new nonhegemonic realm of being and meaning" (313). Carl Malmgren calls *BE* "a kind of narratological compendium." It "incorporates several different forms of textuality," opening with three different versions of its "master narrative" followed by an italicized "overture." It includes "two related kinds of texts variously interspersed": four seasonal sections and seven primer sections. And it is not only multitextual, but polyphonic (251).

The Bluest Eye and African American/Postcolonial Criticism

Twentieth-century African American criticism turns to issues of black identity and community; folk traditions; the idea of otherness; black aesthetics; and postcolonialism. Alluding to Morrison's famous declaration in an interview with Thomas LeClair that she writes what she calls "village literature"—fiction for the tribe—Peter Doughty gauges how *BE* epitomizes Morrison's peasant novels: "They should clarify the roles that have become obscured; they ought to identify those things in the past that are useful and those things that are not; and they ought to give nourishment" (LeClair 20-21). Françoise Clary examines fractured identities in *BE* while R. M. Badode observes the ways in which American society is reflected in the novel.

Five essays appear on folk traditions. After she compares the black population of Lorain, Ohio—perpetuating traditions "that foster black survival, comfort in times of need, and enduring creativity"—with the faulty myth of the North as a place of freedom and prosperity, Trudier Harris addresses *BE* as African American folk culture in progress. The Breedloves "lose their abilities to use the old folk forms that sustained generations of rural blacks, and thus they broke chains of continuity in black culture" (McKay 9). Asserting that, more than just a mode of communication, language "defines a culture's style and method of looking at life and the individual's place within that culture," Yvonne Atkinson determines that Morrison's fiction "dismisses the issue of the correctness of the language but focuses intensely on the communal bonding and artistry evident in the language" (Conner 12).

Allen Alexander observes that nowhere are religious references, both from Western and African sources, more intriguing or perplexing than in *BE*, deeming the most complex Morrison's "representations of and allusions to God." Not limited to characteristics exemplified by the Trinity: Father, Son, and Holy Ghost, Morrison's God "possesses a fourth face, one that is an explanation for all those things—the existence of evil, the suffering of the innocent and just—that seem so inexplicable in the face of a religious tradition that preaches the omnipotence of a benevolent God" (293). As she investigates the ethical value of storytelling, Lyne Terrell uses *BE* as a case study in how a moral sensibility may emerge from a text via the telling of a story. Referring to the novel as a lyrically "songified narrative," Cat Moses suggests that "the catharsis and the transmission of cultural knowledge and values that have always been central to the blues form the thematic and rhetorical underpinnings of *BE*." Its narrative structure "follows a pattern common to traditional blues lyrics: a movement from an initial emphasis on loss to a concluding suggestion of resolution of grief through motion. In between its initial statement of loss and its final emphasis on movin' on, *BE* contains an abundance of cultural wisdom" (623).

Four articles explore black aesthetics, two alluding to Morrison's use of the Dick and Jane primer. Explaining that the "problem of how to represent the black self on the white page, how to overcome the inherent ethnocentrism of the Western literary tradition, is one with which both the critic and the novelist of Afro-American literature must struggle to come to terms," Timothy Powell believes the battle becomes "to de-center the white logos, to create a universe of critical and fictional meanings where blackness will no longer connote absence, negation, and evil but will come to stand instead for affirmation, presence, and good—a struggle for the right/write/rite of Afro-American literature to exist." Powell contends that no one "has accomplished this more fully" than Morrison and that, ironically, Morrison's quest to locate the Word of black culture began with a consummate white text: the Dick and Jane reader (747–48). Adding that *BE* "lays bare the syntax of static isolation at the center of our cultural texts," Shelley Wong claims that Morrison's technique of breaking up and confusing the language of said reader discloses "a two-fold process which marks the trajectory of [her] narrative practice—i.e., the practice of taking apart and then pouring back together to form the ground of a new order of signification" (471–72).

In a text on literature and black aesthetics, Phyllis Hastings allows that *BE* disrupts the American Dream. In another collection on the aesthetics of Toni Morrison, editor Marc Conner submits an essay contradicting the truism of Morrison scholarship that her primary theme is supportive community. Postulating that the community depicted in her early works is actually "predatory, vampiric, sterile, cowardly, threatening," Conner maintains that "Morrison's engagement with the relations between the individual and the community reveals a striking progression" even as her dominant aesthetic concern shifts from the apocalyptic, destructive visions of the sublime to the reconciliation and regeneration that is the beautiful. He tags *BE* to embody the fundamental pattern of the early novels: "an isolated figure, cut off from the community, must undergo a harrowing experience, an ontologically threatening encounter with what is variously described as the unspeakable, the otherworldly, the demonic—that is, the sublime" (49–52).

Toward the end of the twentieth century, international critics began to consider *BE* in postcolonial terms. Suk-Hee Lee and Lothar Bredella deliberate respectively how Morrison's novel internalizes colonial discourse yet contributes to decolonizing the mind. Alluding to Susan Willis's materialist feminist study, which "indicts the hegemonic forces of capitalist America for making many African Americans ashamed of their vernacular culture," English scholar Alan Rice likens the predicament of internally colonized African American subjects to the position of other colonized peoples encouraged to reject their vernacular culture to make headway within majority culture. As he grounds his argument in "a critical paradigm mindful of vernacular black aesthetics in a post-colonial context," Rice asserts that Morrison's efforts to write in a vernacular form arise from a political imperative (133).

Turn-of-the-century African American criticism on *BE* focuses primarily on community, class, and race. Margaret Delashmit presents the novel as an indictment of the African American community. Crystal Lucky prods the scope of its ancestral wisdom. Sara Appel's book chapter includes *BE* in an intersectional analysis that provides a framework for understanding how America's working-class merges with gender and race to create unique modes of discrimination.

Two studies deal with African American marginalization and displacement. In a 2001 book on the literature of marginality, J. Salve proposes black marginality as an important theme in BE. After Jennifer Gillan explains the ways in which "the abstract idea of the bodiless citizen has marked women and non-white Americans as outside the boundaries of full citizenship, because the attention paid to the various markings of gender or race on their bodies precludes them from being categorized as the unmarked, representative norm," she reads BE as "a commentary on the artificial boundaries of citizenship, gender, race, and history." By demarcating the history of the Breedloves' exclusion from the "'terms of full and equal personhood,'" Morrison "demonstrates that this family's unequal position is a product not of their intrinsic inadequacy, but rather of the systematic reinforcement of a racial and gendered criteria for full citizenship. This critique, in turn, disrupts the official stories that feature the United States as a brave defender of democracy and staunch critic of racialized nationalism abroad" (283–84).

Two early twenty-first-century studies approach BE as an African American bildungsroman. As she addresses the black self in a racial world, Irena Ragaišienė considers Morrison's novel to be a terminated coming-of-age story. Describing the traditional bildungsroman as accentuating "a male protagonist who demonstrates 'heroic' achievement by overcoming social and moral obstacles, defining a unified, autonomous self, and developing ethical authority through the narrative," Anne Salvatore includes BE with others in Morrison's oeuvre that "present African American female protagonists who inevitably lose the struggle against the double oppression of gender and race, fail to create authentic identity, and thus falter in the pursuit of ethical and narrative authority." Salvatore goes further, however, arguing that Morrison "creates a hybrid form of the bildungsroman that is simultaneously both ironic and nonironic." To accomplish this paradox, she presents a set of paired characters: "the protagonist, who serves as ironic anti-hero [Pecola] and her nonironic alternate, a secondary character with a seemingly lesser role, who by demonstrating strength and courage, triumphs in some way despite the enormity of cultural and personal obstacles [Claudia]. Thus Morrison de-centers the focus of the traditional bildungsroman, shifting ethical emphasis and authority away from the assumed central subject" (154–55).

Two twenty-first-century international studies, one from Korea and another from Romania, take on issues of black consciousness. Soo-Hyun Lee analyzes the tragic aspects of African American self-consciousness. Examining the first and last of Morrison's published books, Tamara Jovović investigates how Morrison draws upon the social, political, and economic forces that shape contemporary racism in America. Jovović ponders the meaning of self in a culture determined by skin color along with what has changed during the span of forty-five years.

Three twenty-first-century scholars assume a postcolonial attitude. As she includes Morrison among authors whose oeuvre is major enough to merit periodization, Malin Pereira calls for scholars to examine Morrison's "complex relationship to colonization," which has been "radically transformed from her early to more recent work" (71). Piers Armstrong cites *BE* in a study which surveys "the overlap of conceptions of blackness and [Bakhtinian] carnivalesque in a pan-American context, from the popular praxis of Brazil, where carnival stands as a performative narrative" (Abstract). Finally, writing for the *Journal of Postcolonial Writing*, where she applies Kelly Oliver's concept of the "colonization of psychic space" to *BE*, Emy Koopman connects rape to other forms of oppression, suggesting that "incest is at least partly the result of the dynamics of being colonized and 'othered.'" After she explains that "without a positive space of meaning, victims of racial oppression and of sexual violence find themselves among the abjected," Koopman critiques the connections made between colonization and incest for "ignoring the specificity of the processes by which incest and rape function to make one feel abjected" (Abstract).

The Bluest Eye and New Historical/Cultural Criticism

The first critical article on *BE* cited by the *MLA Bibliography* deals with two icons central to early twentieth-century American culture: the popular *Dick and Jane* reader and Shirley Temple—Hollywood's top box-office draw as a child actress from 1935 to 1938. Phyllis Klotman's three-page critique maintains that Morrison uses the contrast between blue-eyed, blond-haired Shirley Temple and Pecola, like her contrasting versions of *Dick and Jane*, "to underscore the irony of black experience. Whether an African American child learns acceptability from the formal educational experience or from cultural symbols, the effect is the same: self-hatred. Pecola's actual experience cannot be found in 'Dick and Jane,' for in the school primer, society denied her existence. In yearning to be Shirley Temple, she denies her own" (124). In 2000, Paul Taylor references contemporary figures like Malcolm X, Arthur Danto, and Spike Lee to explore the longstanding preoccupation by African American activists with standards of physical beauty. Centered on Soaphead Church's description of Pecola's petition, Taylor discusses the existential, social, and psychological conditions that cause this preoccupation and frame his cultural study of black aesthetics.

Scholars have regularly been engaged by the ways that *BE* addresses contemporary commodity culture. Her 1989 book chapter titled "I Shop Therefore I Am," Susan Willis employs Morrison's novel to answer whether it is possible for African Americans to participate in commercial capitalism without being assimilated to it. Giavanna Munafo follows with ways in which the concept of private property has been rendered life-denying to black and white Americans. Bill Brown includes *BE* in a cultural/poststructuralist/Marxist study about things: "If the history *of* things can be understood as their circulation, the commodity's 'social life' through diverse cultural fields, then the history *in* things might be understood as the crystallization of anxieties and aspirations that linger there in the material object. And such a history might yet be explored, however provisionally and problematically, between . . . a poststructuralist epistemology that insists on dispensing with "things" and a Marxian phenomenology that insists that we have no things to dispense with . . ." (935–36).

In a 1996 edition of *Midwestern Miscellany* devoted to Morrison's oeuvre, much of which is geographically connected to or inspired by her small, industrialized Lorain, Ohio, birthplace, Lynn Scott relies on Foucault's analysis of the link between power and knowledge— particularly his theories of "genealogy," "discourse," and "disciplinary power"—to create her own new historicist approach to *BE*. Scott explains that Foucault's genealogy rejects the traditional progressive view of history as well as the inevitability of events: "Knowledge and truth are constituted in discourse, and discourse is both constituted by and constituting of institutions. It is the function of genealogy to unmask discourse by showing its association with the subjugating effects of power." Morrison's novel affirms, according to Scott, that "events can't be traced back to single origins, that history is circuitous, and most importantly that the purpose of historical reflection is not to romanticize the past, or to justify the present, but to unmask structures of power" (10).

Two scholars deal with *BE* as literary jazz. Recognizing the deliberate orality/aurality of Morrison's "village literature," Anthony Berret maintains in 1989 that Morrison reaches beyond merely replacing tribal music with peasant fiction; her work absorbs "many of those qualities which have made music so expressive for black people over the years" as she includes a "sound track of gospel songs, folk tunes, standards, and blues," depicts her characters singing and humming, incorporates images representing village values, and mimics musical sounds and rhythms in her prose (268). Inger-Anne Søfting juxtaposes Bakhtin's culture of laughter with Morrison's utilization of black music as counterculture (1995): "In her novels carnival erupts as an alternative to white bourgeois American culture and signals an ideology which stands as a contrast to the compartmentalization of contemporary commodity society" (81).

Two twentieth-century scholars deal with the film/televisual connections to *BE*. Carol Gerster compares the marginalized treatment of racial stereotypes in film adaptations such as *Imitation of Life* and *The Littlest Rebel* with Morrison's center stage depictions of black people in *BE*. As she distinguishes between shame and guilt and concludes with "observations about the mass-mediation of shame" that saturates everyday American life, Kathleen Woodward focuses on the cultural politics of shame via *BE*: "If shame cannot be said to have a cognitive dimension for the black characters in the novel who suffer from trauma for a multitude of reasons, shame, I argue, can move Morrison's white readers to an understanding of racism and thus to insight that is ultimately moral; a cultural poetics is at work as well as a cultural politics of the emotions" (212).

Twenty-first-century criticism quite naturally includes ideas about *BE*'s reflections of as well as influence on twentieth-century history and culture. Justine Baillie illustrates how "African-American fiction seeks to define and shape an aesthetic in opposition to racial ideologies as diffused through science, education and popular culture." Viewing *BE* through the lens of Morrison's "engagement with nineteenth-century racial theory and its implicit presence within ideologies of beauty and American popular culture of the 1930s," specifically the figure of Shirley Temple, Baillie claims that "Morrison shows how the African-American community's internalization of cinematic images of beauty can lead to a psychosis that leaves identity fractured and the racial self all but erased." In addition to reading Morrison's novel as "both a critique of scientific racism and as an historical novel in sustained debate with the cultural hegemony of the 1930s," Baillie assesses its significance as "a text in dialogue with the social and political milieu in which it was written": Morrison specifically eschews the nationalism of 1960s Black Power politics for a "political contestation of ideologies through the expression of African-American art forms" (Abstract).

Trinna Frever highlights Morrison's implementation of a Shirley Temple doll. In its most literal sense a depiction of usually female humanness made miniature, the doll as depicted in fiction and popular culture becomes "a multifaceted symbol for societal disputes over what it is to be female." Morrison employs her ground-breaking/doll-cracking scene in *BE* to "fuse literary, gendered, cultural, and pop-cultural concerns, played out in the text, and played with by literary girls and their authors" (Abstract). Debra Werrlein is more specific. Acknowledging that Morrison is not the first African American author to disrupt cherished conceptions of national identity, Werrlein asserts that *BE* "challenges America's complacent belief in its benevolent self-image through representations of children who experience race, class, and gender oppressions." Morrison juxtaposes images associated with the Dick and Jane primers, references to Shirley Temple, and allusions to John M. Stahl's 1934 film *Imitation of Life* with child-characters treated as extensions of familial, socioeconomic, and national histories that contradict the ideal of childhood innocence. As she portrays children as recorders, victims, activists, and oppressors, she demythologizes the "innocent" past (53–54).

Several twenty-first-century scholars hone in on *BE*'s concessions to cultural spaces of meaning. After she acknowledges the stereotype of home as safety and protection to be complicit with sexual violence, Minrose Gwin allows that while *BE* shows how "the father's physical and psychological power over the daughter derives from his own disempowerment through historical and material contravention," Cholly nonetheless "feels empowered enough to rape his daughter" (317–18). Such depictions of explicit sexuality earned *BE* a chapter in an edition on censored books (see Luebke).

Alisa Balestra concurs with Swati Samantary that communication is inseparable from culture, so that cultural differences become especially important when we send or receive nonverbal messages. As Samantary turns to the use of color operating as literary symbolism, she contends that Morrison relies on chromatics to convey character and theme in novels such as *BE*. Balestra maintains that Morrison signs her revelations of intra-racial oppression in *BE*, which leads to a disintegration of self and community, in terms of "the destabilized flora": a "loaded phrase used in association with racial, religious, and sexual perversion and the characters' roots to their past." When the novel's black characters initiate black-on-black violence, they effectively negate their African heritage.

While Christopher Douglas observes that forays into family history provide Morrison "standard strategy for establishing character motivation in *BE*," he also notes that said strategy changes midway through the novel. In the scene where Junior hurls a black cat at his mother, Morrison pauses for a startling description of Geraldine as representative of "particular brown girls" that is not familial but typological. One of a category of people losing a cultural identity, she as "they" is caught in a "fundamental ambivalence." *BE* on the one hand "locates funk as a species-wide quality; we all have, or once had, funk." This quality, however, is "understood to have been already lost by white people in a process that was either racial or cultural (perhaps this loss is what makes someone white)." These "particular brown girls" are learning "'how to get rid of the funkiness,'" which is "embodied and racialized through the various phenotypic differences that mark the social construction of race and that threaten to overwhelm the whitening process" (141).

Recent cultural criticism occasionally takes a regional tack. If scholars link Midwestern literature most often to white modernist writers such as Sinclair Lewis, Willa Cather, and Scott Fitzgerald, Lisa Long sets *BE* among this "decidedly white and seemingly static and homogeneous canon" to shed new light on both Morrison's regional affiliations and on Midwestern culture more broadly. Simultaneously proposing that we make Morrison's work central rather than peripheral to understandings of Midwestern literature, Long suggests that "attention to the specificities of Morrison's regional formations yields a new Midwesternism," which "reflects the historical diversity of the region and prompts a rethinking of national-ethnic narratives that rely on a particular version of that history" (104–5).

Finally, twenty-first-century cultural critics have connected *BE* with various media. John Young gauges television host Oprah Winfrey's influence on Morrison and her oeuvre. Explaining the problem of the "double audience" for twentieth-century African American writers, Young tracks the extraordinary movement away from this racialized hierarchy in the twenty-first century, as Winfrey's book club "dramatically shifted the publishing world's balance of power." He goes on to consider the "Oprah Effect" on Morrison's career. Having become after only three appearances on "Oprah's Book Club" the "most dramatic example of postmodernism's merger between canonicity and commercialism," Morrison pooled her canonical status with Winfrey's commercial power to supersede "the publishing industry's field of normative whiteness, enabling Morrison to reach a broad, popular audience while being marketed as artistically important. By embracing 'Oprah's Book Club,' Morrison replaces separate white and black readerships with a single, popular audience" (181). As she welcomed and was welcomed by popular culture, her insistence that her books be read—by Oprah viewers, by her on tape, along with all the usual sites of reading—enabled a significantly different version of textual authority from that previously available to her: "Whereas the original edition of *The Bluest Eye* bespeaks bibliographically a conflicted presence within the mainstream, white publishing structure, Morrison's 'Oprah' editions and audiobooks present a voice of authentically black experience that demands attention, for its words and through its sales, from black and white readers" (199).

Several *BE* scholars explore other cultural venues of spectatorship and performance. Jacqueline Stewart shifts the focus of black spectatorship from individual films and psychological processes to issues of performance, interpretation, and public space. More specifically, she foregrounds "the intersection of two phenomena that profoundly shaped black spectatorship but are rarely discussed together in a systematic way—urban migration and the development of the classical cinematic paradigm." Pauline Breedlove becomes an example of how urban centers as well as classical Hollywood cinema "shaped the ways in which many African Americans both saw movies (for example, accessibility of theaters, types of films screened) and how black people came to understand their public roles as spectators during the first half of the twentieth century" (652–53).

Samy Azouz implicates Hollywood in the perpetuation of a "fallacious ideology, which intends to disseminate a disturbing paradigm of whiteness/beauty" as cinema becomes a machine that targets the psyches of *BE*'s female characters, especially Pauline Breedlove, and the screen becomes a mirror in a Lacanian sense. Azouz's critical lens allows him to discover a multiple pun in the book title: it is simultaneously the eye that Pecola Breedlove most desires; the "bluest I" that narrates Pecola's victimization (Claudia MacTeer); the eye of a white deity; and the eye of a surrogate camera.

As they assess Lydia Diamond's stage production of *BE*, Harvey Young and Jocelyn Prince weigh the challenges of adapting Morrison's work for the stage and other visual media, record how expectations of a "successful" adaptation have altered over time, provide a brief history of Chicago's Steppenwolf Theatre company (the location of the 2005 world-premiere production), especially *BE*'s role in diversifying Steppenwolf's acting ensemble, and showcase Diamond's contributions to her play. They detail the art of translating words across media "not by offering a close reading of the script in relation to the play text, but by revealing the negotiations and investments of the novelist, playwright, producing theater company, and theater critics who played a role in bringing Morrison's first novel to the stage" (143–44).

Including an interview she did with Diamond in an edition on Morrison and her work, Carmen Gillespie relates the visceral transformation the playwright experienced while adapting *BE* for the stage. Gillespie also presents in her 2012 collection an autobiographical essay written by African American scholar Koritha Mitchell, which traces her own upbringing and professional development alongside the narratives of race and gender in Morrison's novels. Interested in transracial performances, on and off the formal stage, Chatard Carpenter traces their roots to the early 1600s when blacks, whites, and Native Americans began to act out their impressions of each other. Moving beyond the various dark faces of minstrelsy, however, Carpenter concentrates on the dramatic iterations of whiteness in African American performance and incorporates Diamond's adaptation of *BE* in a study that looks at "ways in which embodied enactments of white-identified privileges and behaviors expand our understanding of African American performance and cultural expression" (Abstract).

The Bluest Eye and Reader-Response/Pedagogy

BE has provided rich fodder for reader response and/or pedagogical purposes. Writing in 1986 that the book had "not been accorded the attention it deserves," Marco Portales provides a close reading of the effects of a Shirley Temple culture on Cholly, in order to encourage teachers to be more aware of the special needs of black children. Linda Wagner devotes an MLA-published essay to teaching BE. Joyce Middleton explores how discussions of literacy by black feminists and black women writers "help scholars, teachers, and students to interrogate mainstream conceptions of literacy and language use." After she articulates cultural conflicts between Western and African American modes of expression, Middleton presents "Morrison's language issues as pedagogical issues" and turns to BE to delineate strategies that resist assimilation to the dominant, white Western "master narrative" (301–2). If Amy Goodburn employs BE in a project to erase white privilege in pedagogical and research writing about race, Kimberly Hébert submits a chapter focusing on Topsy, Shirley Temple, and Pecola to a book on teaching Stowe's *Uncle Tom's Cabin*.

A 1997 collection of approaches to teaching Morrison's work, edited by Nellie McKay and Kathryn Earle, contains four essays on BE. Rafael Pérez-Torres describes it as a "text that raises critical questions about identity construction," which can be "painful, threatening, or alienating" to non-European American students "who have had to live within a culture that consistently devalues their aesthetics" as well as disturb students "who feel kinship with dominant social values." The best approach, according to Pérez-Torres, would be for instructors to "turn the thematic difficulties the novel presents to good use by addressing them explicitly" (21). Given that racism exists within as well as outside the classroom, Kathryn Earle attempts to enable the white instructor to tackle in multiethnic settings the racial issues unveiled by this "explosive book" (27). Crediting the "controlled anger" in BE with making it a "superb novel to teach," far more than "a cheap way of tapping into youthful rebellion (or facile liberal sentiments)," Thomas Fick and Eva Gold maintain that "Morrison is angry at the destructive presence of authority," which she "grounds in literary traditions and historical contexts" (56). Conceding that the novel confirms for many white audiences negative typecasts of black people, Gurleen Grewal advises teachers to ensure that students understand its complex relations of cause and effect: going well beyond replicating stereotypes, BE highlights "the race-based class structure of American society that generates its own pathologies" (118).

Two twentieth-century scholars apply reader-response theory to BE. Less confident than Martha Nussbaum that habits of subtle perception learned as a reader contribute to the larger moral life, Eileen John proposes "literary fiction as sometimes playing a *subversive* role with regard to subtlety," that "reading fiction can disrupt a working standard of subtlety": "Works of fiction do not provide 'normal' perceptual fields, and readers do not approach them with precisely 'normal' perceptual habits, so, roughly stated, the reader-fiction interaction has plenty of potential for disrupting epistemic standards of subtlety, bluntness, opacity and so forth" (309). John uses *BE*'s scene with Maureen Peale to illustrate two types of such subversions, one of which has moral import. Robin Murray uses *BE* as an example of a readerly/writerly text, which demonstrates textual authority, reader authority, and social authority.

Though enthusiasm has diminished, twenty-first-century criticism continues to provide research on readers' responses to and the teaching of *BE*. Angeletta Gourdine refers to a black vernacular definition of "reading" as "interpretation of the highest order" when, for example, a parent "reads" his child or a teacher "reads" her student in situations that voice critique and insist upon reform. Including *BE* among other "colored readings" of the "raciogendered body," Gourdine explains that the "reader" desires "not only to tell you about yourself but also to craft an other self that amends the self your previous behavior encodes," rendering "an interpretation that supersedes previous interpretations" (60). As Jerome Bump applauds literature that integrates rather than splits feeling/knowledge because "emotions often generate more energy for reform of race, class, and gender inequities than abstractions, and a focus on feelings challenges not just the way multiculturalism is taught today but the foundations of higher education itself," he urges English and language departments to increase students' emotional intelligence by "adopting an 'emotive' literary criticism focusing on the feelings, moods, and emotional fields in readers as well as texts" (147–49). Bump recommends works like *BE* particularly for white readers seeking to understand the subject position of "the other," a prerequisite for moral awareness.

Brenda Daly concludes that for white people to become more effective antiracist teachers and multicultural allies, they "must continue to scrutinize the social construction of [their] white identity—emotional, psychological, and historical." Her attempt to do so required transforming her reading practices, as well as those of her students, into testimonial reading and writing. This approach rejects merely a passive textual analysis of racism; the testimonial reader is equally obliged to examine her own subjectivity. After she studied her socially constructed white identity through an analysis of her relationship—emotional and generational—to the racism expressed in a family memoir (locating this family memoir within the US history of whiteness), Daly gauged the effectiveness of her new pedagogy by evaluating student testimonial readings of *BE*.

Professors and deans promote use of Morrison's work in the twenty-first-century classroom. In a book on reading through the lens of gender, Barbara Waxman offers ways in which teachers might introduce students to *BE*'s issues of culture, nature, dysfunctional families, and racial self-hatred. In a journal that emphasizes reader-oriented theory, criticism, and pedagogy, Jeffrey Buchanan views storytelling as teaching in *BE*. In an article for *MELUS*, Myung Ja Kim focuses on teaching

BE to Korean students. Carole Ferrier contributes a book chapter about teaching African American women's literature in Australia. Citing a variety of ways in which readers can engage with Morrison, "whether sensory, political, affective, or antagonistic," Elizabeth Beaulieu utilizes her position as Dean of the Core Division at Champlain College in 2012 to provide insight into Morrison's continued relevance in the undergraduate classroom, "particularly in a curriculum invigorated by questions of moral and social aesthetics" (Carmen Gillespie 21).

CHAPTER TWO

SULA (1973)

Sula's Critical History as Told by Toni Morrison

Sula, published in 1973, may have been one of ten finalists for the National Book Award in 1975, but its critical trajectory was nonetheless nearly identical to that of *The Bluest Eye* and almost always connected to *The Bluest Eye*.[1] Morrison's foreword to the 2004 Vintage edition of *Sula* attributes this initially rocky path to the New Critical flight in the 1950s away from any accusation of being labeled a politically minded fiction writer, an awkward situation which became acute for African American writers in the racially thorny 1960s. Converting her concerns, per her usual way, into a question, in this case "What could be so bad about being socially astute, politically aware in literature?" she turned her attention to the source of the panic and the ways by which some artists and intellectuals sought to assuage it.

---

1   Standard operating procedure for the National Book Award remains by and large political and financial, calling for publishers to nominate the book, pay the entry fee, and submit the text. Each judging panel is comprised of ten people typically from the monetary end of the book trade: publishers, editors, librarians, booksellers, possibly one creative writer. Although Morrison could have, because she had been a senior editor at Random House since 1965, she most likely would not have nominated her own work for such a highly visible book award. By 1973, however, she was a fiction writer under the roof of Random House, or its Knopf imprint, with former colleague Robert Gottlieb as her editor. It is Gottlieb, then, who would have more likely nominated *Sula* for the National Book Award, Fiction category, given the publicity and prestige for Random House of having its book considered at all, much less landing among the top ten finalists. More significantly, given such careful grooming, we might have expected a softer critical landing for the novel. See https://www.nationalbook.org/national-book-awards/submissions/.

As a classical scholar, Morrison understood that derision toward politics in literature was either undirected at or unheeded by master writers such as Sophocles, Dante, Chaucer, and Shakespeare. Yet she struggled to complete *Sula* hard upon the heels of poor sales of and depressing reactions to *The Bluest Eye* by black and white reviewers alike, who ultimately questioned both books on the grounds that political fiction is not art. Morrison repudiates this critique, denying that fiction alleged political is "less likely to have aesthetic value because politics—all politics—is agenda and therefore its presence taints aesthetic production" (*Sula* foreword xi).

Because so many of these New Critics ignored the formalist criteria they themselves advocated, however, Morrison dismissed most 1970s commentary on *The Bluest Eye* as having little merit: "If the novel was [deemed] good, it was because it was faithful to a certain kind of politics; if it was bad, it was because it was faithless to them." With *Sula*, she continued to disregard the superficiality of such opinions, along with the problematic stigma of being a problem to be solved rather than a writer to be read. Finding herself caught in the no-win Catch-22 of being judged upon whether "Black people are—or are not—like this," she saw no choice but to remain faithful to a sensibility that fuses myth and the fantastic with a deep political sensitivity, acknowledging both artistic and social problems and fixing *Sula*'s narrative in a landscape "already tainted by the fact that it existed" (foreword xii).

She reminds us in "Unspeakable Things Unspoken: The Afro-American Presence in American Literature" (1988) that she began *Sula* in 1969 during a period of extraordinary civil unrest, while *The Bluest Eye* was still in proof. Morrison connects the "political-only" analysis of the worth of both novels to the display of the then-current and tellingly anxious series of questions concerning what should or does constitute a literary canon. Referring to the theoretical fortifications that monopolized the postmodern academy and resisted creative interlopers as the "canon fodder" debate, she ponders the after-boom of power protecting an officially legitimized set of American texts and presumes at least some of the hysteria over this ongoing debate to be a reaction to the successful assault by the feminist scholarship of men and women (black and white) on traditional literary discourse:

> Canon building is empire building. Canon defense is national defense. Canon debate, whatever the terrain, nature, and range (of criticism, of history, of the history of knowledge, of the definition of language, the universality of aesthetic principles, the sociology of art, the humanistic imagination), is the clash of cultures. And *all* of the interests are vested. (132)

Morrison not only commends the "melee" as provocative, explosive, and healthy, but she praises the extraordinarily profound criticism that ensued, which redeployed the political consciousness advanced by widely-accepted-as-canonical American writers. Michael Rogin, for example, produced an exhaustive study in 1983 elaborating how deeply Melville's social thought penetrates his writing. Turning to her own work, she explains that the compulsory separation between politics and aesthetics placed an inordinate burden on African American writers:

> Whether they were wholly uninterested in politics of any sort, or whether they were politically inclined, aware, or aggressive, the fact of their race or the race of their characters doomed them to a "political-only" analysis of their worth. If Phillis Wheatley wrote "The sky is blue," the critical question was what could blue sky mean to a black slave woman? If Jean Toomer wrote "The iron is hot," the question was how accurately or poorly he expressed chains of servitude. This burden rested not only on the critics, but also on the reader. How does a reader of any race situate herself or himself in order to approach the work of a black writer? Won't there always be apprehension about what may be revealed, exposed about the reader? (*Sula* foreword xi–xii)

The 1988 lecture Morrison delivered at the University of Michigan confronts four major charges targeted at African American literature by self-appointed, self-protective defenders of the American aesthetic, attitudes that not only had a direct impact on her approach to *Sula* but had effectively managed to deflect the autonomy of black literature since the seventeenth century. The flood of rediscoveries and reprints encouraged by critical analyses of that literature in the second half of the twentieth century, such as Alice Walker's search for Zora Neale Hurston's grave and literary garden in 1973 or Henry Louis Gates Jr.'s 1982 discovery of Harriet Wilson's 1859 novel *Our Nig*, buried the first charge (no third-world or African American art exists). It simultaneously expanded the traditional canon to include classic African American works, such as *Their Eyes Were Watching God* (1937) and devised critical strategies useful for examining those works, such as Gates's *The Signifying Monkey: A Theory of African American Literary Criticism* (1988). Gates's afterword to the rediscovered, reprinted *Their Eyes Were Watching God* (2003) applauds *Their Eyes* as "a bold feminist novel, the first to be explicitly so in the Afro-American tradition" (187).

Similar close readings and research into the cultural roots of black art silenced the second charge along with its accompanying easy, if not lazy, labels: African American art exists but is inferior—excessive, banal, sensational, unintellectual—though often ardent, genuine, naturalistic, or sociologically revealing ("Unspeakable Things" 134). As Morrison encapsulates in *Playing in the Dark: Whiteness and the Literary Imagination* (1992), a great deal of the negative commentary highlights ways in which black authors address received prejudices and even create alternative terms with which to reevaluate the attachment to or intolerance of the texts and their contexts.

Accusing the third charge (African American art exists but is superior only when it measures up to Western culture's "universal" aesthetic criteria) of producing the most perniciously seductive analyses since such comparisons can infantilize and consequently cripple the literature, Morrison connects this insidious attack with the dangers of a fourth patronizing charge: third-world texts are not so much sophisticated art as rare ore, raw and thus in need of refining by Western intelligences from its natural state into an aesthetically complex form. She counters this double-barreled volley with three cautionary approaches that she finds "neither reactionary nor simple pluralism, nor the even simpler methods by which the study of Afro-American literature remains the helpful doorman into the halls of sociology" ("Unspeakable Things" 135).

The first welcomes a truly accommodating theory of African American literature based on its cultural history and the aesthetic strategies its texts employ to negotiate the world they inhabit. A second examines and reinterprets the founding nineteenth-century canonical works for the ways in which the presence of African Americans has shaped the language, structure, and meaning of American literature, an exhumation and recuperation of the *deus ex machina* into the "ghost in the machine." A third approach sifts through contemporary, generally noncanonical literature for this absent presence, regardless of its classification as mainstream or minority. Permanently astonished at the work African American narratives, persona, and idiom do for contemporary "white literature," Morrison asserts that the questions of essence and difference, in other words what makes a text "black," are critical to African American literature itself:

> The most valuable point of entry into the question of cultural (or racial) distinction, the one most fraught, is its language—its unpoliced, seditious, confrontational, manipulative, inventive, disruptive, masked, and unmasking language. Such a penetration will entail the most careful study, one in which the impact of Afro-American presence on modernity becomes clear and is no longer a well-kept secret. ("Unspeakable Things" 136)

Continuing the examination of African American sisterhood begun "as quiet as it's kept" in *The Bluest Eye* by recasting Claudia and Frieda respectively into aspects of Sula and Nel, Morrison maintains in *Sula*'s 2004 Vintage foreword that she always viewed Sula as quintessentially, metaphysically black, a state attributable neither to melanin nor to unquestioning fidelity to the tribe. When Morrison describes her character to Bill Moyers as representing the "New World Black Woman," she renders Sula daring, improvisational, disruptive, and available primarily to her own imagination. Sula's double dose of biological and chosen blackness, combined with her drive to derive choice from no choice, make her dangerously female and what Philip Page calls dangerously free. Morrison goes on to delineate some of the philosophical and sociopolitical implications of a magnetically charged friction between two types of modern black woman:

> So I was putting together two sort of strands of womanhood: certainly black womanhood is a nurturing black neighborhood woman who relies on that, but without the imagination of the New World, and then Sula, who doesn't have the

other roots, has no seed around which to grow. I happen to think that they need each other. I mean, that the New World black woman needs a little of the Old World black woman in her, and the other way around. I don't think that they are completely fulfilled without the other. I think an ideal situation is a Sula who has some responsibilities and takes them upon herself, but at the same time has this, you know, flair. (Moyers)

While she counts few individuals in 1988 who believed that the body of American literature or its criticism would ever again be confined to what it was in 1965—essentially the protected preserve of the ideas and products and analytical strategies of white men—Morrison nonetheless recognizes the political repercussions of a 900-year-old academy attempting to maintain its "standards" on the literary critical history of books like *Sula*. She also reiterates in *Sula*'s 2004 foreword her one failed effort to resist pandering to this "white gaze": she would not have needed nor would she have provided in 1988 the welcoming "lobby" or short introductory section that constitutes the novel's 1973 opening.

Having initially planned to begin with the brief declaration "Except for World War II, nothing ever interfered with the celebration of National Suicide Day" (7), she persuaded herself to create a bridge in the form of an explanatory threshold between the reader and the African American text, something she did not do with *The Bluest Eye* or with any of her novels subsequent to *Sula*. Although her aesthetic instinct warned her to fling her readers into the midst of Shadrack's fragile, wounded universe to sink or swim—just as he and so many other beautiful black boys were catapulted into the chaos of World War I and allowed no lifeline before, during, or after, Morrison opted not to refuse "the line of demarcation between . . . them and us. Refuse, in effect, to cater to the diminished expectations of the reader, or his or her alarm heightened by the emotional luggage one carries into the black-topic text" (*Sula* foreword xv–xvi).

Having second-guessed her original beginning, she devised an alternative that would usher an outlander into the hilltop black Bottom community yet not abandon the "outlaw" ambiance she desired for the text. She used her fictional lobby to let a stranger in through whose eyes readers can appreciate nostalgia for the history of a neighborhood, the violence done to its nightshade and blackberry patches, and the damaging results of that violence. She still regrets, however, the four pages and three months of nights it took to beckon the outside-the-circle reader into the circle. Confessing to embarrassment at what she views now as a staged opening, she hopes even so that her attempts to explain afterward what motivated her to include the valley man's guidance up to the city upon a hill are "helpful in identifying the strategies one can be forced to resort to in trying to accommodate the mere fact of writing about, for, and out of black culture while accommodating and responding to mainstream 'white' culture." Even if the ploy was successful, it was not the artistic or political work Morrison wanted to do:

> Had I begun with Shadrack, I would have ignored the smiling welcome and put the reader into immediate confrontation with his wound and his scar. The difference my preferred (original) beginning would have made would be calling greater attention to the traumatic displacement this most wasteful capitalist war had on black people in particular, and throwing into relief the creative, if outlawed, determination to survive it whole. Sula as (feminine) solubility and Shadrack's (male) fixative are two extreme ways of dealing with displacement—a prevalent theme in the narrative of black people. ("Unspeakable Things" 154)

The Bottom's stability and creativity in the face of ongoing dislocation are manifested via deliberate references to music, dancing, craft, religion, wit, humor, and language. This softer embrace Morrison ultimately offered in place of Shadrack's painfully remembering/reminding presence presages and complements Shadrack's organized public madness, which also helps to unify the community until Sula's outlaw spirit of black womanhood challenges it.

That encounter becomes another major (political) premise of Morrison's book. It forces readers to ask questions such as: "What is friendship between women when unmediated by men? What choices are available to black women outside their own society's approval? What are the risks of individualism in a determinedly individualistic, yet racially uniform and socially static, community?" (*Sula* foreword xiii). Because female freedom, particularly economic autonomy, has generally been coupled with sexual freedom, Morrison presents Eva, Hannah, Nel, and Sula as points of a cross displaying Eva's physical sacrifices in the name of financial independence; Hannah's noncompetitive claims to personal liberty enabled by her economic dependence upon an in-house female; Nel's position as subdued community standard; and Sula's defiance of both personal sacrifice and cultural accommodation. Relying credibly on a discredited black vernacular neither comic nor exotic, Morrison not only aimed to redirect or reinvent the critical theory imposed upon African American writers, but to reexamine the historical and political status of outlaw women regarded as naturally disruptive when not under the thumb of men. In a literary tradition where women's escape from male rule typically results in misery, regret, or eradication, *Sula* becomes Morrison's reexamination of the consequences of that self-determination on conventional black society as well as on female friendship. The only triumph possible becomes "that of the imagination" (foreword xiv).

Given that Morrison purposely shapes the content and the form of *Sula* by way of such noncanonical themes and language, we may presume, then, that both attack and defense would spill out of the academy into popular press reviews. She agrees. Since she finds the question of whether a literary canon should exist "disingenuous" (because "there always is one whether there should be or not"), Morrison views reviewer resistance to displacement within or expansion of a canon as neither surprising nor unwarranted: "Certainly a sharp alertness as to why a work is or is not worthy of study is the legitimate occupation of the critic, the pedagogue, and the artist" ("Unspeakable Things" 128). Critical response to her voice ultimately enabled recurrent literary canonical inquiry to remain a vested interest of the extended professional critical community.

Sula's Initial Critical Reception History

However, as was the case with inquiry defined by the first wave of Morrison criticism focusing on *The Bluest Eye* (1970–73), the second wave concentrating on *Sula* (1974–77) regularly contains, much to Morrison's sustained dismay, sparse though benignly favorable book reviews printed at first only in popular magazines and newspapers. Jump-started by *Sula*, these responses routinely continue to establish merely that Morrison's are entertaining books that will sell in addition to providing a message, certainly not the serious scrutiny their author had hoped for. Reviews no longer than a paragraph appear in trade journals and are prevalent in publications meant for a general audience, such as *Library Journal* (Aug. 1973); *Kirkus Reviews* (Nov. 1, 1973); *Publishers Weekly* (Nov. 5, 1973; Aug. 4, 1975); *Newsweek* (Jan. 7, 1974; Dec. 30, 1974); *Choice* (Mar. 1974); *New Republic* (Mar. 9, 1974); *Booklist* (Mar. 15, 1974); and the *New York Times Book Review* (June 2, 1974; Dec. 1, 1974). Pronouncing *Sula* an "impressive second novel" (*Kirkus Reviews*), reviewers limit themselves even so to brief synopses about authenticity, characterization, language, and originality (*Library Journal* and *Publisher's Weekly*); friendship, poverty, sexuality, and symbolism (*Newsweek*); authentic dialogue and narrative style (*New Republic* and the *New York Times Book Review*). Later, more in-depth analyses divulge that perhaps the real issue behind what Morrison would deem lightweight investigation is that early, especially white, reviewers were simply at a loss for words.

Whereas Leroy Staggers's doctoral research labels responses to *Sula* as progressively "resolute" in their approval, critics nonetheless continue to restrict theselves to glowing generalities (36). Introductory stands essentially restate that Morrison's language is compelling, as in *BE*, while her narrative highlights the devastation caused by racism. Despite her retraction of previous accolades for *BE* (see chapter 1), *New York Times* reviewer Sara Blackburn reflects initial Morrisonian assessment; her 1973 review on *Sula* gushes that Morrison is "someone who really knows how to clank out a sentence ... and her dialogue is so compressed and life-like that it sizzles" (3). Subsequent second-wave critics commonly praise Morrison's linguistic skill. Margo Jefferson states in *Ms.* that "The language is passionate and precise; lyrical and philosophical" (34–35), and *Newsweek* reports to its readers that the novel's "brevity [is] belied by its surprising scope and depth" (Jan. 7, 1974).

Other critics are equally enthusiastic—as well as vague. Elliott Anderson, writing in the *Chicago Tribune Book World* (Jan. 13, 1974), praises *Sula* as "one of the most beautifully written, sustained works of fiction [he] had read in some time" (33). Some critiques may be described as backhanded compliments repeatedly disguising willful innocence or subtle racism. In an article titled "The Naughty

Lady," for example, Jonathan Yardley says that "*Sula* is rich in mood and feeling, its humor is earthy and delightful, and its dialogue is especially sharp" (*Washington Post Book World* 3). Ruth Rambo McClain claims that the book "command[s] at least a second reading" (*Black World* 51–52); Douglas O'Connor comments that Morrison uses "her playful intelligence to create the circumstances of this striking tale" (*Black Creation* 65–66); and Jefferson adds that "Morrison has a musician's sense of tone, texture, and emotional balance" (*Ms.* 34–35).

While several critics note flaws even as they praise the novel, those who offer little or no positive commentary often expose attitudes ensuing from unawareness and titles signifying privileged inexperience: "Underwritten and Overwritten"; "Something Ominous Here." An article titled "Same Old Story," appearing in Britain's *Times Literary Supplement* (Oct. 4, 1974), dismisses the novel as not worth reading. This terse statement by an unnamed reviewer opens with a short summary of *Sula*, incorrectly referring to it as Morrison's "first novel," and concludes with:

> As a record of a vanished life this is convincing and vivid; it is only the story of Sula herself which is unsuccessful. She is left on the level of allegory in her growing up, her effect on the village and particularly at her death, which seems contrived to coincide with the drying up of the themes she represents.

Granting that a misinformed bibliographical detail does not render the reviewer's assertions invalid, Staggers allows that "it certainly makes them questionable. By suggesting that the story of Sula is 'unsuccessful,' the reviewer tacitly admits a void in his understanding of the pathos inherent in Afro-American culture" (40). Staggers goes on to point out that, just as their criticism reveals the cultural biases of some of the critics, so do the periodicals in which they publish. Frequently, in fact, "the critic's worldview and the publication he writes for are strikingly similar" (40). Three responses increasingly bear out this theory; two clearly rooted in Euro-American cultural tradition echo the London *Times Literary Supplement* in reducing Sula's experiences in *Sula* to extended allegory.

If Blackburn has already conceded in her *New York Times Book Review* (Dec. 1973) that "It's possible, I guess, to talk about *Sula* as allegory" (3), Joanne Temple of the *Village Voice* (Mar. 1974) shows no hesitation whatsoever: "In the end, allegory overtakes the novel, and the mythically large characters, so magnificently drawn, have their reality subjugated to their meaning" (31). While Christopher Lehmann-Haupt claims to have had "glimpses" of what Morrison was "trying to do in her second novel, *Sula*," he blames the author for the critic's inability to fully grasp her ideas: "What Miss Morrison had in mind in writing *Sula* finally remains unarticulated" (29). Staggers attributes these commentators' lack of appreciation, explicitly noticeable in what he calls Lehmann-Haupt's "obtuse assessment," to the cultural gap between novelist and reviewer—and the fact that the critic "has not expended the intellectual effort necessary to begin to bridge the gap" (41). Although Staggers accepts that, as is the case with most dedicated professionals, all the reporters believe they share honest valuations, he cites Blackburn's article as an example of the social distances that prohibit reviewers from free access to Morrison's Bottom community: "Sara Blackburn is really talking about the limitations of cultural experiences—her cultural experiences—when she talks about the narrowness of the novel and 'its refusal to brim over into the world outside of its provincial setting'" (3).

Such a dearth of educated discernment explains why Morrison felt compelled to provide *Sula* with a welcome mat across which white readers would be invited to enter what she would undoubtedly deny being a "provincial setting." Euro-American reviewers acknowledge but reveal limited understanding of the complexities of folks up in the Bottom, focusing primarily on Morrison's narrative skills and the friendship between Nel and Sula, and praising the porch Morrison allowed (and later regretted allowing) them to stand on in the novel's introductory chapter. Apart from Lehmann-Haupt, who dismisses *Sula* based on flawed narration, proponents of the "poetic" also admire what they allow to be rhythmical language rather than typical African American idiom, metaphor, and word play, barely concealing the racist assumption that all black people can sing. Morrison openly admits that she "detests" the title of "poetic writer," viewing the lens on the lyricism of her work as marginalizing her unique contributions and denying her stories their power and cultural resonance (Schappell 62).

Another group of mis[un]informed critics, both black and white, pronounce *Sula* as overly pessimistic and Morrison as responsible for a vision devoid of hope. Blackburn complains that these doomed characters are "locked in a world where hope for the future is a foreign commodity" (3); O'Connor observes that the world Morrison created "is bordered by a vision of hell" (65–66); and Barbara Smith confesses that, while literature is rendered better for Sula's voice, "Sula is frightening" (*Freedomways* 1974). In 2003, *New Yorker* critic Hilton Als recalls one black female reader admiring yet simultaneously frustrated and angry with Morrison for exposing black lives even as Als remembers himself accusing her of "perpetuating rather than dismantling the myth of the indomitable black woman, long-suffering and oversexed": "In a book about real and fictional black women, I wrote that the obsessive 'man love' of Hannah, Sula's mother, was a stereotype. (At the time, I didn't see that Morrison's decision to burn her to death was a moral condemnation, not a melodrama)." Though he appreciates Morrison for being comfortable with challenges and unafraid to confront her detractors ("'I didn't like what you wrote,' she said to me a few years ago"), Als candidly confesses to having been caught off guard by Morrison and confused about *Sula*.

He identifies the *Nation* critic Jerry H. Bryant as coming closest to articulating the confusion: "Most of us have been conditioned to expect something else in black characters, especially black female characters—guiltless victims of brutal white men, yearning for a respectable life of middle-class security; whores driven to their profession by impossible conditions; housekeepers exhausted by their work for lazy white women. We do not expect to see a fierceness bordering on the demonic." His title pronouncing the disturbing quality that he deems "very different" about Morrison as a writer, Bryant denounces her bleak worldview as "ominous." As he explains, "Sula, Ms. Morrison's protagonist, has qualities I have seen in a fictional black female only recently," he expresses his concern that Morrison has "a fascination with evil" and "an interest in the lower layers of the psyche of black characters, in their capacity to hurt and destroy" ("Something Ominous Here" 23–24).

Only the rare academic critic lauds Morrison early on for creating a fresh level of awareness or appreciates her unique rendering of evil: Cynthia J. Smith writes that "Sula is no stereotype. She lives a life that is different" while Patricia Meyer Spacks observes that *Sula*'s "most original aspect is its treatment of the bizarre" (*Cross Currents* 340–43; *Hudson Review* 284). If the overall European assessment in the 1970s appears to dismiss the book based on its having nothing especially new to say, Euro-American critics clearly carry their cultural baggage to their reading of Morrison's *Sula*: their publications promote Euro-American values, and the readership to which they appeal shares this cultural background and experience. We can ultimately weigh the criticism of the novel during this second-wave period as favorable but unspecific, because predominantly Euro-American critics apparently found themselves somewhat awkwardly trying to figure out exactly how to climb to the top of the Bottom.

Sula's Defining Critical Moments I. Feminist Accolades

Agreeing with Keith Byerman that the tradition of black women writers reveals a definite bent toward feminist ideology and with Barbara Christian that race and class remain uniquely and organically connected to the elements of gender embedded within the African American woman's feminist position, Staggers ascribes Morrison's rise in critical stature in large part to feminism and to this novel about female friendship. It was, he notes, after the appearance of *Sula* that feminist critics began to take Morrison more seriously as a writer and, consequently, to examine her writing more carefully. We see this change in attitude most explicitly when the occasional article both longer and broader in scope begins to appear in scholarly journals.

For example, a four-page essay by Barbara Smith appears in *Freedomways*, the leading African American theoretical, political, and cultural journal of the 1960s–1980s. Counting W. E. B. Du Bois among its founders and his wife Shirley Graham Du Bois as its first general editor, the journal continued printing until 1985. While Smith echoes the euphoric but nebulous language contained in many early reviews when she declares, "Morrison is a virtuoso writer," Smith's 1974 piece also places *Sula* solidly and specifically in the feminist literary tradition based on what Smith perceives as one of the dominant themes of the novel: "the link between Black women who share each other's lives," apparent in the special bonds between Nel and Sula; Hannah and Eva; Hannah and Sula; and Nel and Helene.

Cynthia Smith's four-page article in *Cross Currents* (Fall 1976), titled "Black Fiction by Black Females," extends the usual few paragraphs on plot, style, and characterization in *Sula* by examining it from the perspective of "the Afro-American novelistic tradition."[2] Smith compares *Sula* to Alice Walker's *Meridian* (1976) to illustrate how novels by black women deviate from the tradition of African American male writers, particularly Richard Wright and Ralph Ellison. Morrison herself comments in a 2003 interview with the *New Yorker* that she believes Wright, Baldwin, and Ellison were writing for a white audience. Though she certainly appreciates Ellison's *Invisible Man* as a realistic portrayal of black male resistance, Morrison mirrors Zora Neale Hurston's rejection of Richard Wright's militantly antiracist political agenda when Morrison similarly breaks rank and takes issue with Ellison's title: "Invisible to whom? Not to me" (Als).

She also objects to being branded a feminist writer. In a 1971 *New York Times* article, which posits "What the Black Woman Thinks about Women's Lib," her customary comically blunt opener answers her own question: "Well, she's suspicious of what she calls 'Ladies' Lib.' It's not just the question of color, but of the color of experience" (15). The essay explains that attempting to find consensus among African American women on any subject is a doomed prospect because they have consistently, and deliberately, defied classification. However, it also surmises that critiques on masculinity and support for feminist issues, viewed by many black women and men alike as a predominantly white "family quarrel," remain even more elusive because relationships between black men and black women have been historically different from those of their white counterparts. Accused of designing female victims, castrating women, and messed-up men, Morrison retorts that black women have borne their crosses "extremely well" and "everybody knows, deep down, that black men were emasculated by white men, period. And that black women didn't take any part in that" (Stepto 384). Thus, Morrison's version of what Alice Walker would call black "womanism" aligns Morrison with a tradition that refuses to exclude the masculine.[3]

She maintains her wariness toward feminism in a 1998 *Salon* interview with Zia Jaffrey:

> In order to be as free as I possibly can, in my own imagination, I can't take positions that are closed. Everything I've ever done, in the writing world, has been to expand articulation, rather than to close it, to open doors, sometimes, not even closing the book—leaving the endings open for reinterpretation, revisitation, a little ambiguity. I detest and loathe [those labels]. I think it's off-putting to some

---

2 Created in 1950 by the Association for Religion in Intellectual life, *Cross Currents* continues as a peer-reviewed academic quarterly published by John Wiley and Sons.

3 Walker's oft-cited analogy, "Womanist is to feminist as purple is to lavender," appears in the preface to *In Search of our Mothers' Gardens: Womanist Prose* (1983 xi). See also Mayberry, *Can't I Love What I Criticize? The Masculine and Morrison* (2007 1-4) for Morrison's attitude toward feminism.

readers, who may feel that I'm involved in writing some kind of feminist tract. I don't subscribe to patriarchy, and I don't think it should be substituted with matriarchy. I think it's a question of equitable access, and opening doors to all sorts of things.

Sula's Defining Critical Moments:
II. Margaret Atwood on Female Friendships

While recent criticism bears out Morrison's aforesaid declarations of independence, the scant eighteen articles published on *Sula* during the thirteen-year period from 1973 to 1986, mostly focusing on the human devastation caused by racism and the nature of female bonding, would seem to render the writer still somewhat invisible and attached at the hip to the feminist. Margaret Atwood's nuanced race/class/gendered approach to *Sula* in 1986, however, generated a turning point in its critical reception. Having just completed *The Handmaid's Tale* (1985), her dystopian novel on the various means by which women in subjugation set themselves free, Atwood knew better than most that eighteenth- and nineteenth-century English women routinely formed emotional ties with other women. In addition, she understood that, although many collections of letters indicate that such deeply felt same-sex friendships were casually accepted in American society as well, the portrait of a long-lived, intimate friendship between two women was a feature of the female experience that, consciously or unconsciously, the typical male historian and critic had chosen to ignore.

Atwood's *New York Times Book* essay, "That Certain Thing Called the Girlfriend" (1986), reminds us that during the mid-twentieth-century American female novelists derived much of their energy from the forbidden: the sense that they were raising to the level of art, or at least of the written word, material that had been considered "either too dirty or too abnormal or just too trivial to merit inclusion." Hence, these writers have led us,

> with a certain relentless glee, through the scrublands of domesticity, replete with porridge pots and soggy diapers and the thorny jungles of heterosexual relationships; through lush stretches of gynecology and lesbian love, and through the architecture of the family: mother-daughter, father-daughter, sibling-sibling. At no time in literary history have women been examined, from toenails to neuroses, in such microscopic detail. But what lies beyond the last frontier? What turns out to be the latest on the list of unmentionables in female life now seen to deserve mention? Could it be . . . Best Girlfriends?

Identifying female friendship as nothing new to the novel (*Jane Eyre* immediately comes to mind) and citing Morrison's *Sula* on the list of current leading-writer contributions, Atwood also concedes that the conventional novelistic assumption has been that "when you become a woman, you put away girlish things and replace . . . sickly Helen with sickly Mr. Rochester." Adult women, so the novel per Atwood has told it, should focus their energies on men, not only because that was where love and money were to be located, but because women were either minor league, broken plates, or snakes.

If we detect a notable gap between life as it was lived by women and life as portrayed in novels by both women and men, Atwood nevertheless deems the nineteenth century "less queasy" on the topic, in literature and in life, than the mid-twentieth. While Queen Victoria in fact exempted women from anti-homosexual laws because she disavowed the very existence of lesbians, the Queen's attitude prevailed almost to the end of the twentieth century in that virtually all kinds of female bonding remained beyond sexual suspicion. In *Disorderly Conduct: Visions of Gender in Victorian America*, Carroll Smith-Rosenberg chronicles the extent to which real-life American women, trapped in marriages to men from whom they felt estranged because of their widely disparate backgrounds and spheres of activity, relied on fellow women for intimacy and emotional intensity: "Indeed, from at least the late eighteenth through mid-nineteenth century, a female world of varied and yet highly structured relationships appears to have been an essential aspect of American society. These relationships ranged from the supportive love of sisters, through the enthusiasms of adolescent girls, to sensual avowals of love by mature women. It was a world in which men made but a shadowy appearance" (1–2). Given the pervasiveness of these friendships, "both sensual and platonic," Smith-Rosenberg finds the most remarkable aspect of the nineteenth-century novel to be the fact that it doesn't deal with female affairs more fully (4).

Not much more can be said, says Atwood, for twentieth-century literature or literary critical history. Those born circa the fifties may recall the biblical Ruth's pledge of loyalty to her mother-in-law Naomi made popular in the form of a song by Englishwoman Petula Clark, which is obviously directed to a ubiquitous male; mother-in-law jokes told by men; serious literature confined to writers like Hemingway, Fitzgerald, and Faulkner. Female-female relationships came in the cat-fight form of playwright Lillian Hellman's *Little Foxes*; disenchantment by tight-knit members of novelist Mary McCarthy's *The Group*; rival film actresses Betty Davis and Joan Crawford horrifying each other in *Whatever Happened to Baby Jane?* "Best girlfriends were for discussing the real business of life—boyfriends" (Atwood).[4]

The Canadian novelist highlights two 1970s/80s novels by African American women writers, however, which take women's friendships to a more complex level: Walker's *The Color Purple* (1982) and *Sula*. Atwood describes the most enduring relationship in the first book to occur between the protagonist Celie and her husband's former mistress, its complications including but by no means limited to sex; the emphasis in *Sula*, according to Atwood, becomes the girlhood friendship between Nel and Sula, which passes through estrangement caused when Sula has sex with Nel's husband, but returns per Nel's final epiphany after Sula's death, to reveal Nel's unbroken attachment to Sula:

---

4   As late as 1996, some, usually male, high school teachers presented *Sula* as a cat fight over a man, in this case Jude.

> "All that time, all that time, I thought I was missing Jude." And the loss pressed down on her chest and came up into her throat. "We was girls together," she said as though explaining something. "O Lord, Sula," she cried, "girl, girl, girlgirlgirl."
>
> It was a fine cry—loud and long—but it had no bottom and it had no top, just circles and circles of sorrow. (174)

In addition to applauding the novel as "dense" and "tragic," Atwood's most important contribution to revving up *Sula*'s literary critical history becomes her analysis of why African American women writers "were among the first on this turf." Both *Sula* and *The Color Purple* present one of each of their pairs of females as more conventional, what Morrison would call the Old World black woman (Nel/Celie), and the other more exotic and flamboyant, what Morrison refers to as the New World or "outlaw" black woman (Sula/Shug). While each pair shares a man, both novelists establish the female bond as the one that "creates a synthesis, a completion, which is larger than each woman separately."

Assuring readers that these "are not icing-sugar friendships, all sweetness and teacups. They are complex and important, and they include pain, anger, feelings of betrayal, jealousy and hatred, as well as love," Atwood turns to sociology to explain why black women writers were on the cutting edge of this topic, even though meaningful relationships between women were not and are not exclusive to the black community. Could the prevalence of female-headed households provide an answer—with the ensuing need for female support systems? Could black women writers, unable to see themselves in the white fiction available about women, be more likely to insist on recording their own truths regarding the life they experience? The main truth sociology cannot uphold as self-evident is why it took so long for these friendships to appear as central plot lines in mainstream fiction.

Atwood's conclusions make Morrison's truths even more telling:

> Perhaps the reason it's taken women novelists so long to get around to dealing with women's friendships head on is that betrayal by a woman friend is the ultimate betrayal. In sexual love, betrayal is almost expected; if we don't allow for it, it's not for want of warning, because treacherous lovers are thoroughly built into popular mythology, from folk songs to pop songs to torch songs to mom's advice. But who warns you about your best friend? Nell's clinching accusation to the dying Sula is, "We were friends." Because friendship is supposed to be unconditional, a free gift of the spirit, its violation is all the more unbearable.[5]

The literary critical history of *Sula* has borne out Atwood's speculations: *Sula*'s twentieth-century lens on a female fusion that is larger than each woman

---

5   In her foreword to *Love*, Morrison states: "People tell me that I am always writing about love. Always, always love. I nod, yes, but it isn't true—not exactly. In fact, I am always writing about betrayal. Love is the weather. Betrayal is the lightning that cleaves and reveals it" (ix).

individually not only represents one of the first of its kind but enabled women's friendships, despite their late blooming, to become a fixture on the literary map as valid and multidimensional novelistic material. Morrison told Zia Jaffrey in 1998 that she wrote *Sula* based on this "theoretically brand new idea, which was: Women should be friends with one another." Understanding that, typical of dominated people, many women had to be taught to like women, Morrison challenged the belief that a female friend must be consigned to a secondary relationship. Her sensibility was informed by women in her childhood community who "would choose the company of a female friend over a man, anytime. They were really 'sisters,' in that sense."

Now, in fact, as she predicted in a 1992 interview with Elissa Schappell, there's nothing so very astonishing about that connection at all. Although "heterosexual women who are friends, who are talking only about themselves to each other" seemed ... "a very radical thing when *Sula* was published ...,'" she concludes emphatically, "it is hardly radical now." When Schappell adds that "It is becoming acceptable," Morrison notes wryly: "Yes, and it's going to get boring. It will be overdone, and as usual it will all run amok" (79). Yet, having explored the problematical complexities of female relationships since Claudia and Frieda grew up to define Sula and Nel, on into both of her published short stories ("Recitatif" in 1983 and "Sweetness" in 2015); and in *Jazz, Paradise, Love,* and *A Mercy,* the subject apparently still grips Morrison (and us) in her choreo-poem drama, *Desdemona,* and her last novel, *God Help the Child.*

Second-Wave *Sula* Criticism

The four-year period from *Sula*'s publication in 1973 to the publication of *Song of Solomon* in 1977 delivered the scant few reviews and articles described above; the *MLA International Bibliography* begins to list citations on *Sula* in 1978. Since then, roughly 183 scholarly articles, book chapters, and books (not to mention 27 dissertation abstracts and at least 11 re-printings) have been presented by mostly American distributors.

Twenty-one percent of those texts appeared in journals with a multicultural concentration: *Black American Literature Forum* (9), which in 1992 became the *African American Review* (12); *CLA Journal* (11); *SAGE* (2); *MELUS* (1); *Phylon* (1); *Obsidian II* (1); and *Callaloo* (1). Purdue University's *Modern Fiction Studies* offered four essays, which may be ascribed primarily to the keen interest in Morrison scholarship of its assistant editor from 1994 to 99. Nancy Peterson guest-edited the *Toni Morrison* special issue (*MFS* 39.3&4) in the fall of 1993; that double issue was later revised to become in 1997 the first "Modern Fiction Studies Book," also printed by Johns Hopkins University Press: *Toni Morrison: Critical and Theoretical Approaches.*

In addition to the distinct focus on *Sula* via African American and white feminist perspectives, 26 articles have been made available by international journals/

critics from 1990 to 2016. Foreign attention includes the Canadians, Chinese, French, Germans, Greeks, Indians, Japanese, Koreans, Portuguese, Spanish, and Swedes. The Morrison French connection appears to be straightforward; or the French simply fell in love with her. Morrison was, in fact, asked to curate an exhibit for Paris's Louvre Museum and was awarded the French Legion of Honor in 2010. She also won a special place in the hearts of Canadian and Asian academics. Toronto's York University scholar/publisher, Andrea O'Reilly, for example, not only authored a book on *Toni Morrison and Motherhood* (SUNY Press 2004), but her own Demeter Press produced another, edited, volume—*Toni Morrison on Mothers and Motherhood*—in 2017, both of which contain material on *Sula*. Besides an escalating twentieth-century concern about women's rights, the Asian notice may be clarified by Kun Jong Lee's overview of Korean/Asian American literary studies, 1964–2009, in that Asian scholars are drawn to close readings of individual texts and prefer dense narratives like Morrison's to plays and poems.

In sum, approximately 63 English texts explicating *Sula* have made their way into print after *Song of Solomon* won the National Book Critics Circle Award in 1978; 158 more were issued in various languages after Morrison won the Nobel Prize in 1993. Such data suggest that Morrison's third book and her own snowballing popularity allowed her second book new life and newfound, more widespread literary critical awareness. Besides ongoing examinations of previously discredited, particularly twentieth-century female friendships—Elizabeth Abel's very able "(E)Merging Identities: The Dynamics of Female Friendship in Contemporary Fiction by Women" (1981) comes to mind—and the political dynamics in *Sula*, more recent studies emphasize additional aspects of feminist/womanist; psychoanalytic; deconstructionist; structuralist/post-structuralist/postcolonial; new historical/cultural; and African American literary criticism. The various reactions stimulated by these theoretical approaches will be presented chronologically.

Sula and Feminist/Womanist Criticism

Morrison's popularity corresponded with and facilitated the burgeoning popularity of black feminist studies in the 1980s. Over half of the noteworthy MLA bibliographical listings on *Sula* may be catalogued under "womanist" and/or psychoanalytic criticism, categories which frequently overlap. Having depended, often quite heavily, upon Morrison's work to distinguish black from white feminism, critics like Hortense Spillers, Barbara Smith, Madhu Dubey, Margaret Homans, and Deborah McDowell rely on *Sula* to illustrate its defining characteristics:

> Toni Morrison's *Sula* is a rebel idea, both for her creator and for Morrison's audience. To read *Sula* is to encounter a sentimental education so sharply discontinuous from the dominant traditions of Afro-American literature in the way that it compels and/or deadlocks the responses that the novel, for all its brevity and quiet intrusion on the landscape of American fiction, is, to my mind, the single most important irruption of black women's writing in our era. (Spillers 1983, 293)

In addition to being among the first scholars to take Morrison's talent seriously, Barbara Smith has continued to fix *Sula*'s place in the womanist canon, critiquing the novel in "Toward a Black Feminist Criticism" (1978) and including material on it in her edited collection *Home Girls: A Black Feminist Anthology* (2000). Madhu Dubey refers to the Black Nationalist aesthetic as well as black feminism to account for the many oppositions in *Sula*. Exposing the ways in which African American gender oppression cannot be understood apart from racial domination, Sula notably challenges Nel: "You say I'm a woman and colored. Ain't that the same as being a man?" (142). As Margaret Homans compares Eva and Sula Peace's disastrous appropriations of the power of the Logos with Nel's referent-less howl, "which closes the novel with an image of women's language that radically questions compatibility of genuine female self-expression and the use of ordinary (to say nothing of literary or lyrical) discourse," Homans uses *Sula* to differentiate between the two alternative directions in feminist literary criticism represented by the United States and France during the 1980s: while both approaches sought to account for women's relative absence from mainstream culture, they differed over the adequacy of language to represent the female experience. Finally, Deborah McDowell's 1988 study echoes Barbara Smith's rejection of the unwaveringly "positive racial self" promoted by the Black Aesthetic movement as well as Smith's concerns about black women viewing black men as "the privileged centers of the race" (Hull 1982). Claiming that *Sula* "transgresses all deterministic structures of opposition" to enable the "next stage in the development of feminist criticism on Afro-American women writers," McDowell views the novel as "rife with liberating possibilities" that "lead us beyond the descriptions that keep [African American men and women] locked in opposition and antagonism" (79).

Ongoing critiques of *Sula* reflect Mary Helen Washington's 1975 summary of black feminism's defining concerns:

> When I think of how essentially alone black women have been—alone because of our bodies, over which we have had so little control; alone because the damage done to our men has prevented their closeness and protection; and alone because we have had no one to tell us stories about ourselves; I realize that black women writers are an important and comforting presence in my life. Only they know my story. It is absolutely necessary that they be permitted to discover and interpret the entire range and spectrum of the experience of black women and not be stymied by preconceived conclusions. Because of these writers, there are more models of how it is possible for us to live, there are more choices for black women to make, and there is a larger space in the universe for us. (xxxii)

Some second-wave studies of Morrison's novel focus specifically on the maligned black female body. In the essay she writes for her edited collection with Michael Bennett, *Recovering the Black Female Body: Self-Representations by African American Women* (2000), Vanessa Dickerson argues that the body of the black female, unlike that of white women, has "not been interiorized as ideal but localized as thing." Dickerson cites *Sula* as "one of the most powerful and successful reappropriators of black representation" (195–96). Describing the women in Morrison's fiction as signifiers of body difference or deformity, Linden Peach includes one-legged Eva Peace as he surveys Morrison's "exploration of the stigmatization of body difference other than skin color" and ways in which "this process of shaming is countered by a performative view of body identity" (274).

Several 1990s studies highlight *Sula*'s stories about motherhood/ motherlove/ mothering/ mother-daughter relationships. Dayle Delancey and Laurie Vickroy view *Sula*'s portrayal of motherlove as "a killer," depicting how external threats can distort mothers' love. While Lucille Fultz forefronts the mother-daughter conflicts in the novel, Vickroy maintains that, even as it provides a compelling examination of "the murderous extent to which the exercise of power determines the workings of intimate relationships and even constructs versions of self-definition," it nonetheless offers, through daughters' embrace of personal spaces, "new possibilities for reaching beyond those structures of domination which governed their mothers' behavior and conceptions of selfhood" (28).

Martha Satz remains unsurprised in 2017 that a novel about authentic female experience reveals the mothering relationship often occurring between female friends and the "intergenerational effect of positive or negative mothering on the psychological makeup of female beings" as important as the friendship between two female characters (201–2). Calling upon their own maternal history, invoking maternal traditions that are "deep, authentic, mythical, and cultural," Sula and Nel revoke conventional motherhood, midwife each other into self-actualization, mother each other, and mother themselves (212).

Since, as Barbara Smith and Deborah McDowell proposed in the 1970s and 1980s and Susan Mayberry demonstrated in 2007, Morrison's form of black feminism celebrates the interconnectedness and balance between African American women and men, singling out her black men does not negate the preeminence of her black women. Rather, it confirms that black men have "successfully retained their special vitality in spite of white male resistance" and that black women's connections to black men have saved their lives (Mayberry *Can't I Love* 1). In addition to spurring African American masculinity studies, then, analyses of *Sula* have fostered gender and queer studies. Mayberry's "Something Other Than a Family Quarrel: The Beautiful Boys in Morrison's *Sula*" provided the catalyst for a full monograph on Morrison's male characters, *Can't I Love What I Criticize? The Masculine and Morrison*. Set Byul Moon's "A Possibility of Black Manhood through Re-Reading Black Veterans in Toni Morrison's *Sula*" fuses masculinity with psychoanalytic studies, and Kwangsoon Kim's "Playing in the Marginal Space" queers the master narrative Morrison asks us to unlearn in *Sula*.

Sula and Psychoanalytic Criticism

If important aspects of *Sula* have been illuminated by black feminism frequently bolstered by psychoanalytic theory, equally significant analyses of the novel are more heavily dominated by psychoanalytic literary criticism. Naana

Banyiwa-Horne analyzes Sula as the frightening face of Nel's alter-ego (1985). The subtitle of a casebook entry by Houston A. Baker reads "Psychoanalysis and *Sula*" (1997). Mai Boswell (1999) and Jennifer Henton (2012) look to psychoanalytic approaches that both engage the subject in culture and speculate on the possibility of thinking outside that subject position. The agency of Lacan's [black] letter in Eva Peace's outhouse, according to Boswell, comments on the racial "other" of the Western hegemonic system— "with vast implications if we think of problems linked to constructions of postcolonialism, immigration, educational, media, economic, and legal attitudinal and policy decisions" (132). Morrison's take on her Bottom community, per Henton and Kathryn Stockton (1993), becomes her "nigger joke" on Freud's anal stage and on the ways in which psychoanalysis tunes out its own mandate to listen. Its jokes reminding us of Freud's connections between the joke and irony, *Sula*'s humor suggests that psychoanalysis must cure itself of its innate narcissism by listening to the Other. Providing an opportunity for "queer crossings," *Sula* both reveres and degrades Freud: "To debase Freud is to credit his accounts of feces as coins but to make sorrowful what he, with his culture, sometimes celebrated: *how the Bottom was lost*" (Stockton 83).

In a 1990 article, reprinted in 1997 and again in 2000, Diane Gillespie and Missy Kubitschek align the "female component" of a "'second renaissance'" of African-American fiction in the 1970s and 1980s with a new psychology of women via the research of Nancy Chodorow and Carol Gilligan. Finding caretaking and its corresponding emphasis on "empathy, affiliation, nurturance, and a collective vision of social life" central to female experience, these women-centered psychologists challenge the traditional male relationship between the self and other by privileging the mother-daughter relationship. Gillespie and Kubitschek contend, however, that since most of the designated literary models are of middle- or upper-class Euro-American origin and since "Afro-American literature often explores a self-in-community," multiethnic texts offer women-centered psychology another manifestation of the female self "beyond the Euro-American mother-daughter or friend-friend dyad" (21–22). They identify *Sula* as not only expanding the women-centered paradigm, but in its defiance of traditional male-centered interpretations of female development, having anticipated the discoveries of women-centered psychology.

Finally, psychoanalytic critics of *Sula* did yeoman's work to advance serious discussions about African American trauma, which sustain Morrison's assertions that the effects of slavery have created an entire American community that is still suffering the after-boom of abuse. Richard Barksdale (1986) shows how some African American texts by women writers, including *Sula*, invite symbols of castration, acknowledging yet problematizing phallic power. Trevor Dodman (2011) and Manuela López Ramírez (2016) examine Morrison's rendition of post-traumatic stress disorder. Dodman maintains that, even though white and black soldiers alike endured PTSD's "crippling passage," the black shell-shock narrative has long been elided. Insisting that America's scientific study and treatment of nervous breakdowns in the nineteenth and early twentieth centuries do not even attempt to account for the impact of white racism, oppression, and terrorism on black subjects across much of this same period, he claims that, cut out of "official" discourses, African Americans remained victims of America's double-consciousness, left largely to themselves to locate a language for their own suffering. A proper accounting of shell shock in the United States, therefore, needs to address what W. E. B. Du Bois identified as the twentieth-century's singular problem of the color line (151). As an antiwar novel that unpacks the physical and psychological violence racism continues to exert on anti-heroes, *Sula* explores the tensions of this racially prejudiced America and the dire consequences for the black community and self (López Ramírez Abstract).

Evelyn Schreiber and Jaleel Akhtar have produced complete monographs on race trauma and dismemberment in Morrison's novels. In a culture where a white norm leaves the black self marginalized, Morrison explores a range of trauma associated with black experience and the nuances of this marginalization (Schreiber 2010). Just as Morrison presents racial alienation as a complex process, likening its impact on individuals to the splitting of bodies, amputation, phantom limbs, and traumatic memories, approaching dismemberment in Morrison's fiction from an interdisciplinary perspective allows a more rounded understanding of racism and its debilitating effects on the psyche (Akhtar 2014).

Sula and Deconstructionist/Post-Structural/Modern/Colonial Criticism

1980s/90s deconstructionist critics of *Sula* examine Morrison's rejection/expansion of Saussurean binary thinking and semiotics even as she endorses "the presence of absence." Robert Grant argues that *Sula*, as character and text, presents a deliberate conundrum to readers not only because Morrison avoids the conventional rhetorical/polemical features generally associated with African American "protest fiction," but because she attempts to depict black experience via negations and absences that both "enlarge the black female hero and deconstruct the expectation of politicized 'determinacy'" (101-2). Rachel Lee cautions, however, that the more productive endeavor would be to read Morrison's aesthetic of ambiguity not as "apoira to be 'filled . . . by the reader' (Grant 94)," but as dismissal of "an unattainable desire for stable definitions and identities" (571). By enacting the relativity of meaning, *Sula* questions semantic integrity (how can we convey what we mean), epistemological accuracy (how can we know anything since there is no objective perspective and no objective essence to know), and historical truth. Morrison's chronicle thus connects discursive slippage to cultural circumstance. Rita Bergenholtz asserts that, by way of intentionally blurring clear choices and reminding us there is no fixed signification inherent in words or names, only the meanings assigned to them, Morrison's novel ultimately becomes an extended satire on reductive thinking.

Observing that placing and spacing (the opening or closing of distances between things and people) take on urgency in *Sula*, for example the empty space once occupied by Eva Peace's missing leg and "the place where Chicken Little sank" in the river (*Sula* 61), Patricia McKee considers Morrison's use of space and place "both as components of social and psychological order and as components of historical experience" (1). When Morrison identifies empty spaces as emptied space, we realize her resolve to uncover missing experience. Appreciating the similarities between the gist of McKee's post-structuralist argument, that "Morrison's novel seeks to force a confrontation with the losses that have marked African American experience and to insist on their historical particularity," and his own, Phillip Novak furthers the discussion by asking how *Sula* effects an orientation "toward the recognition of such losses" (footnote 7).

His essay an attempt to answer this question, Novak points out that while *Sula* becomes a virtual litany of traumatic experiences, of literal and figurative deaths, so that the novel functions to bear witness, its structure nevertheless articulates an absence. These elements combined cause *Sula* to sanction a sustaining of grief and represent a kind of ongoing wake. Its narrative discards the model for mourning that advocates giving up grieving in the interest of getting on with living as "inadequate to a situation in which the losses endured are cultural as well as individual, public as well as private" (191). To move beyond mourning in the context of continuing cultural fragility may well constitute a surrender to the processes of cultural absorption and diffusion described at the end of the book.

Post-structural critic Cedric Bryant examines *Sula*'s stance toward madness and evil, which concludes that order derives from a person's ability to devise a means of coexisting peacefully with chaos and others. Bryant compares Morrison's embrace of madness with Foucault's theory that history may judge us by how we deal with our "disjunctions": "The community's ability to integrate those individuals who would in the larger world be ostracized is a crucial measurement of both humanity and civilization" (732). 1990s scholars Biman Basu and Michael Wilson refer to Bakhtin's theory of dialogism to distinguish *Sula*'s African American intertextuality. When Morrison attempts to define the discrete blackness of black language, Basu reminds us, she relies on an analogy with music. Claiming that Sula becomes the figure of music/semiotics in *Sula*, Basu quotes Morrison: "There was an articulate literature before there was print. There were griots. They memorized it. People heard it. It is important that there is sound in my books—that you can hear it, that I can hear it" (91).

Wilson illustrates how this [intra]intertextuality encourages affirmations of communities and change:

> *Sula* reminds us that we must be willing to accept the possibility that literary texts, people, and communities sometimes require new or different strategies for reading, which may not in fact equal the complexity of that which we wish to understand. The success of our strategies of reading depends upon our willingness to "listen" carefully to literary texts, to other cultures, to other people—just as we expect others to hear the terms by which we express our own complex lives. (36)

Ceron Bryant applies Homi Bhabha's postcolonial third space theory in 2013 to clarify the novel's respect for difference.

Sula and New Historical/Cultural and African American Criticism

From the beginning, critics have touted Morrison's [re]interpretations of black cultural history. Lounsberry and Hovet maintain in 1979 that no writer better confronts how contemporary African Americans can "preserve some vestige of vital cultural identify from the past and, at the same time, move forward, away from the limitations of any single cultural tradition, toward the multiple perspectives and opportunities of cultural pluralism" than does Toni Morrison in *Sula*. Her ambivalence toward the Bottom's Old World attitudes as well as the reader's skepticism toward the heroine as ambassador of liberating perspectives force us to "see the limitations of the concept of 'multiple perspectives' itself" (126).

1990s scholars explain ways in which the novel values the persistence of the cultural codes that shape our understanding of the social world and underlie the production of literary meaning. Phillip Richards stresses cultural over feminist criticism in *Sula*, insisting that Morrison grasps the endurance of black middle-class culture and its semantics far better than the myriad critics who emphasize reversals of bourgeois social, political, and economic codes in her work. Lucille Fultz juxtaposes a white Southern ethos of hospitality denied to African Americans with a counterculture black ethic based upon necessity and expediency, which is constantly shifting in response to complex, often arbitrary Southern mores. Fultz maintains that individual fulfillment in Morrison's world can be found only within a "collective context, one that insists upon a knowledge of a Southern past that engendered a Black ethic rooted in slavery and harvested in a desire and a press for intra-racial and universal respect" ("Southern Ethos" 93).

Although readers will find major similarities among the ways in which new historicist/ cultural critics and African American critics address *Sula*, we can differentiate African American criticism by the explicit ethnic issues, traditions, and echoes that have informed African American literary history. Critical race theorists, for example, challenge the inherent ethnocentrism of the Western literary tradition. Illustrating how Morrison's work has powerfully influenced the formation of racial identities in the United States, McKee maintains that race becomes visible only through image production/exchange as she illuminates the significance that representational practice has held over the process of racial construction. She views the culture in *Sula* as aural and oral—and often about the absence of the visual. Because Morrison's African American communities produce identity in nonvisual—even anti-visual—terms, McKee argues, they repudiate not just white representations of black persons as objects, but also visual modes of representation that have constructed whites as subjects and blacks as objects (1999).

In 1990, Timothy Powell credits Morrison, and underscores *Sula*, as having more completely than any other writer not only decentered the white logos but also restructured the center by discovering the powers that lie hidden in the black logos: "Morrison rises out of what Houston Baker calls the black (w)hole to create what I will call, in a signifying riff on Baker's term, a (w)holy black text" (748–49). We see the ongoing results of this struggle to depict the black figure on the white page when Mae Henderson's black feminist essay critiquing *Sula* is included in a reader called *African American Literary Theory* (2000). Paraphrasing Morrison's statement that black women writers were not interested in writing about white men and, consequently, freed American literature to take on other concerns, Henderson notes wryly that "if black women writers speak in tongues, then it is we black feminist critics who are charged with the hermeneutical task of interpreting tongues" (366).

The African American critical reception of *Sula* contains significant interest in the African influences on the novel. Vashti Lewis (1987) and Gay Wilentz (1997) applaud Morrison for recognizing African tradition in African American culture and for deliberately opting to write from an African point of view: "In doing so, she removes much of the mystery of black life and answers to some degree, the ubiquitous question: What makes black folk act that way?" (Lewis 97). Lewis joins Karen Stein, Susana Vega-González, and Anissa Wardi in a twenty-six-year exploration (1980–2006) of the emphases on naming and ancestors in *Sula* that result in a uniquely complex and multifaceted culture rooted in an African past.

African American critical gazes likewise spotlight black folk motifs. If Christian introduces in 1980 *Sula*'s many connections between community and nature, Phillip Royster specifically pits a priest and a witch against the spiders and the snakes in the first analysis to focus on scapegoating in *Sula* (1978). Chikwenye Okonjo Ogunyemi treats the entire novel as Morrison's "nigger joke" (1979), and Norris Clark explains its mores on "flying black" (1980). More recent scholarly articles concentrate on African American folklore to explain how *Sula*'s Eva Peace re-embodies the traditional black matriarch (De Angelis 2001); how the depiction of the returned World War I soldier "breathes life into and subversively reconstructs a lynching narrative, one of black modernity's most nightmarish facets," to sustain a metaphor for the modern black male's relationship with and participation in the national public sphere (Jackson 2006); and, finally, how a merger between Stanley Fish's reader-response theory with Roland Barthes's theories of listening and music creates an ideological basis for approaching the musical aspects of Morrison's language that we might call a "listener-response theory" (Glover 2006). Together, such essays reflect Morrison's assertion that, while music historically kept the Bottom community alive, passing on the mythologies that enabled survival for her "peasant people," African American music has been co-opted by others and, so, is no longer sufficient (LeClair 370–71). The literary critical reception history of *Sula* reveals that novels like *Sula* must now do what the music used to do.

CHAPTER THREE

SONG OF SOLOMON (1977)

Song of Solomon's Critical History as Told by Toni Morrison

The critical history of Morrison's third novel unravels itself as a conundrum in more ways than one. The writer confesses to snubbing the writing process in her foreword to the 2004 Vintage edition, which also reveals that her father's death during the creative blackout that occurred after *The Bluest Eye* and *Sula* brought her muse to life. Having "long despised artists' chatter" about those "'voices' that speak to them and enable a vision," Morrison found no access to *Song of Solomon* until her dead father, to whom she had felt closer than she did to herself, answered her deliberate quest for advice: "'What are the men you have known really like?'" Having been blessed by his inspiration, the author trusted her "'bright angel'" thereafter (xi–xii).

His response led to yet another conundrum: "The challenge of *Song of Solomon* was to manage what was for me a radical shift in imagination from a female locus to a male one. To get out of the house, to de-domesticate the landscape that had so far been the site of my work. To travel. To fly" (xii). Known to inform her creative writing students that she wasn't remotely interested in reading about their "little lives," Morrison often declared her personal story uneventful. Since she didn't swim, ski, or skydive, she lived vicariously, and most intensely, through the characters she created, locating her most vital self when she was with them. As a black woman writing about the causes and significance of the "traveling Ulysses scene, for black men," Morrison had to turn her own psyche inside out to dislocate her typical mode of disruption: "I couldn't use the same kind of language at all. And it took a long time for the whole thing to fall together because men are different and they are thinking about different things. The language had to be different" (Gates and Appiah 387–91).[1]

Time and place had to be different, too. With *Song of Solomon*, Morrison interrupts her previous zigzaggy structures, opting for a straightforward chronology and traditional literary realism as she accompanies her archetypal hero on his call to epic adventure. As one of Joseph Campbell's heroes with a thousand faces, her black boy duly departs the ordinary world to be tested by the fires of earth, washed by sacred waters, and ultimately returned home renewed by way of air.[2] In Morrison's hands, however, traditional method and monomyth become a conundrum, since her old-school saga comes with "other meanings": "Opening the novel with the suicidal leap of the insurance agent, ending it with the protagonist's confrontational soar into danger, was meant to enclose the mystical but problematic one taken by the Solomon of the title" (xii).

With Solomon's story, Morrison intentionally embeds an enigma within her theme of flight, representing the concept in *Song of Solomon* as disturbing as it is triumphant. As she recasts "some old folks' lie" about African American slaves who flew back to Africa, her legend of the flying African features Solomon/Shalimar, enslaved patriarch of twenty-one sons by his wife Ryna. Not running away, the baby and the wife right next to him, he "just stood up in the fields one day, ran up some hill, spun around a couple of times, and was lifted up in the air. Went right on back to wherever it was he came from." While the father breaks his shackles and gets to go home, the mother loses her mind, "or died or something"—unable to "live without a particular man"... or "trying to take care of children by [herself]" (*Song of Solomon* 323). Morrison's male myth celebrates the dynamic but oppressed black man's sudden [s]urge toward freedom; it laments, nonetheless, all the women and children who are left to lose sight of him.

The foreword goes on to explicate *Song of Solomon*'s first sentence as an exercise in carefully worded conflict:[3] "The North Carolina Mutual Life Insurance

---

1   *Song of Solomon* becomes pivotal to Susan Mayberry's book, *Can't I Love What I Criticize? The Masculine and Morrison*, which details the conundrum of black men in motion alongside the women and children left at home who need to know their names.

2   Novelist Terry McMillan calls up "zigzagginess" to illustrate how Morrison typically juggles various elements at once. If this dizzyingly "distinctive and undeniably Morrisonian" narrative technique forwards the subject matter and contributes to an element of mysticism in her first two novels, Morrison must reinvent the old-school heroic outlined by Joseph Campbell to do the same for *Song of Solomon* (J10).

3   In her essay "Grendel and His Mother," Morrison defines *conflict*, unlike *crisis*, as "the clash of incompatible forces... a disharmony calling for adjustment, change, or compromise." Recognizing legitimate oppositions, honest but different interpretations of data, contesting theories," conflict in the academy, according to Morrison, must not only not be militarized but must be embraced if education is to occur: "Conflict is not another word for crisis or for war or for competition. Conflict is a condition of intellectual life, and, I believe, its pleasure. Firing up the mind to engage itself is precisely what the mind is for—it has no other purpose" (*The Source of Self-Regard* 262).

agent promised to fly from Mercy to the other side of Lake Superior at 3:00." Designed to "mock a journalistic style," this declarative sentence does double duty sounding like a small-town newspaper announcement of minimal local interest yet containing signs and information crucial to the saga. Morrison clarifies that the corporate name of the insurance company is legendary to African Americans as historically black owned and supported; the words "life" and "mutual" subtly deride the last state to officially join the Confederacy thirty-seven years before former-slave-turned-entrepreneur John Merrick founded his Durham, NC, company in 1898 (xii–xiii).

The place names nod to a lifetime-guaranteed merciful/superior dichotomy connected to slavery and racism, and to the usual south (North Carolina)/north (Lake Superior/Canada) direction for black migration. The direction of the novel's journey, however, takes us from north to south, indicating that the protagonist must return to his roots to mature. Morrison's sentence includes two notions central to that maturation: "fly" suggesting both escape and confrontation; "'mercy' the unspoken wish of the novel's population" and "what the townsfolk believe can never come from the white world, as is signified by the inversion of the name of the hospital from Mercy to 'No-Mercy'" (xiii).

Most telling in the opening statement is its verb: "promise." The insurance agent modestly publicizes his revolutionary act as an implied contract between himself and others, intending his flight, like that of the title character, simultaneously to align with sanctuary and to be interpreted not as the desperation of an unexamined life, but "as a radical gesture demanding change, an alternative way, a cessation of things as they are," as, in other words, "a deep commitment to his people." Gradually acknowledging the suicide note he tacks on his door as an invitation to forgive and a sign of his sacrifice meant to inspire them, they, indeed, come to feel "a tenderness, some contrition, and mounting respect" (xiii).

Morrison waits until the final paragraph of her foreword to actually write the word "conundrum," meaning both "a confusing and difficult problem or question" and "a question asked for amusement, typically one with a pun in its answer; a riddle." Even though all her books celebrate the difficult lives of black men as serious play, and despite her claims that while she has met a lot of dull white men, she has never met a boring black one, as well as her confession that she is delighted that black men will just split at the drop of a hat, her *Song of Solomon* testifies unequivocally to her gratitude for the feisty magic of what she calls the free black male.[4]

Although much of this male magic results from a curiosity about what's around the corner, a great deal comes from a deep appreciation for and continual practice with community word play. The last words of the foreword confirm this paradox. If "Solomon's is the most magical, the most theatrical, and, for Milkman, the most satisfying" of all the flights in the novel, it is, like the insurance agent's

---

4   Even one of Morrison's children's books, co-authored with her son Slade, prefers the playful, artistic grasshopper over the hard-working, steadily saving ant (see *Who's Got Game? The Ant or the Grasshopper?*).

jump and Milkman's leap, ambiguous. Solomon must abandon his family to fly free; guilt and despair accompany Mr. Smith's demonstration of love; Milkman risks his life for his aunt even as he wheels into the killing arms of his brother. Hence these flights, those "erstwhile heroics," come to be viewed "quite differently by the women left behind." Morrison's decision to use song rather than flight in her title; her equivocal epigraph, "The fathers *may* soar/And the children *may* know *their* names" (emphases mine); the daughter's dedication to "Daddy" affirm the dependence of different/mutual understanding on verbal acrobatics: "To praise a woman whose attention was focused solely on family and domestic responsibilities, Milkman summons a conundrum: that without ever leaving the ground she could fly. My father laughed" (xiv).

Song of Solomon's Initial Critical Reception History

The oddly balanced binaries summoned by *Song of Solomon* and highlighted in Morrison's 2004 foreword are reflected in the novel's initial critical reception. Morrison's first two books originally received scholarly short shrift, with most of the responses appearing in publications targeting general readers. However, much of the critical reaction to *Song of Solomon* from late 1978 on was published in scholarly journals, with 1979 finding it a focus of that highly specialized academic genre known as the doctoral dissertation. As Leroy Staggers notes in his dissertation surveying Morrison's critical reception from 1970 to 1988: "The net effect was that Morrison's third novel was recommended, read, and analyzed by both general audiences and scholars." And, interestingly enough, in the years following the publication of *Song of Solomon* in 1977, *The Bluest Eye* and *Sula* accrued further probing examination, with most of the responses appearing almost exclusively in academic journals: "Moreover, in the wake of *Song of Solomon*, these later responses to the earlier novels tend to indicate that they are more profound than some of the earlier criticism had indicated" (Staggers 47–48).

Increasing receptiveness to Morrison's work by professional critics as well as general readers generated a wider readership and a broader volume of response, a majority of respondents echoing Philip Sydney's famous endorsement of the purpose of literature in their descriptions of *Song of Solomon*: it teaches and it delights. Staggers offers three ways in which the reception to Morrison's third novel replicates that of her first two: critical reactions mix praise with reservations; appraisals, along with the vehicles disseminating them, reflect cultural biases; most analysis involves traditional literary techniques and elements.

Two striking differences, however, do exist. If more critics responded to *Song of Solomon* than to *The Bluest Eye* or *Sula*, more critics, including African American critics, vigorously condemned the novel. Nevertheless, by virtue of both the causes and the effects of a swelling audience, the large number of both Euro- and African American respondents, and the scholarly focus, *Song of Solomon* "established Toni Morrison as an American writer," its stature moving critics to recast Morrison's oeuvre in a sunnier light (Staggers 49). With several critics elevating the 337-page effort to an epic that surpasses her shorter good but not great books, its quest theme depicting an archetypal hero, *Song of Solomon* assumes comparisons with classical texts like *The Odyssey*. Writing for *Obsidian*, Charles De Arman presents one such analogy: "Not only do Macon Dead, Jr.'s movements trace a course that parallels that of the protagonist of romance, but when seen in the light of the quest, his trek takes on the wider significance of the archetypal hero, of one whose role it is to restore the 'runes [=mystery or secrets] of wisdom'" (57).[5]

While early critics gradually expanded their scope to subjects like black consciousness, character names and characterization, incestuous relationships, mythology, racism, Morrison's style and artistic vision, her command of language, and her storytelling skills, even trade journals concentrating on immediate commercial success predicated their good-read expectations on the classical quest motif. Short, unsigned reviews linking *Song of Solomon* with popular books like Alex Haley's *Roots* (*Publisher's Weekly*, June 27, 1977; *Kirkus Reviews*, July 1, 1977); placing it within the folklore tradition established by Zora Neale Hurston and Ralph Ellison, which encouraged libraries to buy copies (*Library Journal*, Sept. 1, 1977); and touting it as a Book-of-the-Month Club selection, which insured book sales (*Publisher's Weekly*), resulted in a bestseller and some financial security for Morrison.[6]

Unlike early reviews of *The Bluest Eye* and *Sula*, this novel found prompt notice in influential publications that augmented Morrison's prestige as well. Authoritative vehicles such as the *Chicago Tribune Book World*, *Newsweek*, the *New York Review of Books*, the *Village Voice*, and the *Washington Post Book World*, which target Euro-American readers and shape public opinion, examine *Song of Solomon* in more depth than do critiques of her previous efforts. Maria Mootry argues in the widely circulated *Chicago Tribune* (1977), for example, that by addressing the "need to transcend the bitter legacy of American racism," Morrison provides a resource for self-motivation. Noting that *Song of Solomon* represents a "shift from the woman-centered themes" of her prior two novels, Mootry critiques its message as "unnecessarily harsh" with a "bramblebush plot" that ultimately, cultivated by its author's "tremendous perception and profound intelligence," "blossoms into a rose" (8). Titling her *Newsweek* review "Black Gold," Margo Jefferson compares *Song of Solomon* to a beautifully patterned, perfectly designed quilt. Writing for the *Washington Post*, Charles Larson celebrates Morrison's third novel as the "most substantial piece of fiction since Ralph Ellison's *Invisible Man*,"

---

5   When Nellie McKay asks her why she chose a male protagonist for her bildungsroman, Morrison responds: "Because I thought he had more to learn than a woman would have" (Gates and Appiah 410).

6   Condensed in *Redbook*, *Song of Solomon* became in 1977 the first Book-of-the-Month-Club "main selection" black book since Richard Wright's *Native Son* in 1940. The "same month in which it was published by Knopf, it sold to the paperback [publishing] house, New American Library, for a reputable $315,000" (Dowling).

an achievement that places its author "in the first rank of contemporary American writers." Acknowledging its "black heritage" but insisting that the book will endure because it "says something about life for all of us," Larson implies that the classical quest theme takes universal precedence over narrower renderings of African American life (37).

Although the *Chicago Tribune Book World*, the *Christian Science Monitor*, the *Los Angeles Times*, *Newsweek*, the *New York Times*, and the *Village Voice* listed the compelling literary elements of Morrison's first two novels, critics writing about *Song of Solomon* for these and similar venues actually discuss aesthetic features in detail. Angela Wigan praises Morrison for a vision that encompasses "both a private and a national heritage" (*Time*); Linda Kuehl states that *Song of Solomon* allows "eloquence to black English" (*Saturday Review*); novelist Reynolds Price applauds its depiction of "the possibility of transcendence within human life, on the time scale of a single lifetime," adding that "few Americans know, and can say, more than [Morrison] in the wise and spacious novel" (*New York Times Book Review*).[7] As Collette Dowling, author of best-selling *The Cinderella Complex* (1981), confirms in a 1979 *New York Times* interview with Morrison, "And John Leonard didn't exactly hurt the book's chances when, in the *New York Times*, he put it in the same class with Vladimir Nabokov's *Lolita*, Gunter Grass's *The Tin Drum* and Gabriel García Márquez's *One Hundred Years of Solitude*." Such Euro-American readers become in large part responsible, then, for the third novel's commercial success.

Staggers concurs that many of the critiques on *Song of Solomon* "demonstrably originated in Euro-Americans' minds, with all their cultural biases, and were presented in publications that promote Euro-American cultural biases and assumptions." Mixed, though leaning to the positive like most of these reactions, Vivian Gornick's 1977 article in the *Village Voice* sums up Morrison's novel as a triumph not without flaws. As she explicates its themes to what Staggers calls "Euro-American, upwardly mobile readers" (61–62), Gornick describes characters "who grow up in an emotional vacuum, disconnected, cut off from the immediacy of their lives." Identifying an "emotional emptiness" lingering at the core of the protagonist's adulthood that prevents his "genuine maturity," she goes on to explain that Morrison relies on "mythology" to develop her ideas as Milkman finally sets out to discover himself. Gornick concludes that "Morrison is an extraordinarily good writer," regrets a "manipulativeness in the book's structure" and a "misdirected angle of vision," but claims that despite these shortcomings *Song of Solomon* "yields up moments of rich life" (41).

Interestingly enough, as Staggers points out, neither Gornick nor a number of other reviewers specifies that this rich life is that of an African American family. Staggers proposes that some in fact find *Song of Solomon*'s strengths to arise not from its sensitive portraits of black America, but from Morrison's adroit

---

7   Price also faults Morrison for including no significant white characters in *Song of Solomon*.

manipulation of language and the novel's positive interpretations of American values. As they caution readers about the painful emotions evoked by the novel, various generally positive Euro-American responses, according to Staggers, reflect white guilt as well. Two such reviews provide stress triggers for the *Christian Science Monitor*'s conservative audience (Oct. 20, 1977; Nov. 13, 1978). Underscoring that as a "black novel" and "not light reading," *Song of Solomon* "can hurt," Neil Millar recognizes the culpability felt by some Euro-Americans vicariously witnessing the suffering of American blacks. Novelist Anne Tyler expresses similar discomfiture when she states that its suffering characters are "still haunting my house. I suspect they'll be with me forever" (E-1). Morrison's worldview makes some European critics queasy as well. Writing for the London *Times Literary Supplement*, Harold Beaver dismisses *Song of Solomon* on the basis of its grotesque gothic, claiming that its effect is "freakish, full of verbal gestures and fabricated horrors" (1359).

Contrasting these responses with those from publications dominated by African Americans, Staggers illustrates how the latter not only identify, but also scrutinize African American cultural biases and conventions. Such vehicles replicate the traditional analyses of literary techniques emphasized by Euro-American journals but also contribute assumptions that "can be attributed to the difference in the critic's and the publication's cultural awareness" (61–62). The *College Language Association Journal* (Mar. 1981), for example, describes the novel's representations of pain, folklore, community, and fulfillment of expectations. Other reviews allude to its accents on wit, humor, black awareness, oral history, nature, and the eternal rightness of things. While African American publications often define pathos differently from Euro-American publications, some African American critics nevertheless disagree with what they deem Morrison's negative perspective even as they foreground her gritty presentation of black American life and then generalize about other themes.[8]

Poet Nikki Giovanni, for one, declares up front that *Song of Solomon* is "ultimately a novel of Black men. They are pitiful, Morrison's Blacks, and we know them all. They sit in the barber shops, at the gin mills, on the corners and stoops of their own lives." Despite its depictions of desolation, however, this "profound" book is a necessary addition to American letters (39). Comparing the novel's craftsmanship with Morrison's earlier efforts, Jessica Harris considers it "vaster in terms of time, locales and sustained character development" and Morrison a "master storyteller," but she is less enthusiastic about its change of subject, deferring to the "promise of what [Morrison's] talent will become" (41). Harris's statements reinforce Staggers's observations that reviews, along with the publications issuing them, reflect and promote cultural biases. *Song of Solomon*'s focus on men would likely be of less

---

8   Additional publications providing an African American reaction to *Song of Solomon* include *Black Book Bulletin* (Mar. 1978); *The Crisis* (Mar. 1978); *Freedomways* (Second Quarter 1978); *Obsidian: Black Literature in Review* 6 (1980); and *Umoja: A Scholarly Journal of Black Studies* (Fall 1978).

interest to a critic such as Harris who writes for *Essence*, since *Essence* targets black female readers.

Song of Solomon's Defining Critical Moments

The defining critical moments of Morrison's third book mirror the various conundrums outlined in its 2004 foreword. Providing front-page cover for the *New York Times Book Review*, the novel won a fiction award from the American Academy and Institute of Arts and Letters (1977); Morrison was chosen as a subject for the PBS series *Writers in America* (1978). On January 11, 1978, Toni Morrison accepted the prestigious National Book Critics Circle Award for fiction. Two hundred critics and review editors selected *Song of Solomon* as the best work of fiction for 1977, the decision a definite indication of Morrison's growing artistic reputation, the close decision possibly suggesting the political nature of the award. Either way, articles began to appear that treat the same themes cited in previous accounts in a more scholarly, detailed, and sometimes scathing manner. Ironically, a great deal of the negative criticism derives from African American critics writing for periodicals that target African American scholars.

Echoing the heated 1960s/1970s disputes among Black Arts activists such as Giovanni, along with previous internal discord among artists and intellectuals during the 1920s/1930s Harlem Renaissance and the "protest literature movement" of the 1940s/1950s, these dissenters disparage Morrison for violating traditions of African American fiction, for challenging some basic tenets of the Black Power movement, and for downright belittling black life.[9] Limiting her accolades to Morrison's inventive use of language and "uncommon style of writing," Norma Rodgers, for example, goes on the attack in *Freedomways*, doubting even "the author's seriousness" (1978). Rodgers underscores passages that "insult ... the dignity of black womanhood" because Morrison portrays black women as "mentally disturbed" (107). She goes on to claim that *Song of Solomon* does not "advance the level of consciousness among the [black] readership by creating a work of art based on human experience," that it depicts the black experience "mindlessly," and that it "denigrates life" (107).

Arthur P. Davis agrees that the novel misrepresents African American life. In the *College Language Association Journal* (1978), Davis describes *Song of Solomon* as a "strange novel," its black characters an "'alien' people to [him], with actions that are unreal" because Morrison "lacks a certain depth of insight into human action." Nonetheless, Davis concurs with Rodgers that the "novel is brilliantly written" (475–77). James McClaren laments its lack of optimism: "the predominant

---

9   Although *Song of Solomon* pays tribute to the Black Arts Movement—Morrison concurs that "the best art is political"—it also questions some of the movement's basic principles, including the role of black women in this largely black male-oriented campaign, and reaffirms the place of black vernacular and the blues as an integral part of African American art and culture.

quality of [black] lives often appears marked by hopelessness and the pursuit of temporary gratification" (369–72).[10]

On the other hand, many scholars writing for multicultural academic publications sing Morrison's praises. Writing separately for the *College Language Association Journal*, both Claudia Tate and Jane Bakerman applaud her style and subject: *Song of Solomon* is a "perfectly crafted novel . . . about love" (Bakerman 446–48). Adam Miller admires her characterization and also asserts that the book conveys a "sense of Afro history" (47–50). In a longer essay highlighting relationships between characters and community which result in an African American "value system" (1980), Barbara Christian concludes that like most fables *Song of Solomon* provides moral instruction for people; read sympathetically, it teaches us about the "marvelous resiliency of nature and therefore of human society" (65–78).[11]

By 1979, critical responses to Morrison's third novel, along with her first two, begin to appear in very lengthy academic journal articles, in books (one an anthology) and book chapters, and in dissertations, suggesting that critics since 1970 had been correct in their prognostications of Morrison as a major contributor to American letters.[12] Intense serious treatments, some continue to expand upon ear-

---

10   When Thomas LeClair notes in a 1981 interview with Morrison that some critics condemn her for writing about eccentric, non-representative black people, she retorts: "This kind of sociological judgment is pervasive and pernicious. 'Novel A is better than B or C because A is more like most black people really are.' Unforgivable. I am enchanted, personally, with people who are extraordinary because in them I can find what is applicable to the ordinary. . . . Black readers often ask me, 'Why are your books so melancholy, so sad? Why don't you ever write about something that works, about relationships that are healthy?' There is a comic mode, meaning the union of the sexes, that I don't write. I write what I suppose could be called the tragic mode in which there is some catharsis and revelation. There's a whole lot of space in between, but my inclination is in the tragic direction. Maybe it's a consequence of my being a classics minor" (Gates and Appiah 374). Tessa Roynon devotes a 2013 monograph to unraveling Morrison's complex engagement with ancient Greece and Rome.

11   One of the scholars who refocuses on Morrison's previous books as *Song of Solomon* accrues increasing respect, Christian develops these ideas into a chapter for her *Black Women Novelists: The Development of a Tradition, 1892–1976* (1980). Calling it "The Contemporary Fables of Toni Morrison," Christian contextualizes Morrison via the African American female literary tradition, citing *The Bluest Eye and Sula* as feminist texts: "Both novels chronicle the search for beauty amidst the restrictions of life, both from within and without. In both novels, the black woman, as girl and grown woman, is the turning character, and the friendship between two women or girls serves as the yardstick by which the overwhelming contradictions of life are measured. . . . Often they find that there is conflict between their own nature and the society that man has made, to the extent that one seems to be an inversion of the other" (137–79).

12   Anne Mickelson's *Reaching Out: Sensitivity and Order in Recent American Fiction by Women* (1979) includes Morrison in a chapter titled "Winging Upward: Black Women; Sarah E. Wright, Toni Morrison, Alice Walker" (112–74), which focuses on Pilate in its discussion of *Song of Solomon*. We also find an introduction to Morrison in the anthology

lier notions while others introduce fresh observations. Karen Stein, for instance, returns to *Sula* with an idea overlooked by previous scholars: "Many of the characters' names, like that of Ajax, conjure up heroes of literary tradition" (1980). Going on to "explore the classical Greek and Biblical allusions which they evoke," Stein considers Ajax and Helene from the Greek tradition and the biblical Eva and Hannah (226–29). Norris Clark embraces rather than resists balancing *Song of Solomon*'s traditional epic structure with its critique of the African American experience, insisting that Morrison re-envisions a "universal myth" (51–63). Wilfrid Samuels and Leslie Harris also focus on mythology. Samuels maintains that *Song of Solomon* mirrors the classical mythological search for selfhood. Recognizing that Morrison relies on folklore to undergird her narrative, Harris affirms that she does so without reducing the novel to fantasy or overpowering it with allusion; her structural use of myth, which reflects the reassurance allowed by storytelling, enables her to universalize a single black man's struggle for identity.

Some of the most intriguing ironies linked to *Song of Solomon*'s defining critical moments continue long after its publication. The novel has faced a number of denouncements and challenges throughout the United States since 1993: as recently as 2010 it was banned and later reinstated at Franklin Central High School in Indianapolis, Indiana.[13] On the other hand, it was cited by the Swedish Academy in awarding Morrison the 1993 Nobel Prize in literature. It became the second book to be tapped by television talk-show host Oprah Winfrey in 1996 to feature in the popular book club she began that same year. In 1998, the Radcliffe Publishing Course named it the 25th best English-language novel of the twentieth century. In 2011, Shortlist.com listed *Song of Solomon* in "40 Favorite Books of Famous People" as President Barack Obama's most cherished book, a comment he reiterated when he awarded Morrison the Presidential Medal of Freedom in 2012. Last but not least, the book's protagonist inspired the name of the Philadelphia hardcore punk rock band the Dead Milkmen, formed in 1983 and performing to this date.

Second-Wave *Song of Solomon* Criticism

The bulk of second-wave *Song of Solomon* criticism (135 of 265 publications) appeared between 1990 and 2005.[14] If the critical reputation of Morrison's first

---

Sturdy Black Bridges (Bell 1979), a selection attesting to the significance of her work. The volume credits Morrison for her fiction and for her skill as an editor.

13 Copyrighted in 1994 by the American Library Association, a poster that proclaims "Banned Books Week—Celebrating the Freedom to Read" above a photograph of Toni Morrison explains: "Censors denounced an Ohio library in 1993 for having the *Song of Solomon*, because it contains 'language degrading to blacks, and is sexually explicit.'"

14 Organizing its citations according to decades to include academic journal articles and dissertations, the *MLA Bibliography* lists 37 records from 1980–89; 73 records from 1990–99; 52 records from 2000–2009; and 16 records from 2010–18.

two novels benefited from the publication of her third, the status of her third profited from the appearance of her trilogy on the African American experience: *Beloved* (1987); *Jazz* (1992); *Paradise* (1997). Her endowed professorship at Princeton University in 1989 didn't damage *Song of Solomon*'s standing either, nor did her global recognition via the coveted Nobel Prize in Literature. The *MLA International Bibliography* begins to list scholarly responses to the novel in 1980; 18 of these records may be counted as first-wave *Song of Solomon* criticism (1980–82). Since then, roughly 200 scholarly articles and book chapters (105 in peer-reviewed journals), in addition to 35 dissertation abstracts and 12 books, have been published by mostly American distributors.

Monographs initiating significant analysis on *Song of Solomon* come from small and prominent academic presses alike. Most provide chapters, although the novel did help fuel five monographs centered primarily on Morrison's work and two editions from Nellie McKay on Morrison's oeuvre to 1997 (*Critical Essays on Toni Morrison*, 1988, and *Approaches to Teaching the Novels of Toni Morrison*, 1997) as well as inspiring its own casebook study (*Toni Morrison's Song of Solomon: A Casebook*, 2003, edited by Jan Furman).

Books stimulated by *Song of Solomon* include *Black Time: Fiction of Africa, the Caribbean and the United States* (1981) by Bonnie Barthold; *New Dimensions of Spirituality: A Biracial and Bicultural Reading of the Novels of Toni Morrison* (1987) by Stephanie Demetrakapoulos and Karla Holloway; *Subject to Negotiation: Reading Feminist Criticism and American Women's Fictions* (1997) by Elaine Orr; *Subversive Voices: Eroticizing the Other in William Faulkner and Toni Morrison* (2001) by Evelyn Schreiber; *Trances, Dances, and Vociferations: Agency and Resistance in Africana Women's Narratives* (2001) by Nada Elia; *African American Servitude and Historical Imaginings: Retrospective Fiction and Representation* (2004) by Margaret Jordan; *Toni Morrison and Motherhood: A Politics of the Heart* (2004) by Andrea O'Reilly; *Orphan Narratives: The Postplantation Literature of Faulkner, Glissant, Morrison, and Saint-John Perse* (2007) by Valérie Loichot; *Can't I Love What I Criticize? The Masculine and Morrison* (2007) by Susan Mayberry; *Art and Ritual in the Black Diaspora: Archetypes of Transition* (2017) by Paul Griffith; *James Baldwin, Toni Morrison, and the Rhetorics of Black Male Subjectivity* (2017) by Aaron Oforlea; and *Vexy Thing: On Gender and Liberation* (2018) by Imani Perry.

With the first five articles on the novel published in journals that accent black culture, the trend continues as 26 percent of MLA citations appear in similar venues: *Black American Literature Forum/African American Review* (14); *CLA Journal* (5); *MELUS* (5); *Callaloo* (4); *Griot* (3); *Minority Voices* (2); *Obsidian/Obsidian II* (2); *Journal of Blacks in Higher Education* (1); *Journal of Ethnic Studies* (1); and *SAGE* (1). After translation rights were sold in eleven countries, 36 essays, or 25 percent, were issued by foreign presses from places as diverse as Argentina, Australia, Canada, France, Germany, India, Italy, Japan, Korea, the Netherlands, the Philippines, Portugal, Serbia, Spain, Taiwan, Turkey, the United Kingdom, and West Africa. Second-wave studies, described here in chronological order within categories, emphasize archetypal; African American/postcolonial; feminist/womanist; psychoanalytic; new historical/cultural; and intertextual literary criticism.

Song of Solomon and Archetypal Criticism

A number of scholars succeed Harris, Clark, and De Arman in extending the pervasiveness of myths and archetypes in structuring *Song of Solomon*. Charles Scruggs reminds us in 1982 that Morrison's characters often "suffer from a more fundamental form of dispossession than loss of property or civil rights"; sometimes they are cut off from "the basic myths that place isolated individuals within . . . a rural village, a city neighborhood, or a family" (312). If Jacqueline de Weever presents a 1980 survey on Morrison's employment of fairy- and folktale in the novel, Susan Blake confirms that, by basing it upon a variant of a well-known Gullah story, Morrison "calls attention to one of the central themes in all her fiction, the relationship between individual identity and community, for folklore is by definition the expression of community" (1980). Ironies within her version of the folktale serve to illustrate Morrison's concept of community (77).

Scholars address specific ways in which vernacular myths become structurally significant. Pinpointing *Song of Solomon* to best epitomize its author's conviction that "blacks have to cling to their cultural identity to fight the American system, which threatens to homogenize society by absorbing cultural differences," Chiaro Spallino concentrates on the "temporal progression of the narration" (1985). Although Milkman's subjectivity unfolds from the stories of others, his transformation "is activated by the family past beneath which . . . lies the mythic past" (510–11). Timothy Powell credits Morrison's affirmations of folktale and blues with having decentered the white logos (1990).

Various scholars have noted archetypal connections to names and flight in *Song of Solomon*. In a seminal study on naming, Ruth Rosenberg connects its fascination with its subversions of expectation (1981). Characters with biblical names in a text called after a book in the Bible would logically delineate a biblical allegory. Having "joyously" sabotaged that probability, "gaily frustrating all searches for her onoma in Biblical concordances," the author remarks, according to Rosenberg, on the black use of a white book: "By stressing the self-referentiality of her names, she protects the integrity of her fiction. It can only be explicated in its own terms, not ours" (195). In 1987, Joyce Ann Joyce counters critics who disparage the novel's "meandering and confusing plot" by maintaining that they fail to find its center: Morrison deliberately opts for an omniscient narrator, subplots, and an array of characters to craft a structural frame that fuses themes of flying and naming (185).

While Christian Moraru scrutinizes the politics of the proper name in the text, Judith Fletcher signifies [on] the midwife Circe. Asserting that *Song of Solomon* is a "story *about* naming," in which characters' names frequently "denote their narrative function," Fletcher clarifies that Circe, the only character to bear a name from classical mythology, simultaneously subverts her "Homeric intertext and the patrilineal literary history that is its legacy" (405). Lucinda MacKethan evaluates the overall importance of naming in the African American tradition. Echoing a notion introduced by Ralph Ellison in a 1964 address titled "Hidden Name and Complex Fate" in which Ellison states, "Our names, being the gift of others, must be made our own," MacKethan argues that names in *Song of Solomon* reflect its characters' desire to claim "their own identities as they rebel covertly against a system that would take title to their names and lives as well" (199).

Morrison often associates naming with flying. As Philip Royster points out, until Milkman pays attention to the people and signs around him, that is, regenerates his collapsed imagination "to perceive alternative actions and conditions, and therefore to manipulate as well as to select from the environment," he remains the unconscious scapegoat-victim (1981). His flight, then, becomes a transcendent self-awareness, so that instead of being consumed by the social order, his energy enables self-reliance and self-determination (419–20). Agreeing that Morrison coordinates Milkman's archetypal search for self with the unique specifics of a black American experience, Dorothy Lee insists that his flight "may be duplicated by all who can abandon the frivolous weights that hold them down and, in so doing, ride the air" (70).

In 1986, James Coleman takes to task those critics who view Morrison's conclusion as celebratory. Echoing Guitar's belief that "creative, imaginative, and practical Black survival responses to oppression inevitably merge into strange and destructive behavior that is a consistent and unbreakable cycle in the Black community," Coleman assesses Milkman's death to be "fulfilling in terms of the novel's traditional myth pattern" but also a means of freeing him from a situation in which he no longer fits and, hence, leaving the majority of African Americans in a vicious cycle that minimizes or seriously compromises genuine love and caring (151–52). Richard Heyman opts for up in the air. As he acknowledges the curious kinship of writers marginalized by various modern languages, Heyman counts Morrison's suspended ending as her question to "the validity of both [Milkman's] means of achieving his goal and the search itself" (1995). *Song of Solomon* suggests alternatives to flight delays or cancellations while "avoiding the kind of prescriptive closure that creates centers and margins in the first place" (381). Cedric Bryant puts it this way: "*Song of Solomon* epitomizes subversive closural practices in the African American narrative tradition that . . . denies death's dominion by rejecting the prevailing [Judeo-Christian] cultural constructions of it" (99).

Grace Ann Hovet and Barbara Lounsberry pilot a seminal study on Morrison's use of flight as sexual potency in her first three novels (1983). Judging the commonplace of flying as "'escape' or 'freedom' in Afro-American folklore and literature" too readily accepted, these scholars expand the trope to include Wright's and Ellison's emphases on "equality" and "opportunity" and, more recently, Morrison's negative implications of "free-falling" and, in *Song of Solomon*, affirmative connotations with "identity, community, and creative life." (119–21). Gay Wilentz and James Hall (McKay, *Approaches* 68–72) provide additional discussions on Flying

African myths in *Song of Solomon*. If Diane Bowman determines that Morrison's Icarus figure represents narcissism and immature eroticism, Manuela López Ramírez maintains that, as Morrison rescues those elements of black cultural mythology that are still relevant to blacks and fuses them with evident allusions to Greek mythology, she rewrites the Legend of the Flying African and the Myth of Icarus to create her own myth (2012).

Song of Solomon and African American/Postcolonial Criticism

Since the title of Morrison's third novel privileges Solomon's song over his name or his flight, African American critics measure the thematic centrality of music. Confirming that a positive side-effect of Morrison's increasing critical and popular success became the opportunity to query the author about her fictional purpose, Joyce Wegs reports that Morrison believes the novel must now do for her peasant community what the music used to do (1982). Wegs's essay demonstrates that "Morrison as novelist takes on the role of a blues singer in order both to explore how folk values buried in the past may contribute to a better future for all her people and to describe variations on traditional male and female roles in order that her readers may analyze for themselves which ones appear most valuable" (211-12). Abraham Smith proposes two ways in which *Song of Solomon* employs the blues: "1) to absorb cultural values, and 2) to identify those characters with healthy cultural rootedness" (112). Anthony Berret evaluates how the novel exemplifies literary jazz (1989).

Allison Bulsterbaum and Marilyn Mobley investigate Morrison's use of folksongs such as "Sugarman Gone Home." Bulsterbaum shows that it functions as "a sustaining vehicle for both plot and theme" (15). Mobley allows it threefold significance: "For Milkman, it signals the story of his family; for the community of Shalimar, it functions as a kind of cultural glue through the children who learn, sing, and perform it; and for the reader, it serves as an illustration of Morrison's folk aesthetic and mythic impulse at work (127).[15] While Deanna Garabedian sums up music in the novel as "the language and the expression of the African-American heritage" (313), Vikki Visvis notes its therapeutic usefulness as traumatic testimony.

1980s/90s scholars also probe the importance of story in this story. Claiming that critics have missed Morrison's "profoundly traditional view of the relation between literature and culture," Theodore Mason terms her "an example of the novelist as *conservator*," in this case of black communal practices (564-65). Joyce Middleton agrees that while most praise Morrison for her "modernist" and "experimental" novels, by "drawing on the oldest literary tradition of all, that of oral storytelling," her achievement "has been to illuminate the values of an ancient

---

15 For an extended discussion on the relationship between the oral and literary traditions, see also Trudier Harris's *Fiction and Folklore: The Novels of Toni Morrison* (1991).

form within the modern novel" as she "dramatizes the cultural conflicts between oral and literate traditions." (64)

Research from 1992 to 2002 finds Cindy Burkhalter explicating these various tropes that signify African American wisdom, and Nina Mikkelsen comparing Morrison's narrative structure to "the mathematical 'fractal' visual pattern seen in African architecture and in de-centered kente cloth patterns as a scaling, infinitely repeating design, which corresponds to the social structure prevalent in pre-colonial African culture" (97). After he establishes that *Song of Solomon* shifts Morrison's narrative focus from the tradition of uplift to the anomalies of the American Dream, Dolan Hubbard observes that the philosophical center of the text "makes the connection between sermonic discourse, self-determination, and spiritual authority" as it "engages in a progressive dialectic between memory (Pilate) and forgetting (Macon)" (289).

1990s African Americanists hone in on the significance of memory and bearing witness to the past. As Deborah Guth identifies Morrison's purpose ("to explore and dramatize the complex interaction between a present in search of itself and a past that appears sometimes as nurturing cultural foundation, sometimes as a restrictive tradition to be fought off, and sometimes . . . as a frightening nightmare that imposes itself between the present and a future of freedom and renewal"), Guth examines "three different constructions of this relationship and three aspects of the problem—rejection, reclamation and the dynamics of the remembering imagination—in order to clarify the ramifications and cultural implications of [Morrison's] thought" (575). Robert Holton names *Song of Solomon* along with *Beloved* as Morrison's witness to African American historiography, and Maggie Ann Bowers explains how Morrison creates "an African American cultural memory with her readership" by encouraging "imaginative participation of the reader in the text" (19).

Finally, African American critics scrutinize the text's revelations about its [Southern] milieu and masculinity. Carolyn Jones, Lucille Fultz, Catherine Lee, and Jennifer Terry survey Morrison's landscape. Contributing to a special 1998 edition of *Studies in the Literary Imagination*, Jones designates Morrison's Southern environment as psychic scenery; Fultz connects Morrison's Southern ethos with black ethics; and Lee particularizes *Song of Solomon*'s South as providing initiation, healing, and home. Terry incorporates a broader structuralist approach in 2007 to show that, as the novel contests familiar stories of national belonging and being in the land, it excavates buried perspectives about black displacement, dispossession, estrangement, travel, discovery, connection, and home, which shape an alternative narrative.

While Jackie Thomas examines the symbolic black male ancestor, Rolland Murray deems references to "the debilitating effects of 'strutting' masculinity" Morrison's critique on the emancipatory limits of black patriarchy (121). As he posits an intertextual relation between *Song of Solomon* and *Go Down, Moses*, John Duvall suggests in 1991 that "Morrison's novel reclaims Faulkner's in ways that question the male-centered world of the hunt and that refuse the gambit of tragedy" (95–96). Proposing that the politics of the novel and the politics of pedagogy are closely aligned in *Song of Solomon*, Linda Krumholz adds that "Milkman's initiation into black manhood serves to initiate the reader in the 'discredited knowledge' of African Americans" (551). Susan Mayberry centers her 2007 book outlining Morrison's insights on the black male around Guitar's attitude toward the black female: "Can't I love what I criticize?" (*Song of Solomon* 223).

Postcolonial critics infuse Milkman's flight with an [anti]imperial twist. Citing an African American, a Cuban, and a Jamaican version, Wendy Walters advises that "the legend of the Flying Africans is a canonical tale which resonates throughout the expressive traditions of that part of the African diaspora which has known slavery in the New World" (1997). This "geographic currency" demands both "a pan-American and a pan-African analytic perspective, a theoretical framework which encompasses Afro-Caribbean and Afro-Latin geographic and cultural areas, in addition to looking at the perhaps more commonly cited North American examples" (4). Polycarp Ikuenobe elaborates on how flying and myth underpin *Song of Solomon*'s African cultural and philosophical foundation (2001). Nada Elia asserts that the novel reflects the work of Belali Mohomet, a Muslim African poet: "Morrison took some poetic liberty as she wrote the novel, transplanting Mohomet and his descendants to Virginia and fusing their history with that of the Ibos, to recreate the collective history of the US South's Afrodiasporans" ("'Kum Buba'"Abstract).

Katherine Thorsteinson believes that modern aviation technology "converged with civil rights integration efforts so as to transform the mythic desires for physical escape into aspirations for socioeconomic ascension," shifts that led to increasing connections with the African continent (2015). Thus while the Flying African myth came about under the conditions of slavery, it was "altered under the possibilities that were generated by the very technologies of flight for which it had once expressed an impossible desire" (259). Having defined Morrison's *Playing in the Dark* as "a distinct African-American intervention into postcolonial theory," Justine Baillie goes on to juxtapose a reading of Morrison's *Song of Solomon* with Faulkner's *Go Down, Moses* (2007).

Song of Solomon and Feminist/Womanist Criticism

Four of the first studies on *Song of Solomon* merge archetype with feminist approaches. Acknowledging that the bildungsroman, traditionally a vehicle for male expression, has generally been, for women writers, an apprenticeship involving marriage and motherhood, Carolyn Naylor includes Morrison's novel in Naylor's 1982 study of "the journey motif as it undergirds the theme of the bildungsroman as a vehicle for self-exploration, and of androgyny as it symbolizes the healing, affirming, and humanizing self and others" (27). Explaining that African American literature joins American literature in viewing "movement and change as intrinsically valuable—a process of endlessly becoming rather than progress culminating in a state of completed being" (59), Robert Butler names Pilate among a small number of female characters who "offer proof that the liberating open motion of our picaresque literature is sometimes available to women" (75).

Gerry Brenner proposes that while Morrison shrewdly embraces the saga of the hero's birth on Milkman's behalf, she just as skillfully mocks him and the other male characters in order to reject the sexism of Otto Rank's monomyth along with the expectations of feminists. When he tosses African American theory into the archetypal/feminist mix, Michael Awkward concludes that Morrison intends her novel not only to preserve black culture but also to infuse those traditions with the "new information" necessary for ongoing survival (1990). As she recognizes "a discourse attuned to the intersections between afrocentric and feminist ideologies" (484), *Song of Solomon* both reflects the perspectives of African American culture and "seeks to contribute in significant ways to its transformation" (497).

Re this novel that Morrison dubs her tribute to men, other feminist criticism is sporadic, running the gamut from female initiation to gender politics to women playing the dozens.[16] Jane Bakerman judges Morrison's depiction of female initiation in her first three novels, as fused with her primary concern about "love or its absence," to portray failure (541–42). Though she allows that early reactions focus more on myth than on feminism (1995), Susan Farrell rejects Bakerman's negativity in 1995 to position herself more in accord with Awkward's attitude toward Morrison's feminism than with Brenner's claim that she discards it: "The text of *Song of Solomon* serves as a wonderfully appropriate site for a black feminist criticism" (Awkward 484). Soophia Ahmad is more specific. Describing the novel, and Milkman, "supported by a brilliant cast of female protagonists," Ahmad illustrates how their "race consciousness develops as a result of their experiences—both within and outside the community." While these women lead Milkman toward an understanding of himself, the "search for their own identity and purpose in life, the craving to understand who they are, and what they desire becomes, eventually, the deciding factor between life and death, self-affirmation and self-negation, ecstatic joy or desperate misery. It decides, ultimately, who finds meaning in life and whose years on the earth are a waste—and why" (59).[17]

Those who applaud Morrison's feminism in *Song of Solomon* urge dissenters to consider how "racist and sexist social forces underly constructions of female beauty in the U.S." (Farrell 132). Clarifying that the framework provided by theorist Luce Irigaray for discussing the visual objectification of women in Western culture has focused on the entrapment of white female characters within the "male gaze," Malin Walther argues that Morrison forces a reconsideration of a "universal" standard of female beauty, so defined by white consumer culture, as both

---

16 "The dozens" is a game of wit and spoken wordplay between two contestants, common in African American communities, where participants insult each other until one gives up—or gets angry.

17 Morrison tells Nellie McKay that Morrison the novelist seeks to find out "who survives and who does not, and why" (Gates 402).

racist and frivolous (1990). As she "explores the visual system upon which definitions of beauty are based, identifies the racial underpinnings of visual beauty, and reorients the gender-based construction of the gaze," Morrison has "moved to redefine beauty out of the specular system and into a racial authenticity" (775). Bertram Ashe traces the construction of African American beauty standards via the trope of hair, concentrating on "specific black-male expectations where black-female hairstyles are concerned" (579).

Stephanie Demetrakopoulos and Edith Frampton debate the idea of embodiment in the text. Defining "embodiment" as "the way a woman's body mediates between her psyche and the cosmos," Demetrakopoulos incorporates *Song of Solomon* into her study of the nursing mother and feminine metaphysics (430). Frampton is also interested in the implications of Ruth continuing to nurse a four-year-old Milkman, demonstrating that Morrison cites breastfeeding among the feminine bodily functions inflected by the trauma of racism as she "foregrounds the body as a discursive, racialized construct" (141).

Other feminist critics highlight female positions and interactions. Carmen Subryan examines the mother/daughter relationships portrayed in the novel, showing how societal influences can result in the stagnation of black women's spirits, and how love and compassion can result in the uplifting of those spirits. Deanna Ramey compares the triad of women depicted in *Song of Solomon* with that portrayed in *Sula*. Marjorie Podolsky includes Morrison's third novel in an essay on black women writers playing "the dozens," and Hsin-ya Huang appraises Pilate's healing power particularly as an "Other[ed] woman" and *Song of Solomon* as a critique of imperialism.

Song of Solomon and Psychoanalytic Criticism

As Elizabeth Beaulieu points out in 2003, "Despite the reservations some scholars have expressed about using psychoanalytic theory to discuss the works of an African American author such as Morrison, psychoanalytic critics have successfully highlighted the central place of fantasy in Morrison's novelistic narratives as they have investigated Morrison's representation of the complex inner and social worlds of the individual and family" (38). Those foregrounding *Song of Solomon* begin with questions of subjectivity. Preliminary essays, which emphasize that "the black characters in Morrison's early novels are especially vulnerable to the defeats that accompany isolation," address the "interplay between self-knowledge and social role" (Valerie Smith Abstract). David Buehrer writes two pieces on fragmented characters and the psychological intersections of race, class, and place for the *Journal of Evolutionary Psychology* (1995, 2004). While Aeju Kim investigates the psychological effects of migration on identity, Ashley Tidey recalls Freud's observations about how we get there ("'What we cannot reach flying, we must reach limping...'") as she illustrates the characters in *Song of Solomon* manifesting Du Bois's double-consciousness, that is, different degrees of resolution and balance between Eurocentrism and Afrocentrism (48).

Eleanor Branch and Gary Storhoff ponder Morrison's notions about Freud's oedipal complex as Zhu Yanyan and Quan Wang propose Lacanian readings. Noting how Morrison resorts to "an appropriation and critique of both African and Western mythologies," since her "task in the novel is reparation of the old mythological aesthetic and the production of a new one," Branch attends to "the affinity between Milkman and Sophocles's Oedipus in the way limping characterizes both characters and their search for identity" and on oedipal overtones vis-à-vis Ruth's protracted breastfeeding of Milkman and the Western fairytale of "Rumpelstiltskin" (55). Although he concedes that the dominant psychoanalytic discourse taken toward the novel has been "resolutely Freudian," Storhoff is convinced that too-narrow a lens on oedipal issues leads to oversimplification and suggests critical focus shift "from the intrapsychic to the interpersonal or social dynamic" (1997). There we discover that *Song of Solomon* is a portrait of destructive "enmeshment—the suffocating bond parents occasionally create with their children that Morrison labels 'anaconda love'" (290). Cowriters Yanyan and Wang concentrate on the Lacanian scheme of androgyny in their reading of Milkman (2007); Wang goes it alone to take the same tack toward Pilate (2013).

Song of Solomon and New Historicist/Cultural Criticism

Cultural critics of *Song of Solomon* hone in on its portrait of Black Nationalism and the after-boom of the "Oprah Effect." John Brenkman reminds us in 1994 that Morrison wrote the novel "on the cusp of historic uncertainties": "By 1977, the only New Day to dawn in America was going to be bathed in the murky sunlight of Reaganism illuminating a landscape of decay and sorrow." Nonetheless, Brenkman continues, even though Morrison's story ends in 1963 so that we might view it as avoiding contemporary politics, the years in between not only inform the narrative, but they "infuse it" (57). As she reminds us of Morrison's well-known comment about the relationship between her writing and black music, Laura Dubek identifies 1963 as a time when civil rights activists "felt compelled to choose between two very different ways forward—the integration and passive resistance model advocated by . . . the Southern Christian Leadership Conference (SCLC) and the black power vision promoted by . . . young militants increasingly at odds with SCLC" (2015). Dubek believes that *Song of Solomon* enters this space "by referencing slavery and Jim Crow, linking characters to historical figures in the civil rights movement, and conjuring up the spirit of a gospel singer named Solomon Burke" (91). Writing for a Canadian press and focusing on Guitar and Pilate, Dana Medoro contends that each "articulates and develops a form of justice" in the novel, and that each "informs—or exerts pressure on—the other's configuration of justice" (1).

Four critics scrutinize Morrison's portrayal of Black Nationalism. First up is Harry Reed, who contrasts early cultural nationalist efforts to achieve equality inside the American political system with modern Black Nationalism, which seeks to "control, direct, and shape political destiny" (1988). Viewed through this prism, according to Reed, *Song of Solomon*, simultaneously affirming and criticizing black cultural nationalism, "suggests a need to expand BCN to permit a focus on regenerating the community from within" (50–52). Ralph Story and Nigel Thomas reflect specifically on Morrison's Seven Days. Story reckons that the revolutionary group allows its creator "a microcosm of the two primary ideological streams which have characterized Afro-American political thought in the twentieth century" (150). Encapsulating the dissonance between these two streams in the characters of Guitar Bains and Milkman Dead, Morrison's portraits are based on the historical figures of Malcolm X and Martin Luther King Jr. In a 2001 effort to defend Guitar from "the opprobrium to which he has been subjected," Thomas counters certain aspects of Story's "thorough and controversial" analysis, arguing that Morrison's unsanctioned "warrior-protector" is also "in search of salvation, though of a lesser spiritual kind" (147–48). Meina Yates-Richard concentrates on maternal disavowal and the reverberations of black women's pain in Black Nationalist literature, including *Song of Solomon*.

John Young explores the effects of television talk-show host Oprah Winfrey endorsing Morrison's novel. After he quotes James Weldon Johnson's remark that twentieth-century black writers have had to confront the problem of a "double audience," leading to questions about artistic authenticity when black texts are published for white readers, Young comments: "Oprah Winfrey's television book club has dramatically shifted the publishing world's balance of power" (2001). He goes on to argue that "the alliance between Morrison's canonical status and Winfrey's commercial power has superseded the publishing industry's field of normative whiteness, enabling Morrison to reach a broad, popular audience while being marketed as artistically important. By embracing 'Oprah's Book Club,' Morrison replaces separate white and black readerships with a single, popular audience" (181).

Song of Solomon and Intertextual Criticism

Intertextual critics from the 1980s on apply ideas about genre and authorship to juxtapose *Song of Solomon* with other texts. Perry Nodelman compares it to *M. C. Higgins the Great*, written by children's author Virginia Hamilton. Joe Weixlmann lists Morrison's text together with others he terms Afro-American novels of detection. Ann Imbrie considers it a pastoral novel.

Some employ it to determine Morrison's affinities with other authors. Josie Campbell and Giulia Scarpa emphasize its third-world kinship with the novels of Simone Schwarz-Bart. Gabrielle Foreman and Susana Vega-González contrast its magical realism with that of Isabel Allende and Gabriel García Márquez. Bev Hogue numbers it among novels that accent late-twentieth-century exiles' search for authentic names, homes, and memories, which will lead the body to function as a meaning-making machine that thrives beyond the comprehension of the structured system.

Texts by Joyce and Faulkner are repeatedly compared with *Song of Solomon*. Insisting that the ethnic writer needs as much rescue as the regional writer from "labels that imply diminished importance," David Cowart maintains that *Song of Solomon* deserves attention "as part of intertextual engagement with certain literary predecessors, among the most important of whom are Faulkner and Joyce" (87). Kate Ellis intersects Morrison's hero specifically with Joyce's Stephen Dedalus and "his Greek mythological avatar, both linked by 'the name of the father' to the flying Milkman" (35). Joseph Brown and Lorie Fulton focus specifically on Morrison's interactions with Faulkner. As he unveils these novelists' respective approaches to history, Brown articulates *Song of Solomon*'s comedic vision of life, as opposed to the tragedy dramatized in the lengthy soliloquies of *Absalom, Absalom!*. Fulton's Cornell M.A. thesis expands Alessandra Vendrame's work by connecting Morrison's interpretation of Faulkner to *Song of Solomon*.

Several scholars note the novel's interactions with other African American texts. Holly Fils-Aimé examines spiritual death, initiation, and empowerment in Marshall's *Praisesong for the Widow* and *Song of Solomon* and, subsequently, the roots of the latter and of Naylor's *Mama Day* via the trope of ginger. Fred Metting contemplates the possibilities of flight in all three books. Harold Bloom muses about what he calls two African American masters of the American novel (Ralph Ellison and Toni Morrison) while Valorie Thomas includes *Invisible Man* together with *Song of Solomon* (and *My Life in the Bush of Ghosts* by Nigerian writer Amos Tutuola) in her study of vertigo. Assessing *Song of Solomon* to pick up "where [Ishmael Reed's] *Mumbo Jumbo* leaves off," Michael Rothberg analyzes conspiracy, trauma, and posthumous communication in Morrison's version of the Dead letter office. He urges us to read Morrison's novel not only through its numerous intertexts but also as a commentary on the significance of intertextuality as a literary, historical, and social process (501). Providing bookend essays, Cheryl Wall credits Morrison's novel with re-sounding the African American literary tradition according to Du Bois's *The Souls of Black Folk*, and William Ramsey recognizes *Song of Solomon* along with Colson Whitehead's work as bringing about a time when no single "ideological discourse of the South can claim objectivistic grounding as authoritative history" (769).

No survey of criticism on *Song of Solomon* would be complete without compiling its biblical reverberations. Judy Pocock and Jessica Wierzbinski unearth its typology, the Bible being, according to Morrison, not just "'part of [her] reading . . . it was part of [her] life'" (Taylor-Guthrie 97). Jan Stryz summarizes what Wierzbinski describes and Pocock deems Morrison's "'guerilla' use of typology" (283). If this novel illustrates how she "negotiates the obstacles imposed by the task of freeing her own story from a literary past," it also uses biblical names to "show the impact of the Bible on the lives of black people, their awe of it and respect for it coupled with their ability to distort it for their own purposes." As Morrison "articulates the cosmology of the black people within the bounds of this fiction, the cosmology of her fictional text is reflected here too. Narrative movement reaches a destination that is also an origin and so achieves closure within the field of the text. *Song of Solomon*, even while it repudiates a certain type of 'authorized' writing, tells the story of a writing that is not parricidal, a writing that recovers the story of the father and incorporates it into a text that, while engendered and animated by that story, is in its individuality itself original" (39). In other words, it provokes a conundrum.

CHAPTER FOUR

TAR BABY (1981)

Tar Baby's Critical History as Told by Toni Morrison

Tar Baby, no doubt thanks to the popularity of *Song of Solomon*, received some lengthy, politely worded mixed reviews from the highbrow popular presses when the former was published in 1981 but less literary critical attention until its author received the Nobel Prize in 1993. In 1981, with four novels in print, a frustrated Morrison put one white male interviewer on notice: "I have yet to read criticism that understands my work or is prepared to understand it.... It's like having a linguist who doesn't understand your language tell you what you're saying. [Novelist] Stanley Elkin says you need great literature to have great criticism. I think it works the other way around. If there were better criticism, there would be better books" (LeClair 376–77).

If Morrison determined to amend this dearth of useful African American literary criticism and disrupt the trajectory of her own literary critical reception by including a 1993 afterword to the 1970 edition of *The Bluest Eye*, along with forewords to the 2004 Vintage editions of *Sula* and *Song of Solomon*, the most conspicuous thing about the foreword to the 2004 paperback of *Tar Baby* may be its absence of recriminations. Describing her linguistic choices in *The Bluest Eye* (her "reliance for full comprehension on codes embedded in black culture"; her "effort to effect immediate co-conspiracy and intimacy" without succumbing to what she calls in *Sula* a welcoming introductory "lobby"; her failed effort to "shape a silence while breaking it") as "attempts to transfigure the complexity and wealth of Black-American culture into a language worthy of the culture," she deems her narrative project as difficult in 1993 as in 1973: "With very few exceptions, the initial publication of *The Bluest Eye* was like Pecola's life: dismissed, trivialized, misread. And it has taken twenty-five years to gain for her the respectful publication this edition is" (215–16).

Sula's foreword becomes an endeavor to redress Morrison's embarrassment at what she now views as its staged opening by delineating the strategies African

American writers "can be forced to resort to in trying to accommodate the mere fact of writing about, for, and out of black culture while accommodating and responding to mainstream 'white culture'" ("Unspeakable Things Unspoken" 154). Although the foreword to *Song of Solomon* opens on a similar note of regret, it comes in the form of personal mourning upon losing with her father's death the image of her own best self that had lived inside his head. Ultimately learning to trust him as the muse that made possible her novel about black men, Morrison welcomed the challenge to manage "a radical shift in imagination from a female locus to a male one" (xiii).

The foreword to *Tar Baby*, however, embraces collective listening. If the book's epigraph cautions "brethren" about contentions among the house of Chloe (Toni's given name), its dedication calls out the names of the female ancestors Chloe and company must hearken to: "Mrs. Caroline Smith [great-grandmother]; Mrs. Millie McTyeire [great-grandmother]; Mrs. Ardelia Willis [grandmother]; Mrs. Ramah Wofford [mother]; Mrs. Lois Brooks [sister]; and each of their sisters, all of whom knew their true and ancient properties." For Morrison, all narrative begins with listening, and Morrison's *Tar Baby* critiques a community's infuriatingly self-destructive refusal to pay attention to legends and dreams past and present. Unlike previous codicils to her books, which linger on professional or personal regret in the face of cultural/gendered difference, this 2004 foreword straightway celebrates the mysterious, rejuvenating power of African American myth: "The figure of [the] tar [baby], having done its work, falls out of the action of the tale, yet remains not only as its strange, silent center, but also as the sticky mediator between master and peasant, plantation owner and slave. Constructed by the farmer to foil and entrap, it moves beyond trickery to art" (xii–xiii).

The primordial depiction of black tar, "threatening yet inviting," led Morrison to render her tar baby tale as a story of masks not merely covering what lies hidden beneath but demonstrating how masks exaggerate the tensions between themselves and what they cover and, in so doing, themselves come to life—or take life over. As she pondered the larger-than-life features of African ritual masks which, per cultural tradition, cause the wearer to conceptually lose his or her human identity and turn into the spirit represented by the mask, she transformed their ancient animation into the structure of *Tar Baby*: "All of the characters are themselves masks. And like African masks, the novel merged the primal and the contemporary, lore and reality" (xiii). She exposes her male protagonist's most effective mask to be none at all; she enables other characters to assume masks that take on a life of their own and then collide with the living masks of others. Maintaining in "Unspeakable Things Unspoken" that people may have originally turned to folklore as allegory explaining natural or social phenomena, Morrison argues that folklore can also contain myths which, like masks, perpetually reinvent themselves via the people who repeat, reconstruct, and reinterpret them.

Though once again she uses her public platform to secure her narrative project, the foreword to her fourth novel seems to find Morrison increasingly more at ease with her critical task and the critical appraisal of it: "The texture of the novel seemed to want leanness, architecture that was worn and ancient like a piece of mask sculpture: exaggerated, breathing, just athwart the representational life it displaced. Thus the first and last sentences had to match, as the exterior planes match the interior, concave ones inside the mask." Unlike her revisions to *Sula*, where she ignored her initial hesitancy about the need for her final introduction, she freely altered the first version of the opening sentence of *Tar Baby*, "He thought he was safe," to "He believed he was safe," not because she wanted to make the entry more accessible to white readers, but because "'thought' did not contain the doubt wanted to make the reader uneasy about whether or not he really was—safe." Associating thinking with non-reality and self-control, she opted for belief, as belief implies trust on the part of the speaker and promotes distrust on the part of the reader: "The person [Son] who does the believing is, in a way, about to enter a dreamworld, and convinces himself, eventually, that he is in control of it. He believed; was convinced. And although the word suggests his conviction, it does not reassure the reader" in the way that a flat statement, "He was safe," would have ("Unspeakable Things" 158–59). Clarifying that African Americans have long relied upon tales, gossip, celebrations, and, especially, indigenous music to pass on survival skills and conceding that outsiders have co-opted that music, Morrison proposes that the novel must now keep her "peasant people" alive. Thus her fiction always examines who survives and who doesn't and why (LeClair 370–71).

Tar Baby's people must learn the uneasy lesson that there is no safety. Safety becomes the central desire of its characters. Locating, creating, and losing safety provides the locus for the novel. Morrison underwrites her message by making the last line of the text bookend to the first. "Lickety split, lickety split, lickety lickety split" is not only the final sentence of the folktale, Son's final action, the ambiguous ending that ensues from an unreliable beginning, and the complementary meter to its twin opening, but "the wide and marvelous space between the contradiction of those two images: from a dream of safety to the sound of running feet. The whole mediated world in between. This masked and unmasked; enchanted, disenchanted; wounded and wounding world is played out on and by the varieties of interpretation (Western and Afro-American) the Tar Baby myth has been (and continues to be) subjected to." As the characters creatively wind their way through the traps and escapes induced and produced by their past, nothing is safe. Or, Morrison emphasizes, "should be. Safety is the fetus of power as well as protection from it, as the uses to which masks and myths are put in Afro-American culture remind us" ("Unspeakable Things" 160–61).

Tar Baby's Initial Critical Reception History

The first-wave critical reception of *Tar Baby* (1982–86) certainly proved to be something other than a safe bet. As Leroy Staggers puts it in his 1989 PhD dissertation, "*Tar Baby*, like Morrison's three earlier novels, received both positive and negative critical responses. However, this novel received more negative criticism than the previous three. Nonetheless, *Tar Baby* was still hailed by the critics as another triumphant achievement by Toni Morrison" (87). If *Time* magazine lauded it in 1981 as being "like the rabbit bait in the Uncle Remus tale," as "the sort of novel one can get stuck on" (Sheppard 91), the *Atlantic Monthly* relegated it to Morrison's "weakest book so far":

> With *Tar Baby*, Morrison has attempted to hitch another such bucking bronco of a theme onto a comedy of manners, and they're an odd pair. No sooner have we set up the thrumming poetry, the animistic sense that the clouds and trees are on to something big, than we are exchanging persiflage with some desiccated white folks and their gelded black retainers in a gingerbread house in the Caribbean. (Sheed 119)

Ballyhooed or harangued, *Tar Baby* garnered more immediate response than Morrison's previous three novels, in part benefiting from the enormous popularity of *Song of Solomon* as well as its selection by a close vote among two hundred critics and review editors in 1978 to win the National Book Critics Circle Award for best fiction in 1977. By 1982 Morrison's name was well known in contemporary American literary circles. Her photograph dominating the cover of *Newsweek*'s March 30, 1981, issue attests to her growing appeal to a broad spectrum of readers; the weekly magazine highlights among its trending stories a lengthy article outlining the author's biography and explaining the essence of her oeuvre. The publication of *Tar Baby* spurred reviewer Jean Strouse to clarify in layman's terms to a general audience what some scholars and literary critics had allowed for almost a decade—that Toni Morrison was fast becoming an American literary celebrity:

> In the new novel, "Tar Baby," Morrison takes on a much larger world than she has before, drawing a composite portrait of America in black and white. She has produced that rare commodity, a truly public novel about the condition of society, examining the relations between blacks and whites, men and women, civilization and nature circa 1981. That may sound like it's good for you but no fun, but "Tar Baby" keeps you turning the pages as if to find out who killed J.R. (52)

As was the case with Morrison's previous books, the initial reactions to *Tar Baby* appeared prior to the book itself in trade publications such as *Kirkus Reviews* (Jan. 1, 1981), *Booklist* (Jan. 15, 1981), *Library Journal* (Jan. 15, 1981), and *Publishers Weekly* (Jan. 23, 1981). Staggers reminds us that since the business of trade journals is to promote book sales, touting *Tar Baby* following *Song of Solomon*'s financial success became a win-win prospect. Even so, the steady upshot of *Tar Baby*'s early promotional reviews was that the book is vintage Morrison but better: Morrison takes risks, pulls them off, and, because her milieu and mythology include the Caribbean, New York City, and all-black, small-town Florida, she broadens her scope and our consciousness (Staggers 78).

Conversation about *Tar Baby* shifted from the trade journals that target book dealers as their primary readership to publications directed toward a mass audience. The tenor of criticism in a category that includes *Time* magazine (Mar. 16, 1981), the *Village Voice* (Mar. 18, 1981), the *New York Times* (Mar. 21, 1981), the *New York Times Book Review* (Mar. 29, 1981), *Newsweek* (Mar. 30, 1981), the *New York Review of Books* (Apr. 30, 1981), and *Ms.* (July 1981) is, once more, enthusiastically mixed. Madeline Lee cautions her predominantly white female readers in the feminist *Ms.* magazine: "Ration yourself carefully, or the book will go by too fast. Rich, seductive, and still nourishing, it leaves whatever you are doing in real life looking rather disappointing" (26).

Critics who dubbed the book better than her previous novels describe several significantly new elements. Up to this point, Morrison had focused primarily on the particular concerns of her "peasant people." *Tar Baby* not only addresses multiple settings, introducing African Americans to characters and customs from the Caribbean but includes a wealthy family of white people, whose patriarch takes on as his protégé a light-skinned black woman moving restlessly between black and white worlds. Some, however, deemed the novel overly stereotypical and less than subtle. Anatole Broyard wonders in the *New York Times* (Mar. 21, 1981) "why Miss Morrison, who won an important award with her last novel, has written so poorly in this one." Describing *Tar Baby* as protest fiction, Broyard speculates that the reader may have a few protests, too. For example, "He may wonder why the black characters in *Tar Baby* have all the passion, while the white ones are fit only for sitting in greenhouses, manufacturing candy and sticking pins into their babies." As readers demand what the novel means (and here Broyard riffs on lines from said novel), they "may feel that black folks should sit down with white folks for a frank exchange about the reading and writing of fiction."

Conceding that Broyard may be correct in viewing Morrison's white characters as stereotypes, Staggers maintains that she is nonetheless "being consistent with a tradition in Afro-American fiction according to which black writers portray whites as being capable of enormous cruelty to blacks as well as to other whites." Prompted by his own decision to "pass," biracial critic and writer Broyard may also be overreacting to Morrison's overt censure of white society in America.[1]

---

1 An American literary critic and editor from New Orleans who wrote for the *New York Times*, Anatole Broyard's career turned controversial after his death in 1990 when biographers revealed that he had "passed" for white as an adult. Broyard moved to Greenwich Village, mecca for aspiring artists, to be accepted as a writer, instead of a "black writer." Having acted out of self-interest during a period of increased black communal political activity, the Louisiana Creole of mixed-race ancestry was outed by some contemporary African American political figures for his decision to deny his past. Late twentieth-century advocates of multiracial culture have since praised Broyard as an example of a person insisting on an independent racial identity before it was widely popular in mainstream America. African American critic Henry Louis Gates Jr., swings both ways. Six years after

Since such denunciations had been more implicit in her previous three novels, "some of the Euro-American critics writing in publications, such as the *New York Times*, which promote Euro-American values, condemned *Tar Baby* for its direct criticism of those values" (Staggers 88–89). Although he does not damn the entire novel as a failure, Euro-American novelist John Irving allows in the *New York Times* that "our best and most ambitious writers indulge their vices as freely as their virtues; they are unafraid of them and think it small-minded to exercise restraint" (Mar. 29, 1981). Declaring that "Miss Morrison has been up to this kind of dramatic exaggeration for some time," Irving explicitly cites *Tar Baby*'s excessive use of dialogue and over-the-top lyricism.

While remaining positive overall, publications aimed at a more particular segment of the general American reading public contained more negative commentary than publications targeting a wider mass audience, perhaps because the former solicit more highly educated and thus more discriminating readers. The spectrum of such responses can be found in the *New Republic* (Mar. 21, 1981); the *Atlantic Monthly* (Apr. 1981); the *Nation* (May 2, 1981); the *National Review* (June 26, 1981); *Black Enterprise* (July 1981); *Commentary* (Aug. 1981); the *Progressive* (Sept. 1981); the *New Statesman* (Oct. 23, 1981); the *Spectator* (Dec. 1981); the *Sewanee Review* (Fall 1981); and the *Yale Review* (Winter 1982). Acknowledging (but significantly miscomprehending) Morrison's disruptions of the tar baby tale, Pearl Bell, for example, contributes more specifically to her colleagues' disparaging observations about *Tar Baby*'s "banal" characters (Hutch 793) and Morrison's "self-conscious" style (Milton 259):

> Even the title of *Tar Baby* contributes to the underlying confusion of Miss Morrison's story, her failure to consider the way a metaphor can mislead. In the Uncle Remus story, a tar baby is the black doll a white farmer puts into the cabbage patch to trap the thieving rabbit. As Son hurls the tale at his lover's head in their final quarrel, Valerian becomes the white man who made tar baby Jadine—but how, then, does Son stand for the rabbit who outsmarts the farmer and runs away? Why does he desperately try to find Jadine after she runs back to Paris? None of this makes much sense.... (56)

Broyard's death, Gates wrote a profile for the *New Yorker*, titled "White Like Me," which attacks Broyard for concealing his African American ancestry. Expanding his essay in "The Passing of Anatole Broyard," published the next year in Gates's *Thirteen Ways of Looking at a Black Man* (1997), Gates denounces Broyard for deceiving friends and family by "passing" as white even as Gates sympathizes with Broyard's literary ambition: "When those of mixed ancestry—and the majority of blacks are of mixed ancestry—disappear into the white majority, they are traditionally accused of running from their 'blackness.' Yet why isn't the alternative a matter of running to their 'whiteness'?" (180–214). In his miniseries, *African American Lives* (2008), Gates acknowledges that he learned by DNA analysis and genealogical studies that he himself is ancestrally more than half white.

Analyses of *Tar Baby* gradually made their way into publications devoted to literary critics and academics. This category of journals includes the *College Language Association Journal* (Sept. 1981), *Freedomways* (Fourth Quarter 1981), *Critique* (Spring 1983), the *Mississippi Quarterly* (Winter 1984), *Names: Journal of the American Name Society* (Mar. 1984), *American Literature* (May 1984 and May 1986), *SAGE* (Spring 1985), *Comparative Literature Studies* (Fall 1985), *Black American Literature Forum* (Spring–Summer 1986), and *Studies in American Fiction* (Autumn 1986). As with previous reviews, appraisal varies; unlike cursory immediate reaction, however, the articles in these publications typically contain more detailed, scholarly interpretation.

Staggers references essayists representing both predominantly African- and Euro-American literary journals, who, characteristic of most detractors during the first onslaught of *Tar Baby*'s critical history, attack Morrison's overarching vision for the novel (91). Nieda Spigner argues in *Freedomways*, the leading African American theoretical, political, and cultural journal of the 1960s to 1980s, that because Morrison peopled her book with "a bunch of emotionally stressed jet-setters" whose manipulated characterization rings true "only within the fictional bounds the author has set," *Tar Baby* becomes merely "a dazzling example of marketability" (267). Via the first-wave manifestation of the current *African American Review* (the *Black American Literature Forum*), James Coleman attributes Morrison's "unclear directions and garbled messages" to leaving the reader "in a muddle at the end." Although she continues the immersion into the positive influence of folk values projected by *Song of Solomon*, Morrison pulls "an escape act" by imposing on *Tar Baby* "a superficially good ending that, under analysis, proves unsatisfactory." Its characters neither successfully integrate folk values into the context of a white world nor embody wholeness by assuming white Western sophistication: "*Tar Baby* fails to penetrate the core of such important issues, and, in this sense, is a failure" (72). Cynthia Edelberg secures space in *American Literature*, the journal sponsored by the American Literature section of the Modern Language Association and published by Duke University Press, to accuse Morrison of using *Tar Baby* as a platform to denounce the value of American education.[2]

Clearly miffed, Staggers infers Edelberg's opinion of Morrison as anti-education to imply that she is likewise anti-American. Charging the white critic with misconstruing the black communal values espoused by *Tar Baby*, Staggers takes umbrage with Edelberg's pronouncement that "in contrast to the high premium placed on education in the black community," Morrison "sees the values that western education teaches as demonstrably destructive to blacks" (91). He also considers Edelberg's evaluation of Jadine's Sorbonne education being responsible for saturating Jadine with damaging Western values and forcing her to choose between

---

2   Associated with W. E. B. and Shirley Graham Du Bois, *Freedomways* began publishing in 1961 and ceased in 1985. Founded in 1976, the *Black American Literature Forum* became the *African American Review* in 1992. The first volume of *American Literature* was published in March 1929.

black and white worlds to underestimate Jadine's complexity. Rejecting Edelberg's rejection of *Tar Baby* as "being all style and no substance," Staggers objects to his colleague's overall assessment of Morrison's characters and oeuvre:

> These characters live in a brutal world from which there is no way out. Morrison posits a kind of primitivism as an answer, as something that counters education and works, but this primitivism is rhetorical rather than convincing. She woos us through her style, but cannot enlist us in her cause. In the hopelessness of the human situation she creates, Morrison's values are reduced to wishful thinking. To put it another way, she implies that "ancient properties" are better than education and the work ethic, but dramatically shows us that they are not. (Edelberg 237)

Identifying Edelberg's "us" to signify "whites," Staggers alleges that this critic misuses the authoritative voice of *American Literature* to mislead Euro-American literary scholars—and dismisses her reaction as "overreaction" (92).

Quite a few of the first-wave critics writing for literary journals, however, expressed positive reactions to *Tar Baby*, some introducing topics that would continue to echo through subsequent investigation. Not only is Bonnie Lange one of the first scholars to note Morrison's symbolic use of color imagery, but Lange focuses on the primary color in *Tar Baby* to present it as more optimistic than its predecessors. Explaining that each novel's meticulous depiction of color evokes "a unique and particularly representative response of sensual experience," Lange theorizes why the color code in *Tar Baby* shifts from red to yellow. Since psychological research determines that people's distaste for red can often be connected to personal frustration, Morrison's emphasis on the devastating power of red in her first three novels may partially be the result of her recent divorce contributing to ongoing anxieties about gender and racial oppression. Thus, contrary to Edelberg's pessimistic conclusions about the plot of *Tar Baby*, Lange submits that the dominance of the color yellow, in the form of the tar-black African woman wearing a canary yellow dress and holding aloft three chalk-white eggs, who haunts Jadine throughout the work, not only signals Morrison's celebration of black women's "ancient properties," but also a return to the promise of female energy and vitality (173–82).

Charles Fishman uncovers another recurring trope in the even more specialized *Names: Journal of the American Name Society*. Highlighting the naming process that will prove to be a hallmark of Morrison's oeuvre, Fishman proposes dual purposes for her character and place names. First is her "desire to make clear distinctions, to suggest connections or motifs within the text, or layer patterns that extend between texts, and to erect borders. . . ." This critic points to the onomastics in *Tar Baby* to illustrate his second reason: many of the names "elevate the narrative to a land of myth." L'Arbre de la Croix, for example, is French for "Tree of the Cross," Star Konigsgaarten translates as "King's Great Garden," and Eloe indicates "Elohim" or "God" (33–34).

Tar Baby's Defining Critical Moments

The first wave of *Tar Baby*'s literary critical reception history includes some of Morrison's more broad-minded and enduring Euro-American critics. Intrigued as recently as 2011 with Morrison's interactive narrative of words, music and song, *Desdemona*, Early Modern scholar Peter Erickson initially critiqued *Tar Baby* in 1981. Erickson insists in a *College Language Association Journal* article that the extent to which reviewers designated *Tar Baby* as a sharp departure from Morrison's previous concerns has been exaggerated. Arguing that although we are made more conscious of disconnections than connections between its principal black women (Therese, Ondine, and Jadine), we must nonetheless acknowledge the novel as a feminist text, since "its main issue is the generational continuity among black women" (11). If Morrison centers primarily on ways in which Jadine, even more decisively than Sula, stands for the New World black woman by rejecting maternity in search of originality, Ondine, Therese, and to a limited extent Son, embrace the nurturing role of the Old World black woman. African American theorist Henry Louis Gates Jr., reprints Erickson's essay in *Toni Morrison: Critical Perspectives Past and Present*, edited by Gates and Appiah in 1993.

Literary generalist Terry Otten also defends Morrison's vision for *Tar Baby* in an article published by *Studies in American Fiction* (1986). Her conviction that "evil can be redemptive and goodness can be enslaving," Otten asserts, "does not restrict so much as enlarge the scope of her vision." Illustrating that a full moral awakening entails a necessary mindfulness of evil, the characters Morrison creates who remain willfully innocent, like those of Milton and Dostoevsky, become inhibited because a "fall from innocence is ironically essential to being" (153–63). In contrast to the anti-education approach Edelberg will take in 1986, Elizabeth House's 1984 essay, likewise for Duke University's *American Literature*, aligns with Otten's view that the novel espouses the liberal humanistic values endorsed by Morrison's classical education at Howard and Cornell Universities: *Tar Baby* "affirms the superiority of idyllic values over competition; [Morrison] clearly details the negative consequences of valuing power or wealth more than other people" (195–200).

Especially during late 1983/early 1984, graduate students such as Madelyn Jablon, Shirley Jordan, Geta Lesseur, Charles Nama, Angelita Reyes, Jose Saldinar, and Danille Taylor-Guthrie found enough fodder in *Tar Baby* to concentrate on it in their doctoral dissertations. Typically examining Morrison's previous novels together with her fourth book or analyzing her work along with that of several other writers, research includes one PhD. thesis that developed into a monograph focusing exclusively on Morrison. Danille Taylor-Guthrie's interest, beginning with her 1984 dissertation at Brown University, led to a 1994 edition published by the University Press of Mississippi, which contains interviews given by the Nobel laureate beginning in 1974. The same academic press supported a 2008 collection, edited by Carolyn Denard, which expands upon the 1994 edition by contributing thirty years of interviews and profiles, including those from the 1970s and 1980s that were not collated in Taylor-Guthrie's *Conversations with Toni Morrison*.

Discussions of the novel increasingly made their way into books geared toward literary scholars. Chapters and reprinted articles can be found in texts such as *Black Time: Fiction of Africa, the Caribbean, and the United States* (1981), *The Afro-American Novel since 1960* (1982), *Paradoxical Resolutions: American Fiction since James Joyce* (1982), *Terrorists and Novelists* (1982), *Black Women Writers (1950–1980): A Critical Evaluation* (1984), *Amid Visions and Revisions: Poetry and Criticism on Literature and the Arts* (1985), *Black Feminist Criticism: Perspectives on Black Women Writers* (1985), *Conjuring: Black Women, Fiction, and Literary Tradition* (1985), *Contemporary American Women Writers: Narrative Strategies* (1985), *The World of Toni Morrison: Explorations in Literary Criticism* (1985), *Living Stories, Telling Lives: Women and the Novel in Contemporary Experience* (1986), and *Mythic Black Fiction* (1986).

In *Black Feminist Criticism* Barbara Christian devotes two chapters to Morrison's novels, one a prior review by Christian reprinted from *In These Times* (1981). Chapter 4, "Testing the Strength of the Black Cultural Bond: Review of Toni Morrison's *Tar Baby*," declares that the novel's conflict of values between the "individualistic, materialistic Jadine" and the "roots-bound Son" raises more questions than it answers: is there "a functional black culture in the present-day West, a contemporary black community that is held together by bonds that work[?] Are blacks essentially upwardly mobile? Is color merely a camouflage? Is race in America operating as a communal bond or is it merely an indication of a past history once functional but no longer perceived by contemporary blacks as operative in their responses to each other?" (68–69).

Distinguishing in a foreword to this republished review between the critic's "immediate, succinct response," essential to "the creating of a wider, more knowledgeable audience for the writer's work," and the essay in which critics have "the time and space to analyze [the writer's] craft and ideas," Christian developed her initial reaction to *Tar Baby* into a longer academic conference paper on the concept of class in Morrison's work, presented at a 1981 Pittsburgh Area Philosophy Colloquium and later included as chapter 5 in *Black Feminist Criticism*. In this chapter, "The Concept of Class in the Novels of Toni Morrison," Christian argues that, consistent with the tradition of fiction by African American women, Morrison's four novels constitute her attempt to analyze the relationship between class, race, and gender. As she introduces well-heeled white characters and Caribbean "serfs" into *Tar Baby*, Morrison "may be suggesting not only that class concerns are now more critical than racial bonds, but that women, in their search for autonomy, may be taking on patriarchal values." Her body of work signals that sex, race, and class may be "so organically connected that one must understand their interrelationship in spite of their ever-shifting appearance" (78–79).

Mari Evans's *Black Women Writers 1950–1980* (1984) also contains dual (and dueling) analyses of *Tar Baby*. After Darwin T. Turner impugns its characters as, contrary to those in Morrison's previous novels, "too ordinary, too stereotypical—created solely to demonstrate the clash of class and culture," this respected African American poet, educator, critic, and editor pays Morrison the dubious compliment of achieving status as a major novelist by artfully creating "grotesques destined to live in worlds where seeds of love seldom blossom." Turner determines that in Morrison's four novels to date, "Black men and women—regardless of class or culture—never sustain harmonious relationships in heterosexual love." Thus her class and cultural differences may conceal a "more significant difference—that of their sexes" (369). Taking each of Morrison's four novels as "a part of a whole," however, Dorothy Lee concurs with Christian that Morrison's vision of the human condition is preoccupied with "the effect of the community on the individual's achievement and retention of an integrated, acceptable self" (346). Unlike Turner, Lee regards Morrison's theory of quest that draws recurrently on myth and legend for story pattern and characterization as a motivating device.

The year 1985 produced several books containing notable commentary on *Tar Baby*. In *Contemporary American Women Writers: Narrative Strategies*, edited by Catherine Rainwater and William Scheick, Linda Wagner's "Toni Morrison: Mastery of Narrative" attributes Morrison's genius as a writer to the power of her narrative style: "To read Morrison without attention to her narrative structures and methods is to obscure her always careful relation of character to theme, shape to form, voice to effect." Wagner claims that, contrary to many novelists, Morrison attempts different and usually new techniques with each book, rather than following a traditional pattern of learning from the first novel how to be more effective in the second (191–205). Discussions of Morrison's *Tar Baby* can also be found in chapters 4, 14, and the afterword to *Conjuring: Black Women, Fiction and Literary Tradition*, edited by Marjorie Pryse and Hortense Spillers. Elizabeth Schultz's "Out of the Woods and into the World: A Study of Interracial Friendships between Women in American Novels" differs from Christian and others who insist that *Tar Baby* reinforces stereotypes. Locating the novel's main point in its charge that "racial power plays cannot go unchallenged," Schultz posits that *Tar Baby* establishes the open confrontation of ethnic stereotypes as the necessary basis for an interracial interrelationship: "If the white and black women in *Tar Baby* move toward a friendship in the novel's conclusion, it is because they have confronted head-on the stereotypes and emotions generated by racism" (76).

First-wave book critics disagree, however, about the tenor of *Tar Baby*'s conclusions. In chapter 14 of *Conjuring*, "Trajectories of Self-Definition: Placing Contemporary Afro-American Women's Fiction," Christian reasserts her previous criticism of *Tar Baby* as overly "pessimistic." Fixed primarily upon Jadine, the "Afro-American princess" whose focus on security and comfort causes her to take a position so far removed from her community that she "succumbs to the decadent Western view of woman," Christian states: "In [Jadine's] search for self she becomes selfish; in her desire for power, she loses essential parts of herself (243–45). Another 1985 book, the first devoted entirely to Morrison's oeuvre at this point, takes a different tack. In *The World of Toni Morrison: Explorations in Literary Criticism*, Bessie W. Jones compares *Tar Baby*'s "exotic Caribbean island" with Milton's Eden in *Paradise Lost*. This critique of the book's symbolic landscape touts *Tar Baby*'s closing as upbeat: "Morrison's moral vision is reflected in the optimism with which the novel ends" ("Garden Metaphor and Christian Symbolism" 115–24).

Defining first-wave criticism determines that *Tar Baby* signaled a noteworthy expansion of Morrison's perspective not only in its inclusion of commentary on white characters for the first time but also in its effective juggling of several complex literary techniques at once, which makes the novel appealing to a broader audience. Unlike the works of many African American writers at this time, Morrison's political protest, while compelling, is subtle, objective, and mostly without moralizing. Her characterization is skillful, her language lyrically precise, her accent on feminist issues decisive but not obsessive. Staggers credits Morrison's adeptness with allowing readers representing the three prevalent literary critical emphases (Euro-American, Afro-American, and feminist traditions) to "find the novel interesting as well as intellectually stimulating" (107–8). Unique in their simultaneous appeal to all of these readerships, the books and book chapters devoted to *Tar Baby* indicate that it, along with Morrison's previous novels, had come to be perceived as major contributions to American letters.

Second-Wave *Tar Baby* Criticism

The bulk of second-wave *Tar Baby* criticism (64 of 89 publications) came out between 1990 and 2009 (1990–99 accrued 40 publications, and 2000–2009 accounted for 24). The *MLA International Bibliography* begins to list scholarly responses to the novel in 1984; 10 of these records, including 2 dissertations, may be counted as first-wave *Tar Baby* criticism (1982–86).[3] Since then, roughly 73 scholarly articles and book chapters (in addition to 8 dissertation abstracts and at least 8 reprints) have been published by mostly American distributors. Thirteen percent of MLA citations appear in journals with an American multicultural concentration: *Black American Literature Forum* (4); *CLA Journal* (2); *MELUS* (4); *Callaloo* (1); the *Black Scholar* (1); and *In Process* (1). Purdue University's *Modern Fiction Studies* has provided four essays.

The official publication of the Modern Language Association's Division on Black American Literature and Culture, *African American Review* (*AAR*), titled *Black American Literature Forum* from 1976 to 1992, has featured prominent African American cultural critics and writers, including Toni Morrison. The College Language Association (CLA), established in 1937 by a group of black scholars and educators, is an organization of college teachers of English and foreign languages, which serves the professional priorities of its members and their

---

3   Organizing its citations according to decades, the *MLA Bibliography* lists 19 records from 1980–89; 40 records from 1990–99; 24 records from 2000–2009; and 16 records from 2010–19.

collegiate communities. Founded in the San Francisco Bay Area in 1969, *the Black Scholar* is one of the first journals of black studies and research, and *In Process: A Journal of African-American and African Diasporan Literature and Culture* has been produced since 1996 by current graduate students at the University of Maryland, College Park. The four articles on *Tar Baby* offered by *Modern Fiction Studies* become a byproduct of the continuing focus on Morrison scholarship by its assistant editor from 1994–99, Nancy Peterson. Reprinting an essay on *Tar Baby*, Peterson's 1997 edition (*Toni Morrison: Critical and Theoretical Approaches*), which promises to take "the process of reading Morrison's works seriously," situates Morrison's works "in relation to various theories of the post- that have come to proliferate at the end of the twentieth century in America." (1).

To accommodate the many teachers who assigned Morrison's novels long before she won the 1993 Nobel Prize and prior to the existence of a significant body of secondary literature on the author, Nellie McKay and Kathryn Earle include three essays on *Tar Baby* in their *Approaches to Teaching the Novels of Toni Morrison*, printed in 1997 by the MLA as part of its series Approaches to Teaching World Literature. Madelyn Jablon's "*Tar Baby*: Philosophizing Blackness" demonstrates how that instructor uses Morrison's fourth novel, a "high point of the course," to do what "Morrison herself seems to do": examine more closely and carefully the themes and motifs contained in *The Bluest Eye* and *Sula*. Agreeing with Stephanie Demetrakopoulos that Son and Jadine become each other's tar babies (Holloway 136), Jablon privileges a philosophy of blackness "that celebrates difference, one that acknowledges and accepts contradiction" (73–76).

In "Telling Stories" Marilyn Mobley opts for a cultural studies approach to teaching *Tar Baby*, defining African American literature as "an inherently interdisciplinary field that has always provided a political critique of representations and discursive practices." Gaging the novel as "disconcerting" for many students, Mobley admits that, while her approach makes it no less so, she hopes to help us to "make our way individually and collectively through the difficulties of our own cultural moment" (141–46). Ann Jurecic and Arnold Rampersad agree that, because *Tar Baby* is perhaps the most problematic of Morrison's early novels, it has likewise been the least acclaimed and considered. Their essay enables teachers to recognize the controversial elements that alienate readers, and proposes, as does Morrison, "places and spaces so that the reader can participate" and the text itself become a kind of tar baby (Morrison, "Rootedness" 341).

McKay also includes two essays on *Tar Baby* in her previously issued *Critical Essays on Toni Morrison* (1988). Other scholars who have made space in subsequent editions for chapters specifically on Morrison's fourth novel are Marc Conner (*The Aesthetics of Toni Morrison: Speaking the Unspeakable*, 2000); Harold Bloom (two books in his Bloom's Literary Themes series: *The Trickster* and *Exploration and Colonization*, both edited by Blake Hobby in 2010); and Carmen Gillespie (*Toni Morrison: Forty Years in the Clearing*, 2012).

Morrison's Nobel Prize provided the catalyst for international interest in *Tar Baby*, too. The novel has been notably popular since 1993 with foreign journals and scholars, twenty-three articles having appeared from 1993 to 2016. Overseas attention consists of critics from China, England, Germany, India, Japan, Korea, Spain, and Taiwan, as well as Central and West Africa. Second-wave studies, summarized chronologically within categories in the following sections, accentuate psychoanalytic; Marxist; archetypal; African American; postcolonial; and additional aspects of the body of criticism most influential in providing substantive readings of Morrison's novels: womanist/ black feminist literary criticism.

Tar Baby and Womanist/Feminist Criticism

Tar Baby lends itself to discussions stimulated by womanism/feminism, particularly issues of motherhood and mother-daughter relationships. Lucille Fultz addresses the tension produced by a culturally enforced emotional distance between African American mothers and daughters, while Andrea O'Reilly distinguishes Morrison's as a philosophy of African American mothering that outlines a liberating, generative experience connected to her larger political stance on black womanhood in America. Arguing that material barriers (economic limitations and race/class/gender biases) to expressions of love cause daughters to rebel against mothers who view their sacrifices as substitutes for affection, Fultz explains that, denied tenderness, daughters do not learn to transfer tenderness to their daughters (1996) Confrontation erupts in *Tar Baby* when Ondine, rejoicing in Jadine's independence yet resenting Jadine's disregard of Ondine's maternal support, blames herself for not exposing Jadine to the African American community. O'Reilly celebrates Morrison's belief that, because black women traditionally view freedom as merely choice of responsibility, they have freely and less problematically than white women inhabited concurrent domestic and public spheres (2000). This emphasis on and ease with responsibility make maternal commitment to kin and community central to Morrison's definition of black womanhood in *Tar Baby* and elsewhere.

Three essays extend the novel's presentation of black woman and female sexuality. Ann Rayson posits Morrison's as a "sad indictment" of said woman's position, caught between foreign exotic and domestic drudge. Continuing the first-wave critical conversation about *Tar Baby*'s depiction of the negative consequences of Western education for African American females, Rayson adds that in the late twentieth century, it is "the African American male who is trapped"; Jadine simply "gives up the soul of a black folk culture she never knew, one which Son has romanticized, in order to survive" (97, 99). As Judylyn Ryan examines Jadine's missed experiences, she turns to W. E. B. Du Bois's concept of double consciousness to explore the multifaceted conflicts between Jadine and Son. Ryan proposes that *Tar Baby* illustrates the importance of considering gender and class in tandem with Du Bois's focus on race and suggests ways in which Du Bois's definition of a debilitating "double consciousness" can be transformed into an empowering "double-vision" when choice and agency underpin competing visions. Paul Mahaffey further complicates womanism by rethinking *Tar Baby*'s inquiries into biracial female sexuality.

Tar Baby and Psychoanalytic Criticism

More recent psychoanalytic lenses on *Tar Baby* rebut first-wave commentary that the novel fails to answer satisfactorily whether African Americans can seek emotional wholeness, much less locate self-identity while edified by modern Western values. Margo Backus conducts a feminist/materialist psychoanalysis of fiction to determine how the post-capitalist Anglo-American family has been shaped and supported by the reproduction of capitalism, directing particular attention in *Tar Baby* to the incestuous and pornographic views of women that reflect and maintain prevailing social relations within late industrial capitalism (1994). Susana Vega-González prefaces her essay with Morrison's quotation: "No Black woman should apologize for being educated or anything else. The problem is not paying attention to the ancient properties." Because spiritual death for Morrison comes from the negation of culture and community, which results in the loss of self, Vega-González views *Tar Baby* as a "cautionary tale," with Jadine's college education failing to fill in for her racial ignorance (1996). The solution becomes privileging balance over binary: "There must never be a total detachment from the cultural roots from which the black woman has stemmed, nor an absolute submission to the canon and the establishment within the community" (150).

In a 1996 issue of *Midwestern Miscellany* devoted entirely to Morrison's works, Mary Beth Pringle asserts that Jadine manages to journey through art toward freedom, eluding so far as possible the sticky embrace of the Candy King. In the process, she "turns placelessness—a seat in an airplane far above the sites on earth that would entrap her—into a home of sorts" (37). Urging us to be generous with our definitions of "success," since most female quest heroes never even dare to try, remaining, as they do, inhibited by the patriarchy, Pringle measures Jadine's accomplishments fruitful in "instants and potential" (49).

Two psychoanalytic studies include the author in their speculations. Agreeing with Pringle that the success of Jadine's quest for self-discovery must be evaluated in terms of black experience, Krishnamoorthy Aithal credits *Tar Baby* with revealing that Morrison accepts but moves beyond racial, political, and ideological self-definition to embrace personhood first. Her own self-awareness coupled with her ability to connect with the complex identities of others, whatever their race or color, encourages diverse readers to feel deeply involved in the fate of her black protagonists so that her art becomes universal (1986).

John Duvall adds that when she wrote *Tar Baby*, Morrison may have been, like Jadine, struggling with her own "night women," those "internalized voices that might question her for layering nontraditional roles onto her maternal one." Having in 1981 left her birthplace along with her birth name, she was rearing two sons by herself while giving priority to a career that "made her as much the cultural as the natural creator." Thus *Tar Baby* "confirms Morrison's refusal to endorse an African American identity that would allow black men—in unacknowledged complicity with white patriarchy—to assume property rights over black women. Black women, the text also submits, need not be tied to an agrarian community in order to partake of the ancient properties but, like Jadine (or indeed like Toni Morrison), may migrate freely, with or without men, to the city and beyond" (347).

Tar Baby and Marxist Criticism

The lone Morrison novel containing fully developed white characters, *Tar Baby*, unsurprisingly enough, has inspired more Marxist criticism than any of Morrison's works. Angelita Reyes reminds us of Morrison's declaration in "Rootedness: The Ancestor as Foundation" (1984): "If anything I do, in the way of writing novels, (or whatever I write), isn't about the village or the community or about you, then it is not about anything. I am not interested in indulging myself in some private, closed exercise of my imagination . . . which is to say yes, the work must be political" (Evans 345).

Doreatha Mbalia, John Lutz, and Jean Wyatt weigh *Tar Baby*'s discerning critique of capitalism. Mbalia's essay commends Morrison for maturing in her understanding that capitalism and imperialism have caused the oppression of African people, meaning anyone of African descent, everywhere. Perceiving the novel to censure the United States as the African's worst enemy, Mbalia praises Morrison's heightened class consciousness, apparent through her postcolonial setting, her inclusion of Euro-Americans as major anti-heroes, and her thematic concerns with the schism that exists in the African community over identifying with the oppressor or the people (1997). Lutz appreciates Morrison's use of the original tar baby story to underscore the relationship among commodity consumption, exploitation, and social/economic domination. *Tar Baby* presents commodities as a dual snare, causing characters to repress the exploitative origins of wealth as they pursue individualistic, self-negating activities (2013). Wyatt insists that while Morrison's modes of attack on capitalist values are many and varied, her primary weapon is satire (2014). The "follies and extravagances of her characters constitute an indictment of capitalism: their actions dramatize the ways that capitalist entanglements warp people's feelings, desires, and thought processes" (30).

Another group of Marxist critics note *Tar Baby*'s emphasis on agricultural and environmental consumption, investigating the dynamics of economic power and social class in a modern/postmodern context. Eleanor Traylor introduces *Tar Baby* as an exquisitely told story about nourishment: "the devastation caused by its lack and the regenerative power of its presence" (148). In his 2004 book on food and resistance in twentieth-century African American literature, Andrew Warnes argues that black writers have consistently found associations between hunger and illiteracy and by extension between food and reading. As he examines food as a metaphor for race relations in America, exposing the irony of American slaves laboring to produce food surfeit while enduring personal food shortage, Warnes explains how the trope of food implicitly politicizes hunger, revealing it to be an avoidable, imposed condition. Morrison's depiction of her characters' strategies of pilfering and foraging suggests a kind of hunger that could be abolished were it not useful as a means of enforcing submission and dependency. Warnes connects his readings to such diverse sources as Frederick Douglass's slave narrative, Ntozake Shange's cookbook, and Stanley Kramer's film *Guess Who's Coming to Dinner?*

Susan Mayberry alludes to Kramer's film in the title of her 2012 essay on *Tar Baby*, which maps Morrison's navigations of contemporary theoretical currents. Mayberry finds food and its consumptions functioning in the novel as signifiers that enable Morrison "to address complex modern philosophical dilemmas about conditions of knowledge, cultural hybridity, rejection of fabricated history, and uncertainty of language." Referring to Morrison's claim that ". . . Black people were the first modernists" (Randolph 106), Mayberry credits the attitude of Morrison's characters toward appetite, food, and eating with redefining "race, class, and gender constructions against and within the context of a modernism that questions traditional values and assumptions and the rhetoric by which they were sanctioned and communicated" (213). As it explores the relationships among food, racial identity, and an emerging modernism, Mayberry's analysis identifies in *Tar Baby* the tenuous, and indeed vexed, link between what we consume and what consumes us (2012).

Alison Carruth and Anissa Wardi calculate *Tar Baby*'s ecocritical politics. Although written nearly thirty years before the United Nations Food and Agriculture Organization issued a report that attributes a pressing environmental crisis of food hunger to globalization, *Tar Baby*, according to Carruth, presciently frames the food system in terms of environmental justice (2009).[4] With every character a consumer, plentiful food images allow the novel to "imagine the contemporary era through an entwined narrative of hunger, consumerism, and environmental exploitation" (596–97). Wardi includes *Tar Baby* in the first sustained treatise on watercourses in the African American expressive tradition, inter-accentuating the ways that water acts not only as a body of resistance but as a site both material and metaphorical of trauma, memory, and healing (2011).

Tar Baby and Archetypal Criticism

Several second-wave critics foreground the mythological aspects of *Tar Baby*. Aeju Kim maintains that Morrison's oeuvre endorses Barthes's concept of myth as a value system, which changes according to time and place, over Jung's concept of archetype as sacred, irreducible narrative. *Tar Baby* particularly imposes new meaning on the black experience by reshaping traditional Western mythologies. Lauren Lepow, Craig Werner, Angelita Reyes, and Patricia Magness approach the novel respectively as Edenic, modernist, paradoxical "other," or courtly love myth. Pointing out that Morrison continually requires us to confront the self-defeating qualities of binary thinking as she demonstrates that half a reality is insufficient for

---

4   The 2008 FAO report ascribes increasing world hunger to a food system that consolidates agricultural production and distribution in corporations headquartered chiefly in North America, Europe, and Asia. Environmental justice is a social movement that asserts the interdependence of class, ethnicity, and ecology.

anybody, Lepow establishes that *Tar Baby* attacks dualism on every front, recasting the Genesis story "in such a way that its dualism is upset and its moral absolutes evaporate" (365). Werner states flatly that "Toni Morrison remakes (post)modern myths." Labeling *Tar Baby* "postmodern meta-mythology," he shows how the novel "highlights the link between Barthes's theory of myth and the Afro-American folk tradition that precedes, echoes, and revises it," apprehending myth "both as a tool of Euro-American power and as a reservoir of historical knowledge capable of resisting that power" (150–51).

Reyes and Magness agree that a major concern for Morrison is the search for a myth adequate to experience. Reyes contends that *Tar Baby* juxtaposes tales of the ancient properties, or the "sacred and psyche-cultural bonds of the Past" centered in African tradition, with New World folklore about the tar baby. As Morrison relies on the significance of the "other" that is not seen and the motif of tar that both entraps and bonds, she "represents myth and folklore with a modern sensibility," which attempts to be "'the useful conscience of the community'" (25). Unsurprised by her application of the tar baby story from black folk tradition, Magness proposes that Morrison counterpoints the African American myth with the European model of courtly love by inserting constant reminders of royalty, chivalry, and courtly life. Since both tar baby and courtly love clichés continue to sustain the mystery necessary for expressing new experience, *Tar Baby* subsumes the clash of black and white worlds into its mythic structure. Morrison uses the courtly love model "not to endorse it as a pattern for life, but to show its inadequacy." She conjures up two magic kingdoms "in which we would like to believe," only to remind us that neither is for us. She "offers no comforting conclusion in this clash of values, dreams, and goals, only hard choices" (98–99).

Tar Baby and African American/Postcolonial Criticism

A great deal of criticism on *Tar Baby* stresses Morrison's mindfulness of Africa, culminating in monographs by La Vinia Jennings (2008) and K. Zauditu-Selassie (2009) on that subject. Cynthia J. Smith recaps Morrison's employment of intertexuality as agent of representation in the novel. Marilyn Mobley and Sandra Paquet concur that Morrison identifies a link between folklore as a repository of inherited wisdom and the use of an ancestral figure as a barometer of cultural integrity in contemporary African American literature. Mobley exemplifies critics who not only censure Jadine for her "negative, stereotypical attitudes toward Afro-American and African culture," but for her "attempts to justify her distance from that culture" (765–66). Underscoring the necessity of acquiring self-knowledge in familial terms, Paquet identifies Thérèse as *Tar Baby*'s dominant ancestral figure but also grants Son with instructive and protective ancestral qualities.

Alma Jean Billingslea, Susan Edmunds, and Yvonne Atkinson single out African American history and language as bearing witness to black power. Billingslea considers Morrison's "return to the source" to be an affirmation of cultural continuity. Reversing and revising the historic African passage of forced migration to the New World, *Tar Baby*'s voluntary journeys across spatial, temporal, and cultural borders enable its characters both to reclaim an African and diasporic folk heritage and to subvert the distorted meanings imposed on that heritage along with the effects of Euromerican cultural dominance (1999). Edmunds suggests that "*Essence* magazine provides a crucial intertext for understanding Toni Morrison's engagement in *Tar Baby* with the political debates that surrounded the 'Black Is Beautiful' slogan in the black power era and her use of the Tar Baby story to dramatize and interpret those debates" (2018 Abstract). More generally, Atkinson reflects in 2000 on Morrison's longing for a critic "who will know what [she means] when [she says] 'Church' or 'community' ..." since her books "come out of those things and represent how they function in the black cosmology" (McKay "Interview," 407). Because language moves beyond mere communication to define a culture's style, Atkinson determines that "the oral tradition of Black English is the foundation of Morrison's work" (12).

Linda Krumholz details how Morrison explores "blackness" in *Tar Baby* to illustrate that we are all implicated in its production and to introduce ways that black art can unveil and transform those fabrications (2008). As Morrison immerses readers in competing concepts of blackness to show the pitfalls in constructing meanings of blackness, while at the same time requiring us to participate in those meanings, Krumholz concludes that the novel is ultimately "about the need for self-consciousness regarding our constructions of meaning. When we create meaning in order to make ourselves safe, to ensure our innocence and purity, then we are in the greatest danger of self-deception." *Tar Baby* urges all people to "accept their complicity, immerse themselves in blackness, and learn blackness as a way of seeing that might transform racial meanings, relations of power, and people's lives." *Tar Baby* allows Morrison to illuminate her "artistic beliefs and purposes; she dramatizes theories of hegemony that link art to power and thus delineate the high stakes of cultural representations, and she highlights aesthetic and rhetorical strategies that give the work of art the potential to transform readers and, consequently, to transform the cultural and material world" (263–90).

As she fixes the novel in its historically sociopolitical context, Evelyn Hawthorne defines *Tar Baby* as a genre piece: "a Diasporean novel which forsakes boundaries to transcend cultural insularity and promote an inclusive vision of African peoples and cultures" (1988). Developing a Diasporean voice "significant for its integrative vision" when creative writers began to play an increasingly important role in Diasporean dialogue, Morrison uses the historic past as a regenerating spring (100). Although critics typically read *Tar Baby* as a fairly straightforward defense of tradition in which Morrison "warns against the dangers of losing touch with racial and ancestral memories, by way of a symbolic contest between a black man in tune with nature, family, and history, and a modern, cosmopolitan and rather shallow woman, who refuses to acknowledge the value to any of these" (393), Yogita Goyal cautions in 2006: "Neither can be upheld as a reliable authority on race or gender, as Morrison uses the two to displace the other's certainties and to reveal their limitations" (406). Unique in Morrison's oeuvre for its overt references to the concept of diaspora embodied by Jadine, the novel skirts the simplicities of Afrocentrism and Son's Black Nationalism and navigates the anti-essentialist ground of black Atlantic studies to "delineate complicated, shifting, and deeply equivocal interactions between nationalism, gender, and diaspora" (393).

Alan Rice includes African Americans among the colonized who disown vernacular traditions to make headway within predominant majority culture (1999). Crediting Susan Willis's materialist/feminist approach with revealing ways in which Morrison indicts the hegemonic forces of capitalist America for making black people ashamed of their vernacular heritage, Rice riffs on Willis's concept of "funk" (the "intrusion of the past into the present" 108), turning to the jazz aesthetic in *Tar Baby* to show how Morrison's foregrounding of vernacular modes like jazz becomes a "funky," decidedly political response to demands for conformity to Anglo-American modes.

Three postcolonial critics evaluate the postmodern/early modern echoes between *Tar Baby* and *The Tempest*. Malin Walther reads Morrison's novel as a revision of Shakespeare's play in which Valerian is the artist-magician Prospero, Jadine the bereft Miranda, and Son the savage Caliban (1993). Walther creates a compelling argument that "Morrison targets colonialism as the root of aesthetic hegemony, revealing art's inherent politics" (138). Maintaining that *Tar Baby* "depicts the struggle over cultural definitions and identifications in a postmodern world," Gurleen Grewal claims in 1998 that the twentieth-century author relies on Shakespeare's "prototype of a colonialist narrative" as she places the African American crisis of identity and alignment in a colonial and postcolonial context (79, 83). Elizabeth Gruber compares the two texts in ecological terms (2010). Reading *Tar Baby* alongside *The Tempest* illuminates the (post)modern novel's tenet that "environmental devastation works in tandem with social injustice," as forecast by the intellectual traditions that took shape in the early modern period (223).

* * *

While *Tar Baby* has maintained a fairly steady, if slow, scholarly drumbeat as part of Morrison's overall oeuvre, it did not benefit as much as its predecessors from the devotion heaped upon her next book. *Beloved* becomes the watershed moment during which Morrison begins to be satisfied that not only are her critics learning to talk her talk, but also better criticism has, indeed, enabled her to better walk her walk.

CHAPTER FIVE

BELOVED (1 9 8 7)

Beloved's Critical History as Told by Toni Morrison

Regardless of the fact that a cottage industry of readers regularly dub *Beloved* Morrison's masterpiece, its author wastes few words in reconfirming the book. If the forewords written for *Sula* (2004) and *Paradise* (2014) take up the most pages of the seven novels reprinted with a Morrison introduction, *Beloved*'s 2004 foreword ranks among the shorter of the Vintage reprints. We might ascribe her brevity in part to Morrison's increasing comfort with the abundance and diversity of scholarship on her oeuvre, particularly after the 1985 publication of the first monograph devoted to her in its entirety—Bessie W. Jones and Audrey L. Vinson's *The World of Toni Morrison: Explorations of Literary Criticism*.

Concerned prior to the publication of *Song of Solomon* in 1977 that comparisons made between herself and white male canonical writers were tantamount to imposing an adverse methodology on her efforts, Morrison maintains in a 1983 interview with Nellie McKay: "I am not *like* James Joyce; I am not *like* Thomas Hardy; I am not *like* Faulkner" (Taylor-Guthrie 152). By the time Morrison writes *Beloved* and delineates the process of doing so in a 2004 Vintage foreword, she appears to be far more satisfied that profoundly serious and honestly nuanced criticism of her novels and those by other black women writers was being made possible by the development of a critical tradition rooted in black culture. As Nancy J. Peterson points out, "given the profusion of such scholarship by even the mid-80s, it is no wonder Morrison took the opportunity to comment upon the (in)appropriateness of some of these approaches" (6).[1]

---

1   Peterson's collection reflecting Morrison's critical history to 1997 draws heavily on a special double issue *of Modern Fiction Studies*, devoted to Morrison and edited by Peterson (vol. 39, nos. 3-4), that appeared even as Morrison was awarded the Nobel Prize for literature in 1993.

CHAPTER FIVE

In "Rootedness: The Ancestor as Foundation" (1984), Morrison remarks: "My general disappointment in some of the criticism that my work has received has nothing to do with approval. It has something to do with the vocabulary used in order to describe these things. I don't like to find my books condemned as bad or praised as good, when that condemnation or that praise is based on criteria from other paradigms. I would much prefer that they were dismissed or embraced based on the success of their accomplishment within the culture out of which I write" (Mari Evans 342). While we might interpret Morrison's rebuke to mean that she "claims only African-American culture as the relevant context for her work," she would continue to ponder questions of cultural affiliation and connections between black and white America via her literary investigations of nonblack texts such as Melville's *Moby-Dick* and its ideology of whiteness ("Unspeakable Things Unspoken: The Afro-American Presence in American Literature" 1989) and of white authors such as Cather, Poe, Twain, and Hemingway, published in 1992 as *Playing in the Dark: Whiteness and the Literary Imagination* (Peterson 6).

In reversed Morrisonian lingo, the relative absence of [verbal] presence in *Beloved*'s 2004 foreword may indicate significant presence unto itself—in more ways than word count. Morrison begins her foreword, in fact, by recounting a loss. Or a gain: "In 1983 I lost my job—or left it. One, the other, or both." She goes on to explain why she thought leaving was a good idea: after four novels, she had good reason to believe writing to be her profession, and, while releasing some spectacular talent, her editing gig was not bringing in much money, because even in the late 1970s book sales outranked abilities or needs. So Morrison opted to try to live, "like a grown-up writer," off her royalties (xv–xvi).

Her history of fabricating *Beloved* proceeds with descriptions of hidden presences urgently making themselves heeded. Relaying an edginess occurring instead of the calm she expected a few days after she left Random House, she was sitting on the pier in front of her Hudson River home when she heard and felt the violent thumping of her heart. Rejecting such apprehension on an otherwise perfect day as fear, she went back to the house to examine this odd sensation, finally diagnosing herself to be "happy, free in a way [she] had never been." It was "Not ecstasy, not satisfaction, not a surfeit of pleasure or accomplishment. It was a purer delight, a rogue anticipation with certainty. Enter *Beloved*" (xvi).

Jobless, single-mother Morrison channeled her newfound shock of liberation into thoughts of what being "free" meant to other women—in the 1980s and earlier, particularly to black women, for whom assertions of motherhood proved impossible, even illegal, under the laws and logic of institutionalized slavery. She despaired of finding a canvas and characters that could capture the destructive [il]logic of parenthood under the peculiar institution until she remembered one of the books she helped to publish back when she had a job. *The Black Book* contains a newspaper clipping from the February 12, 1856, issue of the *American Baptist* relating the story of Margaret Garner, a calm, quite sane, totally unrepentant twenty-five-year-old black woman who decides to kill her children rather than see them returned to enslavement. Succeeding in killing her baby daughter, Garner becomes a cause célèbre for abolitionists, who want her tried for murder instead of the "real" crime, as defined by Fugitive Slave laws, of stolen property. She is ultimately returned with the rest of her children to the owner's plantation, still insisting upon her right to risk everything for what she deemed the necessity of freedom.

Beloved becomes a book not only about the visceral compulsion of freedom, but about the lengths people will go to obtain it. And Morrison not only opts to liberate her imagination by inventing Garner's thoughts, emphasizing historical, political, and social truth over factual information, but also decides that the book's central figure would have to be the murdered, not the murderer: the powerfully absent presence of the baby ghost come back to life. Accustomed to calling upon concrete fact to manifest abstract truth, Morrison gazed out of a swing on her porch toward giant stones protecting her property from the river's possible onslaught, a path through her lawn, and an ironwood gazebo surrounded by shade trees: "[Beloved] walked out of the water, climbed the rocks, and leaned against the gazebo. Nice hat" (xviii).

Unlike the slight defensiveness suggested by her protracted *Sula* foreword, we observe here the author's self-possessed ease with her creative practice in action. From the subconscious come characters "there from the beginning," and out of specific but minimalist detail will evolve complex, contradictory, even terrible experiences: the intimate sense of slavery being both under and out of control; ordinary, everyday life violently disrupted by the claims of the past; the determination to forget interrupted by the demands of memory. Unlike the welcoming entrance she felt obligated to provide for *Sula*, there would be no extended lobby into this haunted house, no introduction to the novel: "I wanted the reader to be kidnapped, thrown ruthlessly into an alien environment as the first step into a shared experience with the book's population—just as the characters were snatched from one place to another, from any place to any other, without preparation or defense." After four novels Morrison can allow the presence of absence: "To render enslavement as a personal experience, language must get out of the way." After dragging readers, sometimes kicking and screaming, into a critical world beginning to acknowledge African American culture, she can embrace the absence of presence—with few but prescient words: "Nice hat" (xviii–xix).

Beloved's Initial Critical Reception History and Defining Critical Moments

If the endorsement of four novels prior to *Beloved* meant that anything Morrison wrote after 1983 drew critical attention, the appearance of *Beloved* in mid-1987 no doubt became a defining moment in her overall reception history. When it failed to win the National Book Award during the fall of 1987, outrage among black writers and scholars was so great that forty-eight of them, including Maya Angelou, Houston Baker, Toni Cade Bambara, Amiri Baraka, June Jordan, Paule Marshall, Alice Walker, and John Edgar Wideman, signed an open letter, published in the *New York Times Book Review* (Jan. 24, 1988), which celebrated Morrison's writing and condemned the "oversight and harmful whimsy" that had denied her "the keystone honors of the National Book Award or the Pulitzer Prize" ("Black Writers"). These well-respected members of the black intelligentsia vigorously maintained that despite her international reputation Morrison had not received the national recognition she deserved for writing five major novels.

Although what *Times* editor Walter Goodman termed "literary lobbying" may have influenced the decision to award *Beloved* a Pulitzer in 1988, previous reviews had already offered a positively unified front. Early accolades appear in numerous venues both popular and professional: *Booklist* (July 1987); *Kirkus Reviews* (July 15, 1987); *Library Journal* (Sept. 1, 1987); the *New York Times* (Sept. 2, 1987); the *New York Times Book Review* (Sept. 13, 1987); *Time* (Sept. 21, 1987); *Newsweek* (Sept. 28, 1987); the *U.S. News & World Report* (Oct. 19, 1987); the *Listener* (Oct. 29, 1987); *Ms.* (Nov. 1987 and Jan. 1988); the *New Yorker* (Nov. 2, 1987); *Commentary* (Dec. 1987); *The Nation* (Dec. 26, 1987); *Choice* (Jan. 1988); *Callaloo* (Spring 1988); the *Hudson Review* (Spring 1988); and the *Southern Review* (Summer 1988). Ann H. Fisher's timely assessment in *Library Journal* speaks broadly yet for most: "Powerful is too tame a word to describe Toni Morrison's searing new novel" (201).

Other reviewers quick to echo Fisher's praise include Paul Gray, Walter Clemons, and Margaret Atwood. Gray posits in *Time* magazine how in Morrison's hands the familiar subject of slavery "does not reinforce received opinions but disturbs them" (75). Clemons's *Newsweek* article goes further to say that Morrison achieves with *Beloved* what "no novelist has ever approached before" by recreating the "interior life" of slaves and releasing the outrage so often repressed by "tactful" black people hesitant to offend sympathetic white listeners (74). Perhaps fellow novelist Margaret Atwood best captures the tenor of *Beloved*'s preliminary critical responses. Crediting Morrison's fifth novel with showcasing her versatility along with her extensive technical and emotional ranges, Atwood asserts: "If there were any doubts about [Morrison's] stature as a pre-eminent American novelist, of her own or any other generation, *Beloved* will put them to rest. In three words or less, it's a hair-raiser." Atwood is particularly impressed with Morrison's "antiminimalist prose that is by turn rich, graceful, eccentric, rough, lyrical, sinuous, colloquial and very much to the point" (*New York Times Book Review* 7.1).

Reviewers frequently mention that the author's trademark themes and narrative strategies reappear in *Beloved*. *Waiting to Exhale* writer Terry McMillan notes that Morrison's fifth book characteristically manages various elements at once, mixing "folklore, legend, myth and surrealism with realism to pull the reader into her world. And without fail it works." McMillan goes on to explain that this dizzyingly "distinctive and undeniably Morrisonian" narrative technique urges the subject matter forward, contributing to an element of mysticism:

> Most of what happens in this novel happens in the past. It's [sic] zigzagginess provides a dreamlike, eerie quality. The past is constantly relived in the minds of characters, and it is alive. Sometimes, one may seem to have missed something, because the story line is like a spider spinning its web, round and round to the center. Prose of this nature is explosive and dense. Things happen over and over again, from different angles, different perspectives, so much that one sometimes has to exhale or even cry. (J10)

Influential *New York Times* critic Michiko Kakutani appreciates the adroit blend of myth and surrealism as well: "These events unfold before us, like dream images, in a succession of lyrical passages that jump back and forth in time, back and forth in point of view from one character to another. As a result, there is a contemporaneous quality to time past and time present as well as a sense that the lines between reality and fiction, truth, and memory, have become inextricably blurred: by the end, we see Beloved as Sethe herself does, as both daughter and ghostly apparition" (C24). Making sure to accentuate *Beloved*'s uniqueness as an historical novel in Morrison's existing canon, McMillan concurs: "A novel of this magnitude and scope, tackling and unveiling the intimate thoughts, fears, feelings and hopes of slaves, far surpasses any documentation seen in a history book" (10J).

Despite approaching the novel with differing expectations, Leroy Staggers and Marilyn Atlas discover plenty of common ground: both insist that *Beloved*'s appearance essentially becomes a watershed in Morrison's literary critical reception history. Staggers clarifies in his 1989 doctoral dissertation on Morrison's reception from 1970 to 1988 that, because it was awarded the prize that in the United States "distinguishes a writer as no amount of other positive criticism can," *Beloved* "must be placed in a different category from Morrison's previous four novels." Concluding his study with the year in which she received the Pulitzer Prize, he maintains that criticism from 1987 to 1988 consists primarily of book reviews, relays "only a few negative comments," and suggests her "new and loftier status." He predicts accurately that "undoubtedly, the lengthier, scholarly, and more scrutinizing critical reactions will be forthcoming" (109). Precisely 916 citations are listed on *Beloved* by MLA to date.

Staggers's dissertation also demonstrates that *Beloved* appeals at once to Euro-American critics, to Afro-American critics, and to feminist critics. Though Trudier Harris contends that *Beloved* mainly addresses black feminist issues, she joins African American scholars in connecting the novel's concerns about motherhood with its issues of slavery. We certainly see the strength of an injured, eight-month-pregnant eighteen-year-old girl in her determination to escape schoolteacher's Sweet Home—in the mother's attempt to prevent her children returning to enslavement, and in the woman's defiance of the communal label of "murderer."

Nevertheless, Harris argues, "the greater power of black womanhood comes in the women who exorcize Beloved from 124 Bluestone Road. They are initially reminiscent of the women in *Sula*, those who were strong enough to let evil run its course. The women here finally conclude, however, that Beloved has overstepped her bounds in making demands of the living." Refusing to tolerate even the abused undead assuming the right to punish Sethe, they apply both pagan and Christian methods to banish the pregnant Beloved: "In this rite of exorcism, this restoration of the status quo, the women favor the living over the dead, mother love over childish punishment of parents, reality over the legend of which they have become a part" (387–89).

Harris's reaction confirms Atlas's premise that good book reviews are not only rare, but "important reflectors of politics and culture and, like books themselves, they help shape the ideas and art of a particular culture's values" (46). Concerned with her own resistance to a book written by a hitherto favorite author, Atlas collated approximately twenty such reviews published before the results of the 1988 Pulitzer Prize were announced. In so doing, she converts an essay on *Beloved*'s reviews into a meta-review, which reveals that, between its writer's prestige, her race, and its complicated subject of American slavery, *Beloved* was "difficult to evaluate with even a semblance of objectivity" (47). Some, like Harris's, were actually review essays, attempting to analyze as well as articulate the nature of Morrison's style and content—and directly contesting Barbara Christian's characterization of the book review's purpose: to provide "an immediate, succinct response to a writer's work, quite different . . . from essays in which one has the time and space to analyze their craft and ideas" (65).[2]

Allocating to the critic responsibility to create "a wider, more knowledgeable audience for the writer's work," Christian laments reviews written about African American texts that indicate little awareness of an African American intellectual practice (65). Atlas locates reviews on *Beloved*, however, that concentrate on placing the novel within the context of Morrison's previous efforts and/or an African American literary tradition; several reject any obligation for convincing others to read the work. Rosellen Brown states, for example, "Can we not assume that most people interested in new fiction will want to read Toni Morrison's latest book, drawn to it not by rave reviews but by an understanding that she is a gifted novelist who always has something to say?" (*Nation* 418). Most accord with Thomas Edwards: "A novel like Toni Morrison's *Beloved* makes the reviewer's usual stereotypes of praise and grumbling seem shallow" (*New York Review of Books* 18).

---

2   Euro-American *Ms.* magazine's more typically succinct review asserts that all of Morrison's novels embrace all women: "Morrison's women—some are big, powerful people, others shadows and totally powerless, some risk takers, others safety seekers. But through all of them, Morrison asks us, What's power? What's love? What's the real cost of living? Who and what can you claim and/or control? What tricks do you have to play in order to get through? How do you define yourself?" (Marcia Gillespie 60–61).

Staggers and Atlas diverge significantly, and perhaps tellingly, on their assessment of *Beloved*'s negative reviews. Staggers describes the "few" condemnations of the novel to be relayed almost apologetically, often in the form of acknowledgments construed by some as drawbacks. A *Choice* review, for example, claims that "the continued employment of flashbacks in [*Beloved*] leads to confusion" (768). If Judith Thurman finds Morrison's language "powerful but manipulative," Carol Iannone more explicitly contends that "the book grows massive and heavy with cumulative and oft-repeated miseries, with new miseries and new dimensions of miseries added in each telling and retelling long after the point has been made and the reader has grown numb. The graphic descriptions of physical humiliation begin to grow sensationalistic and the gradual unfolding of secret horror has an unmistakably Gothic dimension which soon comes to seem merely lurid, designed to arouse and entertain" (59–63).

While they certainly provide answers as to why Morrison became so frustrated by reviewers unacquainted with black culture, these are by no means the only skeptical interrogations into *Beloved*'s depiction of African American blues.[3] Atlas agrees with Staggers that most major reviewers such as the *Chicago Tribune*'s Charles Lawson and the *Wall Street Journal*'s Helen Dudar have no difficulty declaring Morrison's fifth novel her masterpiece. Atlas does uncover, however, considerably more than Staggers's "few" objectors.

Reviewers disagree about the quality of Morrison's realism, some describing its repetition as cloying, along with her use of the supernatural. If *Time* magazine's Paul Gray finds Beloved's flesh-and-blood presence roiling the novel's realistic surface, with Carol Rumens of the *Times Literary Supplement* calling the ghost's travails non-resonating and the *Village Voice*'s Anita Snitow reducing it basically to "a drag," Rosellen Brown of the *Nation* deems Morrison's unwillingness to explain the walking dead a successful ploy that increases reader intimacy: "Haints and spirits routinely walk the roads of the black South; to explain would be to acknowledge that outsiders were listening" (418). Atwood likewise has no problem with the ghost: "In this book, the other world exists, and magic works, and the prose is up to it. If you can believe page one—and Ms. Morrison's verbal authority compels belief—you're hooked on the rest of the book" (7.1).

Staggers, deliberately or not, omits mention of the African American critic most famously refusing to be hooked. The *New Republic*'s Stanley Crouch defines *Beloved* as nothing more than another "Blessed are the victims" novel, a custom

---

3   We might compare Morrison's annoyance with critics who describe slavery's too "oft-repeated miseries" as "lurid" to a Jewish writer's disgust with critics who dub graphic depictions of Holocaust humiliation as sensational. Defining blues moments like those found in *Beloved* as "an impulse to keep the painful details and episodes of a brutal experience alive in one's aching consciousness, to finger its jagged grain," Ralph Ellison explains the blues attempt to transcend pain by "squeezing from it a near-tragic, near-comic lyricism" (129).

in black literature begun, he asserts, by James Baldwin and perpetuated by Alice Walker's "sentimental feminist ideology." Crouch considers such a practice not only so poor for the soul, but so exploitive of it that it should not be emulated (1–3). He judges Morrison's folk material "poorly digested," her feminism "rhetoric," and her use of magical realism "labored." If he concedes that she has "real talent," an ability to "organize her novel in a musical structure, deftly using images as motifs," he resents that she "perpetually interrupts her narrative with maudlin ideological commercials." Most disconcertingly, he feels "distant from the horrors of slavery as presented" in this "blackface holocaust novel." Lacking "a true sense of the tragic," Morrison asks in *Beloved* merely "that her readers tally up the sins committed against the darker people and feel sorry for them, not experience the horrors of slavery as they do" (3–4). Crouch reckons Morrison's work "melodramatic"; "trite"; "contrived" and "counterfeit"; its "protest pulp fiction" containing too many tries at "biblical grandeur"; and finally lacking in "the courage to face the ambiguities of the human soul, which transcend race." He determines Morrison to be American in the ugly-American sense—as "American as P. T. Barnum" (6–7).

Writing her meta-review to help her understand her initial discomfort with *Beloved*, Atlas finds answers in this the angriest, ugliest and, she concludes, most self-protective reaction. She confronts the wild critical mood swings in which one reviewer cherishes the book that enables readers to discover wisdom where another reduces *Beloved* to little more than "New York glitz and cheap thrills Afro-American style" (51):

> Perhaps the contradictions reflect the novel's emotional atmosphere—perhaps *Beloved* simply makes some reviewers extremely uncomfortable, forcing confrontations not usually required by literature. These critics do not want to reflect upon these particular human issues and they are unable to see how exploring these new details from new perspectives permanently expands the tradition of American literature, and allows valuable characters into the world, ones they can see no value in examining. Not every reviewer wants his or her consciousness transformed by these particular insights, and Morrison's prose in this novel is pushy. (51)

A nursing mother herself at the time, Atlas just could not finish the novel, unable, unlike with Morrison's previous female characters, to imagine Sethe getting up off her bed to resume a normal family life. She was not yet ready to let this book transform her consciousness through the telling of the tale.

If Staggers's choice, or oversight, is to ignore Crouch, Maria Diedrich insists that the backlash must be confronted as more than merely "a feminism that aroused the ire of male competitors":

> The second bone of contention for black critics is this self-proclaimed female griot's radically revisionist discourse on black history and life. Two major sources of dissent will be identified: 1. Morrison's treatment of the Western concept of time and reality, and 2. her decision not to respect the self-protective taboos of

traditional black historiography and literature, i.e., her determination "to rip that veil drawn over 'proceedings too terrible to relate.'" (Abstract)

Atlas ultimately lets Morrison have the last word. And Morrison, in a 1988 interview with Marsha Jean Darling, returns that responsibility to the reader:

> They always say that my writing is rich. It's not—what's rich, if there is any richness, is what the reader gets and brings him or herself. That's part of the way in which the tale is told. The folktales are told in such a way that whoever is listening is in it and can shape it and figure it out. It's not over just because it stops. It lingers and it's passed on. It's passed on and somebody else can even alter it later. You can even end it if you want. It has a moment beyond which it doesn't go, but the end is never like in a Western folktale where they all drop dead or live happily ever after. (4–5)

Having made her peace with a book that does not stop and makes her squirm, Atlas makes her recommendation "as a reviewer, as a critic, as a fan of Morrison: read it and grow" (55). This Pulitzer Prize-winning novel, however, might not even and of itself be the last word on the subject. Having discovered, together with her readers, wisdom hidden within *Beloved*'s tales of misery, Morrison suggests in a 1987 interview with Miriam Horn that the proverbial "fat lady" may not yet have sung: "So I'm not finished with these people, and they are not finished with me. We have this hiatus right now. But I guess they are all waiting out there for me to come back" (75). Some say they didn't have to wait long—for *Jazz*.

Beloved Criticism

Morrison also guessed that *Beloved* would be the least popular of her novels because readers would perceive it as dealing with that peculiar American institution readily placed under erasure by what she calls a "national amnesia": "I thought this has got to be the least read of all the books I'd written because it is about something the characters don't want to remember, I don't want to remember, black people don't want to remember, white people don't want to remember" (Angelo 68). Writing in 1993, Barbara Christian counts the number of critical essays on *Beloved* to rival in a mere six years those written on just "a few other contemporary African American novels: Ralph Ellison's *Invisible Man* (1952), a favorite of American English departments, and Alice Walker's *The Color Purple* (1982), a favorite of women's studies departments" (5). Angeletta Gourdine states in 1998 that "*Beloved* has been discussed perhaps more than any other novel of the late twentieth century" (13).

The *MLA International Bibliography* identifies 890 citations issued on *Beloved* between 1988 and 2018. 440 of these are printed in academic journals (367 peer-reviewed), and 285 appear as book articles. 45 books include examinations of

Beloved, 6 focusing specifically on that novel;[4] MLA lists 120 dissertation/thesis abstracts to date. Scholarly attention comes primarily from English and American sources with 827 analyses written in English. Interestingly enough, this Pulitzer Prize-winning fifth novel, unlike the books Morrison wrote before or after, originally drew attention from the broader, more "established" academic publishing community: *Modern Fiction Studies* (8); the *Arizona Quarterly* (6); *College Literature* (5); *Cultural Critique* (5); *Literature Interpretation Theory* (5); *Studies in American Fiction* (4); *American Literature* (3); and the scholastically prestigious *PMLA* (4) and its subsidiary SAMLA (2), altogether providing 42 articles.

Academic journals with an American multicultural concentration, however, soon got on board to announce their enthusiastic support: *Griot* (9); *MELUS* (8); the *CLA Journal* (7); and *Callaloo* (4) for a total of 28 articles. With an astonishing 35 articles in print on *Beloved*, the *African American Review* rose to become the preeminent journal highlighting African American literature, in part by promoting Morrison studies and putting its stories with hers.[5] Foreign and online publications contributed a healthy 14 percent of journal articles: the *MLA Bibliography* lists 61 texts in venues sponsored by France (15); China (8); Spain (8); Japan (7); Italy (5); Germany (4); Korea (4); Finland (2); Poland (2); Portugal (1); and Sweden (1). Two essays are composed in Persian, one in Dutch, and one in Serbo-Croatian.

Because so many provocative analyses on *Beloved* exist, this survey will tap those that hold the greatest impact. Such journal and book articles, précised chronologically within categories, stem primarily from intertextual; feminist/womanist; African American/postcolonial; new historical/cultural; and psychoanalytic theoretical approaches. Initially inspiring structuralist critiques of its narrative, *Beloved* continues to provoke current interests in queer and ecocritical studies,[6] and several scholars use it to experiment with reader-response or pedagogical strategies.

---

4   Scholars continue to produce book-length studies on *Beloved*: *Toni Morrison: Beloved* (Carl Plasa, ed., 1998); *Toni Morrison's Beloved and the Apotropaic Imagination* (Kathleen Marks, 2002); *Beloved: Character Studies* (Nancy J. Peterson, 2008); *Toni Morrison's Beloved Origins* (Justine Tally, 2009); *Reading Toni Morrison's Beloved: A Literature Insight* (Paul Penrith McDonald, 2013); and *Beloved* (Maureen N. Eke, ed., 2015).

5   Founded in 1967 as *Negro American Literature*, the journal appeared under the title of *Black American Literature Forum* from 1976 until the year prior to Morrison receiving her Pulitzer Prize when it became the *African American Review* and subsequently the official publication of the Modern Language Association's Languages, Literatures, and Cultures African American.

6   Andrew Levy and Philip Page pioneer the critiques on *Beloved*'s narratology: the former tracing its multivocality (1991), the latter proposing a year later that a structuralist analysis of its "explicit and implicit circles and their implications reveals the subtle relationships between the novel's content and its form" (31). Insisting that writing, including scarred slave bodies, is as central to *Beloved* as speaking, Anita Durkin cites critics occupied with its forms of self-expression (2007). Scholars applying queer theory include Gene Jarrett, Rebecca Balon, and Juda Bennett in a 2015 book on Morrison's spectral sphere as

Beloved and Intertextual Criticism

Given Morrison's protests about her work being likened to other, particularly more canonical American writers, it comes as no surprise that most preliminary *Beloved* criticism is intertextual. Of the 367 peer-reviewed articles printed on the novel, 68, or 19 percent, focus on intertextual juxtapositions. They include the works of various African/African Americans (24); Faulkner (7); Hawthorne (5); Native Americans Leslie Marmon Silko and Louise Erdrich (5); Twain (4); Browning and the English Romantics (3); and Morrison herself (7). Intertextual scholars are also interested in Morrison and the Bible (8) as well comparing *Beloved* with other American novels such as *Uncle Tom's Cabin* and *Gone with the Wind* (5).

John Duvall's 1989 analogies between *Uncle Tom's Cabin*, *Absalom, Absalom!*, and *Beloved* represent the earliest analysis on the latter book. Viewing *Beloved* as a Morrisonian rewriting of Stowe's novel that allows mythological depth but refuses her Christian vision of the world, Duvall notes overt parallels: a tranquil state that terminates suddenly, and a desperate escape. While *Uncle Tom's Cabin* shifts quickly, however, from the horrors of slavery to a wish-fulfillment fairytale, *Beloved*'s reunions are more ambiguous. Thus Duvall finds *Beloved*'s "more covert" dialogue with *Absalom, Absalom!* more aesthetically satisfying. The foremost critic to stress Morrison's 1955 Cornell University master's thesis, "Virginia Woolf's and William Faulkner's Treatment of the Alienated," he claims that *Uncle Tom's Cabin*, *Absalom*, and *Beloved* "raise questions about the abuse of patriarchal authority, an authority that finds its clearest instance in slavery.... In all three narratives 'ghosts' are produced as a response to patriarchal oppression. Taken together, the various haunted houses—Legree's, Sutpen's, and Sethe's—form an intertextual space that variously questions the patriarchal values that attend slavery" (84).

Duvall's essay sparks a number of intertextual approaches to Faulkner and Morrison.[7] In two additional *Faulkner Journal* pieces, Philip Goldstein looks at *Absalom* and *Beloved* through the lens of black feminism, addressing both as Gothic romances, while Peter Ramos believes that the ghosts in both function to ease trauma. After an African American woman in his Faulkner and Morrison class [mis]interprets his use of the terms "Standard English" and "Black English" as racially denigrating, William Dahill-Baue opts to investigate black dialect in *The Sound and the Fury* and *Beloved*. Claire Crabtree determines the American frontiers in *The Bear* and *Beloved* to be interiorly located, and Rie Makino reconstructs Faulknerian masculinities in *Beloved*.

Several studies emulate Duvall by similarly connecting Morrison's novel with *Uncle Tom's Cabin*. Lori Askeland turns to the architectural building and dwelling

---

already outed—a provocation and challenge to heteronormativity. Ecocritical theorists include Reginald Watson, Tuire Valkeakari, Tadd Ruetenik, Deborah Bailin, and Molly Hall.

7 So many scholars agreed about the overlaps between Faulkner and Morrison that courses with that title were introduced across the American academy in the 1990s. This impulse subsequently led to individual classes entirely on Morrison's oeuvre.

metaphors embedded within critical theories like structuralism and poststructuralism, linking these tropes to the model home supposedly meant to empower women like Harriet Beecher Stowe (1992). Askeland contends that *Beloved* becomes a remodeling of the Victorian domestic ideal, revised "in a way that avoids reification of a patriarchal power structure" (787). In another *American Literature* article (1998), Lauren Berlant underscores the unfinished business of sentimentality. Exposing a particular form of American liberal sentimentalism that "promotes individual acts of identification based on collective group memberships," she, like Crouch, cautions that the practice has "been conventionally deployed to bind persons to the nation through a universalist rhetoric not of citizenship per se but of the capacity of suffering and trauma at the citizen's core" (636).

Concluding her analysis with *Beloved*, Berlant, unlike Crouch, views that novel as a "postsentimental project," which "would have you refuse to take on the history of the Other as your future"; it refuses the "too-quick gratification after the none-too-brief knowledge of pain; . . . it understands that whatever transformation we might imagine being wrought from the world-making effects of identification must start right here, in the place of corporeal self-knowledge . . ." (665). By way of an addendum to her political history of the novel, *Desire and Domestic Fiction* (1994), Nancy Armstrong references *Beloved* as she examines the racial logic behind the sentimental narrative exemplified by *Uncle Tom's Cabin*.

The majority of intertextual studies emphasize intersections between Morrison's novel and other African American texts. Even as she juxtaposes *Uncle Tom's Cabin* with Melville's *Benito Cereno*, Sarah Robbins compares *Beloved* with Charles Johnson's *Middle Passage* to situate the history of the antislavery narrative within the context of gender; Vincent O'Keefe looks at offstage violence in the two African American novels; and Timothy Parrish illustrates how both authors [re]imagine slavery. Several scholars note the associations between *Beloved* and the works of other black women writers. Two contributors to the *CLA Journal*, Madelyn Jablon and Reginal Watson, respectively analyze rememory in it and Walker's *The Temple of My Familiar*, and milk/motherhood as images of deconstruction in it and Walker's *The Third Life of Grange Copeland*. Shu-li Chang associates historical trauma with the ghosts of daughters in it and Kincaid's *The Autobiography of My Mother*; Glenda Weathers links biblical trees with *Beloved*'s literary landscapes and those in Hurston's *Their Eyes Were Watching God*; Elizabeth Hayes designates 124 Bluestone Road and Naylor's "the other place" as extraordinary domestic dwelling become radical discourse space for the named and the nameless; and Caitlin O'Neill establishes how the visionary creativity apparent in Jacobs's *Incidents in the Life of a Slave Girl* serves as an antecedent to novels such as *Beloved*.

Anne Goldman investigates [re]production in *Beloved* and Williams's *Dessa Rose*, while Kristine Holmes considers the body and embodiment, and Mark McWilliams the physical cruelty of slavery in the same texts. Adam McKible reconsiders history through the names of characters in those novels together with Gayl Jones's *Corregidora* and Octavia Butler's *Kindred*; Clara Escoda Agusti studies the deconstruction of madness in *Beloved* and Jones's *Corregidora* and *Eva's Man*; Solomon Omatsola Azumurana discloses the problems of Western education via Aidoo's *Changes: A Love Story*, Naylor's *The Women of Brewster Place*, and *Beloved*; and Donna Winchell records the use of history in *Beloved*, *Dessa Rose*, and Styron's *The Confessions of Nat Turner*.

Others place *Beloved* in the context of an intertextuality that includes male writers. In fact, studies following most immediately upon the heels of Duvall's Faulkner/Morrison research focus on relationships between *Beloved* and texts by the English Romantics, Browning, Hawthorne, Twain, and Melville. If Martin Bidney demonstrates Morrison's implementations of Blake, Keats, and Wordsworth to create a "Feminist-Communitarian Romanticism," her intersections with Hawthorne and Twain receive the most attention. Jan Stryz and Wesley Britton highlight the Hawthorne/Morrison hauntings, Stryz viewing the specter of *The Scarlet Letter* as the other ghost in *Beloved* and Britton imagining *Beloved*'s black Gothic in light of *The House of the Seven Gables*. Acknowledging that several readers, such as Jürgen Wolter, have detected allusions to Hester Prynne in Sethe's "crime" and its aftermath, Caroline Woidat argues that *Beloved* represents Morrison's challenge to Hawthorne's politics while "claiming her own authority as an African-American writer" (528). Charles Lewis couples the two novels to explore the relations and resemblances between historical romance fiction and new historicist criticism.

Twain connections counterpoint the journey from slavery to freedom in *Beloved* and *Huckleberry Finn*. Like many, Richard Moreland believes that putting Twain's story beside Morrison's "shows not only the economic, political, social, and cultural forces (ranging from slavery to patriarchy to capitalism) that make working together ... difficult, isolating us from each other and from the others within ourselves; it also shows more particularly how the discourse of American romance both relies on these same disciplinary and normalizing structures and enables us to reimagine and renegotiate our encounters and interactions" (523).

Other intertextual analyses include twentieth- and twenty-first-century black male writers. Anissa Wardi, for example, classifies Gaines's *A Gathering of Old Men* and *Beloved* as ancestral requiems. Helen Lock observes the process of oral memory in three written African American narratives, including *Beloved* and David Bradley's *The Chaneysville Incident*. Sarah Wyman examines the imaging of separation in Morrison's book and that of children's author and illustrator Tom Feelings (*The Middle Passage: White Ships/Black Cargo*). Two further intertextual approaches involve children's literature. Gail Sobat compares the ghosts in *Beloved* with those in Virginia Hamilton's *Sweet Whispers, Brother Rush*, and Nina Mikkelsen applies the concept of rememory in Morrison's novel to ethnic children's texts such as Hamilton's. If three readings associate Morrison with Wright and Ellison, another recognizes the more contemporary Colson Whitehead. Both writing for the *African American Review*, Cedric Bryant surveys the African American Gothic in three texts, including *Beloved* and Wright's "Big Boy Leaves

Home," while William Ramsey maintains that, as they render Dixie a postmodern social construction of contested stories, Morrison and Whitehead confront an end of Southern history.

Hermeneutics intertextualists outline various ways in which biblical texts influence *Beloved*. Carolyn Mitchell underscores its biblical revisions; Shirley Stave traces its vindication of the apocryphal figure of Lilith; Carolyn Jones tallies its images of Cain; Robert Broad looks at haints, history, and Hosea in *Beloved*. Asking "Who are the Beloved," Danille Taylor-Guthrie investigates, together with Old and New Testaments, old and new faith communities; Emily Griesinger answers why Baby Suggs quit preaching the Word. Demonstrating that Morrison draws religious inspiration from both Africa and the West, Christina Lake views Beloved as much the grotesque as a ghost. Her necessary exorcism tells us, then, where Morrison locates divine activity in the world: "There is never a *deus ex machina* in Morrison's work; God manifests Himself in an accepting, loving, and charitable community." *Beloved*'s triumph is "to show that evil, when perpetuated by a community motivated by fear, is also best defeated by a community motivated by the baptizing power of love. But [Morrison] also lets the demonic show its grotesque face just long enough to prove that it was in the service of the divine all along" (76–77).

Finally, if intertextuality is the shaping of a text's meaning by another text, reverberation between *Beloved* and Morrison's other novels also intrigues her critics. Deborah Guth sees the past as both a blessing and a burden in *Sula*, *Song of Solomon*, and *Beloved*. Considering *Beloved* alongside *Sula*, Rachel Lee argues that more productive than Robert Grant's postmodern approach of transforming Morrison's absences into presence would be to read the ambiguities of her texts "not as aporia to be 'filled ... by the reader' (McKay 94) but as signifiers of an unattainable desire for stable definitions and identities" (571). Anne Salvatore treats Morrison's paired characters and antithetical forms in *The Bluest Eye*, *Sula*, and *Beloved* as a new expression of the bildungsroman. Pointing out that the intertextuality between *Beloved* and *Jazz* has thus far received short shrift, Martha Cutter submits that Morrison returns the character of Beloved to *Jazz* as Wild, forcing readers to reexamine the previous novel and its conclusion, an examination "crucial to an understanding of how Morrison creates narrative designs that avoid immobilization" (62). Noting how little critical attention has been given to suicide in Morrison's oeuvre, Katy Ryan establishes that the bodies in *The Bluest Eye*, *Sula*, *Song of Solomon*, *Beloved*, and *Jazz* "do not tell a history of capitulation to dominant powers but comprise one part of a larger multivalent narrative of black survival in North America. The act of self-destruction overtly participates in racial and class struggles, revealing, to borrow a phrase from Michel Foucault, "a body totally imprinted by history" (390).[8]

---

8   Ryan agrees with Dara Byrne that, since slaves were "guided by an African world view that did not perceive death as the culmination of the spiritual being," death allowed the slave freedom to deny "the supremacy of the nineteenth-century American public sphere

Beloved and Feminist/Womanist Criticism

The majority of *Beloved*'s feminist scholars concentrate on its ideas about mothers and daughters. Three additional groupings surface repeatedly, however: its feminist methodology and discourse, its attitude toward the female body, and its approach to manhood/masculinity. Denise Rodriguez rejects Stanley Crouch's famous detraction of *Beloved* on the basis of his pejorative definition of sentimentality. Rodriguez proposes that Morrison reinscribes domestic discourse to reconsider sentimental literature, using its tropes "as part of a larger effort to extrapolate what it reveals about slavery and slavery's articulation as a literary subject" (40). Showcasing *Beloved* as Morrison's most extraordinary womanist remembrances of things past, Bernard Bell believes that her neo-slave narrative privileges the multivocal discourse of black and third-world women in America. Leah Milne contends that the women of *Beloved* reclaim their voices by renaming often unspeakable hardships. Naming the one perspective often overlooked regarding the often-explored subject of motherhood as that of the mother herself, and highlighting *Beloved* as one of a very few examples of literature written in a maternal voice, Colleen Cullinan observes how women's experiences as mothers clarify redemption not as "endings and cancellations, but . . . continuity and wholeness" (78).

Scholars engaged with *Beloved*'s mothers and daughters highlight the effects of history on motherlove. Barbara Mathieson confirms that Morrison pairs the tensions contained in the elemental mother/infant dyad with the pain of memory so that each "mirrors the other's anguish and ambivalence" and together they create "a shared avenue for hope and growth" (1). Stephanie Demetrakopoulos couches the idea similarly: as Morrison suggests that maternal bonds can obviate a woman's sense of self, her book "problematizes the conflict between history/culture and maternal instincts," its conclusion effecting "a resolution of the tension between history and nature which underlies the movement of the work as a whole" (51). Maintaining that Morrison both participates in and theorizes about the black aesthetic of remembering as she constructs from an historical African American victim of racist ideology "a hopeful presence in a contemporary setting," Ashraf Rushdy demonstrates that *Beloved* "create[s] daughters Signifyin(g) history" (568).

Some feminists call attention to Morrison's renderings of women. Ralph Story discusses Sethe's character, Maria Aristodemou writes about Baby Suggs as mother-in-law, and Nicole Coonradt takes on Amy Denver. Lorraine Liscio refers to *Beloved*'s revelation of the essential meaning of slavery for black women (their reproductive value) as "writing mother's milk" (34); Michele Mock considers the trope of breastfeeding to embody its dominant theme: the sacred union within the mother and child cosmos disrupted by the unnatural force of slavery. Susan Babbitt and Renee Gardner note Morrison's use of motherhood to undermine patriarchy. Babbitt alludes to Drucilla Cornell's work on the myth of Medea in

---

by removing its agency and authority in defining that particular individual as moveable property" (26).

Beloved to urge feminists to foreground the kinds of relations that identify the relevant political consequences of what Cornell labels a social unconsciousness. Gardner allows that, as *Beloved* dismantles the motherhood mandate, it subverts patriarchy with vulnerability.

Others expose a "deeply encoded rejection of the body" that "drives the highly pressurized haunting in *Beloved*" (Lawrence 189). As much about language's ability to maim spiritually as about the physical trauma of enslavement, claims Anissa Wardi, the novel "highlights the play between word and flesh in the symbol of *Beloved*, a physically wounded body that is offered as a site of linguistic violence.... As Morrison ruptures the parameters of discourse to include the body, she attempts to heal the wounds of the flesh" (44). Cynthia Dobbs argues that as *Beloved* "transforms many prevalent critical notions of American modernism by infusing that modernism with the figures of repressed and oppressed black bodies-in-pain," Morrison "radically dismantles conventional constructions of the birth of modernity and modernism as an early-twentieth-century phenomenon" (563).

Jean Wyatt names *Beloved*'s embodiment of the word "the maternal symbolic," indicating that Morrison deviates from Lacan's depiction of a child's entry into language as a patriarchal symbolic order. Explaining how Morrison "foregrounds the body as a discursive, racialized construct" inflected by trauma, Edith Frampton explores what she calls *Beloved*'s "incorporeal breastfeeding subjectivities" (141). Thomas Girshin furthers its application of incorporeality by proposing that Morrison "blurs the boundary between the 'body' and the 'Earth'"; thus, she "constructs an ethic of corporeality as an antidote to the Western tradition based on rationalism—an ethic that is in alignment with the interests of much of the contemporary environmental justice movement" (151).

Feminist/womanist critique on *Beloved* is not limited to its females.[9] Deborah Sitter, in fact, insists that "the ghostly subtext of *Beloved* is an intense debate over the meaning of manhood and the possibility for enduring heterosexual love" (1992). The full meaning of Sethe's story made possible only in relation to Paul D's, his desire to "put his story next to hers" is not merely a clever way of bringing closure to the novel (*Beloved* 273). The dialogue between their two stories "constructs the context in which Morrison conducts a deeper dialogue with the social meanings of words which have the power to liberate or enslave" (Sitter 17). Maintaining that Paul D's parallel story mirrors the structural and thematic core of the novel, Steven Daniels notes the juxtaposition of Sethe's choice of death for herself and her children, rather than returning to slavery, with Paul D's decision to live when he finds himself in similar circumstances. Herman Beavers argues that Morrison revises scenes from *Uncle Tom's Cabin* "in order to foreground the anxieties that

---

9   As defined by Alice Walker's epigraphs to *In Search of Our Mothers' Gardens*, "Womanist" connotes "a black feminist or feminist of color": a woman who is audaciously, courageously, or willfully committed to the "survival and wholeness of entire people, male *and* female" (xi).

occur at the intersection of race and masculinity, for both white male characters like Mr. Garner and black male characters like Paul D and Stamp Paid" (Enke viii).

Observing the relative dearth of criticism that "explores the matrifocal *Beloved* as a masculinist text, or conversely, one informed by highly misandric (or androphobic)" impulses, Nancy Kang interrogates in 2003 "the possibility of a misandric impulse that accompanies the novel's well-documented engagement with specifically woman-centered issues like motherhood" (836). Susan Mayberry begs to differ. Her 2007 book on *The Masculine and Morrison* refuting Kang's "exact why of the misandric impulse in *Beloved*" as "an open question," Mayberry turns to Morrison for answers (852): "Accused of designing female victims, castrating women, and messed-up men, Morrison retorts that black women have borne their crosses 'extremely well' and 'everybody knows, deep down, that black men were emasculated by white men, period. And that black women didn't take any part in that.'" Morrison's review of black masculinity, in *Beloved* and elsewhere, thus affirms that "not only have black men successfully retained their special vitality in spite of white male resistance; their connections to black women have saved their lives" (1).

Doreen Fowler agrees, pointing to "the critical role in *Beloved* of a father figure or third party in helping to form boundaries that both distinguish an autonomous subject and allow for alliances with others" (2011). Revealing the paternal function as "an ongoing socializing process that can and should be performed by both men and women and by people of all races and ethnic groups as different relationships with others develop new, different social identities," Morrison "intervenes in a theoretical debate about the father's role in socialization and counters a white Western, phallocentric, exclusionary model of identity formation" (14–16).

Beloved and African American/Postcolonial Criticism

Although pleased that *Beloved* entered so early and easily into mainstream university curricula, Barbara Christian christens herself "perturbed" in 1993 that its feminist and multicultural discourses outweighed a much-needed African American approach ("Fixing" 6). Christina Davis and Mary Paniccia Carden signal such a change in direction. In fact, Davis's "*Beloved*: A Question of Identity" (1988), an essay that expands her 1986 interview with Morrison about Morrison's attitude toward the black experience in the United States, is the first peer-reviewed article published on the book.[10] Pointing out that history has assisted the basic and horrifying facts of black American enslavement to emerge, Davis credits her colleague with giving voice to those details: "But up until now not much has been said about what it felt like in the much-denied heart of the human being summarily dismissed under the term slave. Morrison's accomplishment is not only to

---

10   Interestingly enough, international journals published the first three articles on *Beloved*.

have taken the individual out of the mass of statistics, but also to have displaced the tone of the prose from the third person into the first." Sethe's final victory becomes, then, "recuperation of her own identity" (151, 154). Carden insists that, for "an African American woman addressing a 'dominant narrative' in which black women have been secondary or invisible, 'writing beyond the ending' means interrogating the historical implications that romance assumes when infused with ideologies of race." *Beloved*'s "intersecting narratives of romance and slavery lead to dual endings, which, in their refusal of resolution, represent the double dilemmas of divergent narrative perspectives and goals" (402).

As scholars extend and intensify their gaze, they tag various features of the African American tradition. Several perceive how naturally the supernatural becomes incorporated into nature. Explaining that Morrison "dissolves chronological sequences and interweaves multiple narrative voices in a radical redefinition of narrative structure," Carol Schmudde particularizes how *Beloved* is informed with at least one conventional formal pattern: "At the most basic level of plot and setting, *Beloved* is a ghost story" (409). Deborah Horvitz believes that as the "powerful corporeal ghost who creates matrilineal connection between Africa and America, Beloved stands for every African woman whose story will never be told," empowering words to heal flesh (157). Pamela Barnett allows that "*Beloved* is haunted by history, memory, and a specter that embodies both; yet it would be accurate to say that *Beloved* is haunted by the history and memory of rape specifically" (418).

Two readers question the straightforwardness of the ghost theory: Elizabeth House asserts in 1990 that "the uniform acceptance of this notion is surprising, for evidence throughout the book suggests that the girl is not a supernatural being of any kind but simply a young woman who has herself suffered the horrors of slavery" (17). Because *Beloved* exemplifies the griot method of storytelling, however, resisting narrative closure and lending itself to rereading, Cutter claims ten years later that the text "balances between realistic explanations of Beloved's presence (she is an escaped slave woman who has been sexually abused by a white man) and supernatural ones (she is Sethe's dead child come back to haunt her), and is therefore an excellent example of . . . the fantastic" (62).

Beloved scholars also recognize the importance of family, home, and community to African Americans. Charles Scruggs associates Morrison's focus on intimacy with what he calls the "invisible city"—her signs of the domestic in *Beloved*: "Morrison documents the redemption of the house, the origins of community, and the integration of the individual within the community's life-sustaining body" (99). Maggie Bowers proposes that Morrison creates collective memory by acknowledging ambivalence while Robin Blyn insists that "*Beloved* reconnects memory to African American ethics and aesthetics and, simultaneously, it connects that memory to the Western tradition's long history of philosophical inquiry into the status and value of the past" (114). Dana Heller looks at ways in which the book's narrative reconstructs family; Nancy Jesser enumerates the effects of violence on its fictionalized home and community; Alexis DeVita views Beloved as the sacrificial child that completes its circle of redemption.

Many count the ways in which Morrison re-envisions the slave narrative. Identifying *Beloved*'s mixed genres, Carl Malmgren describes it as part ghost story, part historical novel, part love story, and part slave narrative. After Molly Travis examines the causes and means of silencing black women in historical and literary narratives, she reaffirms Davis's opinion by demonstrating how *Beloved* speaks from "the gaps within and between these prior narratives" and "acts as a necessary supplement" (69). Sherryl Vint discusses the limits of realism in neo-slave narratives. Alluding to the children's ability to negotiate their surroundings in *The Bluest Eye* via the certainty in sound, Peter Capuano shows how Morrison furthers slave narrative song in *Beloved*.

According to Madhu Dubey, Morrison's neo-slave narrative ironically disavows the literary mode she takes as her chosen medium of expression; she signals her skepticism toward the emancipatory promise of print literacy that fueled the modern African American tradition by her discomfort with her own literary modality. Cynthia Hamilton contends that "the primary generic template for *Beloved* is the gothic, which Morrison uses to overcome the limitations of the slave narrative, the genre which provides the generic focus of interest," and to expose its partisan agenda (445). William Andrews is interested in "not how much or what kind of influence the slave narrative may have had on *Beloved* but rather what kind of influence this novel may have on our reading of the slave narrative" (115).

Other readers note *Beloved*'s nod to the importance of spirituality, orality, and music in black American culture. Explaining how the entire novel can be regarded as a spiritual (1990), Karla Holloway unveils in a second essay (2014) its descent from the African "talking book," and Joanna Wolfe defines song as key to *Beloved*'s narrative revision. Several examine Morrison's treatment of the African American call-and-response structure, Jean Daniels highlighting responses to Baby Suggs's call and Maggie Sale going so far as to designate call-and-response as critical methodology. If Cheryl Hall and Lars Eckstein record Morrison going beyond the "literary habit" to utilize jazz in *Beloved*, Lenore Kitts urges scholars to unearth its "subterranean music" like the railroad holler "Sis Joe" so as to "appreciate the depth and conviction of Morrison's reckoning with slavery" (495). Edward Dauterich dubs her intermingling of verbal and written "hybrid expression." Bärbel Höttges and Hannes Bergthaller produce their own call-and-response analysis with Bergthaller resolving the paradox of Höttges's "written sounds and spoken letters": "but all in print." Roxanne Reed stipulates the novel's power of sound as instrument for black communal catharsis.

A number of articles accentuate symbols that are especially reflective of the African American community. While Wendy Harding and Jacky Martin address the cultural interface provided by corn tropes in *Beloved*, Jane Hindman and Janice Daniel consider quilting as metaphor and storyteller respectively. Several critics perceive the significance of trees to the book. For Michèle Bonnet, the sanctified referent that Morrison measures sin against is not Western religion or even some secular yet sacred human law, but man's natural environment, specifically the tree, which in African religion often plays the role of intermediary between God and man. Hence transgressions perpetuated against trees in *Beloved* "can be construed as violations of the natural law they embody" (41–42). Lorie Fulton complicates Bonnet's argument by claiming that "trees remain conflicted images" as Morrison associates "the key issues that each of her characters struggles against with a tree of some kind" (189). Sandy Alexandre links *Beloved*'s trees to iconography and gender in representations of violence: "tree imagery signifies a male-female continuum between assaulted black slave bodies" (916).

Two critics concentrate specifically on Amy Denver's [re]invention of the pustulous wounds on Sethe's back as a beautiful chokecherry tree in bloom. Gina Greenway unpacks the multilayered image, and Heike Härting construes the metaphor as a performative material palimpsest for Sethe's memories. Finally, Samira Kawash once again restructures the race[d] house, "which draws our attention to the 'architectural imaginary' of race and its alignment with the structure of property and the definition of person. The materiality of the color line as figured architecturally suggests that racial division in contemporary American culture cannot so simply be reimagined as cultural difference but must equally be understood as embedded in the forms and structures whereby property, subjectivity, and belonging are determined and negotiated" (84).

Such scholarship moves us into the realm of postcolonial discourse. In 2014 Biman Basu puts *Beloved* on the postcolonial world literature shelf. If Satya Mohanty speaks on its resonances with the postcolonial condition, Lynda Koolish applies postcolonial theory to analyze fictive strategies and cinematic representations in this text she identifies as postcolonial. Using a "cinematic reading" of what was at the time a never-filmed text, Koolish argues that Morrison's narrative strategy is clearly postcolonial "in its assertive re-framing of the world from a locus of language, the known, and history, to a locus of the visual, the impossible to be named, and a new historicism that honors the individual and fictive narrative as a collective and truth-telling one" (421).

William Handley uses "Nommo," or West African ancestral spirits, to guide the book's ethics of reading; Marygai McNamara, Maria Simms, and Pat Skinner connect it to aboriginal Australian discourse. As Morrison wields language "so that it circumvents traditional ideas of past, present, and future" in a text of margins that "plays with the efficacy of language itself, demonstrating how utterly powerful and powerless language is," she uses, according to Sharon Holland, bakulu or ancestor discourse, that is, the language between two states of existence (89). While Lay Sion Ng and Rusbeh Babaee agree with Alan Rice's 1998 consideration of cannibalism as a meta-discourse in *Beloved*, they go further in 2017 to propose that cannibalism and slavery relate not only to the domination of black slaves by white masters, but also to black mother-child/sister-sister relationships. Ironically, the system of slavery deconstructs the images whites have built of themselves, making them little more than cannibals.

Because postcolonial studies is a relatively recent phenomenon, much of the most current *Beloved* criticism is, understandably, postcolonial. Theresa Washington addresses Morrison's call for an analysis that complements her art "by using an Africana theoretical perspective centered on a force called *Ajé* to interpret the intricacies of the mother-daughter relationship in *Beloved*" (171). As she shifts the theory to a domestic setting, Mary Jane Elliot considers the novel in the context of commodified subjectivity. Malini Schueller specifically includes it as an articulation of African Americanism in South Asian postcolonial theory; Kathryn Rummell traces how it transforms the African heroic epic. Clarifying that the reborn denizen abiku/ogbanje evokes the separations and instability of the past, Chikwenye Okonjo Ogunyemei maintains that this child spirit serves as "a springboard for examining issues of memory . . . that link West Africa with the Americas." Hence Morrison employs it in "writing postcolonial theory and narrative, rooted in African mythologies of kinship and community, to speak to complex African and African American relationships" (663).

As *Beloved* leads him to diagnose the self-centeredness of trauma, Petar Ramadanovic determines "the entanglement between the Oedipal narrative and narratives of Western modernity, trauma, and post-coloniality" (178–79). Explaining that Beloved has been convincingly described "as a ghost, a reincarnation, a vampire, and a manifestation of repressed trauma," Robert Yeates goes beyond these Euro-American interpretations to present "compelling evidence that African religious concepts of the living-dead, the Caribbean concept of the zombi, and the American adaptation of the zombi as zombie all bear profound influence on the composite identity of the character" (515).

Naeem Nedaee counters the increasingly common tendency to approach *Beloved* from a postcolonialist viewpoint. Exploring Morrison's novel via "Deleuze and Guattari's concepts of nomadic subjectivity, war machine, and becoming-other," Nedaee illustrates how the book "opens lines of flight/possibilities of emancipation and constitutes a discourse of resistance and affirmation" (39). Because Morrison positions her female characters as both mothers and daughters, simultaneously past- and future-oriented, and "gestures toward a posthumanistic articulation of becoming-subjectivity," Kristen Lillvis defines *Beloved* as "a precursor of Afrofuturist literature." Its liminal space "suggests that black power need not be rooted solely in the past: the future can serve as an accessible site of authority and resistance as well" (Abstract).

Beloved and New Historical/Cultural Criticism

Though the majority of new historical/cultural criticism on *Beloved* involves its influence on popular culture, Maria Margaronis recaps in 2008 the fundamental position of its new historicists:

> To write a historical novel is to enter a no-man's land on the borders of fact and fantasy. All fiction is written on this territory, but when the work explicitly

> engages with historical events—when it is part of the writer's project to reimagine them—the ground becomes a minefield of hard questions. What responsibility does a novelist have to the historical record? How much—and what kinds of things—is it permissible to invent? For the purposes of fiction, what counts as evidence? What are the moral implications of taking someone else's experience, especially the experience of suffering and pain, and giving it the gloss of form? Can imaginative language discover truths about the past that are unavailable to more discursive writing? (138)

Acknowledging the dangerous allure of violence to those who set their novels in times of war or political brutality, as well as the contemporary confluence of two strong and sometimes conflicting currents (modernism/postmodernism and the question of who is qualified to break the silence of unspeakable horrors), Margaronis gives Morrison credit for engaging so deeply with "the purposes and processes of writing historical fiction" that "questions of authority, responsibility and authenticity are absorbed and expressed in [*Beloved*'s] form" (140). Three new historicists note how the novel reconsiders spaces of history and loss: Jeanne White includes it in a study of four slave narratives that depict the problem of place and the presence of absence. Caroline Rody maintains that Morrison's "prose-poem" brings "history to an unclosed closure and the haunt to our own houses" (113). Emily Budick submits that "*Beloved* remembers, not through telling a single story . . . but by placing one story next to the other, insisting that each of these stories register and respond to each other. . . ." In this way the book concurrently creates the story of family, community, and history, which recalls the past, "not by literally re-membering it, but by gathering together its pieces, placing one next to the other, and letting these pieces freely generate the future, that hopefully will remember them" (136).

Cultural critics often juxtapose *Beloved*'s horror stories with those of modern American society. Kathryn Stockton displays them, like the AIDS Memorial Quilt squares, in the cybernetic age of AIDS where "untimely deaths and dangerous transmissions are broad surroundings": "Writing out of her fictive interval (*Beloved*'s 1873), Morrison makes herself a prophet of the future ills of 1987, making a teenage infant—pregnant, disappearing—her book's most infectious idea" (435). Laurie Vickroy, Lisa Garbus, Lois Lyles, and Naomi Mandel focus on commonalities with the Holocaust, Vickroy and Garbus specifically comparing *Beloved* to the nine-hour, 1985 French documentary *Shoah*, directed by Claude Lanzmann. After Mandel cites critics uncomfortably reminded by *Beloved*'s dedication to "sixty million and more" of the approximately six million Jews murdered during World War II, she allows that Morrison evokes "a sense of the limits of language in order to establish that slavery shares, with the Holocaust, a certain quality of horror that exceeds representation." Her "figure and the slippage of its referents eloquently emphasize how, in light of such significant absence of historical documentation, the numbers themselves are clearly not the point. Human suffering is" (583–84).

Three scholars accent *Beloved*'s reminders of and resistance to ongoing white supremacy. Peggy Ochoa believes that Morrison's allegorical revision in *Beloved* of the Old Testament *Song of Songs* and other Biblical passages constitutes "a type of minority discourse related to, but not symptomatic of, the dynamics of religious and/or cultural 'othering,'" resulting in a subversive alternative language that attempts to keep the WASPS at bay (107). Proposing that Morrison conceptualizes the desperate attempt of "whitepeople" to control and dictate the knowledge of *Beloved*'s black folks as an ironic reinvention of the Garden of Eden story, its malevolent fallen angel re-imagined as a KKK dragon, David Cosca states that said dragon is not only representative of disgruntled reactionary white terrorists rampaging through Reconstruction South, but of white supremacist beliefs and values dismissed, ignored, repressed, and/or revised—then and now. Nicole King reads *Beloved* in its 1980s context when the American conservatism that fractured black communities and challenged black identity produced a resurgence of nostalgic affirmations. Morrison prevents her readers from substituting the fantasy of black community for the reality of black neighborhoods even as she calls attention to their possible investment in recalling such a past.

Some of the 1980s nostalgia may have resulted from recurring backlash to Senator Daniel Patrick Moynihan's 1965 document, "The Negro Family: The Case for National Action." James Berger, Mabel Khawaja, and Jon-Christian Suggs discuss how *Beloved* takes up debates that emerge but are suppressed in the wake of what came to be called "the Moynihan Report," which depicts the African American family as a site of violence resulting both from a racist society and from within the family. Berger reads Morrison's novel as "an intervention in two ongoing debates about American race relations." It "opposes neoconservative and Reaganist denials of race as a continuing, traumatic, and structural problem in contemporary America but also questions positions on the left that tend to deny the traumatic effect of violence within African American communities" (408). Additionally, it corrects the liberal mistakes of negating African American culture and agency and slighting African American women (408). Khawaja and Suggs respond in Letters to the Editor. Khawaja appreciates that "interdisciplinary scholarship is almost indispensable in the analysis of race relations" but calls for reconsideration of Berger's biblical allusion to the apocalyptic moment (115). Jon-Christian Suggs maintains that Berger underestimates the frequency of slave infanticide.

Much of the cultural criticism on *Beloved* involves its interactions with popular culture. Lydia Magras argues that "BUPPIES (Black Urban Professionals), children of the turbulent sixties as readers, were meaningful precursors to the appropriately serious literary (aesthetic) reception of Morrison's work. In the case of the novel and the film, this popular reception was actually an embryonic response that bolstered an academic one, resulting in considerable overlap between these two interpretative communities." Magras connects "the American Black Power Movement of the 1960s and the subsequent emergence of Black Studies programs to the reception of the text and its film adaptation, as well as incorporating Morrison's own words on interpretative interaction between readers and her work" (Abstract).

Critics often mention *Beloved*'s impact on female pop culture. Praising the novel's "multivocality," Jeffrey Insko urges readers to include among its voices "those of the women writers who have produced the long tradition of popular writings in America labeled 'sentimental'" (427). Others hone in on the effects of TV talk-show host Oprah Winfrey's interest in all things Morrisonian. Including reaction to *Beloved* in her analysis, Kimberly Davis offers a reception study of Winfrey's televised Book Club programs, focusing on white female fans discussing black women's fiction. Davis's conclusions about fiction reading's influence on political change underscore "the important role that empathetic crossings within cultural space can play in the development of anti-racist coalitions" (Abstract).

Several cultural critics notice that Winfrey's melodramatic interpretation of Sethe contributed to the authenticity of Oprah's star persona. In his review essay on director Jonathan Demme's 1998 film of *Beloved*, John Tibbetts provides details of Winfrey's investment in the project. An "unabashed act" of Morrison worship, Winfrey's portrayal of Sethe marking her first return to film since her 1985 performance in *The Color Purple*, she optioned the book rights from a supposedly reluctant Morrison and supported at least three writers for a decade to produce the screenplay. His primary objection the "monstrous" depiction of Beloved, Tibbetts pronounces the outcome "literal-minded and arty" but a dazzling visual display bent more on impressing than moving its viewers. Anne-Marie Paquet-Deyris agrees that the director's violent and nonlinear approach is not only "debatable," but redefines the moral implications of Sethe's infanticide and the screen representations of distress and survival.

Anissa Wardi is less restrained: "This is not right. It's too Hollywood." Hoping on opening night to be thrilled by Beloved as enacted rememory, Wardi the fan grudgingly concurs with a reductive whisper from the row behind her: "'This chick's fucked up.'" Wardi the scholar dispassionately concludes that "*Beloved* failed not because of its divergence from the novel, but because there is no representational analogue to Morrison's textual project, specifically insofar as Beloved herself evades cinematic representation." With the film "bereft of the novel's metaphoric power, watching the resurrected baby becomes a voyeuristic exercise" in a grotesque movie accenting freak shows, spectacles, and carnivals (513–14).

While associations with American culture continue to draw the broad interests of *Beloved*'s cultural critics, including relationships as varied as *Beloved* and Bessie Smith, and prison brutality and *Beloved*, several have settled upon connections between *Beloved* and the opera *Margaret Garner* (2005), music by Richard Danielpour, libretto by Toni Morrison. Catherine Kodat appreciates Morrison's efforts to reintroduce to the twenty-first century an unknown slave woman who was an abolitionist cause célèbre in the nineteenth and the inspiration for scores of essays, poems, pamphlets, and engravings; however, Kodat is disappointed with the outcome for two reasons. Having sympathized with the almost immediate manipulation of Garner's story—the appropriation of her voice among the most ironic of her many oppressions—Kodat not only judges the opera "an unfortunate production in many respects," but thoughtless in "its approach to the central ethical problem of ventriloquizing its subject," especially surprising given Morrison's "scrupulous handling" of this issue in *Beloved* (161). Kodat also feels that singers as well as operagoers have been "shortchanged" by Danielpour and Morrison's lack of vision:

> We should rethink the entire treacherously seductive nineteenth-century structure underlying grand opera itself: not only its appropriateness as a vehicle for contemporary representations of certain kinds of historical narrative, but also the strongly racialized and only occasionally questioned notions of verisimilitude and authenticity that structure opera productions even to this day. (169)

If the Margaret Garner opera did not enjoy a particularly long run, it did inspire a book, edited by La Vinia Delois Jennings, and with a foreword by Denyce Graves, who played the title role. Recording key events, debates, and assessments of Garner's story in sound, *Margaret Garner* (2016) includes contributions by individuals who helped bring the opera to the stage as well as literary and opera scholars and American slavery specialists.

Beloved and Psychoanalytic Criticism

Psychoanalytic criticism on *Beloved* may be arranged into five major categories. Several scholars present an overview of its structures of psychoanalysis. Asserting that Morrison's narrative strategy, like psychotherapy, "acts as a conditional operative, offering her creative opportunities to deal with the real, the fantastic, and the possible events that make up slave history," Lyunolu Osagie maintains that Morrison relies on psychoanalysis to excavate the "buried stimuli" of the slave past and [de]construct historical records (423). Three scholars confirm Morrison's Lacanian methodology. Referring to what she calls "Lacan's gaze qua object," Evelyn Schreiber suggests that *Beloved* "illustrates how identity components intersect in the maintenance of subjectivity. A multiplication of identities occurs on several levels: within the text, character identity alters according to changing interactions with others; simultaneously, the reader's subject position fades, then reinscribes itself as a result of encountering the text" (445). Helene Moglene uses Lacan to identify how Morrison reconceptualizes "the power of the fantastic to map the social and psychological relations of self and other" (18). Sheldon George highlights Morrison's presentation of Lacan's "Real." Jan Campbell contends, however, that Morrison's psychoanalysis challenges not only the Freud/Lacan "paternal metaphor," but sanctions the language of the mother. Jennifer Fitzgerald uses object relations theory to explain how *not* to draw on hegemonic psychoanalysis to explore the aftermath of appalling physical and psychic hurt.

Most psychoanalytic critics address Morrison's ideas about the (coherent) self. Because an autonomous identity demands "the recognizing response of an other," external enslavement, which denies recognition of a human subject, also prohibits internal freedom (1991). Hence, *Beloved* illustrates that subjectivity "cannot be achieved independently of the social environment" (Schapiro 194). Jennifer Holden-Kirwan presents a general examination of the characters' search for subjectivity.[11] If Carolyn Jones associates the psychic landscape in *Beloved* with the South functioning both as site for disjunction and for reunification with the self, Howard Fulweiler examines how this "fictional re-creation of the slave experience from within illuminates both the experience of the slaves themselves and the larger consciousness of which it is a part" (332). Alluding to Morrison's claim that fiction provides the possibility of "becoming coherent in the world," Betty Powell proposes that reshaping fragmented life stories into a lucid whole allows *Beloved*'s characters to "free themselves to yoke together stories and bodies, spirit and flesh, and to begin forging a sense of self that holds the promise of the future" (105).

Her reification of pain as "venom," according to Kristin Boudreau, permits Morrison to counter Western culture's long tradition of romanticizing suffering and to correlate being human with occupying an ever-shifting identity. Jeanna Fuston-White indicates that in telling the stories of the unspeaking enslaved, Morrison also "ties her work to the production of critical theory as she deconstructs the Enlightenment notion of subjectivity to make room for what bell hooks calls a "radical black subjectivity" (461). By addressing its conflict of interpellating or competing systems, Arlene Keizer demonstrates how *Beloved* "intervenes in current debates about black subjectivity, helping to define a position for the black subject between essentialism and postmodern fragmentation" (105).

Several scholars weigh the ramifications of self-lessness. Gloria Randle takes a social psychology approach to show that "what constitutes good mothering, good neighboring, or even good mental health" in the powerless world of enslavement becomes inextricable with how a well person operates in an unhealthy society (302). The damage caused by slavery is so traumatic that *Beloved* raises questions about the ability of ex-slaves to become persons in a moral sense, submits Thomas Lineham, in an essay concerned with the psychological and especially moral constituents associated with becoming a person. Cynthia Wallace concludes that only by reading the psychoanalytic and the religious *together* can we "do justice to the novel's provoking paradoxes of religious and linguistic hope" (269).

Others consider Morrison's historical recovery as psychoanalysis. Explaining that she "reconceptualizes American history" through the perspective of its slaves so that "history-making becomes a healing process," Linda Krumholz points out that *Beloved* "constructs a parallel between the individual processes of psychological recovery and a historical or national process" (395). Going further, as he references Morrison's self-described tactic of placing her readers inside the novel's

---

11 Nancy Peterson's 2008 monograph connects *Beloved*'s characters to its key issues and themes.

circle of intimacy, Hannes Bergthaller associates the reader's activity of synthesizing a coherent story with the psychological recovery of the characters as they work through their repressed memories. Michael Kreyling believes that, even as the novel enacts rather than describes or analyzes collective memory cum psychic survival, Morrison is "conflicted about what makes the past matter now," creating *Beloved*'s "power through irresolution," which has produced one of the most extensive critical bibliographies in American literary criticism (2007, 118–19).

Reactions to Morrison's fifth novel have contributed extensively to trauma studies. While traditional psychology associates the repetition compulsion exhibited by the neo-slave narrative with senseless and potentially destructive behavior, Naomi Morgenstern asserts that novels like *Beloved* "make possible a reading that calls into question such an understanding of psychopathology" (Abstract). Endorsing Valerie Smith's argument that "Morrison's method of circling her story back upon itself marks a suspicion about the 'limits of hegemonic, authoritarian systems of knowledge,'" Clifton Spargo investigates the "explicit tension between trauma as a trope for recovered history and those therapeutic, empiricist-minded narratives that require a subject to progress beyond and locate herself rationally outside the traumatic moment" (113; headnote). Alluding to the 1980s introduction of post-traumatic stress disorder into the American lexicon, a condition increasingly described as "one in which the encoding of memory rather than its retrieval is affected," Joseph Flanagan lists *Beloved* as "perhaps the best portrayal of how a theory of traumatic history is presupposed in the experience of personal trauma" (387).

Agreeing that both are personal and communal, Rossitsa Terzieva-Artemis illustrates how memory and trauma "shape—through language—the psychohistory of the individual" (125). Emma Parker utilizes French feminist ideas about hysteria to suggest that *Beloved* explores the means by which the disempowered express personal dissatisfaction and enact political dissent; she also indicates that in its exploration of the politics of gender and race, the book "challenges both Freudian and French feminist theories of hysteria" (1). Using *Beloved* to test a model that recognizes in Charles S. Peirce's idea of abductive inference a hitherto unrecognized understanding of trauma, Barry Stampfl declares that "the effortless translation of rhetorical patterns that are ubiquitous in the novel makes clear Morrison's tacit agreement with the proposition that there is indeed a substantive relationship between abductive reasoning and traumatization" (132). Belinda Du Plooy uses anthropologist Mary Douglas's theory of dualistic and symbolic embodiment to investigate historical embodiment and memory in *Beloved*.

Andrew Ng focuses on "*Beloved*'s representations of space as dimensions to register trauma" (231). Surveying Morrison's elaborate use of colors, Florian Bast concludes that the color red "is employed most conspicuously, and it is this color which is intricately connected to the novel's portrayal of trauma" (1069). Asma Hichri "traces the various manifestations of the hunger/ingestion motif in *Beloved* and its implications at the psychological and diegetic levels, mapping out the alliances between hunger and storytelling as a form of resistance" to conclude that a rewriting of black history requires a visceral reliving of its traumas (Abstract).

Associated with this motif of trauma and hunger is a fifth psychoanalytical topic involving Morrison's reflections on grief and mourning. Even as we dread the loss which ironically places the dead other closer to us than ever before, existing only in us, Christopher Peterson believes that *Beloved*'s conclusion advocates historical indigestion: allowing some trace to remain unincorporable and unmournable. Roger Luckhurst contends that the work of "impossible mourning" for the kind of genocide expressed by *Beloved* must be ongoing. Teresa Heffernan agrees: "Morrison's novel is a testament to this untranslatable loss, a loss that is embodied in Beloved, and that explains, in part, why Sethe cannot tell her story" (561). Referring to the concept of melancholia, Victoria Smith develops a feminist analysis of loss, positing a relationship among women's subjectivity, loss, and literary representation, and asserting that *Beloved* offers "a strategy of resistance—stagings of loss—to effect compensation" (headnote); Olivia Pass explains that Morrison relies on Elisabeth Kübler-Ross's five stages of grief to depict Sethe's process of accepting her daughter's death.

Finally, to read Beloved as epitaph, to read *Beloved*'s epitaph, is, according to Jeffrey Weinstock, "to confront the haunting limitations of language and to engage in a process of mourning that inevitably will fail to capture or reconstitute the other. However, the frightening recognition of loss that the epitaph compels serves as the precondition for learning to live and for the opening of the future as something other than a repetition of the present" (130–31). After Dean Franco clarifies that "scores of critical articles and book chapters have been devoted to describing the machinations of the novel's mourning, its role in cultural healing, its quest to rebury the dead, or its program of redeeming black female subjectivity from the damning criticism of analyses like the Moynihan report and its bastard children, the Reagan-era bashing of 'welfare queens' and Dan Quayle's pathologization of single-motherhood," the critic urges his colleagues to "show how psychoanalytic discussions of agency in *Beloved* can be translated into an activist public-sphere" (2006). To do so "will not undermine the value of such trauma studies readings"; on the contrary, "we can arrive at a critical approach that both advances the ethical and political claims a literary text such as *Beloved* has on its readers—the claims of the past on the present—and acknowledge the limits of reader-text identification, or the otherness of text and reader" (415).

Beloved and Reader-Response/Pedagogy

Teacher/scholars consider this text's nuanced layers ripe-pickings for reader response and pedagogical purposes. Because twentieth-century "social models of reading response ignore race" and, thus, reveal little about "'an American act of reading,'" Molly Travis compares *Beloved* with Charles Johnson's *Middle Passage* to convince us that identity politics and competing models of multiculturalism must be weighed as we construct "an adequate social model of reading response" (179). Angeletta Gourdine weds reader-response critique with black linguistic "Reading" and mestiza conscience/consciousness to make sense of Beloved as the central focus of the novel. James Phelan finds the experience of reading *Beloved* so "dynamic and profound" that he "theorizes a new approach to literary analysis — 'rhetorical reader-response criticism' — to do it justice" (N. Peterson, 12). Suggesting that Morrison's rapid entry into the literary canon "at precisely the same moment as the rise of political criticism in the academy" was "no coincidence," Timothy Aubry explains *Beloved* as universally beloved not only because Morrison gave us a book whose "unflinching portrayals of racism, sexism, and other kinds of oppression made reading itself feel like a socially responsible act," but because *Beloved* is also aesthetically pleasing.

To address a problem of "mutual analytic ineffectuality" between "scientistic" and "reader-critic" literary approaches that effectually suppress the role of the author, Sundeep Bisla recommends a return with *Beloved* to the kind of close reading which enables empathy. Two other critics underscore the ethical upshots of readers responding to Morrison's words. Yung-Hsing Wu concurs that because Sethe poses an ethical dilemma for all those who read about her, *Beloved* causes us to be "caught up in an ethics that requires 'the continuum of history' to be 'blast[ed] open'" (783). Also agreeing that "empathy is suddenly hot in the academy—as a topic of inquiry if not a professional practice"—and that "*reading literature* makes us more empathic," Ann Jurecic outlines opposing schools of thought about how to deploy said empathy. She includes *Beloved* in a discussion that proposes to "resolve the disagreement about empathy's ethics by grounding our understanding of this social emotion in neuroscience rather than culture" (11).

American compulsory educational policies that introduce "representative" texts calculated to promote empathy and pluralism have "failed, for the most part, to anticipate the contestations which arise among school actors when issues of race, gender, sexuality and so on are raised" (Doyle 364). Both college and secondary school professionals, however, deem reading *Beloved* helpful in addressing these and related issues. Mary Ann Doyle passes on the question-hypothesis-questions approach of a university professor teaching Morrison's novel. Assigning it to give high school students access to voices rarely in full cultural consciousness, Vicky Greenbaum illustrates how its powerful imagery shifts from devastation to transcendence; Laura Beliveau shows how connecting literature to history enhances students' understanding of Morrison's text; and Elaine Wang culminates students' close reading with an art-based project. Solomon Azumurana reminds us that Morrison's book also reveals her concern with ways in which US-American education "messes up" the minds of blacks.

Donna Schuster relies on developing scholarship and sequenced pedagogical strategies ending with rememory as elegy to "interrupt common pitfalls associated with overgeneralizing" (123). Convinced that an uncritical understanding of multiculturalism causes a "paralysis of relativism," Laurie Grobman brings Satya

P. Mohanty's postpositivist realism to bear and finds *Beloved* "especially useful" in leading students in composition classes "to a more reflective and complex awareness of ethical issues and multiculturalism itself" (208). A Canadian professor is surprised at how often she looks to Morrison's writing "when it is not even on the syllabus." Explaining that "Morrison's fictions both 'know' and challenge what literary theory has to offer us" and examining how *Beloved* can be used in teaching literary and psychoanalytic theory, Naomi Morgenstern turns "the relation between enigmatic text and theoretical elucidation on its head" (816).

If Tayana Hardin meditates upon *Beloved* as a way "to speak of the inheritances that shape [her] work as a teacher—inheritances bequeathed by a peculiar institution that (according to historical record) is by now long gone," that is, as a way to learn from acts of remembrance, Claudia Eppert wonders whether Morrison's bildungsroman "might not also be orienting us toward a curriculum and pedagogy of (a subsequent) just practice of forgetting? And, insofar as this is the case, what would be the implications of such a pedagogy for school, college, and university educators committed to teaching narratives that reference events of historical trauma in their classrooms as a means of initiating and supporting social responsibility?" (185). Eppert concludes that "educators might accomplish much by opening the doors for students to embrace an ethics of forgetting and forgiveness in their remembrance-learning while concurrently initiating classroom dialogue concerning inevitably difficult questions of amnesiac trespass" (193). Ingrid Reneau calls up West African cultural choreography and Baby Suggs's ritual at the Clearing to develop what Reneau calls a "Ringshout Aesthetic" as we move forward with intellectual inquiry. This approach formulates "an intellectual/spiritual aesthetic that affords an enabling and liberating African Diasporic vision for the ways in which we can conceptualize and do intellectual work in the twenty-first century academy and beyond" (Abstract).

CHAPTER SIX

JAZZ (1992)

Jazz's Critical History as Told by Toni Morrison

Jazz, published in 1992, continues to be listed by book sites as "historical fiction." Morrison may have concurred. Instead of attempting to control or recast its critical reception, as she sometimes does with retrospectives on previous novels, her foreword to the 2004 Vintage edition of *Jazz* focuses on its process of production "where the project came as close as it could to its idea of itself—the essence of the so-called Jazz Age" (xviii). By reflecting her own reiteration about the significance of absent presences, she indicates via her lack of concern with the book's interpretive labels the fact that she has become more comfortable with its—and her—place in literary critical history.

This second of stories in Morrison's trilogy on the African American experience came five years after what we have called the "critical watershed moment" of *Beloved*'s publication. Awarded the Pulitzer Prize for fiction, *Beloved* cinched Morrison's nomination for the Nobel award she received the year after *Jazz* appeared, an upwardly mobile trend from which critical momentum on *Jazz* certainly benefited. Its subsequent 2004 foreword describes the development of the book as an urtext. Morrison wanted her words to "reflect the content and characteristics of [jazz] music (romance, freedom of choice, doom, seduction, anger) and the manner of its expression" (xv).

To pull this off, she turned, as with *Beloved*, to a compilation of images narrating black life in America—and to memories of her mother. If *The Black Book* presents a scrapbook of mostly painful African American existence to its 1974 date, including an 1856 article titled "A Visit to the Slave Mother Who Killed Her Child," the collection from which *Jazz* takes its inspiration, more specifically a photograph from James Van Der Zee's haunting *Harlem Book of the Dead*, represents the most comprehensive documentation of black middle-class New Yorkers and their death rituals during the Harlem Renaissance. Akin to Morrison's effort with her ur-*Jazz*, Van Der Zee's portraits not only recognize the Harlem Renaissance but essentially helped generate it. Recalling herself as a child daring to open a forbidden trunk that contained, sitting on top of crepe dresses, a tiny, fringed, and glitteringly glass-bejeweled evening purse belonging to her mother afforded Morrison the necessary imaginative entry into the roaring twenties of that mother-as-girl.

Van Der Zee tells his coeditor Camille Bishops what he remembers about the death of a pretty girl he photographed in a coffin: "She was the one I think was shot by her sweetheart at a party with a noiseless gun." After she complained of being sick, friends helped her to lie down and saw blood on her dress. When they questioned her, she replied, "'I'll tell you tomorrow, yes. I'll tell you tomorrow.' She was just trying to give him a chance to get away" (*Jazz* foreword xv–xvi). Typically permitting her imagination free rein from minimal fact, Morrison perceived in the girl's acceptance of a lover's vengeance as legitimate, and her willingness to put herself at risk to save him, signs of the sacrifice demanded by tragically romantic love: "The anecdote seemed to me redolent of the proud hopelessness of love mourned and championed in blues music, and, simultaneously, fired by the irresistible energy of jazz music." If *Beloved* attempts to capture love as the perpetual blues bereavement resulting from a rural slave culture, *Jazz* anticipates modernity as the unreasonable optimism of urban love liberated: "Whatever the truth or consequences of individual entanglements and the racial landscape, the music insisted that the past might haunt us, but it would not entrap us. It demanded a future—and refused to regard the past as '. . . an abused record with no choice but to repeat itself at the crack and no power on earth could lift the arm that held the needle'" (xvi).

Because romantic love seemed to her "one of the fingerprints of the twenties, and jazz its engine," Morrison intended to follow *Beloved*'s focus on mother love with an emphasis on couple-love— "the reconfiguration of the 'self' in such relationships; the negotiation between individuality and commitment to another" (xviii). She would cast an older couple, born in the post-Reconstruction South, who are emotionally unprepared for the new freedoms made possible by the post-WWI North. She would introduce a new kind of risk into their lives, psychological rather than physical, in the form of a young flapper. Satisfied with her characters, her concept, its context, the plot line and details, she despairs for the structure "where meaning, rather than information, would lie. . . ."

> The moment when an African American art form defined, influenced, reflected a nation's culture in so many ways: the burgeoning of sexual license, a burst of political, economic, and artistic power; the ethical conflicts between the sacred and the secular; the hand of the past being crushed by the present. Primary among these features, however, was invention. Improvisation, originality, change. Rather than be about those characteristics, the novel would seek to become them. (xviii)

Once again Morrison relied on memory, this time of her mother's enthusiastic engagement with all sorts of music: "She sang, my mother, the way other people muse. A constant background drift of beautiful sound I took for granted, like oxygen.... Like the music that came to be known as Jazz, she took from everywhere, knew everything—gospel, classic, blues, hymns—and made it her own" (xix). Morrison signals her fusion of memory and meaning with her choice of *Jazz*'s prefatory segment from *The Nag Hammadi*'s "Thunder, Perfect Mind." An extended riddling monologue in which an immanent divine savior speaks a series of paradoxical statements alternating like *Jazz* between first-person assertions of identity and direct addresses to her audience, the exhortatory gnostic poem reminds us of the inclusive, seemingly instinctive improvisations of jazz and *Jazz*.[1]

Music critics distinguish American jazz as arising from a friction between two different harmonic systems: "that of the European tradition and that found in African music" (Bastien and Hostager 164). Influenced by European harmonies and African rhythms, emerging from various regional combinations of blues and ragtime, it has frequently been called America's classical music. Additionally, jazz is one of the most abstract of musical forms: rather than permitting its listeners to "arrive at a firm external objective, such as emotional climax or denouement," it allows them to "experience fully the multiplicity of the moment" (Brown 631–32). Claiming no conductor, created out of individual variations on a collective theme, jazz depends upon sensitive, concentrated listening to and between multiple perspectives. Morrison likewise identifies the music as "having a quality of hunger and disturbance that never ends. Classical music satisfies and closes. Black music does not do that. Jazz always keeps you on the edge. There is no final chord.... I want my books to be like that.... They will never fully satisfy—never fully" (McKay 411).

Initially unsatisfied herself by her inability to locate *Jazz*'s narrative voice or position its reader's eye, Morrison recollects throwing down her pencil and exclaiming to herself in frustration: "Oh, shoot!... I know that woman." As those words effortlessly written were easily followed by others, the "I," or the narrative voice itself, began to "parallel and launch the process of invention, of improvisation, of change." Explaining that she had previously utilized structure merely to enhance meaning, she now encouraged structure to equal meaning: "The challenge was to expose and bury the artifice and to take practice beyond the rules. I didn't want simply a musical background, or decorative references to it. I wanted the work to be a manifestation of the music's intellect, sensuality, anarchy; its

---

 1   Privileging personal experience or perception, *gnosis* is mystical or esoteric knowledge based on direct contact with the divine. In most Gnostic systems, this inward "knowing" becomes sufficient cause of salvation. *The Nag Hammadi Library* (also known as the "Gnostic Gospels") is a collection of early Christian and Gnostic texts discovered in 1945 near the Upper Egyptian town of Nag Hammadi.

history, its range, and its modernity" (xix). Morrison's employment of an epigraph from *The Nag Hammadi* predicts *Jazz*'s successful structural synthesis of language and sound:

> I am the name of the sound
>   and the sound of the name.
> I am the sign of the letter
>   and the designation of the division.

Jazz's Initial Critical Reception History

Jazz hit the [reviewer] ground running, a variety of well-respected critical venues finally eager in 1992 to throw full-on defensive and offensive punches Morrison's way. *Kirkus Reviews* deemed her sixth book one of her richest yet, "with its weave of city voices, tough and tender, public and private, and a flight of images that sweep up the world in a heartbeat: the narrator (never identified) contemplates airships in a city sky as they 'swim below cloud foam . . . like watching a private dream. . . . That was what [Dorcas's] hunger was like: mesmerizing, directed, floating like a public secret.' In all, a lovely novel—lyrical, searching, and touching."

The *Village Voice* asked us to "imagine a world in which love never dies, only fades in and out like a musical phase, varying and deepening with each return," proclaiming this the place that Morrison creates in her "supple, sophisticated love story which explores the possibilities of romance as both a natural phenomenon and a literary form." More improvisational than Morrison's previous works, *Jazz* riffs on her favorite subject, human freedom, to spin out of it "not only an inventive story but also a new way to write" (Mendelsohn).

Jane Mendelsohn asserts that Morrison makes this happen largely by creating a nameless half-gossip, half-visionary narrator, who interrupts the account, reimagines entire passages, calls attention to herself and then submerges herself into the story: "In the process, Morrison realizes her own limits, and sets her characters free." Her New York setting similarly embodies the liberated/liberating jazz spirit: "Free, but frightening in its freedom, it's a place where the night sky 'can empty itself of surface, and more like the ocean than the ocean itself, go deep, starless.'" Such passages of carefully fashioned poetry, occasionally "disjointed, unconvincing, even irritatingly repetitive" but always memorable, make us want to read the "almost painfully exciting" novel for the first time more than once. Like us, though, *Jazz*'s protagonists must accept that they can live their story for the first time only once. As she imagines their adult love, Morrison "reaches to find a language that will harmonize doubt and desire. The voice she discovers is sumptuously incomplete, quavering between happiness and despair. It is enough simply to listen."

The *New Criterion* agreed that, given Morrison's ongoing preoccupation with jazz and her belief that the novel must replace music as the healing art form for black people, it was probably inevitable that she would publish a novel called *Jazz*.

Bruce Bawer counters Mendelsohn's accolades, however, arguing that Morrison's trademark excesses are likewise those of "black" music: "at its weakest, her fiction can be as monotonous as the most pointlessly protracted of modern jazz improvisations, as melodramatic as the most maudlin blues ballad, as mindless as the most hackneyed spiritual. Yet she has risen less and less frequently to the wit and facility of the greatest jazz, the expertly modulated passion of the greatest blues, or the sincere devotional fervor of the greatest spirituals."

Bawer cites *Jazz*'s first half-dozen sentences reason enough "to step out for some air." Assessing the narrative voice as "meant to be rich in personality and atmosphere—meant to suggest, perhaps, a woman of a certain age sitting at a Harlem window, her voice warm and husky and lilting (rather like Morrison's—or, perhaps, Sarah Vaughan's) as she tells her neighbors' story," the voice of this unnamed, unreliable narrator, Bawer cautions, "is just a bit *too* rich, its general effect that of a somewhat too heavy perfume." Its sophisticated diction and syntax, its descent from "vibrant authenticity into glib detachment," and its propinquity to magical realism muddle the narrator's image; a long second-act digression coupled with the characters' utter lack of humor and intermittent forays into "anachronistic pop-psych chitchat" muddy the narrative waters. Even as The *New Criterion* critic attributes the Golden Gray segment to "some musical analogy or other (is Morrison trying to out-Coltrane Coltrane?)," he maintains that "lovers of Ella, Billie, Carmen, and Mahalia may find that *Jazz* doesn't quite put songs in their hearts."

The *New York Times* and the *Washington Post* moseyed down middle ground. Writing for the *Times*, Edna O'Brien commends Morrison for her linguistic analogy with music as a means for African Americans to communicate among themselves and reimagine their history, the riffs and cadences of her language testifying to the centrality of song in black culture. The Irish novelist lauds Morrison's consummate skill "not just to compel involvement from the very first sentence or paragraph, but to sustain a reader's curiosity." She praises the "sharp compassionate vignettes, plucked from different episodes of [characters'] lives," people "enthralled then deceived by 'the music the world makes.'" Nonetheless, for O'Brien something significant is missing. She interprets the absent element as the emotional nexus found in the greatest of Faulkner, Joyce, or Tolstoy novels, that "moment shorn of all artifice that brings us headlong into the deepest recesses of feeling." Sensing that *Jazz* moments are merely trying to tell her something, O'Brien is not moved to feel nor to extend her pity: "It is as if Ms. Morrison, bedazzled by her own virtuosity—a virtuosity that serves her and us and contemporary fiction very well—hesitates to bring us to the last frontier, to a predicament that is both physical and metaphysical, and which in certain fictions, by an eerie transmission, becomes our very own experience. Such alchemy does not occur here. What remains are the bold arresting strokes of a poster and not the cold astonishment of a painting."

Representing the *Washington Post*, David Nicholson first addresses literary factionalism and his position as white male reviewer of Morrison's fiction by applauding *Jazz*: much of the "new novel about love and desire in 1920s Harlem, is beautifully written, filled with powerful, visionary language. There are moments in it that cut as close to the heart of the matter—love, sex and the whole damn thing—as any great work of art." But we can hear the "but" coming: "*Jazz* is also a maddening book, disjointed and digressive, testimony to the limits of language and of unconventional narrative forms." Its idiosyncratic construction renders it a "homemade quilt of a book, mixing high and low styles, like a sweet potato pie topped with whipped cream and Grand Marnier." Recognizing Morrison's intention to linguistically embody via content and structure the ensemble essence of the great 1920s jazz bands and locating the book as the second in her cycle of works on African American life and the nature of love, Nicholson maintains that when Morrison is good, she is very, very good. But another "but" here, "what keeps *Jazz* from being a great book, instead of merely a good one, is the pointless and seemingly random digressions . . . this is, in the end, not so much a novel as a tale or series of tales." Echoing O'Brien, Nicholson attributes the problem to a distance from the characters and an ensuing lack of feeling: "Thus, while not without resonance and meaning, those moments of revelation and catharsis seem unearned—they are what Morrison wanted to have happen, rather than the result of a process the characters have undergone."

Anticipating the *Independent*'s tribute to Morrison's nourishing wisdom and its assessment that "you can hear blues and jazz in her writing: it's oral and musical" (Busby 1993), Nicholson acknowledges that *Jazz* is as much concerned about the power of words as words as a realistic depiction of people and events. Now the "but" becomes "And yet . . . And yet, in the end, I'm not sure Morrison's suppleness with language, the facility with which she weaves her tale, make up for the digressions and the structural flaws. On so many levels Morrison is telling the truth about love . . . and yet *Jazz* founders under the weight of its own artistic devices."

Jazz's Defining Critical Moments

Because *Jazz* emerged after and thus could ride the crest of *Beloved*'s enthusiastic critical reception, *Jazz*'s defining critical moment, in synchrony with Morrison's nod toward the presence of absence, may well be not swelling a wave of second-thought reaction. Initial reviews, several wedded to conversations with the author, were followed quickly by scholarly analysis. Because it was born into a burgeoning data-driven Internet age, *Jazz* accrued statistics that allowed *Publishers Weekly* to record it as an "authoritative novel"—a Book-of-the-Month-Club main selection and a seventeen-week *PW* bestseller in cloth (Apr. 1993). The book has since received 17,704 ratings and 907 reviews on Goodreads, translating into a 3.8-out-of-5-star recommendation.[2]

---

2   If the origins of the Internet date back to research commissioned by the United States federal government in the 1960s, the linking of commercial networks and enterprises in the early 1990s marks the beginning of the transition to the modern Internet, which

Goodreads enabled the layman reviewer's blog. His website dubbing him "writer, reader and all round music lover," and his spelling identifying him as British, Rob Maher elected to accord *Jazz* five stars in 2014. His Goodreads review explains that his attraction to jazz as well as to literature that alludes to Dante's *Divine Comedy* led to his interest in Morrison's depiction of the Great Migration to the Jazz City as an African American *Purgatorio*. Admitting that he has not read her renditions of Dante's *Inferno* (*Beloved*) or *Paradiso* (*Paradise*), Maher reveals his amateur standing through his erroneous summary of *Jazz*'s conclusion: "The couple grow old together in stagnation." While he should be commended for attempting to correct his "myopia" with respect to reading "far too many books written by white men" and for accurately citing Morrison as winning the Nobel Prize just after *Jazz* was released, our layman places "very little stock in awards ceremonies. Awards are all about opinion, perspective and, certainly with the Nobel prizes, politics." He does, however, find it "nice to veer away from the same old authors and reach out to discover somebody new or unfamiliar." We can conclude that, for better or worse, *Jazz*-age venues have most definitely moved Dante's rendition of Shakespeare's many-headed monster to claim their mob voices.

Jazz Criticism

The increasing availability of Internet communication during the 1990s encouraged an explosion of nonprofessional reviews on *Jazz*. The *MLA International Bibliography* identifies 180 citations (including four reprints) on the novel between 1992 and 2017, but only 92 of these (including one reprint) are peer-reviewed. The bulk of peer-reviewed comments (41) appeared between 1993 and 1999, with 10 records in 1995. Fifty-seven percent of citations that include non-peer-reviewed comments (102) appeared between 1992 and 2002, with 24 records in 1997 appreciating the surge of online options, and a resurgence of interest (14) occurring in 2006. Unlike Morrison's literary critical reception prior to *Beloved*, scholarly articles appeared almost immediately upon *Jazz*'s publication; 12 doctoral dissertations were written between 1995 and 2009.

Like criticism prior to *Beloved*, however, scholarly attention on *Jazz* remains concentrated in academic journals with an American multicultural focus. Of the 92 peer-reviewed responses, 18 (or 20 percent) can be found in publications such as the *College Language Association Journal* (3); *Callalloo* (1); *MELUS* (2), with most, and the most significant, of the articles appearing in the *African American Review* (12). Assistant editor of *Modern Fiction Studies* Nancy Peterson stayed on high alert, with her journal producing 4 articles on *Jazz* between 1993 and

---

generated rapid growth as institutional, personal, and mobile computers were connected to the network. By the late 2000s, its services and technologies had been incorporated into virtually every aspect of human lives, including how and what we read. Launched in 2007, Amazon's Goodreads is the world's largest website for book recommendations.

2006.[3] Perhaps the most intriguing critical reception phenomenon enhanced by the Internet is the proliferation of foreign publications, frequently disseminated online. Forty-nine articles and book chapters on *Jazz* have been published in Australia, Canada, China, Estonia, France, Germany, Great Britain, Hungary, India, Japan, Malaysia, the Netherlands, Pakistan, Poland, Scandinavia, South Africa, Spain, and Taiwan. While overseas articles appear as early as 1993, they increase exponentially in the late 1990s with the rising predominance of Internet communications and continue into the present. Amassed theoretical approaches, addressed here chronologically within category, include reader response; intertextual; structural; deconstructive; womanist/feminist; and African American/postcolonial criticism.

Jazz and [Rhetorical] Reader-Response Criticism

Many scholars find the experience of reading Morrison sufficiently dynamic as to require a new approach to literary analysis; James Phelan, for example, suggests "rhetorical reader-response criticism" (Peterson 225). The experimental nature of Morrison's linguistic project in *Jazz* has led some to improvise a critical vocabulary suited to the novel's jazzy language and structure. Eusebio Rodrigues "ear-reads" the novel as though it were a musical score, celebrating "Morrison's ability to turn language into a musical instrument that trumpets the desires, disappointments, and triumphs of African Americans" (Peterson 12). Nicholas Pici proposes that *Jazz* begins with a "head melody," that while Morrison's style mirrors the sounds and rhythms of jazz music, *Jazz*'s structure reflects the patterns and configurations of jazz compositions. Pici concludes that the authority of Morrison's musical motif lies not in its omnipresence, but in its malleability: "Much like members in a jazz quintet 'trading fours' between themselves—one musician throwing out musical questions and phrases that are promptly deflected by another's musical responses and counterpoints—this novel, particularly in its treatment of jazz, constantly oscillates between several different meanings. Ultimately, then, Morrison might well be viewed as a literary musician, 'trading meanings' between herself and the words she writes" (396).

Anthony Berret adopts a comparative music-and-literature approach in 1997 to show his students how Morrison facilitates the transition from music to literature by carefully inserting musical images. *Jazz* signals that, having realized music can no longer provide a sufficient survival manual for her community, Morrison trusts her novels to recreate black culture (McKay, *Approaches* 113). Barbara Lewis illustrates how the uncertainty of *Jazz*'s narrative voice, calculatedly unresolved in a jazzlike fashion, establishes not only the presence of jazz as a thematic element but also serves as a metaphor for the shifting demographic conditions of migratory blacks.

---

3   See previous chapters for pertinent information about these journals.

Keren Omry compares the affinity of Morrison and James Baldwin for 1940s bebop, a musical moment where past and present meet, to clarify their depiction of cultural identity as an infinitely dynamic process (2006). Bebop as central trope "becomes a conceptual model by which these two authors seek productive ways to consider ethnic identity and rewrite the historical processes that laid so much stress on the biological conceptions of race." From their explorations of "the tensions between a culturally imposed collective and a socially constructed individualized identity" emerge "the beginnings of a new formulation of blackness that incorporates communal consent as one of its defining features" (12). Chad Jewett, however, locates Morrison's experimentations with form and narrative more fully in post-bop jazz movements, specifically that of modal jazz (2015).

Paula Eckard identifies the music itself as the book's narrator (1994): "Like a jazz performance, [the narrator] creates a montage effect in its storytelling. It improvises on itself, utilizes the language of music and syncopated rhythms, and sings classic blues themes of love and loss.... Music, language, and narrative come together in *Jazz*, and their interplay provides the real dynamics of the text" (11). Alan Rice cautions critics who rush to foreground the impact of jazz on Morrison's *Jazz* to be "wary of isolating this novel as her only jazz-influenced work" ("Jazzing It Up" 423). He elaborates in "It Don't Mean a Thing If It Ain't Got That Swing" that Morrison consistently utilizes a radical style to embrace radical ideologies within American letters (2000). Deliberately eschewing traditional literary form to privilege a vernacular analogous to her own people's musical tradition, *Jazz* manifests Kimberly Benston's idea that "black language leads toward music, that it passes into music when it attains the maximal pitch of its being. This belief contains the powerful suggestion that music is the ultimate lexicon, that language when truly apprehended, aspires to the condition of music" (416).

Jazz and Intertextuality

Morrison's *Jazz* has inspired quite a bit of noteworthy comparative criticism. After discovering and translating a previously published novel titled *Jazz*, written by Hans Janowitz, a German-speaking Jew born in Bohemia, Jürgen Grandt assesses the 1927 version as containing very different themes, setting, and characters (including no major black figures) yet virtually the same techniques employed by Morrison to achieve "the translation of the world into jazz music" (Janowitz 24). Grandt thus calls for a new critical template not, like most contemporary jazz critiques, predicated primarily on form and language (2004): "If a critical jazz aesthetic is to be useful for the study of African American literature, it must incorporate a firm knowledge of the music's technical aspects as well as an equally firm sense of the history of both the music and the people who have been creating it" (304).

Comparative critic Anna Kérchy contributes an essay outlining the commonalities between Morrison and Baldwin. Jane Lilienfeld alludes to Angela Burton's assertions that Morrison's narrative strategies expose communal complicity in generating abject pariah figures to ascertain the asymmetric parallels in the constructed personae and narration of Woolf's *To the Lighthouse* and *Jazz*. Roberta Rubenstein and John Duvall examine Faulknerian connections to the novel. Several scholars focus on its [pre]classical influences. Pointing out that the *Jazz* narrator challenges traditional Western epistemology by providing alternate ways of knowing or not knowing in fiction, Vincent O'Keefe asserts that Morrison's resistance to the traditional epistemology of scientific materialism in realist novels compares with the resistance of ancient Gnosticism to the theology and institutionalization of Christianity. Gnostic intuition and agnostic doubt regarding the representation of others' lives and histories inform Morrison's readers, especially African Americans, that they can follow the fresh tracks of Joe, Violet, Felice, and the narrator "only by resisting traditional Western tracks and creating their own or, even better, by recognizing the potential oppression inherent in all track-making" (347).

Kathleen Morgan and Marc Conner perceive Morrison riffing on features of *The Odyssey* and *The Winter's Tale*. While Morgan looks to Homer's presentation of the man-eating Cyclops to explain the concept of "Otherness" in *Jazz*, Conner turns to Shakespeare to propose that in *Jazz* Morrison offers a new direction for the African American novel, heretofore dominated by a realist/naturalist or modernist aesthetic, by imagining it as Romance. Conceding that jazz music does in many ways structure *Jazz*, Conner insists that its engagement with music is simply its first and perhaps least interesting attribute. He argues that *Jazz* converts a human and temporal art into "an inhuman, eternal, and in some sense maternal art that both transcends and unites its various human representations." Hence the novel becomes "an aesthetic quest, moving beyond the constrictions and reductions of race, gender, politics, and history, and gesturing finally toward an aesthetic realm that is far more ancient, fundamental, and redemptive than any earthly corollary could be." In so doing, *Jazz* represents "its own rejection and its own fulfillment, a complex quest tale for a fundamental mothering figure who harmonizes the human, the natural, and the supernatural. In this figure Morrison finds the source of healing for which her tortured characters yearn throughout each of her novels, and she discovers the source for her own art" (341–42).

Martha Cutter concentrates on Morrison's own [intra]intertextuality. Cutter proposes a *Jazz* retake on *Beloved*, ascribing Morrison's reliance on techniques that resist the totalizing impulse of narrative, and closure by readers, to her investment in the griot, the oral African American tradition of storytelling (2000). Although close examination of chronology in *Beloved/Jazz* prohibits an interpretation of Beloved's resurrection as Wild, Cutter's conclusion that "Beloved returns in *Jazz*, yet she remains a mystery" is partially valid. *Jazz* does, indeed, ask us to "start over—reading and rereading, motioning to future readings as well as contemporary ones, creating and recreating that ... endlessly changing text that is storytelling itself" (72). Agreeing that Morrison's fiction is known for evoking African

American folklore as well as recoding black oral traditions, Darryl Dickson-Carr adds that Morrison concurrently and satirically subverts African American (and other) mythologies, especially those of communities in the urban North, the rural Midwest, and the South. Mahboobeh Khaleghi reminds us in 2011 of the contradictory narrative voices (one gossipy and reluctant to reveal its lack of omniscience, another making no claims to complete knowledge), who chime in to tell the *Jazz* story.

Jazz and Structuralist Criticism

Structuralist critiques on *Jazz* primarily accent the operations of its narrative. Even as she identifies narration in *Jazz* as a "problem," Katherine Mayberry asks readers to step back from traditional interpretations involving character, context, or language to consider the relation between chronicle and ideology (1997). Mayberry contends that Morrison deliberately adopts an ambiguous narrative in all her work not because it imitates black storytelling, but to reject the tendency of dominant cultures to co-opt narrative and use it to inscribe hegemonic values. She chooses to return power not only to traditionally silenced figures but also to the authority of her readers. Dale Pattison points out twenty years later that the novel's representations of city space, intimacy, and erotic transgression are mirrored in its narrative architectures, which invite readers into transgressive reading postures. A 1999 collection of essays presenting a variety of perspectives on the forms and functions of narration, written by some of the leading scholars of narratology, includes a study of *Jazz*'s narrative patterns co-authored by one of those theorists (Shlomith Rimmon-Kenan). Matthew Treherne extends Rimmon-Kenan's interpretation of the novel's concluding mind dance with its reader by reminding us that "the signifying process is not one-sided; the freedom to make and to be remade through narrative is a reciprocal process" (199).

Drawing upon the work of postcolonial scholar Homi Bhabha, Treherne suggests that *Jazz* not only underscores the possibilities of a strategic deployment of negotiation but indicates how negotiation can "generate new understandings of narrative and can lead to a new participation in otherness which alternative narrative models might deny." If Morrison's narrative aim is not the reification of other people, their shared humanity, nor a destabilization of the narratives which have led to such reifications, but "an openness to the possibilities of negotiation and renegotiation of the signifiers which might be the building blocks of identity to find and form relationship with otherness," the loss of stable discourses no longer leads to the dearth of an emotional nexus as described by reviewer Edna O'Brien. Rather it leads to a new identity represented in the narrative inflected with otherness: an inconclusive voice that "gets a kick out of talking to you and hearing you answer. The work of narrative is not complete at the end of *Jazz*, but is only beginning: the rest is talking" (210–11).

Jazz and Deconstructive Criticism

Four critics note the unmistakable references to French philosopher Jacques Derrida in the novel and thus Morrison's nod to the claims of deconstructionist scholars that language is not the reliable communication tool we have supposed it to be, but rather a fluid, ambiguous domain of complex experience in which ideologies determine us without our being aware of them. Philip Page is among the first to spot the infusion of Morrison's work by postmodern influences reflected in other African American art forms, such as the deliberate spaces provided for call-and-response in jazz and preaching (1995). If binary oppositions, the presence of absence, and characters trapped in the process of becoming prevail throughout Morrison's oeuvre, postmodern alienation is particularly evident in *Jazz*. Page believes that Morrison's direct allusions to Derridean concepts of the différance, the trace, and the breach become useful in understanding characters who, in their displacement, tend to overemphasize one or the other of opposites instead of seeking a healthier location within the play of oppositions.

Marilyn Atlas and Carolyn Jones examine cracked integrity, verbal putty, and the influence of narrative on identity in the novel. Observing Morrison's practice of embedding geographical images in her work, Atlas states that with *Jazz* location becomes as mental as physical. Charting the landscape means exploring characters' psychological realities to transform cracked psyches into flexibly viable spaces. Language, imagination, and music help characters avoid being run to ground, as they, not geography, assume the controlling position. Jones maintains that Morrison redefines narrative, voice, and identity with the traces and cracks in jazz/*Jazz*. Her concept of self can tolerate "'the polyphony of many voices playing off against each other, without . . . the need to reconcile them just to hold them together'" (494).

Susan Mayberry attributes the development of Joe Trace not only to the disruptive Derridean breaches that contribute to his process of identity formation, but to Morrison's reverence for the divinity of comedy (2007). As her *Jazz* characters "train dance on into the city, it turns the rhythms of country blues into urban jazz and transforms suffering into information." Morrison "relies on various techniques of classical tragedy to relay her men's continuing pain. As blues evolves into jazz, however, the focus and tone of her writing shift from the sights and sounds of tragedy into the tragicomedy that embodies the jazz experience" (*Can't I Love* 194).

Jazz and Womanist/Feminist Criticism

Because *Jazz* inspires critiques focusing on the import of its experimental structure, less feminist criticism has been written about it than is typical for Morrison's oeuvre. Doreatha Mbalia, Drucilla Cornell, and Angelyn Mitchell begin the conversation in the 1990s with Morrison's praise of sisterhood. Just as story and storytelling become one in jazz, so in *Jazz* theme and structure blend to suggest the unification necessary for African Americans to survive. Morrison understands that oppression disrupts this unity, especially releasing the feral in women who experience the triple tyranny of class, race, and gender: "These wild traces may be submerged, but under the right (that is, wrong) conditions, they will emerge" (Mbalia 625).

Proposing that the allegory of the Wild Woman lies at the heart of *Jazz* by way of the destructiveness of the split self, Cornell offers a rereading of this psychical fantasy, who figures as the woman beside herself in two ways: "she refuses both the very limitations of ego identity we call a self, and challenges the ordered world of established meaning imposed by the masculine symbolic" (15). Mitchell believes that Morrison's art embodies her conservation of African American history and culture as she "reinterprets, re-evaluates, and rediscovers Black life as lived, particularly but not exclusively as lived by Black women" distorted by the nucleus of black culture that is the South (49). In this novel that deals directly with Southerners who leave the ancestral home, Morrison offers a generational examination of three black women whose lives are shaped by gendered and racialized Southern history.

Aoi Mori demonstrates that, "committed to reconstructing the history of African Americans who have been excluded from mainstream discourse," Morrison creates *Jazz* to rewrite the Harlem Renaissance from the female perspective that has largely been disregarded, including its armed women and motherless children (320). Stephen Knadler, Leila Tafreshi, and Wan Roselezam Wan Yahya acknowledge the trauma allied with the Jazz Age's jazz impulse. Knadler reconsiders *Jazz*'s attitude toward domestic violence while Tafreshi and Wan Yahya identify major elements of trauma theory and explore the coping strategies utilized by female characters to deal with the post-traumatic stress disorder accompanying migration (2014). Sarah Aguiar and Andrea O'Reilly foreground the mother's voice in *Jazz*. Revealing that self-love depends on the self being loved by another self, Morrison emphasizes how essential mothering is for the emotional wellbeing of children. O'Reilly's reading of *Jazz* explores how loss of the mother fractures and displaces the child's developing self: "Only when Violet and Joe mourn the loss of their mothers is recovery of the child's 'me' made possible" (368).

Additional feminist readings uncover desire, clothing, beauty culture, and the body. Elizabeth Cannon describes *Jazz* as theorizing the nature of female desire, specifically "that sexual desire becomes the only desire operative when the fulfillment of other desires is denied and that what African-American women currently most desire, and what is currently most denied to them, is . . . the consciousness needed to act as a subject" (235). Natalie Stillman-Webb determines sartorial details in *Jazz* to be an intervention in these controversial debates regarding the relationships between African American subjectivity and mass culture. Richard Pearce traces Golden Gray to the complex development of the African American beauty culture emerging during the Jazz Age through a series of negotiations; Pearce then relates those cultural tactics to the narrative tactics Morrison employs in *Jazz*. Katherine Boutry explains Morrison's novel as representing both the female body and the body of blues music: "It is precisely this living, stimulating, and 'indefinable' (nonlinguistic) quality of jazz that connected it to the body and made it both threatening and attractive to listeners" (91).

Two other critics who examine *Jazz*'s musical references from a twenty-first century feminist perspective are Tracey Sherard and Brittney Cooper. Sherard points out that most critical analyses take some account of jazz's role in the novel yet pay only marginal attention to its pervasive signification on women's classic blues—an African American, female-migration, musical crossroads—as well as Morrison's allegorical use of the narrator as technological composite of the phonograph and record that "plays" cultural narratives to which its characters both respond and resist. In her essay on hip-hop feminism, Cooper treats *Jazz* as a literary antecedent to Sapphire's 1996 novel *Push*, a "bridge text to the works of more canonical black women writers" (59). Cooper concludes that, though *Jazz* centers on 1920s New York City jazz culture, it mirrors the broader social anxieties in the early 1990s about the role of rap music in African American culture.

Jazz and African American/Postcolonial Criticism

Finally, some critics have accentuated the African American aspects of the novel. Nancy Peterson touts *Jazz* for "offering an intervention into the writing of African American history," working toward a model that, like jazz, "conceives of black history not as a fixed record of past events, but as a dynamic, collective, and improvised narrative" (11). Roberta Rubenstein views it as Morrison's means of not only culturally mourning the lost possibilities produced by slavery, along with the loss of cultural productions through appropriation by white culture, but of re-claiming black music by re-envisioning the Jazz Age and employing the literary equivalents of its musical forms. Construing the Golden Gray episode as an imaginative reworking of the American tall tale, Jennifer Andrews observes that Morrison disrupts the traditional white-male triumph over nature with her biracial male hero and a black female trickster.

Richard Hardack and Michael Nowlin discover the novel's take on double-consciousness. Hardack claims that its exposure of "quiet as it's kept" in American literature makes *Jazz* a dramatization of self-alienation and double-consciousness in the African American experience. Nowlin explores how, as Morrison's expanding vision "transfigures her usual subject matter, the complex world of black Americans, into a synecdoche for America," she preserves her authority as an American writer without sacrificing an identity predicated upon race: in other words, how "blackness" and "Americanness" become simultaneously antithetical, as in DuBois's formulation of double-consciousness, and, as Ralph Ellison suggests, ironically identical (152). Nowlin maintains that these notions dominate *Jazz* and that Morrison addresses the ambiguity with her equivocal narrator.

Several critics focus on African American relocation. Deborah Barnes and Madhu Dubey examine Morrison's take on migration. Defining Morrison's as a unique depiction, which "interrogates the destructive and distorting effects of physical and emotional dislocation on culturally mobile blacks," Barnes claims that *Jazz* demonstrates the culture shock too often accompanying their social, economic, and political "progress" (284–85). Madhu argues that *Jazz* both resists and underscores the impossibility of resisting the hybridizing consequences of commodification, and thus compels us "to confront the full complexity of the history of migration" (310). Postcolonial scholar Gurleen Grewal completes with *Jazz* her monograph on Morrison as historiographer attempting to bridge the gap between emergent black middle-class America and its subaltern origins.

Jocelyn Chadwick-Joshua, Anne-Marie Paquet-Deyris, and Andrew Scheiber spotlight urban folk. Chadwick-Joshua presents the rhetoric of Morrison's City in terms of metonymy/synecdoche; Paquet-Deyris understands it to encode a space of resistance in which all sorts of cultural practices resurface under oppressive conditions; and Scheiber concludes that *Jazz* revisits the Black Aesthetic argument, which relegates blues to "an artifact of an abjured Southern past" and jazz to "an expression of urban-revolutionary modernism" by "placing it in the context of the Black urban diaspora of the early 20th Century, troubling the boundaries between blues and jazz, cultural tradition and innovation, and vernacular and commodity culture" (Abstract).

Perhaps most significantly, *Jazz* has inspired some theorists to revisit literature as the supplement to living speech that calls into question both the limits of traditional conceptions of African American textual studies and the narrow ontologies of personhood. Veronique Lesoinne, Judylyn Ryan, and Craig Werner note Morrison's attraction to traditional call-and-response structures, which characterize the author and the reader as "partners in the dialectical creation of the text and of its meanings" (McKay and Earle, *Approaches* 154). Ryan and Werner rely on this participatory reading emerging from African diaspora oral conventions to introduce *Jazz* in the contemporary classroom.

Caroline Brown views the Golden Gray segment as the voice of the non-hermeneutic and Morrison as the symbolic African griot. Jennifer FitzGerald and Marjorie Pryse note *Jazz*'s allusions to African "Signifying." *Jazz* itself becomes Henry Louis Gates Jr.'s Signifyin(g) Monkey; the talking book/*Jazz* narrator discovers ways in which reading itself can become a site within which to work through distrust and arrive at reparation. Maurice Wallace taps *Jazz* to illustrate that while "the facts of blackness exceed the printed page" (804), print's "prosthetic (im)personation" affords entry for contemporary efforts in literary and cultural studies, as Sarah Kaplan recaps, "to amend—if not transfigure—existing conceptions of personhood." Wallace's genealogy of the fetishization of print, particularly in African American texts, suggests "an understanding of literacy as a mode of power enacted through the technology of print and materialized in the form of literature" (Kaplan 807). *Jazz*'s trope of the Talking Book illustrates the extent to which print's perceived potential and limitations may owe as much to its magical as technological function, since with its ability to faithfully replicate the aural, the literary text takes on the alchemic power to fulfill on the page the voices of the absent and the object as it renders people out of property, humans out of things.

Morrison puts it more succinctly: "What has already happened with the music in the States, the literature will do one day" (Busby).

CHAPTER SEVEN

PARADISE (1997)

Paradise's Critical History as Told by Toni Morrison

If the second book in Morrison's self-termed African American trilogy, *Jazz*, looks backward to her mother's 1920s music-as-muse/musing, its third installment, *Paradise*, nods its 2014 foreword to her grandfather's war on illiteracy, a discriminating resistance that resounded when *Beloved*'s Sixo declines to learn to read.[1] Although, unlike most of her critics, Morrison considered her seventh novel her masterpiece, *Paradise* continues to rank among experimental narratives utilizing modernist and postmodernist techniques that challenge, indeed deter readers. The author intentionally withholds racial information that readers are accustomed to being spoon fed and thus consider vital to their understanding of the text: "I was eager to simultaneously de-fang and theatricalize race, signaling, I hoped, how movable and hopelessly meaningless the construct was" (Origin 66). While even veteran critics can and did ignore or misinterpret the vital signs that do appear in *Paradise*, its literary critical history, and her Vintage encapsulation, nonetheless reveal that Morrison relied on her masterpiece to teach us a new way to read (see the coda on "Recitatif" at the end of this chapter).

An oft-told family story portrays Morrison's "Big Papa" attending school for a single day to "tell the teacher he wouldn't be back because he had to work. His older sister, he said, would teach him to read." Given that six years after his birth in 1864, a year after the signing of the Emancipation Proclamation, the location of said school and its indubitably revolutionary teacher would need to remain a

---

1   When Sixo's slave master offers to teach him to read, Sixo refuses: "it would change his mind—make him forget things he shouldn't and memorize things he shouldn't and he didn't want his mind messed up." Eventually he stops speaking English altogether because "there was no future in it" (*Beloved* 208, 25).

secret as "black people's access to education in general and reading specifically was violently discouraged and, in most of the South, teaching African Americans to read had been illegal," Big Papa's saga applauds both female and male victory. Rural Alabama would no doubt reflect 1831 Virginia law: "Any white person assembling to instruct free Negroes to read or write shall be fined not over $50.00 also be imprisoned not exceeding two months'; 'It is further enacted that if any white person for pay shall assemble with slaves for the purpose of teaching them to read or write he shall for each offense be fined at the discretion of the justice . . .' ten to one hundred dollars" (foreword xi). Against all odds, Big Papa's big sister taught him to read.

But of necessity he pored predominantly over one book and a few preciously hoarded ethnic newspapers. Because most African American family libraries consisted solely of the Bible, Big Papa could boast of having perused the King James Version of that volume cover to cover five times. Newspapers devoted exclusively to African American affairs were dog-eared from repeated use by multiple readers. Morrison makes clear that reading and cursive writing were prized in her family not only for purposes of instruction and delight, but as deliberate political acts, which defied prior restrictions on learning and released banned truths about being black in America.

It follows logically, then, that the composite record of African American experience Morrison solicited from private collectors, edited, and named *The Black Book* would contain numerous enlightening snippets from the nineteenth-century black newspapers printed around the time her grandfather had his few minutes of school fame. Having located some fifty such newspapers produced in the Southwest during Reconstruction and succeeding the Reconstruction Treaties' forced displacement of Native Americans from Oklahoma Territory, Morrison learned the meaning of African American Utopia: "The opportunity to establish black towns was as feverish as the rush for whites to occupy the land. The 'colored' newspapers encouraged the rush and promised a kind of paradise to the newcomers: land, their own government, safety—there were even sustained movements to establish their own state" (xii).

Frequently defining her novels as public investigations of private questions, Morrison found herself intrigued by a theme running throughout those newspapers—the admonition echoed in articles and headlines: "Come Prepared or Not at All." She interpreted "Prepared" to imply two commands: 1) Do not come if you have nothing and 2) Utopia is only for the few, translated in sum as "no poor former slaves are welcome in the paradise being built here." She also noted the light complexions of landowners photographed in the newspaper advertisements and concluded that "skin privilege" must be a feature of said special few. Although Morrison originally planned to call *Paradise* "War" (and recurrently questioned her decision not to), her ultimate title frames a subject that she claims has chronically fascinated her and that served as the seed for her book: "why paradise necessitates exclusion" (Murline 71). In a 1998 *New York Times* interview, she states that "all paradises are described as male enclaves, while the interloper is a woman, defenseless and threatening. When we get ourselves together and get powerful is when we are assaulted" (Dinitia Smith).

The segregation that accompanied these initial attempts to achieve black paradise, which ironically replicated the white racism from which the town leaders were running, led Morrison to explore the reverse:

> ... exclusivity by the very black-skinned; construction of their very own "gated community," one that refused entrance to the mixed race. Considering the need for progeny in order to last, how would patriarchy play and how might matriarchy threaten? In order to describe and explore these questions I needed 1) to examine the definition of paradise, 2) to delve into the power of colorism, 3) to dramatize the conflict between patriarchy and matriarchy, and 4) to disrupt racial discourse altogether by signaling then erasing it. (foreword xiii)

Her 2014 foreword continues to elaborate on the aims she set out by turning in detail to John Milton's *Paradise Lost*. Here she illustrates for us the kind of careful sign reading that many reviewers and scholars failed to utilize in their responses to Morrison's *Paradise*. She compares the currently over-imagined and thus trivialized idea of paradise with its historical images, intended to be "grand but accessible, beyond the routine but imaginatively graspable, seductive as though remembered" (xiii). Easily available today either as tangible real estate owned by the two percent or luxurious parks visited by the other ninety-eight, or metaphorically as commonplace desire, John Winthrop's City upon a Hill shares with Milton's Paradise the characteristics of beauty, plenty, rest, exclusivity. Only immortality is absent from the modern American Dream.

Definitions of paradisiacal traits, however, have changed considerably. Contemporary beauty resembles that coveted by Milton's Mammon: "benevolent, controllable nature combined with precious metal, mansions, finery, and jewelry." Plenty in an already excessively vacuum-packed world becomes obscene materialism, shamelessly preened before the envious dispossessed. Because today's rest denotes isolation, lazy avoidance of labor, or punishment, it becomes an undesired "desire-less-ness that suggests a special kind of death without dying." Because the unworthy are not there, exclusivity, on the other hand, remains compelling—sought by the wealthy and the middle class alike: gated enclaves, clearly marked boundaries, security systems, and volunteer watchdogs. The term "public" itself a virulent site of contention, citizens squabble over open space, the homeless spoil the sidewalks, and young people up to no good prowl the streets. Rendered insignificant by secular, scientific arguments, eternity becomes earthbound, heaven a matter of "'Only me or us forever,'" and hell merely something less boring than the perdition of everyday life (foreword xiv–xv).

Big Papa's newspapers promoted black hegemony by recruiting light-skinned applicants. Familiar with illogical racist power in political and social arenas, Morrison attempted to counter its undeserved intellectual weight by disrupting assumptions of racial discourse in *Paradise* with a "race-specific/race-free prose, language that deactivated the power of racially inflected strategies," transforming them "from the strait-jacket a race-conscious society can, and frequently does, buckle us into—a refusal to 'know' characters or people by the color of their skin." She credits this challenge to the linguistic pinnacle of white universalism, its effort "to exorcise, alter, and de-fang the white/black confrontation and concentrate on the residue of that hostility," with her artistic liberation (xv–xvi).

Paradise's shocking opening ("They shoot the white girl first. With the rest they can take their time.") signals race as both hierarchy and unreliability. The men in an all-black community, one chosen by its members, make war on the women in a race-less one, also self-selected. As details unfold, "traditional grounds for black vs. white hostilities shift to the nature of exclusion, the origins of chauvinism, the sources of oppression, assault, and slaughter" (xvi). Distinctive rites of racial purity and preservation in the segregated town of Ruby are juxtaposed with the deliberately withheld racial codes in the Convent as Morrison shifts the racial onus onto her readers. Because we "slot and characterize people when we know their race," she denies readers their "usual comfort" (Smith).

For some "this was disturbing and some admitted to being preoccupied with finding out which character was the 'white girl'; others wondered initially and then abandoned the question; some ignored the confusion by reading them all as black. The perceptive ones read them as fully realized individuals—whatever their race." Once Morrison unencumbered her language from the vocabulary of racial domination, the conflicts became gendered and generational, and the narrative freed itself from "the narrow imagination that conceived and betrayed paradise" (foreword xvi–xvii).

The coda to the *Paradise* foreword serves as her illustration of race-specific/race-free prose. We know that "Big Papa" is African American only because Morrison has previously described the homeschooling of her paterfamilias. Avoiding the typical white male author's obvious iteration of Other[black]ness, her last section merely highlights details that will allow us to understand why she drew on her grandfather to design the men in Ruby — "their easy assumption of uncontested authority." If we follow the signs, we will determine that Big Papa was "eccentric, formidable, playful, stubborn, learned. A survivor." He ate raw slices of yam pulled from the family garden and peeled with his pocketknife, "slowly, carefully." He stood silently in front of the person in the chair that he wanted to sit in until s/he got the message and got up. He drew portraits of his granddaughters and gave them "the gift of chewing gum." "Too religious for any church," he drew deference to wherever he was: "He didn't exert power; he assumed it" (xvii).

Morrison's penultimate vital sign tells us the most: "He left me his violin." When we recall that one of the children's books she co-authored with her son Slade, *Who's Got Game? The Ant or the Grasshopper?* (published in 2003 along with Morrison's next novel, *Love*) turns the traditional tale upside down by rendering the lively hopper/artist the hero, our close reading concludes that, though she does not directly say so, Big Papa is undoubtedly something else. Nonetheless, Big Papa's composite drawing should not and cannot be reduced to his Other[black] ness. This multifaceted man not only provided *Paradise* with the model for a captivating patriarch; he set Toni Morrison free to write (xvii).

Paradise's Initial Critical Reception History and Defining Critical Moments

Numerous readers, however, could not break her race-specific/race-free code. Four years after its appearance, Peter Widdowson noted that the novel had yet to receive the critical attention devoted to preceding books in Morrison's trilogy: "Apart from some heavyweight early reviews, especially in the American press (not all favorable, by any means), and a few scrambled 'first-off' essays since, a novel which strikes the present, admittedly white, male, English, critic as raising contentious historical and political issues in a most powerful and complex way has been met with relative disregard" (313).

Speculating that its stylistic complexity had diverted readers from addressing its polemical queries about race, gender, and American history, Widdowson set out to untangle the novel's narrative filaments to expose its ideological positions. Apparently, his detailed effort made little headway, given Adam Langer's vague comment from a 2003 interview with Morrison, which summarized initial reviewer response to her first book printed since she received the 1993 Nobel Prize in Literature: "an ambitious but unrelentingly grim exploration of guilt and revenge, [*Paradise*] received some rave reviews but also some of the worst of Morrison's career" (Denard, *Conversations* 206).

US News & World Report's Anna Murline had already confirmed that early reviews for *Paradise* were "less than stellar"; critics who applauded the book's lush lyricism panned heavy-handed foreshadowing and artificial plot devices. While *Kirkus Reviews* portrays the opening of "Morrison's rich, symphonic seventh novel" as a scene of "Faulknerian intensity," for example, it cautions: "Only her very occasional resort to digressive (and accusatory) summary (e.g., 'They think they have outfoxed the whiteman when in fact they imitate him') mars the pristine surface of an otherwise impeccably composed, deeply disturbing story. Not perfect—but a breathtaking, risk-taking major work that will have readers feverishly, and fearfully turning the pages." Although Louis Menand, writing for the *New Yorker*, calls *Paradise* "the strangest and most original book Morrison has written," dubs it formally her most Faulknerian novel, describes its "genius" as prohibiting the biblical subtext from intruding on the reader's attention and its author as "one of the creators of the taste by which she is appreciated" at her "novelistic best" in *Paradise*, revered principal book critic of the *New York Times* Michiko Kakutani took it to task.

For the most part a Morrison advocate, lauded especially for her keenly incisive commendation of *Beloved*, Kakutani wrote a scathing 1998 review of *Paradise*, which has proved to be its defining critical moment. Comparing it to Morrison's "powerful" *Sula* and weighing its numerous parallels with her "masterpiece"

Beloved, the reviewer tersely concludes: "Unfortunately, *Paradise* is everything that *Beloved* was not: it's a heavy-handed, schematic piece of writing, thoroughly lacking in the novelistic magic Ms. Morrison has wielded so effortlessly in the past. It's a contrived, formulaic book that mechanically pits men against women, old against young, the past against the present."

After Kakutani dismisses its men as "uniformly control freaks or hotheads" and its female characters as two-dimensional clichés, "thin and papery and disposable," she deems the language of *Paradise* comparable to "the hectoring, didactic voice that warped [Morrison's] 1992 essay *Playing in the Dark*," its plot developments a forced "series of random dominoes, falling over noisily, one by one by one," and Morrison's efforts to embed a symbolic subtext "hokey":

> Whereas earlier Morrison novels like *Beloved*, *Song of Solomon* and *Sula* fused the historical and the mythic, the mundane and the fantastic into a seamless piece of music, this novel remains an earthbound hodgepodge, devoid of both urgency and narrative sleight of hand. It's neither grounded in closely observed vignettes of real life, nor lofted by the dreamlike images the author has used so dexterously in the past to suggest the strangeness of American history; the novel's one surreal set-piece feels like a hasty afterthought, clumsily grafted on to try to kick the story to another level.

Kakutani magnifies *Kirkus Reviews*' sole criticism of *Paradise* (sporadically "having [Morrison's] characters spell out the meaning of her story") to a constant matter of making matters worse. She judges such blunt announcements "unnecessary, indeed annoying"— "portentous footnotes in what is a clunky, leaden novel."

To recognize the 2017 retirement of "America's most powerful literary critic," colleagues toasted a remarkable career characterized by "intra-literary rows" and "razor-sharp responses," which "inspired both admiration and fear in the hearts of the writers whose books she reviewed" (Nevins). Jake Nevins describes Kakutani's critique of Morrison's *Beloved* as a superb illustration of the positive book review that incites readers to buy the book even as it displays the critic's unique adeptness "at taking a true work of art—Toni Morrison's *Beloved*, for instance—and writing a review nearly as trenchant and skillful as the novels about which she opined." Kakutani's review of *Paradise* succeeded most famously, however, at provoking the wrath of its writer. Morrison extends an equally no-holds-barred retort when *Salon* interviewer Zia Jaffrey mentions Kakutani's "extremely unflattering" account of *Paradise*: "And I thought, more to the point, it was not well written. The unflattering reviews are painful for short periods of time; the badly written ones are deeply, deeply insulting. That reviewer took no time to really read the book" (Denard 140).

International reaction turned out to be equally contentious. If the *London Telegraph* circulated in its entirety Morrison's foreword to the 2014 reprinting of *Paradise*, followed by a URL for the purchase of tickets to hear her speak in Haymarket, English journalist/novelist Zoë Heller, writing for the *London Review of Books*, begins her 1998 critique of the novel by burlesquing what had become Morrison's "amazing" US reputation:

> Over the last ten years, since the publication of *Beloved*, her fifth novel, she has been catapulted from the teeming ranks of well-known, well-respected fiction writers, to the thin-aired plane reserved for America's deities and seers. Winning the Nobel Prize in Literature in 1993 had something to do with this of course, but Morrison's status in American culture goes beyond, and is certainly not reducible to, the approbation of the Swedes. She appears on the cover of the *New York Review of Books* and *Time* magazine. She is required reading in American schools and colleges, and very probably the subject of more doctoral dissertations than any other contemporary American writer. . . . In the great halls of the New York Public Library, an extract from her Nobel Prize acceptance speech has been graven on the stone wall.

Two impassioned Letters to the editor of the *London Review of Books* (*LRB*) reveal that Heller's disparaging analysis of *Paradise* had become a lightning rod. Maud Sulter, founder of Blackwomen's Creativity Project at the University of Central Lancashire, curtly dismisses the white female writer's qualifications to assess black female writing: "Zoë Heller an authority on Blackwomen's writing . . . ? I think not. If the *LRB* does not take our writing seriously enough to be reviewed by the same criteria of scholarship and prior knowledge that you privilege white authors with, then do not bother to review it at all."

Several weeks later Kym Martindale of Bristol continues to find unsettling Sulter's "assumptions and appropriations":

> Certainly, the review was less than sympathetic, and seemed to argue that Morrison's work is increasingly unworthy of the accolades accorded her. This may or may not be the case, but I did not feel that Heller was claiming to be an authority on black women's writing; nor, indeed, that such a position would be helpful. Heller was responding to *Paradise* in tones of critical disappointment. Sulter's stance implies that Morrison's work can only be viewed in relation to its place in the canon of black women's writing, a reductive approach which valorises commonality at the expense of diversity. Nor does it change the possibility that Heller is right, and that Morrison has fallen prey to the kind of cloying "woman-imagery" in which Adrienne Rich glories. Feathers, wombs, fiddle-headed ferns—mercifully, this is not the sum of what women, black or white, write about.

In a special for the *Christian Science Monitor*, Ron Charles acknowledges Morrison's escalating role as literary rock star and provocateur. Although her demands on her language and her audience make reading any of her novels "an act of faith," Charles deems *Paradise* to reward that faith in a manner that would not only generate "volumes of feminist appraisal" but also produce effects both stunning and bewitching. Conceding the difficulty of connecting with characters amidst its bewildering swirl of names, so that the novel fails to reach the emotional heights of Morrison's best early work, he nonetheless describes it "more articulate than her rich, exhausting *Beloved*." This current reviewer for the *Washington Post* adds that television talk-show host Oprah Winfrey had already tapped *Paradise* to be the next selection for her book club. By 1998 a burgeoning phenomenon in American literary criticism, Oprah.com, in fact, deemed *Paradise* "a bravura performance," its powerful mystery "richly imagined and elegantly composed."[2]

The swelling influence of "Oprah's Book Club" on Morrison readership became apparent when reviewers both professional and amateur mentioned it by name. Heller dubs Morrison "Oprah Winfrey's Favourite Author. (In gratitude for which honor, she has, by the way, made several Papal appearances on Oprah's *Book Club*, delivering gnomic verities about Literature and Life to a slightly confounded, but droolingly reverent studio audience.)" Focusing on the unusual character of the *Paradise* book-club episode, academic critic Timothy Aubry wrote an article for *Modern Fiction Studies* in 2006, explaining how the *Paradise* discussion discloses interpretive inclinations that are broadly characteristic of middlebrow reading culture. Designating Morrison "the patron saint of the Oprah Winfrey Book Club," Keith Phipps observes in an AV Club book review that, as per usual, the author does not make her intentions clear until halfway through *Paradise* but that, also as usual, it becomes clear halfway that "she's doing it very well. If there's a weakness ... it's in the book's sheer abundance"; its "strange satellite[s] aren't treated with quite the intensity of some of Morrison's past creations" so that it "lacks the visceral impact of its predecessors." Phipps concedes, however, that "the historical sweep," which "takes the place of some of the more personal, psychological aspects," compensates for any occasional loss.

Agreeing that casual readers may struggle with *Paradise*, Murline recalls that members of Winfrey's book club resisted even Morrison's most straightforward novel when *Song of Solomon* was introduced—and that Morrison expresses some limited sympathy: "People's anticipation now more than ever for linear, chronological stories is intense because that's the way narrative is revealed in TV and movies. ... But we experience life as the present moment, the anticipation of the future, and a lot of slices of the past." Having learned from the best to tolerate disparagement ("I've stopped dreaming about kneecapping."), Big Papa's granddaughter prefers readers to contend with her prose, not merely revere it. Morrison found herself delightfully surprised while perusing Internet chatrooms devoted to her work: "'The sort of lively, intelligent conversations going on there are something,' she says. 'They *are* articulate about what they loathe.'"

---

2   A recurring monthly segment of *The Oprah Winfrey Show*, "Oprah's Book Club" highlighted novels selected primarily by its television host. Winfrey started the club in 1996; it ended its fifteen-year run, along with *The Oprah Winfrey Show*, on May 25, 2011, having made a significant impact on American readership. Introducing a total of seventy books, it made even obscure titles into bestsellers, increasing sales in some cases by as many as several million copies. Some books, like *Beloved*, were adapted into films.

Paradise Criticism

Nonprofessional reviews on *Paradise* increased in proportion to the expanding popularity of the Internet. Although the *MLA International Bibliography* identifies 176 citations published between 1998 and 2017, only 73 of these are listed as peer-reviewed. The bulk of peer-reviewed comments (62) appeared between 2000 and 2011, with 9 records in 2002 and 8 in 2011; 99 of 176, or 56 percent, of citations that include non-peer-reviewed comments appeared between 2000 and 2008, with a spike of 16 records in 2011 and 20 records from 2013–14. Thirty doctoral dissertations on or including *Paradise* were written between 1999 and 2015, with a third of those generated between 2006 and 2008.

Scholarly attention continued to be concentrated in journals with an American multicultural focus. Of the 73 peer-reviewed responses, 22 (or 30 percent) appear in publications such as the *College Language Association Journal* (2), *MELUS* (4), and especially the *African American Review*, which produced an impressive 16 articles. Purdue's *Modern Fiction Studies* sustained its Morrison contributions with 5 essays. Demographics otherwise pointed South with the *Faulkner Journal* issuing two articles dedicated to William Faulkner's influences on *Paradise*; Johns Hopkins University Press printing an article from *Studies in American Fiction* and one from *College Literature*; one article published in Duke University's *American Literature* and one in its *Twentieth Century Literature*; one in *Studies in the Novel* (University of North Texas); and one in the *South Atlantic Review*. Foreign journals continued to focus on Morrison: the *MLA Bibliography* lists 14 peer-reviewed essays involving *Paradise* in venues from China, England, India, Korea, Spain, and Turkey. Theoretical approaches, described chronologically within each of the following categories, include reader response; new historical/cultural; intertextual; feminist; psychoanalytic; and African American/postcolonial criticism.

Paradise and Reader-Response Criticism

Whereas Charles predicted that Morrison's seventh novel would create a surfeit of feminist reaction, as her books generally do, *Paradise* initially stimulated reader-response criticism, attributable to its provocative race-specific/race-free prose. Peter Kearly, Philip Page, and Linda Krumholz were all immediately intrigued by its opportunities for active construction by interpretive communities. Shortly after its distribution, Kearly credited the frustrations expressed by members of Oprah Winfrey's Book Club to a deliberate tactic on Morrison's part. Citing several readers' displeasure and speculating that rejection of *Paradise*'s "heavy-handed prose and jumpy and hard-to-follow timeline of events" may have led to empty seats at contemporary showings of the film of *Beloved*, Kearly insists that readers are "actually participating in the language of struggling to understand" (9–10) that is Morrison making storytelling arc "toward the place where meaning may lie" (Nobel Lecture 20). With *Paradise*, "the struggle to form mutual communication with the strange and complex and articulate a clearly defined sense of bonding with what the words are conveying is precisely the activity of struggling to form a community where people understand each other and accept differences that the novel's narrative draws" (Kearly 10). In other words, *Paradise* embodies Morrison's challenge for readers to embrace the unfamiliar and relinquish some of the conventional and exclusionary.³

In 2001 Page scrutinized how Morrison's text places heavy interpretive demands on readers even as her plot juxtaposes two opposing sets of characters who frequently [mis]interpret each other. Because she stresses readers' involvement over their enjoyment, she parallels narrative complexities with thematic issues of interpretation: "As the text requires readers' participation by forcing them into complex acts of interpretation, the characters struggle with interpretations of their worlds and each other. All the participants' brows are furrowed in hermeneutic concentration" (638).

And in 2002, Krumholz clarified Morrison's recap of the murder scene in *Paradise* to underscore, as with *Beloved* and *Jazz*, the significance of *Différence et Répétition* (Deleuze). If *Paradise* doubles various scenes, characters, and points of view, which effects a consistent process of repetition with a difference for the reader, it also considers the dangers of repetition if difference is rejected in the name of perfect harmony. Since repetition without a difference maintains itself through rigidity and exclusion, yearning for utopia ironically destroys the ideal it seeks to preserve. As readers are obliged to construct a process of revelation that is "best understood as a vision of the many veils of history, ideology and desire" (21), they come to understand that "Morrison's paradise is not a peaceful utopian moment of eternal sameness; it is a complex, dynamic, and challenging process in which insight informs action and responsibility" (31).

Paradise and New Historical/Cultural Criticism

New historical/cultural critics have produced the bulk of *Paradise* commentary, often related to communal insight. The *MLA Bibliography*'s first peer-reviewed article on the novel, in fact, analyzes its associations between history, memory, and performance. Chiji Akoma argues that *Paradise* "marks Morrison's clearest delineation of the uses of memory in representing the black experience in America, both as an alternative to the privileged medium of writing and to the hegemonic power conferred on written and lineal history" (4). Moving beyond *Beloved*'s nod to the centrality of memory to black consciousness, *Paradise* foregrounds the very process of narrating what is remembered when a communal narrative generated by a common response to a past becomes the catalyst for individual narrative performances that compete for recognition. Town historian Patricia Best finally burns her incomplete genealogical tree project as "Morrison directs her artistic vision

---

3   Lucille Fultz devotes a monograph to uncovering the interplay between differences that unite and divide characters in all of Morrison's novels to *Paradise*.

to the unknown quantity in African American experience, the 'trick' of life that defies any unitary narrative" (23). Rob Davidson goes further to investigate how the Ruby-centered narratives in *Paradise* uphold patriarchy by imposing a "rigidly controlled communal historiography predicated on the subordination of the individual to the group" (356). Proposing the town of Ruby as collective protagonist, Davidson concludes that the town's narrative reply to the Convent massacre, as well as Deacon Morgan's rebirth and Reverend Misner's decision to remain, suggest Ruby's patriarchs can change.

Several cultural critics focus on Morrison's remapped geographies of paradise. Katrine Dalsgård, Marni Gauthier, Channette Romero, and Patricia McKee, for example, examine its presentation of [African] American nationhood. Dalsgård reads Morrison's depiction of a small, western, African American community, "whose contemporary members understand themselves in relation to an historical narrative of ancestral perseverance, idealism and triumph," to deconstruct the American Dream since "the price of Ruby's insistence on maintaining a morally superior master narrative may well be the sacrifice of that very narrative":

> By molding Ruby's self-narrative in the cast of an ancestral heroic commemoration of the success of the community's founding fathers in establishing a covenanted community in an inhospitable western landscape, by dramatizing the angry accusations made by the community's contemporary patriarchs against the younger generations when the discrepancy between its morally superior master narrative and its actual cultural practices becomes too vast to ignore, and by ultimately having Ruby scapegoat a group of unconventional women for its internal problems, Morrison invites us critically to acknowledge the presence of one of the most canonical European American narratives—that of American exceptionalism, in African American discourse. (233–34)

Gauthier, Romero, and McKee agree that, despite its conciliatory conclusion, *Paradise* continues Morrison's efforts to complicate sacred (African) American myths. Gauthier explains that it not only divulges how national history becomes inscribed in the popular imagination as mythic history but also deconstructs founding American master narratives beyond the exceptionalist paradigm. Because violence and exclusivity remain linked to counter-discursive national histories, Morrison, unlike other writers of the exceptionalist tradition, refuses to impose an African American palimpsest upon the American Dream. Locating *Paradise* as the final leg in Morrison's exploration of black identity and community, Romero deems its chief contribution to be making religion and spirituality central to questions of history. As Morrison highlights "the historic importance of Christianity for mainstream American and African-American nationhood and community building," she reveals not only the power of non-institutionalized belief in constructing human communities and worldviews, but also the capacity of story to recommend new ways for disparate peoples to heal, connect, and generate social change.

McKee credits the novel with underwriting Morrison's ongoing reconsideration of American history by inserting a past omitted from the record and raising suppressed enquiries about the exercise of freedom in American cultures. As this critic explores "the radical geographical imaginaries at work in *Paradise*," she examines its revisions to the "spatiality of social meaning" that make the practices of freedom possible. Alluding to Morrison's appeal for spaces free of racial hierarchy in her essay "Home," also published in 1997, McKee clarifies that Morrison locates freedom in a "borderlessness" both conceptual and practical that lies within as well as outside of places, a social space both psychically and physically safe. These "spatializations of freedom reinforce revisions of modernity" proposed by African American cultural theorists, who argue that "concepts and experiences of home cannot be separated from discourses of freedom" (197–98). *Paradise* defines freedom not as moving through space, but as approaching that which occupies space, including plants, animals, and absences, in a manner that renders it safe. Sheri Evans adds in 2013 that, ritualistically inhabited, constructed space comes to appear natural. When we overlook the practical planning involved in its creation, its ideological program often controls how we live in it. Evans treats *Paradise* as Morrison's endorsement of Foucault's non-hegemonic heterotopias, her argument that "a morally defensible ethics of home emphasizes open-ended interpretation and individual agency in resisting and revising programmed space" (381).

Scholars also note the novel's cultural or pop-culture implications. In an article that addresses US domestic policy toward crimes and criminals, Megan Sweeney says that in 1998 the Directors' Review Committee of the Texas prison system banned *Paradise* from Texas prisons in the belief that its historical references to whites' oppression of blacks is "designed to achieve a breakdown of prisons" by inciting riots. Sweeney believes, however, that Morrison's novel indirectly contributes to prison abolitionism as it "foregrounds the historical and ongoing ways in which racial and economic inequalities contribute to highly disproportionate rates of incarceration for poor people and people of color" (40–41). Sharon Jessee provides information and images detailing what is now called the black town movement of the American West, within which Morrison situated *Paradise*. As Jessee juxtaposes its complexities with critical and popular texts about the all-black towns, she concludes that *Paradise* "constructs an imaginative historiography which nevertheless yields significant perspectives for the study of non-fictional accounts—from academic to personal ones—of the intersections between race, class, gender, and citizenship; between identity and entitlement; and between community and memory" (87).

Susan Mayberry explains that, because they take experience ever so seriously as strictly black or white, *Paradise*'s controversial male characters categorize women into telling binaries: provocative prey or pedestal adornment (2010). Its abusive husbands, absent fathers, untrue lovers, stalkers, rapists, manipulators, and molesters also suggest types from American frontier pop culture. The lone rangers, paladins, and good/bad/ugly hombres in *Paradise* allude respectively to a long-running radio and 1950s black-and-white TV western (*The Lone Ranger*); to the gentleman gunfighter/frontier knight Paladin from the 1960s television western *Have Gun—Will Travel*; and to the most successful of Clint Eastwood's 1960s "Spaghetti Western" films (*The Good, the Bad and the Ugly*), all of which associate masculinity with aggression. *Paradise*'s urban cowboys/mystical horse whisperers reflecting titles of 1980s/90s movies, the edgy urban cowboy takes a top-down attitude while the horse whisperer gentles his charges; both approaches nonetheless use dominance or manipulation to control. The black men who wash out of *Paradise*'s light/dark negative and are "'brought to you in living color'"[4] retain or regain their sense of humor, find their balance connected to a feminine flexibility, and unsettle the violent frontier ("Putting Down" 86).

A quartet of critics focus on *Paradise*'s revelations about current events. Observing that it illuminates the historical coincidence of two national political texts regulating intimate life in the postwar US (the landmark Supreme Court decision in *Griswold v. Connecticut* and a document issued by the Department of Labor known as "the Moynihan report"), Eden Osucha considers the novel to be "Morrison's most forceful rejoinder to the report's legacies" (2015, 257). Daniel Grausam insists that a complete account of *Paradise*'s allegorical content must add its complex assessment of contemporary foreign relations to prior studies examining its appraisal of American settlement myths and Black Nationalism. To cope with what he deems the "hostile takeover" of family values by the radical religious right, resulting in an "ethico-spiritual predicament," Johnny Griffith sees *Paradise* as a model for "embracing the challenges of living morally in this new milieu"—for developing "a readiness to live with uncertainty, ambiguity, and differences of opinion, navigating and negotiating rather than simply negating such differences by refusing to play if *we* can't make the rules" (583). Finally, Mark Tabone links its exploration of utopia with the novel's publication on the threshold of a new millennium and a new emphasis on globalization, arguing that Morrison dedicates its critique to showing readers how past modes of imagining and representing utopia were pathologically insufficient, her evaluation occurring at an historical juncture when that form has reached its limits.

If *Paradise*'s first peer-reviewed article took a new historicist turn, so did its latest. With interpretations ranging from counter-narrative to the contemporary Black Nationalism that victimized black women and to allegorical representation of the United States's economic policy regarding its third-world neighbors, Ubaraj Katawal's 2017 essay wonders that none of these notes the legacy of the Enlightenment in the men's action against their Convent neighbors. Referring specifically to the work of Max Horkheimer and Theodor Adorno, who clarify that the

---

4   Mayberry notes that the first American color television broadcasts began with this announcement and a still frame of the NBC peacock, in 1957 gloriously animated. Morrison associates American masculinity with violent competition and the desire for luxurious safety represented by the bejeweled tail-spread of a male peacock as early as *Song of Solomon* (1977) when Guitar exhorts Milkman to eat the white bird.

logic behind the Enlightenment project relies on the will to control and contain, Katawal believes that "the seeds of the domination of others can be traced back in the mythic and magic world of the pre-Socratic times" (34).

Paradise and Intertextual Criticism

Twenty-first-century scholars have cited *Paradise*'s numerous allusions to texts classical and contemporary. Jennie Joiner declares that despite Morrison's stated uncertainty about Faulkner's influence on her writing, both Morrison and Faulkner critics "have established that his work has in fact 'challenged and nurtured' hers" even as her work has "enlightened understanding of his" (53). Joiner and Jill Jones propose discernible dialogues between Faulkner's *Go Down, Moses* and *Absalom, Absalom!* and *Paradise*. More specifically, Joiner maintains that by expounding on the themes of the former in *Paradise*— "such as relinquishment and preservation of heritage, withdrawal and social seclusion in response to racial trespasses, and fear of miscegenation—Morrison fills in gaps and reimagines alternative viewpoints of black masculinity" (53) while Jones argues that we can read *Paradise* as a reworking of *Absalom, Absalom!*, especially in its style and emphasis on empire building.

Susan Mayberry locates a literary relationship between Morrison and Joyce Carol Oates. A Princeton University colleague of Oates from 1989 to 2006, Morrison would have undoubtedly read Oates's often anthologized short story "Where Are You Going, Where Have You Been?" in which Arnold Friend pays a call on fifteen-year-old Connie. Although *Paradise* converts adolescent female reveries into those of menopausal women (one called Connie), both writers convey the desire for doppelgangers that comes from feeling foreign at home. All mysterious strangers, the *Paradise* friends riff on aspects of Arnold, whom Oates based on a 1960s serial killer: his shaggy hair, mirrored sunglasses, striking footwear, knowing ways, and musical language. Because she feels like an outsider in her own body, alienated from family and friends, Oates's white girl longs for the dangerous freedom offered by a destructive male. Learning painfully that "most scary things is inside," Morrison's black women, on the other hand, accept the blissfully impermanent home within themselves as they embrace their benign opposites ("Everything about" 39).

Morrison's observations about displacement enabled burgeoning criticism on African American-South African and black-Indian literature. Native American scholar Craig Womack singles out *Paradise*, set in Indian Territory and recalling the history of African American self-rule towns, to "advance new methods for studying the intersections of African American and Native American representations in both fiction and criticism." While he acknowledges some recent studies that construe *Paradise*'s treatment of Native characters as affirmations of Native culture, Womack notices the tensions between African Americans and Native Americans inside and outside of Morrison's work. His position lies "somewhere in between dismissal of Morrison for missing the boat on Indians and ecstasy over any mention of Native people whatsoever, no matter the quality of her depictions" (20).

Two final intertextual analyses link Morrison with Thomas Pynchon and William Carlos Williams. David Schell maintains that both *Paradise* and Pynchon's *Mason & Dixon* are preoccupied with time—as they query whose time it is and how we use it. Succeeding other works by these writers about history, communities, and foundational narratives, *Paradise* and *Mason & Dixon* share a "hyperawareness" of the issues that is atypical for the 1990s. During a period where ideologies deem history exhausted, in cultural spheres that "petrify it for the purposes of commodification," Morrison and Pynchon wonder about the critical human factor prompting history's dynamic possibilities (92).

Calling up the "patient eye" required of Morrison readers, Jason Barr looks to a single reference, the town where Mavis's mother lives, to pronounce *Paradise* Morrison's reply to Williams's *Paterson*: "There are so many resemblances that *Paterson* can be considered as a 'father' text to *Paradise*" and *Paradise* as a "metatextual feminist response to *Paterson*." Barr claims that juxtaposing these works not only encourages us to explore the rich intertextuality of both but also clarifies that *Paradise* is Morrison's attempt to critique and amend Williams's sometimes contradictory views in *Paterson* on the forging of identity, gender, and historical narrative. Morrison not only "returns a wholly feminine identity to her own female characters, but perhaps to the female characters in *Paterson* as well" (421–22, 432).

Paradise and Feminist Criticism

As with Barr's analysis, *Paradise*'s feminist appraisal is often subsumed by other critical schools. Nevertheless, twenty-first-century essays by Magali Michael, Justyna Sempruch, Carola Hilfrich, Stéphane Robolin, Majda Atieh, Deborah Mix, Sarah Aguiar, and Kristin Distel suggest unique directions for feminist inquiry. Pointing out that the prevailing conception of coalition politics has been masculinized, Michael states that *Paradise* alternatively "explores coalition processes that are more accommodative, caring, and loving, rather than exploitative, and that are aimed principally at survival and at moving toward a new, alternative form of non-hierarchical justice, rather than at maximizing power and winning" (643–44). Referring to theorists Julia Kristeva and Catherine Clément, Sempruch considers the subversive household a locus of spirituality and the political influence of mothering—as the home of female drifters and cultural transgressors counters the traditional exclusion of women from the sociopolitical power structures and reinscribes phallocentric authority with spiritual values of the maternal. In her assessment of mother and sibling relationships, Distel posits ways in which the attachment between sisters is a privileged relationship that provides a love that mothers fail to give.

Hilfrich discusses the novel's critique of covenanted politics, focusing on the experience of being excluded from a given social contract, and the challenge to seek out partners and sites for an alternative sociomoral bond, in this case a "blessed malelessness" (177). Appearing in *Modern Fiction Studies* together with Hilfrich's piece, Robolin's essay highlights *Paradise* and Zoë Wicomb's *David's Story* as part of a transnational black feminist literary tradition. As she offers examples in which women and memory in both texts represent potential threats to stabilized order and established truth, Robolin notes that the management of collective memory peculiarly resembles the containment of women in racialized societies like the United States and South Africa.

Atieh compares *Paradise* to a "harem narrative" celebrating the mystical Islamic theosophy that forefronts orality and invites a constant pursuit toward divine discovery and freedom from human limitations. Examining Sufi subtexts in *Paradise* allows us to comprehend female empowerment from an Islamic perspective that focalizes women's resistance and liberation. After she scrutinizes Western culture's "tendency to ascribe superiority to a construction of spirit that detaches it from the body," most insistently enforced "in relation to bodies that are female and/or non-white," Mix attributes *Paradise*'s catastrophic violence and suffering to efforts to uphold the (false) opposition between body and spirit, and defines the necessary work of Morrison's paradise as the dismantling of the binary. Countering Justine Tally's conclusion that "Consolata finally adopts a fusion of the spirit and the flesh in her search [with the women] for wholeness and integrity" (17), Aguiar contends that *Paradise* ultimately argues for a division of body and soul. As the inhabitants of Ruby—and its female double— "deny the processes of death and regeneration" and refuse to let time soften the edges of history's indignities, Morrison demonstrates unequivocally that "the acceptance of mortality is a critical aspect of life's and death's journeys" (513).

Paradise and Psychoanalytic Criticism

Psychoanalytic criticism on *Paradise* accentuates its recommended treatments of individual and cultural divides. Keren Omry explains that, since Morrison realizes the trauma of loss makes impossible a return to the state of innocence, she turns to a "free jazz" aesthetic as the only medium that enables movement beyond the social and individual paralysis of history; she rewrites the concentration on loss/absence/trauma into a new utopian vision that reconfigures racial and ethnic ideologies (2007). As Gurleen Grewal approaches *Paradise* via Dominick La Capra's theories about trauma and healing, she observes how the Convent women work out and through the violence of their past (Fultz, ed.).

Reminding us that Morrison's critics often disregard methods of investigation apart from identity politics and postmodernist cultural critique, James Mellard finds in Žižek's post-Lacanian examination of the concept of fantasy another productive path into her novels. Proposing the concept of Lacanian fantasy, which divides the subject but also protects it against the real, as fundamental to all psychical work, Mellard declares that as we "once used myth and related concepts, we now may use fantasy more deeply to explore elements of culture, such as political ideology, and those features of characterization, such as sexuality—and more— often made fully accessible only through psychoanalysis" (466). In a second essay about *Paradise*'s projection of ideological fantasy, Mellard identifies its Other with Žižek's figure of the "conceptual Jew," the "fantasmatic Jew of the anti-Semite": "The Jew thus stands for all those figures of alien others who block our fulfillment within a social structure.... As Morrison suggests of 'paradise,' the obstacle to fulfillment, in society as in the subject, always already exists. The obstacle comes first. The need to rationalize it comes second. The Jew serves as that rationalization in fantasy and ideology" (351).

Paradise and African American/Postcolonial Criticism

Scholarship based on postcolonial and critical race theoretical outlooks appeared early and stayed late in *Paradise*'s critical reception history. Both Ana María Fraile-Marcos and Cynthia Dobbs defer to postcolonial theorist Homi Bhabha. Drawing on his notion of mimicry as resistance to explain Ruby's manifestation of the Puritans' "City upon a Hill," Fraile-Marcos concludes that, despite its efforts to preserve a homogeneous cultural identity, Ruby exemplifies Bhabha's definition of nation as a "'heterogeneous, changeable grouping, ambivalent in its constitution, split by otherness within, and hybridized at its every contact with the Other (over)lapping its borders'" (4). Dobbs turns to Bhabha's ideas about the meanings of home for the exiled: recognizing a true sense of home by its absence and acknowledging that "a physical house does not guarantee a sense of safety and belonging, with every domestic space remaining vulnerable to 'history's invasions.'" Morrison's *Paradise* "amplifies and extends Bhabha's perspective, giving the theme of an 'unhomely' domestic space her own African Americanist, feminist, and womanist twist" (111). Situating the novel specifically within the context of westward expansion and perceiving *homesteading* as "a euphemism for settler colonialism," Holly Flint analyzes *Paradise*'s comments on black cultural citizenship in the American empire (585). Lastly, Richard Schur locates it in the post-civil-rights era by categorizing its place within contemporary debates about the legacy of the movement: "*Paradise* is but one instance of an ongoing conversation among critical race theorists about the possibility of social, cultural, and legal reform" (276).

African American criticism embraces the novel's attitudes toward black masculinity, the ancestor, spirit work, and inter-intra-racial politics. Andrew Read contends that, as it reenacts the efforts of African American men to establish their masculinity under extreme pressure, *Paradise* "also enacts Morrison's own struggle to articulate black masculinity in ways that reveal problems of patriarchal concepts of manhood without reproducing racist stereotypes." Rejection from Fairly, OK, becomes enduringly unendurable for Ruby's patriarchs because it "profoundly challenged their concept of what it means to be a man, a concept grounded in white American ideals of masculinity" (528). Using as his point of reference Morrison's essay "Rootedness: The Ancestor as Foundation," Timothy Robinson relies on the ancestor figure in *Paradise* to initiate classroom discussions about African American culture. He agrees with Morrison that the fictional ancestor is "an indispensable presence that determines the success or failure of the central character" and "creates a space for interrogating generational influences and examining tensions that arise from the relationship between the past and the present" (41).

Katherine Bassard and Melanie Anderson address aspects of African American spirituality. To deal with the dilemma she calls "the problem of justice and the sign of the cross," in which "African Americans that reembody the cross with a black messiah find themselves performing a counter-Reformation move that cuts across the central tenets of Protestantism," Bassard believes *Paradise*'s engagement with Christianity evidences a historical "shift in the figuration of the Cross from a more orthodox African American Protestantism to a displacement of its meanings out onto the African American (women's) community itself" (98). As she demonstrates that Morrison's fiction not only recovers black histories ignored by dominant Western traditions but also uncovers those memories, practices, and desires that have remained undocumented, Anderson focuses on *Paradise*'s place and purpose within contemporary haunted literature, the spirit story as challenging alternative to "official" history.

Finally, Candice Jenkins and Dana Williams adopt an African American critical approach to deconstruct black intra(inter)racial politics. Jenkins remains surprised that critics who have concentrated on *Paradise* as commentary on various interracial issues have overlooked its quintessentially intra-racial questions about black racial loyalty and the internal complexities of African American identity. She reads the novel "as precisely what it seems to be: that is, a deeply flawed model of African American community building, driven by what is undeniably a black nationalist impulse." Ultimately, *Paradise* reminds us that in the United States the concept of a monoracial blackness "holds within itself the notion of interracial contact and (acknowledged or unacknowledged) kinship, sexual and domestic overlap and confusion" (274, 290).

Williams remains convinced that, because they mirror white American character so obviously, the coal-black patriarchs of Ruby are little more than white men in blackface. When considered through the lens of blackface minstrelsy, *Paradise* corroborates that neither blackness nor whiteness is a fixed biological category, rather an effected social construction so unstable that it often collapses under pressure. Even as studies of the content, music, and social setting of minstrel shows indicate that they served to assuage cultural anxieties, false identities arising and ultimately dissolving in response to the presence, transgression, and containment of fear, reading Morrison's novel through its contemporary engagement with blackface divulges "the truth that minstrelsy inadvertently discloses—all that is constructed can, as easily, be deconstructed." Hence, "the only indelible and, arguably, significant identity is that of humanness" (198).

Coda: "Recitatif" (1983)

"Recitatif" can be viewed as a dress rehearsal for Morrison's appropriation of language in *Paradise*.[5] Because "Recitatif" signals a new way to read, its brief literary critical history can be contained within a close reading of the short story.[6] Critiquing her 1983 text as an "experiment in the removal of all racial codes from a narrative about two characters of different races for which racial identity is crucial," she remarks in the 1992 Preface to her lectures on literary criticism: "The kind of work I have always wanted to do requires me to learn how to maneuver ways to free up language from its sometimes sinister, frequently lazy, almost always predictable employment of racially informed and determined chains" (*Playing in the Dark* xi).

Since most critics have answered Morrison's call to focus on the unfastening of racial fetters as the primary way to understand the text, criticism regarding "Recitatif" often interprets the desire to assign races to the protagonists as reflection of readers' own preoccupation with racial categorization. Marie Knoflíčková claims that "the centrality of racial identity to one's personal identity is questionable as there are no objective foundations for drawing the color line"; Morrison's story accordingly "challenges readers' preconceptions about race" (22–23). Insisting that morality is predicated on an acting subject, Miehyeon Kim maintains that "Recitatif's" ambiguity allows the gift of sympathy. Trudier Harris suggests that its readers join the characters "in being placed in positions that border upon voyeurism. We watch characters being shut out of one another's lives even as we are titillated by the events of those lives.... Readers of 'Recitatif' reach again

---

5   Kathryn Nicol records Morrison's similar treatment of racially ambiguous characters in "Recitatif" and *Paradise*. Her 2002 book article contends that the questions of racial identity in Morrison's texts "deliberately place the reader in a position of doubt rather than mastery, a position which forces self-consciousness into the reading process" (209–10). The French form of *recitative*, even Morrison's title underscores the in-between: a style of musical declamation that hovers between song and ordinary speech.

6   "Recitatif" is one of two short stories ever issued by Morrison. Intended as a screenplay requested for but rejected by two actresses—one black, one white—Morrison "eliminated color altogether, using social class as a marker" because she "didn't know which actress would play which part" (*The Origin* 52). She converted the material into the short story first published in *Confirmation: An Anthology of African American Women* (1983), a collection edited by Amiri Baraka and his wife, Amina Baraka. MLA cites only twelve academic articles and eight book chapters on the piece, with Elizabeth Abel's 1993 essay marking the defining moment of "Recitatif," like that of *Paradise*, as an attempt to discern which girl is white.

and again for the racial markers that will enable them to familiarize characters into the racial pigeonholes with which they are most comfortable, while those characters keep slipping... just out of our grasp.... What we think we know, or what we may want to know, may guide our reading responses, but an elusive, unknowable quality still holds sway" (103–4).

Consequently, as they do with the white girl in *Paradise*, some critics concede that it is impossible to assign race conclusively; others wonder initially and then abandon the question for another tack.[7] Susana Morris is among the few who argue that "the imperative to go through the motions of assigning (or attempting to assign) race to the characters, only to decide (in most cases) that their race is indeterminable, promotes a sort of tunnel vision" (163). Morrison might call it a lazy eye. If she defines one of the most demanding aspects of her job as deconstructing racial signifiers and replacing them with alternate indicators, she certainly expects readers to go the distance to sort out the signs.

She also contends that, since "everything leads to something else," the writer must "know everything" about the site she's constructing: "I have to know how far things are. I have to know what color green their curtain is. I have to know the name of all those tools. I have to know what the name of the railroad was. Everything. So it's all details that contribute to the authenticity and the credibility of the period" (Spain 2:55). She relates working extensively on several scenes in *Paradise* "to make sure that the palette was right, that the same colors that were in the scene were also in another scene": It "may not look comparable in terms of the two scenes," and "the reader may not even know that they're getting the nature

---

[7] If James Phelan illustrates how rhetorical and cognitive theorists can collaborate to show that Morrison constructs a single narrative and uses racial politics to deny our access to part of it, Helane Androne and Javier Monzón adopt purely psychoanalytic approaches. Androne determines the protagonists to be trapped in traumatic mothering situations that reveal an absence/presence paradigm. In his 2016 conference paper ("'I Wonder What Made Me Think You Were Different': A Relevance-Theoretic Account for an Interpretation of 'Recitatif' by Toni Morrison"), presented at the international Poetics and Linguistics Association, Monzón defines "Recitatif" as a short story of childhood trauma. Howard Sklar, Sandra Stanley, Robyn Warhol, and Amy Shuman consider the text's contributions to disability studies. Sklar argues that "Recitatif" "makes a significant move in guiding readers toward a more complex view of Maggie's identity, as well as a level of sympathetic engagement that effectively transcends her apparently prosthetic function" (Abstract). Stanley adds that "Morrison's narrative invites an exploration of the intersecting identity markers associated with disability and race, as well as a critique of the social processes and practices that shape these constructs" (72). Warhol and Shuman merge linguistic and literary feminist narratologies to demonstrate how, "instead of ending on a 'relatable' epiphany, 'Recitatif' presents two protagonists ashamed of their failure to read disability (or even to have understood that disability is neither self-evident nor transparent), just as the story's readers are shamed for their assumption that race shouldn't need to be read, because—as the narrator's silences imply—it supposedly goes without saying" (Abstract).

of the comparison because I have painted them that way.... But I do believe that because I painted the scenes the same colors, there's this sort of undertow or urtext" (Denard 176–77).

In both *Paradise* and "Recitatif," we need to unearth the details and then test Morrison's currents for undertow. Not all critics agree that race is unknowable in the short story. David Goldstein-Shirley, for example, claims that Roberta, "as the master storyteller, is black" (89), with Ann Rayson asserting that "Morrison makes Roberta wealthy and black to overturn our class assumptions" (41). Goldstein-Shirley adds that Morrison's collective tactics of "eliminating explicit racial labels, bracketing gender to focus exclusively on race, using ... an African-American storytelling tradition in order to train the reader to become a competent hearer, and staging within the text the extratextual debate about desegregation" enable the reader to "become an accomplice in the deconstruction of racism" (95).

Ultimately concluding that Morrison's project is not about assigning race but rather about readers recognizing their own possible desire for a more transparent racial taxonomy, Elizabeth Abel deals with her indecisiveness about capsizing the intentional fallacy by writing to Morrison:

> Her response raised as many questions as it resolved. Morrison explained that her project in this story was to substitute class for racial codes in order to drive a wedge between these typically elided categories. Both eliciting and foiling our assumption that Roberta's middle-class marriage and politics, and Twyla's working-class perspective, are reliable racial clues, Morrison incorporated details about their husbands' occupations that encourage an alternative conclusion. If we are familiar (as I was not) with IBM's efforts to recruit black executives and with the racial exclusiveness of the firemen's union in upstate [Newburgh] New York, where the story is set, we read Roberta as middleclass black and Twyla as working-class white. Roberta's resistance to bussing, then, is based on class rather than racial loyalties. (476)

Arguing that twentieth-century criticism "reifies readings of 'Recitatif' along racial binaries by focusing on the racial codes that supposedly label Twyla and Roberta as white or black," Shanna Benjamin believes scholars like Abel, Rayson, and Goldstein-Shirley "miss the brilliance of Morrison's experiment." By challenging race as a literary trope, Morrison deconstructs the black-and-white of the story "to reveal the limitations of America's rigid racial discourse." The narrative that defies classification and suggests the requisites for interracial humanist connection rests in between that of Twyla and Roberta. The story of Maggie, "the 'kitchen woman' who functions as an imperfect yet 'archetypal mother figure,'" embodies the elusive truth behind Twyla and Roberta's traumatic pasts and inspires them to "collaboratively rewrite their shared history" (88–91). In other words, as with *Paradise*, Morrison aims for the possibilities both inside and out there.

Ivan Delazari cautions us that "we have to face the fact that responsibility for attaching racial tags to the characters is ours rather than the text's (or 'reality's')

... since Morrison's point is to reveal how much racist stereotyping there is in the reader's head and how superfluous this stereotyping is. Having made up our minds after recognizing certain details of a character's looks or behavior as the clue, we are repeatedly forced to question our view when new contradictory evidence appears, then return to the former piece of information and see how it did not really exclude the alternative solution, and thus was perhaps no 'clue' at all. No matter whether we decide to cancel an earlier conviction, stick to it, or refrain from judgment altogether, we need to consider not so much the text's deliberate controversy as our own grounds for reading race through cultural and social stereotyping" (199–200).

While we decide on which is the true reading, then, intentional fallacy and reification vie with Morrison's account of herself as "a very controlling person" vis-à-vis her work (Spain 00:23:50). If we take her at face value, "Recitatif's" vital sign unveiling racial identity turns out to be nothing less or more than dusting powder.[8] Mentioning that "every now and then [her mother] would stop dancing long enough to tell [her] something important," Twyla helps us connect two essential identifiers with Mother Mary's active olfactory sense: one is racist but unreliable, and one is reliable but frees up language from its lazy and predictable employment of racially determined chains.

Because Morrison has neither named nor coded her race, Mary's description of "them" smelling "funny" calls up either racist white disdain of black "funk" or racist black disdain of white "nastiness" (438). The twice-repeated reference to Mary's heavy use of sweet-smelling Lady Esther dusting powder, however, plus its association with white apple blossoms accentuate Morrison's avowed fondness for "dusting off" clichés, help to establish the urtext, and infer Mary as white. Though Delazari insists, "It is not that no clues are given; on the contrary, there seem to be too many textual cues, all contingent, insufficient and indecisive" (199–200), putting Bridal Pink Lady Esther dusting powder on a black woman's skin would be as disturbingly shocking as giving a little black girl blue eyes.

From the beginning Morrison has applied cosmetics to character, imagery, theme, symbol, and sociopolitics. Openly resistant to the sixties "Black is Beautiful" mantra, on grounds that waving the flag of this fact deprives it of its obvious truth, she had long assimilated what a lengthy bus tour of the vibrant African and African American scene in Paris taught Toni Morrison Society members during their Sixth Biennial Conference in November, 2010, when Morrison was made an officer in the French Legion of Honor: skincare products for black people were accessible enough in the early twentieth century that an African American female would not wear Lady Esther. Established circa 1908, Château d'Eau in the 10th arrondissement remains a flourishing commercial district specializing in an astonishing array of hairdressing and cosmetics for dark skin.

---

8   Thanks be unto Lib Hayes for this insight.

Morrison's oeuvre also uncovers black American cosmetic availability. The first female self-made millionaire in America, known as Madam C. J. Walker (1867–1919), was an African American entrepreneur and philanthropist, who made her fortune by developing and marketing a line of beauty and hair products for black women under the company she founded in 1910, Madam C. J. Walker Manufacturing Company.[9] Walker's birth name, (Sarah) Breedlove, appears as the surname of the black family convinced of their unique ugliness in *The Bluest Eye*. Having linked the pernicious impact of cosmetics with destructive ideals about physical beauty and romantic love in that first novel, and via Hagar in *Song of Solomon* and Jadine in *Tar Baby*, Morrison calls up this literary trope again in her last book, *God Help the Child* (2015).

Founded by Syma Cohen and her siblings in 1913, the Lady Esther Company was incorporated in Illinois in 1922 to become America's top-selling brand of cosmetics for white women. Capitalizing on the publicity of national radio broadcasting, Lady Esther, Ltd. sponsored a live CBS Radio series in 1941, "The Orson Welles Show," also known as "The Lady Esther Show." After Welles's ill-fated filming trip to Brazil stalled his career, Lady Esther sought another prestigious broadcast to showcase its products, settling on the Screen Guild Theater, sponsored by Gulf Oil. The Lady Esther Screen Guild Theater brought movies to radio from 1942 to 1947, with segments starring popular white actors such as Ingrid Bergman, Humphrey Bogart, James Cagney, Bing Crosby, and Dinah Shore. Hence, even if we agree with Benjamin that "What the hell happened to Maggie?" is central, not peripheral to "Recitatif," it is clear that with respect to a text wherein she privileges race yet removes stereotypical racial codes, Morrison expects us to pay attention to the crucial yet less obvious identification signs she has substituted (453). In other words, our sign won't make sense without hers. If Morrison successfully generated new strategies to replace the old racial "shortcuts," we can't be lazy about language either. Dismissing generalizations about black people as "burdensome," she asks readers to sort through the racial designations in "Recitatif" so that we can more readily locate the significance of class affiliations. She likewise disrupts racial stereotyping in *Paradise*, as she provides multiple identifiers simultaneously. Not signaling race frees her "to talk about the characters in all sorts of ways" so that while "the reader knows that the majority of those women are black, they just don't know which ones." By paying attention to to her emphatic codicil, "*I know*," however, and to her self-acknowledged perfectionism, we know that we can realize what Morrison knows via a close reading of her non-racial routes and the literary critical history of her oeuvre (Denard 166).

---

9 In 2020 Netflix released an eight-episode historical TV drama *Self-Made: Inspired by the Life of Madam C. J. Walker*, with Octavia Spencer in the title role.

CHAPTER EIGHT

LOVE (2003)

Love's Critical History as Told by Toni Morrison

Having functioned as a primary source for both *Beloved* and *Paradise*, *The Black Book* provided an equally vital absence in the literary critical history of Morrison's eighth novel, *Love*. Jettisoned in 2009, the foreword to *The Black Book*'s composite record of African American experience, which Morrison solicited from private collectors and coedited, was authored in 1974 by then adored African American comedian/actor Bill Cosby, the odds-on prototype for *Love*'s Bill Cosey: friend, father, philanthropist, phantom, pedophile, and "*ordinary man ripped, like the rest of us, by wrath and love*" (*Love* 200).[1]

As L, the priestly woman in the chef's hat at pre-integration Cosey's Hotel and Resort, concludes about her charismatic, deeply flawed employer, "*You could call him a good bad man, or a bad good man. Depends on what you hold dear ...*" (200). Likewise, Bill Cosby's productive career and positive image were irreparably damaged in the mid-2010s amid numerous highly publicized sexual assault allegations, the earliest of which date back decades. More than sixty women have accused him of rape, drug-facilitated sexual assault, sexual battery, sexual misconduct, and child sexual abuse, although the statute of limitations was expired in nearly all claims.

A popular stand-up comic during the 1960s, Cosby acquired a part in *I Spy*, the first weekly dramatic television series to feature an African American in a starring role, followed by his own sitcom, *The Cosby Show*, which was ranked America's number one comedy program from 1984 through 1989. Like Cosey a highly successful, hands-on advocate for family-oriented entertainment, Cosby coproduced the series, retained creative control, and involved himself in all aspects

---

1   Mayberry's chapter 9, note 9 in *Can't I Love What I Criticize?* (2007) suggests Bill Cosby as a possible contemporary source for Bill Cosey.

of production. His special interest in educating poor black children akin to *Love*'s Heed-the-Night Johnson continued with the "Fat Albert" character developed during his stand-up routines. His 1976 doctoral dissertation involved the use of the Saturday-morning cartoon based on his childhood, *Fat Albert and the Cosby Kids*, as a teaching tool in elementary schools. Vida Gibbons's comment about Cosey applies equally to Cosby: "His pleasure was in pleasing" (33).

Cosby's various pleasures earned him numerous awards, including a Presidential Medal of Freedom from George W. Bush; he was included in a scholarly book, *The 100 Greatest African Americans*. When he was convicted of three counts of aggravated indecent assault and given a prison sentence, however, over fifty of Cosby's more than seventy honorary degrees were rescinded, along with his Kennedy Center Honor and his Mark Twain Prize for American Humor. His honorary appointment as Chief Petty Officer was revoked by the US Navy. As with Cosey, Cosby's defenders include his wife, who equates him to a "lynching victim" convicted by "mob justice" ("Bill Cosby's wife") and female coworkers, one of whom maintains: "What you're seeing is the destruction of a legacy. And I think it's orchestrated. I don't know why or who's doing it, but it's the legacy. And it's a legacy that is so important to the culture." *The Cosby Show* "represented America to the outside world. This was the American family. And now you're seeing it being destroyed. Why?" ("Phylicia Rashad"). *Love* not only forecasts answers to this question but predicted the question itself.

Most significant to Morrison's critical life, and to *Love*'s critical reception history, Random House issued a 35th-anniversary edition of *The Black Book* in 2009, "with a new Foreword by Toni Morrison." When Morrison Society members queried her during their 2016 conference "Toni Morrison and Her Role as Editor" about the deletion of the original Cosby foreword, Morrison admitted that she objected to such deliberate alterations of history but relented to keep *The Black Book* in print. In her 2007 book on Morrison and the masculine, which notes the resemblances between Cosey and Cosby, Susan Mayberry highlights L's ironic practicality when she confesses to killing Bill Cosey because she "*Had to*" (200)—even as L[ove] reveals that Bill "*helped more colored people here than forty years of government programs*" (9).[2]

If Morrison locates in *Paradise* an innovative language for relaying America's history of race by ignoring racial signifiers, *Love*, its 2005 foreword identifying its subjects only by gender, enables her to find inventive, often subversive expressions of love. Its commentary on the destruction of a black male legacy focuses on the fall-out: battered African American females, incandescent children turned prematurely by abuse into pessimistic old souls. A "mournful sympathy" infecting the distant smile of the pretty twelve-year-old who is indifferent to boys and

---

[2] Other of *Love*'s multiple ironies find Phylicia Rashād, who played Claire Huxtable on *The Cosby Show*, a 1970 magna cum laude graduate of Morrison's alma mater, Howard University, as well as a former member of the Toni Morrison Society's Board of Directors.

whom Morrison resurrects from her childhood to prepare us for the irretrievable losses exposed in *Love*, the "She" in *Love*'s foreword becomes any girl betrayed by adult sexuality: "Before we even knew who we were, someone we trusted our lives to could, might, would make use of our littleness, our ignorance, our need, and sully us to the bone, disturbing the balance of our lives as theirs had clearly been disturbed" (x).

As with eleven-year-old Pecola's repeated rapes in *The Bluest Eye* by the dangerously free father who "loves her enough to touch her, envelop her, give something of himself to her," such disruptions clearly disturb *Love*'s readers (206). As is generally the case with guilt about not paying attention, much less loving enough, angry gossiping bystanders blame someone else, in most cases the victim's mother. *Love* becomes another Morrisonian attempt to put the blame where it belongs—on unyielding American soil. Denying the claim that she is "always writing about love," Morrison explains that, in fact, she writes about betrayal: "Love is the weather. Betrayal is the lightening that cleaves and reveals it" (foreword x). In *Paradise* she foregrounds intra-racial betrayal; in *Love* it becomes, "And a man's foes *shall be* they of his own household" (Matt 10.36).

Because she enjoyed breaching conventional rules of composition in *Jazz*, Morrison adopts a comparable authorial freedom in *Love* by creating a narrator unrestricted by space or chronology, "or the frontier between life and not-life," who would observe and interrupt the damaged, partially unveiled interior lives of the household. Dedicated to and based like *Paradise* on a powerful elder, *Love* is dominated by a voice who is "For and with [Morrison's grandmother] Ardelia" [R]. The character L[ove] "is meant to exhibit and represent the imaginative and transformative nature of her name along with its constructive and destructive talents" (foreword xi).

Concerned about reception to the rape scene by her "village people," many of whom felt as if they had lived through that destruction, Morrison took tea in Brooklyn with thirteen Mocha Moms, a nationwide support group for at-home, often single parents of color. When the similarly solo parent asks her audience, "So, . . . what did you think?" one mother of two confesses that she became so upset about the book's opening gang-rape scene that she burst into tears: "'It made me reflect on my life and situations where it could have been me,' she tells Morrison. 'You helped me to clear my mind about my own fears, my past, my present, my future. . . . And I am so grateful to you for that.'" Morrison is equally appreciative of her readers: "'They relate. It's all very deeply personal, and that's good. I'm very accustomed to the lit crits (literary critics), which is fine, but this level of reading, which is the first level, is the heart for me.'" Serving during the ninety-minute session as both author and sage, Morrison ultimately reaches the Mocha Moms on both levels. "'She seems to understand the breadth and depth of life,'" one woman says. "'She has such a well-rounded picture of relationships and how they function. . . . We can take what she has written and apply it to our own lives'" ("Morrison Gets").

While Morrison attended to the "bromide" that the bitterest betrayal comes from those closest to the self, or from the self itself, she divulges that she could hardly ignore "the parallels between those specific [character's] lives and wider cultural ones," the ways in which "African Americans handled internecine, intraracial betrayals, and the weapons they chose in order to survive them." In this way, *Love*'s narrative contributes specifically to critical race theory, discussions initiated in the 1970s when the decades-long battle over civil rights, requiring for success like other radical changes mutual respect, ceased to be a political or social force. Because "dissension, healthy or malign, was frequently understood as betrayal, as lethal as apathy," *Love*'s account of the effectual revolt against a common white enemy in the struggle for black integration parallels a story of disintegration, the disruptions in traditional relationships and class alliances that signal both deliverance and separation: "Heed and Christine live in the easy weather of pre-civil rights intimacy until they are explosively interfered with. The fault line between them was drawn by the ability of power to satisfy its whims and ignore the consequences" (foreword xi).

Love teaches us that the terrible personal consequence caused by such systemic betrayal becomes mutual distrust, which, unmonitored, leads to scorn, hatred, self-delusion, illogical exceptionalism, violence, and, most dangerous, the renunciation of a common tongue. When the novel's three generations of female children, emotionally unprotected by adults, lose their innocence and their faith from an absence of parenting, "they give themselves over to the most powerful one they know, the man who looms even larger in their imagination than in their lives" (foreword xii). The arsenal that wards off such Cosey/Cosby manhandling, Morrison asserts, contains weapons of knowledge and communication, in other words requires retrieving and sustaining that shared language.

Love's Initial Critical Reception History and Defining Critical Moments

First reaction to *Love* was positive. *Kirkus Reviews*' introductory description, "A black patriarch's obsessive domination of the many women in his life is relentlessly scrutinized in the 1993 Nobel winner's intricately patterned eighth novel," continues with a comment on the "gorgeous deployment of enigmatic flashbacks" and concludes: "Incorporating elements from earlier Morrison novels (notably *Jazz*, *Paradise*, and *Sula*), *Love* is an elegantly shaped epic of infatuation, enslavement, and liberation: a rich symbolic mystery that grows steadily more eloquent and disturbing as its meanings clarify and grip the reader. One of Morrison's finest, and a heartening return to Nobel-worthy form."

The *New York Times* got second dibs, and Laura Miller's opening becomes an ominous signal of *Love*'s impending critical moment:

> No living writer truly benefits from assuming the leaden mantle of Greatness. The perils are many. It may be that the road of excess leads, as Blake insisted, to

the palace of wisdom, but you can be sure that the road of self-importance does not. Writers seldom do their best work when they've decided they're addressing the ages rather than the reader at their elbow: they nurse misbegotten caprices into full-grown enterprises; they speechify. Readers begin to approach their work outfitted with elaborate prejudices.

Going on to reproach Morrison for all-too-predictably taking the part of "aggrieved" female and African American groups, Miller accuses particularly her "spotty" post-*Beloved* fiction of tilting toward "the grand and the instructional," vulnerable, therefore, to "prostrate worship and gleeful nose-thumbing." The *Salon* critic also recognizes, however, the danger of dismissing Morrison, "even if it does offer the petty satisfaction of sticking two sacred cows—the Nobel committee and multiculturalism—with a single pin," and concedes that she "does her best writing about bad people, and her new novel, *Love*, hooray, has plenty of those." As Miller dismisses the middle-class blacks in Morrison's book, who "lose in vitality, in wildness and perhaps in truth" what they "gain in order, stability and mutual support—no small blessing in a hostile, white-run world," she nonetheless lauds Morrison's notions about love as "nearly classical; the emotion is as much affliction and delusion as joy."

Love prompted misgivings from the international crowd, too, though Anita Sethi's review in the [London] *Observer* is more summary than assessment. Describing love as "conspicuously absent" from Morrison's eighth novel, the word spoken only once by a living person, Sethi notes that the stylistic removal of that emotion "leaves the book lacking in the sustained intensity of *The Bluest Eye* or *Beloved*." Its power lies "in the luminosity and energy of its poetic images, set off against the narrative obscurity and laced with horror and beauty: crayon-coloured dreams, cotton-mouth snakes, collapsing hotel attics, the pervasive smell of cinnamon and citrus."

Writing for the *Guardian*, Elaine Showalter adopts a more caustic tone. Stressing that "No less a literary critic than Morrison herself has pronounced . . . *Love* to be 'perfect,'" Showalter allows that it is, indeed, "a disarmingly compact, unpompous book, less in love with the sound of its own metaphors than Morrison's last novel, *Paradise*." When she compares *Love*'s life history, on the other hand, to others affording "opportunities for rich, sardonic and profound reflection on human experience in the 20th century, beyond nationality, race, sex, age, class, and ethnicity," Showalter contends that "Morrison's imaginative range of identification is narrower by choice; although she would no doubt argue—and rightly—that African American characters can speak for all humanity. But in *Love*, they do not; they are stubbornly bound by their own culture; and thus, while *Love* is certainly an accomplished novel, its perfection comes from its limitation."

The *New York Review of Books* opted for a revival of the positive. Darryl Pickney's inaccuracies and tendency to blame the victims, however, make his essay difficult to endorse. *Love* is set in Florida, not North Carolina, as Pickney states; L's real name is not Estelle; and Bill marries Heed at eleven, not twelve.

While Morrison might agree that the book tells the "tale of a harem's end," she would likely balk at the oversimplification that "mostly, Morrison asks us to think about" women complicit "in their own unhappiness, how ill prepared they were to shape their destinies." We can appreciate, though, Pinkney's praise of "Morrison's straightforward but richly gentle prose" and his pleasure in the effortlessness with which "she merges the threads of her story of damaged women, leftover pals, and newcomers." Razor-sharp observations "hidden in her softest lines," *Love* is "modest in length, but constantly suggestive, a beautiful, haunting work about two wasted lives that also mourns for a certain time in black life."

Love Criticism

Reaction to *Love* marks another watershed in Morrison criticism. The first of four novels published after the *Beloved/Jazz/Paradise* trilogy, it begins a trend of books that are markedly slimmer than their predecessors and, according to some critics, in substance and/or development. Showalter remarks that "In 'Father,' the section mainly devoted to Christine's past, Morrison condenses material that would easily provide a dozen novels for another writer." With increasing Internet ease, layman reviews on *Love* become status quo, starting with its 2003 publication. Keith Phipps, writing for the AV Book Club, refers to it as Morrison's "slim new tour de force," prohibited from being labeled horror fiction only because "horror writers don't win Nobel Prizes." Nevertheless, Phipps concludes, "few writers have such a strong sense of how memories linger in a place, or how the worst bits of the past keep bubbling up into the present. Fewer still have Morrison's gift for conveying the horror of a mind divided against itself."

Representing an "online community for reading groups," Stephen Deusner's generous remark that Morrison "transforms her stories into masterpieces" contrasts with a codicil about *Love*: "Too often Morrison seems too willing to let *Love* descend to the level of 'pointless malice,' which infects her prose and her themes with soap-opera formulas." Like Phipps's piece, Deusner's prose reveals the curious juxtaposition of effusive rhetoric and down-to-earth opinion typical of nonprofessional commentary. Even as Deusner commends Morrison's catalogue of the many forms of love in "a concatenation of elegant structure," he feels "compelled to share [his] impressions of her from the two times [he] was honored to have been in her presence. . . . On the continuum of her work, *Love* is the next logical leap in her immutable search for the answers to the questions of life that interest her."

If the *MLA International Bibliography* identifies a mere 54 citations issued on the novel between 2004 and 2017, only 26 of these are listed as peer-reviewed. Almost half of the peer-reviewed comments (11) appeared between 2005 and 2007, with renewed interest, another 6 records, in 2013/14. Six doctoral dissertations on or including *Love* were written between 2004 and 2012, with 4 of those produced between 2010 and 2012. Scholarly attention began to extend beyond journals with an American multicultural concentration, though *MELUS* provided

1 article and *African American Review* retained domination with 5. *Modern Fiction Studies* continued its ongoing interest in Morrison's work, sponsoring 2 pieces, and a 2013 book edited by Lucille Fultz contains 3 chapters on *Love*. Foreign and online journals increased their percentage of contributions: The *MLA Bibliography* lists 16 essays in venues from England, France, Germany, Korea, Spain, and Taiwan, nearly one-third of the total MLA citations. Published articles and book chapters, abridged here in chronological order, derive primarily from African American/ postcolonial, intertextual, new historical/ cultural, feminist/womanist, psychoanalytic, and structuralist theoretical approaches.

Love and African American/Postcolonial Criticism

The first essay focusing explicitly on *Love* connects it via its water imagery to West African and African American cultures, where water represents a complex symbolic element. Associated with memory, love, and freedom, water tropes in *Love* likewise suggest postmodern ideas about fluidity, instability, dynamism, and potentiality, which subvert fixed, monolithic worldviews and transcend the limits of literary discourse. Susana Vega-González relies once more on African American theory when she proposes another reading of *Love* as a trickster novel. Characterized by ambiguity, indeterminacy and transgression, and pervading Morrison's fiction, the trickster paradigm empowers her challenge to unquestioned univocal concepts and certainties; two of its female characters, Celestial and Junior, reflect Morrisonian tricksters like Pilate or Sula. As a writer of such fiction, Morrison becomes a figurative trickster herself, playing with language and endorsing paradoxes, like those produced by a multidimensional concept of love. Defining the "trickster aesthetic" as both a linguistic and stylistic principle rooted in Black English vernacular as well as a figure emphasizing cure by community, Lily Wang Lei explains how it acts as an agent of memory, which enhances spirituality and healing in *Beloved* and *Love*.

Mar Gallego surveys the disruption to female friendships in *Love* caused by the loss of traditional black communal values. Bill Cosey's life should be interpreted, Gallego asserts, as a "'cautionary lesson in black history'" because he "represents the far-reaching effects of African Americans' adoption of a dominant value system that systematically calls into question the very foundations of the black family and community" (Tally 99). In her edited collection on *Paradise/ Love/A Mercy*, Lucille Fultz introduces Carolyn Denard's chapter as relying on "the leitmotif of silence to examine the role of secrets" in *Love* and, "coextensively, in African American culture" (76). Describing L's embrace of silence as agency rather than disempowerment, Denard calls it "willful resistance and cultural decorum," which can serve both good and ill (79). L's withholding of information from Heed and Christine protects both women while Cosey's clandestine pedophilia destroys their friendship and their childhood.

Since most critics agree that *Love* also "explores the losses that went with the gains brought about by the Civil Rights era," some, including Fultz, scrutinize the novel beneath the lens of critical race theory.[3] As she is driven by a former dancer and "kept woman" to witness "her Houston" along its once "magnificent mile" of Dowling Street, major artery of culture, entertainment, and commerce for the 1950s African American community, Fultz simultaneously re-envisions a thoroughfare once "teeming with some of the 'who's who' in African America" and laments the losses resulting from desegregation/integration. Her memory reminds her that as *Love*'s narrative switches back and forth through its span of approximately sixty years (1930s to 1990s), it, too, reveals the "inexorable but unintended outcomes of civil rights," raising questions about "a unitary vision or a united front within the African American community" and concurrently undermining the notion that "black people were ever of one mind" (94–95).

G. Neelakantan and Sathyaraj Venkatesan concur that in critiquing the American Civil Rights Movement, *Love* "not only reformulates some of the crucial issues that impinge on African-American interests within American politics but also departs significantly from the normative triumphalist discourses of the Civil Rights movement" as it evaluates aspects of the movement that had a devastating impact on the successful pre-World War II black community (139). Susana Morris foregrounds the novel's indictment of paternalistic leadership figures such as Bill Cosey and Fruit, demonstrating that "the consequences of their destructive behavior, especially regarding issues such as rampant classism and unmitigated sexual violence against women and girls, are insidious and far-reaching." *Love* not only participates in contemporary black fiction's engagement with civil rights, then, but presents "a paradigm shift in contemporary delineations of African American leadership"; it encourages us to reject the allure and glamour of charismatic paternalism "in favor of recognizing or resuscitating modes of masculine leadership not built on the nostalgia for an ever-present past or on problematic power dynamics" (320, 335–36).

Love also provided a lobby for diaspora studies. In an attempt to counter accusations of the African American literary canon as merely a response to racial oppression and/or a sociopolitical showcasing of racial achievements, the editors of *Contemporary African American Literature* begin with Houston Baker's argument that *Love* exemplifies a tradition that "cannot be fully understood or appreciated outside of what he refers to as an *oceanic critical consciousness* or a consciousness attuned to the resonances of the transatlantic slave trade and its continuing effects as 'a prerequisite for analyzing Black creativity'" (6). Baker challenges the "intellectual shallowness and implicit critical contempt that are hallmarks of journalistic reviews of Black expressivity," exemplified when Miller, Showalter, and Kakutani mistake modernism for "products of 1920s London intellectuals" instead

---

3   "Toni Morrison: Words of Love." *CBS News* (Apr. 7, 2005).

of "resonances of the Transatlantic Slave Trade's violent concatenations" ("Point of Entanglement" 17–19).[4]

Love and Intertextual Criticism

Anissa Wardi claims that Morrison weaves *Beloved* intertextually into *Love*, "as *Love*/love, linguistically and thematically, are part of *Beloved*/beloved." If a dead baby's ghost embodies the heart of *Beloved*, the murdered dead also occupy center space in *Love*. It becomes the depth of mother love and its manifestation, however, which haunt both novels. Perceiving that we have become numb to the word *love*, Morrison turns to the deed. Substituting hands for speech, *Love* moves us out of the emotional sphere into the material: "Rather than seek love's perfection, Morrison examines love's work, work that renews, recovers, and heals" (201, 215). Benjamin Burr contributes to *Love*'s intertextuality when he concludes that all of Morrison's texts help us "to better understand the Bible and deconstruction." Arguing that by the time she writes *Love*, she "calls into question the relevance of mythological paradigms in general," Burr uses Derrida's second definition of hospitality, which acknowledges the possibility of theft and violation, to explore how *Love* functions as a "deconstructive hermeneutic commentary on Paul's Other-oriented model of love" (Stave 159, 167–68).

Tessa Roynon's intertextual analysis of *Love* underwrites her ongoing study of Morrison and the classics. Reminding us that Morrison was a classics minor at Howard University, Roynon regards Morrison's ambivalent relationship with the classical tradition and revisionary deployment of the cultural practices of ancient Greece and Rome as fundamental to her radical project. Since she "repeatedly subverts the central role that Greece and Rome have played in American self-definition and historiography," it comes as no surprise that *Love* "further develops the transformative engagement with America's Graeco-Roman inheritance" ("A New 'Romen'" 31–32). Structured, like much of Morrison's oeuvre, around acts of rape, unified by anxiety about rape, *Love* demythologizes and reconfigures the history of the country's colonization by comparing its "discovery" to a glorious rape ("Sabotaging" 47). Longtime engaged, like Roynon, with ways in which Morrison's novels represent an extension/subversion of a subject, characterization, and/or themes, John Duvall approaches her texts as "rejoinders to Faulkner's great novel on the 'dark house' of race and family dynasty, *Absalom, Absalom!*" While Faulkner's rendition ends in violence, failure, and tragedy, however, Morrison's

---

[4] Fultz's ". . . Elegy for the African American Community" counters these reviewers' concerns about *Love*'s "slimness" as well by declaring that Morrison achieves its powerful sense of immediacy through "brevity, condensation, and a plethora of allusions" that presume or require the reader's scrutiny, knowledge of cultural and social history, and active participation (96–98). Tessa Roynon allows that because of the complexity of *Love*'s classical references its cup runneth over.

treatments, in *Love* specifically of Christine and Heed, "eventuate in reconciliation, peace, and understanding" (Hamblin 12–13).

Finally, Courtney Thorsson addresses *Love* in the context of black women writers who rework James Baldwin's troubled relationships into "a female critique of heteronormativity," use his "interest in complex relationships among men to explore female coalescence," and create communities that "succeed or fail almost directly according to their ability to make room for romantic relationships among women." (619, 616). After she notes the striking absence of characters in Morrison's early fiction whom we might readily identify as lesbians, and the author's rejection of Barbara's Smith description of *Sula* as a "lesbian novel," Thorsson proposes that *Love*'s Christine and Heed share a "womanbond that proves more important than any other relationships in their lives." Like Baldwin's depictions of "binding, conflicted, and erotic" friendship, the novel's central connection is not a heterosexual marriage, but a complicated tie between women, which makes *Love*, by Smith's definition, a "lesbian novel" (626). Privileging Heed and Christine's bond over men's desires would have protected both from a lifetime of pain and betrayal and provided the basis for a sustaining black community.

Love and New Historical/Cultural Criticism

Brooks Bouson confirms that Morrison retains her familiar role of cultural historian in *Love* by placing the personal stories of two warring women, Heed and Christine, against a broad history of the black experience in twentieth-century America. As we consider Cosey's Hotel, "which thrives as an elegant and fashionable East Coast playground for wealthy blacks in the segregationist 1940s; is in decline by the integrationist 1960s; and, by the 1990s, is an abandoned ruin haunted by the spirit of Cosey's former cook, L," we unravel "the exclusionary politics of class and caste in the African American community" (359). Morrison depicts Cosey's widow and granddaughter as mortal class enemies, saved only when the reliable but hidden "Beloved" within is set free by the healing power of the ancestral and artistic imagination.

Several scholars analyze *Love* via the history of falsehoods we tell ourselves regarding American crime, justice, fatherhood, and family. Megan Sweeney explores how Morrison's later fiction questions concepts of justice that rely on "a logic of commensurability (that is, punishment equal to the crime, redress adequate to the injury, and benefit corresponding to the desert)." *Love* questions US measures that have regulated norms of justice, how the language and institutions that "privilege a logic of commensurability risk replicating slavery's logic of commodification" (441). Explaining that modern legal discourse leans toward a fundamental opposition between law and justice, and that American law contains fallacies that in the end offer little satisfaction to ordinary people who seek justice, Jacqueline Berben-Masi establishes that, as representative of final causality (the end or goal of action or development), *Love*'s narrator L resolves the inherent friction between chaos and order, positive and natural law, law and justice.

Elaborating on Susan Mayberry's proposed connection between Bill Cosey and Bill Cosby, Mary Carden suggests that Morrison's reliance on the popular entertainer known as "America's Dad" for *Love*'s portrait of Big Daddy results from "the models of masculinity around which hegemonic conceptualizations of family stability, secure homes, and socioeconomic ethics circulate." Morrison's subtle comparison between Bill Cosby and Bill Cosey "critiques ideologies that situate the family as a national institution of patriarchal ownership, ideologies that have dominated and defined U.S. discourses on race." Arguing that "the preoccupation of many black leaders with racial uplift ideology as a sign of respectability restricted possibilities for effective resistance and constituted a measure of ideological collusion with discriminatory ideologies and practices," Carden asserts that *Love* offers a "historical parable that disputes the notion that the father-dominant model of home and family is a panacea for the problems afflicting many African American communities in the twenty-first century" (131). Morrison intends *Love* as "a challenge to *Father Knows Best*: the assumption that the answer to longstanding and multifaceted social and economic problems is a fatherhood modeled on patriarchal ownership" (143).

Love and Feminist/Womanist Criticism

In a collection that demonstrates the extent to which spatiality has ethical, political, historical, and cultural implications, Jae Eun Yoo shows how *Love* activates a spectral space, which "intrudes into the reader's safe reading space, revising the text's relationship with the reader." Through the fissure opened by the visitation, the reader witnesses a murder committed to redress the historical processes by which American daughters become re-subjected to their fathers. As Morrison portrays African American women's inability to develop autonomous individuality because of this subjection, the reader not only "indirectly witnesses the harm this failure has done, but also partly experiences the harm her/himself, as the fracture in the representation of the black American women characters troubles her/his reading experience." The in-between spectral space thus becomes "a haunted site of crime, and the text positions the reader as a witness, accomplice, and victim all at the same time, pressing her/him with the complex and vital responsibilities that each of the positions entails" (154). Lee Baxter's analysis of identity formation looks to Julia Kristeva's alternative account of (m)othering and patriarchal ideology. Baxter surveys how patriarchy causes women to approach one another as Other, thus creating a divide between women, mothers, and daughters, and maintains that not until the Cosey women "recognize both their selves as other, as well as the other in the Other," can they "learn to love truly and break free from the idealized social constructs of femininity and maternity" (88–89).

Interested in the cultural project of making space for hip-hop music begun by Morrison in *Jazz*, Brittney Cooper notes that Sapphire's novel *Push* critiques Morrison's dismissiveness of hip-hop feminism and literary aesthetics, which appeared a decade later in *Love*. Heather Humann foregrounds the depictions of domestic abuse that Cooper alludes to in *Push*, particularly the long-term effects of such violence. Humann analyzes *Love*'s preeminent sociopolitical message, echoed by so many of Morrison's novels: "that the domestic sphere is a breeding ground ... for violence, that viewing the domestic sphere as a 'private' space works to alternately hide and legitimize the violence that takes place there, and that, rather than existing and operating separately, the larger social problems that plague twentieth century American society—including sexism, racism, and poverty—are tied directly to the sexual objectification, commodification, and violation of women by those intimately acquainted with them" (246–47).

After she establishes that an early American inheritance crisis left its stamp on American literature, Stéphanie Durrans includes Valérie Croisille's chapter on *Love* to illustrate that women's treatment of inheritance often suggests variations on the American Dream as an alternative way of reaching self-fulfillment. Croisille investigates the complex interaction between family and national inheritance when the hopes generated by the Civil Rights movement sour in a narrative reiterating the bitter fight of two women over a dead man's inheritance. As Morrison "deconstructs the conclusions of the 1965 Moynihan Report, which argued that the matriarchal structure of the black family emasculated black males by denying them any chance to stand as authority figures," she turns Bill Cosey into a representative of both black and white exploitation of women by exposing the fallacious nature of his black Eden. The name of the prostitute to whom he bequeaths his property, Celestial, encourages an allegorical reading "if we choose to read Cosey's sexual achievements as a stand-in for the white man's conquest of a virgin land later to be despoiled" (13–14).

Finally, Mecca Sullivan explains how secret languages, invented vocabularies, and recast idioms figure prominently in the writing of contemporary black women. Terming these imagined systems of speech *interstitial languages*, Sullivan believes they enable artists such as Morrison to "wage important critiques of gender, sexuality, and erotic desire while mobilizing those critiques to forward models of black female intimacy rooted in difference." Subversive poetics like those found in *Love* "1) express intersectional identity and complicate it by articulating the often underacknowledged differences among black womanhoods; 2) forward models of black space and community shaped by the nuances of black female difference; and 3) engage in dialogues about intersectionality and black female erotics in pop cultural spaces beyond academic and literary audiences" (705–6).

Love and Psychoanalytic Criticism

Mayberry observes that as Morrison's eighth novel explores looking for [L]ove in all the wrong places, it also relocates [L]acan's Other. Since Morrison contends that Old World black women like her maternal grandmother, Ardelia Willis, constitute the essence of love, *Love*'s Up Beach L could be viewed as the swamp women of *Tar Baby*, or Ardelia [R?], reincarnated—enduring, nurturing females out of the house of Chloe who embrace and transfer their ancient, sacred properties.[5] The "sign of [L's] letter" might also represent the healing language of laughter, in this case a comic inversion of French psychoanalyst Jacques Lacan's singularly serious theories about Sex and the Word (*Jazz* epigraph). While all of Morrison's novels slyly undercut white male authority, *Love* takes a direct stab via the black vernacular; it reduces Lacan's mighty Law of the Father to pesky Police-heads. Indicating that white masculinity assumes the rules of patriarchy, Police-heads establish a frame of empowered masculinity against which *Love*'s feisty black male characters can be considered. Whatever the sound of her name, L reveals that when African American women search for "Big Daddy everywhere," they lay down (to) the Law of the Father instead of "living [their] lives hand in hand" (*Love* 189).[6]

Stephanie Li goes on to show how Morrison's juxtaposition of Heed and Christine's private language against the patriarchal law of the father reflect Julia Kristeva's notion of the semiotic ("a state of undifferentiated plenitude based in the fusion of female bodies") ruptured by entrance into the symbolic's oppressive hierarchy: "*Love* undermines the Lacanian conflation between language and the law of the father by presenting idagay, a female-identified language developed by the two girls, as a discourse independent of the constraints of patriarchy." Unfortunately, however, idagay also repeats Heed and Christine's ultimately segregated unity, a friendship that "fails to allow for the dynamic and generative possibilities of human difference." Morrison's exploration of "how semiotic impulses can be mapped onto language demonstrates the need for a mode of communication that moves beyond the engrained dichotomies and antagonisms of gender associated with the symbolic's power to name and categorize." She embodies such a liberating discourse, reflected by the indirection and possibility of the character's own unarticulated name, into what L calls "humming," a language that "revels in the ambivalent experience of longing rather than in definitive acts of fulfillment and closure" (27–28).

Evelyn Schreiber, Katrina Harack, and Jean Wyatt stress trauma studies. Schreiber approaches the novel by way of psychoanalytic theories of identity, including Lacan's, which enable us to comprehend the sweet Cosey child traumatized by adults who place personal gratification and economic gain above the needs of children. Accentuating the destructive aspect of secrets, Schreiber surveys

---

5   *Love* remains complicatedly "For and with Ardelia." Morrison's parents, George and Ramah Wofford, originally named their daughter, who became a grandmother herself, Chloe Ardelia Wofford after Ramah's mother, Ardelia Willis. The title page of Morrison's 1955 Cornell University M.A. thesis on alienation records "Ardellia" [sic] as her middle name. Thus the narrative voice of *Love*'s author not only answers to Ardelia in the same fashion that *Tar Baby*'s narrator is accountable to its dedicatees, but *Love*'s L *is* [the black grandmothe]R, both Willis and Morrison.

6   Both black and white Southerners often refer to a family's male elder as "Big Daddy" (see Tennessee Williams' *Cat on a Hot Tin Roof*). "The Man" signifies mostly white authority (see James Baldwin's *Going To Meet the Man*).

the process of intergenerational harm (Fultz, ed.). Describing Morrison's oeuvre as an effort to revisit the past "in order to uncover possible futures," Harack focuses on "concepts of witnessing, primal scenes, screen memories, and testimony, as well as the contrast between productive and unproductive (or cyclic) memory," to illustrate how Morrison "constructs a world in which only those who break free of the cycle of unproductive memory can heal and look forward to the future" (255–56).

Wyatt affirms that formal breaks in *Love*'s chronological sequence reflect its characters' psychic dislocations. Like captive Africans aboard the slave ships, early traumatic separation from the love grounding their childhood development causes Heed and Christine to lose connection with their past and consequently become disoriented about their present and future. Just as narrative displacements reflect the protagonists' temporal disorientation, so that the reading is itself discontinuous, we witness the effects—the wasting away of Heed and Christine's lives—before we determine their cause. Thus *Love*'s structure around "narrative time lags that reflect the protagonists' temporal disorientation suggests a new perspective on Freud's model of Nachträglichkeit (variously translated as deferred action, après-coup, and afterwardsness)—and new ways of using that temporal paradigm to illuminate reader response to the asymmetries of nonlinear narrative structures like Morrison's" (194).

James Mellard provides two articles that view *Love* under the theoretical lens of Lacanian psychoanalyst Slavoj Žižek. The first unveils "the intricacies of the concept of identification." Specifically, Morrison's relationship between two girls, who, despite social and economic change, violent outbreaks, and a conflicted adulthood, never outgrow their attachment to each other, suggests not Freud's more common oedipal identification but a narcissistic one, "whose paradoxical expressions . . . avail themselves to analysis through Žižek's mediation of Freudian and Lacanian ideas" (699). Mellard's second essay alludes to Žižek's belief that the subtexts of many popular as well as highbrow films and fictions divulge the conflict of social forces, especially family dramas. Mellard includes *Love* as one such "family chronicle, often quite Gothic in its details," whose social superstructure discloses "how the functioning of paternal authority rears its obscene head." The most powerful narrative in the novel, Heed and Christine's love story, exposes images of the father "as the rotten core of the family mythology that reflects the historical context identified by Žižek and others as the postmodern crisis of paternal authority" (234).

Claiming that *Love* dramatizes Foucault's connections between power and pleasure, Herman Beavers concentrates on the positive adult behavior that allows young people an ethical system. To examine the undertones of excessive pleasure that masquerade as fulfillment, Beavers focuses on Bill Cosey and Romen, characters who must decide between surrender to immediate gratification or yielding pleasure for moral purposes; between seeking pleasure by means of dominance and betrayal or choosing selflessness for a higher cause. Adhering ultimately to values instilled by his grandparents, Romen stands alone as the character whose growth is significant and whose values are worth emulating (Fultz, ed.).

Love and Humanistic Poetics

Several critics join Beavers in highlighting what Shirley Stave calls the "humanistic poetics" embedded in the novel. Aware that Morrison has expressed an ongoing distrust of the concept we call love, Stave maintains that *Love* explores the Christian sense of the term, "particularly as articulated by St. Paul and that, with her usual discernment and penetration, [Morrison] probes the fault line, the overlooked flaw in Paul's articulation of the love humans should bear one another." Specifically, she is bothered by the way in which "Pauline love forecloses political action and therefore, in the context of a racialized and gendered world, precludes any possibility of disabling the power dynamics in place to arrive at any kind of social justice" (183). Mariangela Palladino adds that, as Morrison's fiction delineates a problematic portrait of human experiences in African American history, it urges us "to consider the interactive mechanisms of ethics, narrative, and aesthetics." Since Morrison inscribes the ethical in narrative forms, Palladino gauges *Love*'s narrative ethics by proposing the narrator L as a reconfiguration of the Greek goddess of love, Aphrodite, and investigating how *Love*'s modes of narration affect the reception of the text (334–35).

Finally, Cynthia Wallace reiterates Morrison's remark to Claudia Dreifus in 1994: "The plot, characters are part of my effort to create a language in which I can posit philosophical questions. I want the reader to ponder those questions not because I put them in an essay, but because they are part of a narrative." Recalling Barbara Christian's warning to critics in 1987 that "'a takeover in the literary world by Western philosophers' was 'coopting' the more beautiful and concrete theorizing of marginalized writers and scholars," that "just as 'minority' literature was finally moving into 'the center,' its political power was diminished by rising theories that emphasized textuality and questioned reality," Wallace notes that in making these claims, Christian "articulated not only some of the key tensions in the late twentieth-century academy, but also some of the key terms in what many scholars have called the 'ethical turn' in literary criticism." Wallace's essay considers *Love* in concert with Morrison's Nobel lecture and demonstrates how "*Love* addresses these tensions, forwarding a far more robust literary ethics than the disciplinary debates acknowledge" (375).

Like evaluating the Cosey/Cosby legacy via black vernacular as "good bad" or "bad good"—that is, everything but lifeless—Wallace's conclusions about literary criticism become telling with respect to literary critical contributions on *Love*: "The role of the critic, then, is to expose dead language or narrative for what it is, to recognize it when we see it, to read not just with open minds but also with open eyes. The stories we submit to and celebrate, then, are the ones that challenge and quicken" (387).

CHAPTER NINE

A MERCY (2008); *HOME* (2012); *GOD HELP THE CHILD* (2015)

The Critical History of *A Mercy*, *Home*, and *God Help the Child* as [Not] Told by Toni Morrison

If the forewords/afterword to all the Penguin editions of her novels except *A Mercy*, *Home*, and *God Help the Child* represent Morrison's elusive rendition of an autobiography, they also function as the author's subtle attempt to control her literary critical reception history, compelling readers in a way that no scholarly introduction could ever do.[1] The question becomes, then, why is there no Morrison telling on *A Mercy*, *Home*, and *God Help the Child*?

This issue becomes particularly intriguing given that an assistant editor for UK Vintage, Frances Roe, returned British scholar Tessa Roynon's queries about the prefaces with a reply as enigmatic yet enlightening as Morrison's typically calculated revelations:

---

1   In her 2014 article on Morrison's Vintage forewords, Tessa Roynon focuses on the "new perspectives that the forewords provide on Morrison's narrative project, the insights they contain about American and transnational historical, political and literary cultures and the rare glimpses into her own life story they afford." Roynon also explores what might be lost as well as gained by the forewords' existence, given "the potentially problematic conflicts and inconsistencies that the appearance of these prefatory essays has engendered about audience and reception, about definitive and 'indefinitive' editions, and about the empowerment or disempowerment of the reader" ("Lobbying the Reader" 86).

> It appears Toni Morrison took it upon herself to write the forewords and requested that Vintage US publish them in new editions to her paperbacks. However, the precise background to this will need to be checked with Vintage US or Toni's agent. It appears that they were described as the closest we're ever likely to have to an autobiography from Toni Morrison. ("Lobbying the Reader" 87)

Roynon's subsequent inquiries to Morrison's fiction editor at Vintage USA remain unanswered. The critic concludes that if "Morrison's forewords constitute her attempt to influence (or even dictate) the reception of her work, she is unable to control the reception of the forewords themselves," response having been mixed especially toward what a number of readers perceive to be their unfortunate didacticism and the unusual haste with which they appear to have been designed and written (87).

Authors known for writing prefatory essays to their own work, such as Dryden, Dr. Johnson, and Wordsworth and, more recently, Walt Whitman, Henry James, and Ralph Ellison, might be construed as displaying an implicit self-assurance in the ongoing importance of that work or, equally often, an anxious desire to achieve an impossible influence over the public reception of a text. These motivations exist simultaneously, Roynon believes, in the Morrisonian prefaces: "a wish to consolidate her position and the significance of her works; a continuing perception of a political urgency that necessitates her project and its clarification; and a desire to ensure that readers appreciate the scope of her artistry and her vision to the full" ("Lobbying the Reader" 88).

Morrison long ago took upon herself the mission of teaching us how to read her writing, standing firm on the elliptical "readerly" construction of her texts as one of the characteristics that renders them "Black." When the *Paris Review* editor Jean Stein quizzed curmudgeonly William Faulkner about his famed abstruseness, "Some people say they can't understand your writing, even after they read it two or three times. What approach would you suggest for them," Faulkner's curt retort is comical: "Read it four times" (46). When talk-show host Oprah Winfrey made a similar observation to Morrison, she concurs: "Yes, my dear. That is called r-r-r-r-eading!" Troubled afterward, however, that she may have sounded pompous, Morrison describes herself as a "teacher" (Spain 14:17; 1:12), adding that she regards the reader as a companion in her books: "It's a very intimate relationship that reading provides. I like books that insist on a certain kind of meditation, books that put the reader in a position where they might think about something a little bit differently, that capture the warp and woof of a particular time and place" (Denard 200).

In her extended meditation on the art of reading, Morrison becomes even more ardently elaborative, lamenting language proficiency as an imperiled survival skill. *The Dancing Mind* (1996) offers two anecdotes. One expresses the desperation of a "splendidly educated woman living in a suffocating regime," who fears that her writing will cost her her life. The second bemoans the disability of "a comfortable, young American, a 'successfully' educated male, alien in his own company, stunned and hampered by the inadequacy of his fine education." Resorting to "autodidactic strategies to move outside the surfeit and bounty and excess and ... the terror of growing up vacuum-pressured in this country," he must teach himself the old-fashioned skill of sustained reading with no companionship but his own mind. Comparing this "dance of an open mind when it engages an equally open one" to a peace "that is not merely the absence of war," Morrison claims that it occurs "most naturally, most often in the reading/writing world we live in" (7–13). Her 1993 *Nobel Lecture in Literature* reduces the disparate scenarios to a compelling roux: "We die. That may be the meaning of life. But we do language. That may be the measure of our lives" (22).

Since she has consistently represented herself as an educator who requires her audience's reciprocal participation in the imperative "word work" that is the interpretive process, we ask why she felt impelled, at the peak of her career and at this cultural moment, "to tell us so definitively what her novels are about" (Roynon "Lobbying the Reader" 90). We might understand her concern about her critical reception in the 1980s and 1990s, when she defined her difficult, demanding style by its "reliance for full comprehension on codes embedded in black culture" ("Unspeakable Things Unspoken" 23). But why so determinedly refuse then to provide a supportive entrance into her literary world and undo that determination now?[2] More pertinent to this chapter, why allow the comforting lobby with all her novels but three: *A Mercy*, *Home*, and *God Help the Child*?

Part of the answer may simply lie with their more recent publication. Roynon reminds us, however, that previous forewords "present to Morrison's readers a valuable clarification of the complex ways in which multiple timeframes operate in her *oeuvre*. There exists a productive friction between the time in which a novel is set and the time in which it is written" ("Lobbying the Reader" 94). The forewords emphasize this relationship, add the immediacy of the third (twenty-first century) timeframe in which they were composed, and engage in noteworthy dialogue with novels apart from the ones the forewords specifically precede. Certainly, the fact that no forewords exist for *A Mercy*, *Home*, and *God Help the Child* indicates that the teacher knew she had done her job. Morrison was finally convinced that most of us are now familiar enough with the linguistics of African American culture to read her texts on our own. However, one further impetus may have come into play with respect to each of her final three novels: something already done would do.

A Mercy (2008)

Morrison's principal foray into literary critical theory, an adaptation of three lectures she delivered at Harvard University in 1990, published in 1992 by Harvard Press and titled *Playing in the Dark: Whiteness and the Literary Imagination*,

---

2   Though she sometimes wishes that Morrison's forewords would get out of the way, Roynon's conclusion in "Lobbying the Reader: Toni Morrison's Recent Forewords to her Novels" summarizes Roynon's insights as to why they exist.

serves as an apt introduction to her ninth novel. Collectively, the lectures wonder whether the "major and championed characteristics of our national literature—individualism, masculinity, social engagement versus historical isolation; acute and ambiguous moral problematics; the thematics of innocence coupled with an obsession with figurations of death and hell—are not in fact responses to a dark, abiding, signing Africanist presence" (5). *A Mercy* not only locates the metamorphosis of Old World serfdom in the New World, but it also highlights the origins of American masculinity. Maintaining that she wanted to tell the other story about the development of racism in the United States, not just "the Puritan, Plymouth Rock stuff" (Nance 48), Morrison wrote a book that critiques nation-building as it confronts America's foundational myths, including the proposition of equal manhood. She wanted to explore a historical period "before racism was inextricably related to slavery... before a race hierarchy was established legally and later culturally in the states" (Brophy-Warren 5). Mulling over the brutal colonial uprising that has come to be known as Bacon's Rebellion, *A Mercy*'s newly arrived European male remembers the militia that pitted "blacks, natives, whites, mulattoes—freedmen, slaves and indentured" against the local gentry and the ruling class. The colonial elites responded by passing laws that hardened the racial caste as a way of controlling the colony's marginalized people:

> By eliminating manumission, gatherings, travel and bearing arms for black people only; by granting license to any white to kill any black for any reason; by compensating owners for a slave's maiming or death, they separated and protected all whites from all others forever. Any social ease between gentry and laborers, forged before and during that rebellion, crumbled beneath a hammer wielded in the interests of the gentry's profits. (11–12)

Playing in the Dark prepares us for *A Mercy*'s depiction of the New World white male as "ratty orphan become landowner, making a place out of no place, a temperate living from raw life" (13). Morrison's novel dramatizes her theories: that attitudes toward a permanent Africanist presence in America arose from the need to establish individuality among European males who came with nothing to discover a New World; that "cultural identities are formed and informed by a nation's literature"; that "the image of reined-in, bound, suppressed, and repressed darkness became objectified in American literature as an Africanist persona." Because a Greek shipbuilder's primary connection with an Irish farmer or a Puritan preacher proved to be the color of his skin, blackness became a readily available and subjectively inscribed "Other." Morrison the critic projects into her novel what has been on the "mind" of US literature since Emerson's "The American Scholar"—the "self-conscious but highly problematic construction of the American as a new white man" (*Playing in the Dark* 38–39).

Playing in the Dark takes on double duty as foreword to *A Mercy* by articulating Morrison's fictionalized speculation that collective hardship forces disparate but displaced Europeans to establish solidarity despite difference. In so doing, new North American arrivals constitute American Africanism as darkness and savagery, a characterization that not only shapes and makes possible white desires for autonomy, authority, and absolute power, but also embodies major themes in American literature. A rebellious but serviceable black slave population, more accessible than the non-white indigenous population, handily enables otherwise disconnected white men to create bonds of privilege based on differences. In other words, the need for New World manhood and the color of their skin transform European immigrants like Jacob Vaark into a new American male. Whatever his social status in London or Amsterdam, the white male immigrant becomes more of a "gentleman" in the New World. Shared guilt about being invigorated by rawness as he struggles to survive in a hostile environment, that is, "collective needs to allay internal fears and to rationalize external exploitation," persuades him that dark savagery is "'out there'" and that his house upon a hill makes him *the* Man (*Playing* 44–45).

A Mercy's Initial Critical Reception History and Defining Critical Moments

A Mercy occupies a unique place among the final four of Morrison's canon in that it has accrued as many responses as the rest of the volumes put together. Although critics include it as another instance of Morrison's increasing tendency toward slim output, initial reactions were largely positive: first responders were more apt to rank this 2008 novel with "masterpieces" like *Song of Solomon* and *Beloved* than any of the other three books.

The *New York Times* sponsored two reviews. Michiko Kakutani's comparison of *A Mercy*'s core premise to that of *Beloved* represents one pearl in a string of accolades for "Ms. Morrison's remarkable new novella . . . a small, plangent gem of a story that is, at once, a kind of prelude to *Beloved* and a variation on that earlier book's exploration of the personal costs of slavery—a system that moves men and women and children around 'like checkers' and casts a looming shadow over both parental and romantic love." Explaining that the novel invokes the beautiful but untamed landscape of its colonial setting with the "same sort of lyrical, verdant prose that distinguished" the previous Reconstruction era novel, Kakutani waxes ecstatic over what is missing: "Gone are the didactic language and schematic architecture that hobbled the author's 1998 novel, *Paradise*; gone are the cartoonish characters that marred her 2003 novel, *Love*. Instead, Ms. Morrison has rediscovered an urgent, poetic voice that enables her to move back and forth with immediacy and ease between the worlds of history and myth, between ordinary daily life and the realm of fable." Kakutani concludes that this choral tale about the shattered innocence of orphans not only exemplifies a heart-wrenching account of lost dreams, but "stands, with *Beloved*, as one of Ms. Morrison's most haunting works yet."

Pointing out that the Greek-invented genre that idealizes rustic life has found its real home in America, *New York Times* reviewer David Gates deems Morrison "a conscious inheritor" of the American pastoral even as she "implicitly criticizes it." If *A Mercy* tells the story of two original sins—the near genocide of the native population and the importation of African slaves by white colonialists, Gates weighs it as having "neither the terrible passion of *Beloved* . . . nor the spirited ingenuity of *Love*, the most satisfying of Morrison's subsequent novels." He finds this, "her deepest excavation into America's history," not a polemic but a tragedy in which no character is wholly evil but all are damaged goods. Morrison's "postcolonial pastoral" maintains that "only mercy or the lack of it . . . makes the American landscape heaven or hell, and the gates of Eden open both ways at once."

The *Guardian* likewise produced two reviews. Tim Adams recognizes the many connections between *A Mercy* and *Playing in the Dark*: that *A Mercy* distills Morrison's theories about American ideals of political and economic liberty being contingent upon bonded labor; that "the history and literature of America were predicated on the exclusion of the black part of its population"; that "the myths of nation-building contained an explicit or an unspoken 'us' and 'them.'" He predicts, in addition, the "fundamental resonance" between this prequel to the book chosen by the *NY Times* in 2006 as the greatest American novel of the last twenty-five years (*Beloved*) and the 2009 election of an American president who could eclipse that divide. Nonetheless, Adams cautions, Morrison's willingness to assume the voice of America's conscience occasionally reduces her to spokeswoman instead of writer.

Dame Hilary Mantel's denunciations are less measured. Agreeing that *A Mercy* allows us the preconditions for *Beloved*, this novelist contends that when Morrison eliminates Vaark, "the narrative also loses the firm, directed feel of the early pages." Fate and fortune bring barely sketched characters together only long enough for them to acknowledge common victimhood. If Morrison avoids sentimentality, she does not escape the portentous: "at its worst, this is a book of ritualised postures and cut-rate epiphanies." Mantel appreciates the book's "supple, graceful and inventive" language but laments its unchanging pace and tone, "and a certain authorial weariness behind the whole enterprise. *A Mercy* is a shadow of the great novel it should be; its half-told tales leave cobweb trails in the mind, like the fragments of a nightmare."

Two additional UK reviews came from the *Independent* and the *Telegraph*, the first glowing, the second mixed. Acceding to the "difficulty" of Morrison's writing and the "tenacity" required to finish more recent work such as *Paradise*, Andrea Stuart terms this ninth novel a "seductive read" with an ending "both devastating and satisfying." Rendering pioneers not featured in popular history, "*A Mercy* is a stunning and significant book that fills an essential gap in the American story." The *Telegraph*'s Caroline Moore, on the other hand, believes that this "historical fable" displays both Morrison's genius and its flaws. Her limitations include "writing convincing historical fiction that resurrects the flavor, linguistic textures and mindset of a past era," and her sometimes ludicrous "attempts at historical or cultural ventriloquism." If the scenes with the women on the boat from England display some of the most "unconvincing Cockney sprightliness since Dick Van Dyke in *Mary Poppins*," Moore understands "Morrison's cavalier attitude to historical nuances" to be "forged on the anvils of ideology": "She found her literary voice in an era that proclaimed that all history was 'his-story' (written by white men); and that the English language was 'smitheryed' (Morrison's term) into an instrument of patriarchal and racial oppression." At her best, however, Morrison creates a "genuine, dense idiom, both her own and evocatively 'black,'" in a fictional world "that is not dead history but living fable." Never prescriptive, her books always allow the possibility of human resilience. Her symbolism can appear simplistic: the human ramifications, never: "Emotions run deep and twisted in Morrison's fiction; and their outcome is superbly traced in this powerful, flawed and genuinely creative novel."

One of the most entertaining of Morrisonian reviews was written on *A Mercy* by John Updike for the *New Yorker*. Perhaps expressly to Morrison's consternation, Updike attributes several of her writing habits to the "pernicious" influence of William Faulkner: her heavy reliance on *in medias res* and her belief that the past is not past.[3] Some of Updike's comments sound snarky: "This author's early novels were breakthroughs into the experience of black Americans as refracted in the poetic and indignant perceptions of a black woman from Lorain, Ohio." Some, like his inclusion of the three-hundred-page *Paradise* among "the shorter novels that have followed" *Beloved*; his identification of Jacob Vaark's homestead as "Protestant Virginia"; and his claim that "the insemination that produced [Sorrow's] two pregnancies is mysterious, at least to me," are careless or downright misinformed. In short, Updike's thinly abrogating assessment of his colleague's new novel appears partly sour grapes:[4] "In *A Mercy*, Morrison's epic sense of place and time overshadows her depiction of people; she does better at finding poetry in this raw, scrappy colonial world than in populating another installment of her noble and necessary fictional project of exposing the infamies of slavery and the hardships of being African American. The white characters in *A Mercy* come to life more readily than the black, and they less ambiguously dramatize America's discovery and settlement." Updike's ambiguity is mostly not subtle; he pointedly undercuts his praise of Morrison's "noble and necessary fictional project" when he reduces *A Mercy* to merely "another installment."

A Mercy Criticism

The *MLA International Bibliography* identifies 85 citations issued on *A Mercy* between 2009 and 2018. Forty-two of these are published in peer-reviewed academic journals, and 36 appear as book chapters/sections. While a significant number of books either focus on (2) or refer to (6) *A Mercy*, MLA lists no dissertation/thesis abstracts to date. Scholarly attention comes primarily from English

---

3   In a 1983 interview with Nellie McKay, Morrison forcefully signaled her desire to distance herself from major canonical writers: "Our—black women's job is a particularly complex one. . . . I am not *like* Faulkner. I am not *like* in that sense" (Gates 408).

4   Updike's *American Pastoral* was runner-up to Morrison's *Beloved* in 2006 as the *New York Times* winner for best single work of American fiction published since 1980.

and American sources. Journals with an American multicultural concentration sustain their interest—*African American Review* (1), *Callaloo* (1), *CLA Journal* (1), and *MELUS* (4), as does *Modern Fiction Studies* (3)—providing a total of 10 articles. Foreign and online journals maintain their percentage of contributions: the *MLA Bibliography* lists 14 essays in venues sponsored by China, Finland, France, Germany, Korea, India, Israel, Spain, Taiwan, and Turkey. Published journal and book articles stem primarily from African American/postcolonial; feminist; psychoanalytic; ecocritical; intertextual; and new historical/cultural theoretical approaches. Several scholars use *A Mercy* to endorse pedagogical strategies.

A Mercy and African American/Postcolonial Criticism

Initial scholarly reactions to *A Mercy* were not clustered but ran the gamut of critical models. The first published study, in fact, appears in a book with a current theoretical emphasis. For this edition, which offers a variety of cultural narratives of diverse border crossings, Cathy Waegner uses *A Mercy* to illustrate the intricacies of constructing ethnic identity, challenging the view that migrants belong to a single nation-state.

Mina Karavanta believes that Morrison's preoccupation with what comes next for the United States as a nation, given the myths that continue to represent its origins even during a period when globalization, transnational capitalism, and transcultural/intercultural communities predominate, contributes to the development of a post-national novel: "By narrating the story of a counternational community of interracial, interethnic, and intercultural features formed not only by economic and political need but also by errancy and transfiguration—the transfiguration of debt into gift—that counters the 'Puritans' divinely ordained errand into the wilderness of the New World,'" *A Mercy* unveils the "history of other, forgotten communities and their abandonment by the mythogenetic processes of the American nation" (Abstract). Reemphasizing that national sovereignty was weaker in chaotic colonial America and has been limited by today's hyper-connected globalization, so that the political concept of space has become more fluctuating, Morten Hansen understands *A Mercy* as "a meditation on aesthetic and political worldmaking." He cautions us not to ignore its questions of gender or race, but to situate Morrison's illustrations of white supremacy and patriarchy in "a larger historical and spatial context than the history of the United States" (210).

Wen-ching Ho applies three postcolonial ideas to Morrison's exposés of American slavery: double coding, counter-hegemonic representation, and resistance to closure. After analyzing Morrison's use of hybridity, including shifting narration and multiple perspectives, Ho concludes that both *Beloved* and *A Mercy* provide an "emancipatory vision that holds out 'a sense of possibility' for the colonized" (Hamblin 18). Sun-ok Kim maintains that both the political and religious dogma of America's colonizers created American racism. If Morrison explores the historical fact that racism was not an inherent American ideology but resulted from the political power of white colonists who feared the alliance of poor whites and black slaves, especially after Bacon's Rebellion, she similarly critiques how Christian discourse based on the exceptionalist myth differentiated colonists from native and black people. She divides *A Mercy*'s major characters into colonizing or colonized subjects according to their positions in the dominant discourse based on race, gender, and class. Caught in the crisis of a loss of self, caused by racism and slavery, the colonized subject can resist racism and sexism only by reconstructing a positive, definable, irresistible identity.

Two critics recognize the diasporic influences on *A Mercy*. Artress White examines how it, together with Maryse Condé's *I, Tituba, Black Witch of Salem*, highlights an African spiritual cosmography where community remains central to healing. Countering the tendency of classic slave narratives to cite Christianity as the protagonist's primary solace, these novels portray a spiritual quest grounded in African practices, with the mother figuring as spiritual storehouse. Despite the legacy of their mothers' violence and trauma, the heroines reach a healed selfhood and a sexual autonomy that defines female desire as enlightening and positive. Marie Sairsingh presents another comparative analysis that develops the diasporic connections between Morrison and Jamaican writer Erna Brodber.

A Mercy and Feminist Criticism

Feminist critics offer their word work on the novel. Tessa Roynon states that the prevalence of male sexual domination becomes one of the unifying preoccupations of Morrison's oeuvre. Roynon's 2010 essay on *A Mercy*, which determines that rape and the fear of rape largely define the lives of its female characters, finds company in a volume that not only analyzes narrative strategies employed by international writers when dealing with rape but also describes the subversive work being done on retheorizing sexual violence to establish new dimensions of healing. Susmita Roye uses *The Bluest Eye* and *A Mercy* to demonstrate that Morrison's expressed desire to locate a black female like herself in literature sculpted her into a writer: "Morrison's feminist ideology accommodates universal girlhood, crossing frontiers of race, class, culture, ethnicity, continents, and centuries. . . . If the disturbed girlhoods of her disrupted girls express her anger, then brave endeavors by some of these girls to survive their amputation constitute not only a message of hope but also an agenda of action" (225). Rashad Mohammed Moqbel Al Areqi uses the novel's depictions of the human rights violations inseparable from past slavery to enlighten us about the inhumanity of contemporary slavery, particularly with respect to the vulnerability of women.

Cheryl Emerson homes in on Rebekka Vaark's question, "What complaint would a female Job dare to put forth?" (*AM* 107). Challenging Job's status as the archetype of human suffering, characters in *A Mercy* embody the message that shocked Job into humility and renewed fidelity: the awareness of invisibility. Job underwent an existential moment that a slave would have experienced since birth;

he is physically alive but socially dead. Morrison likewise calls attention to the implication of "invisible ink," challenging readers to decipher structures that can't be seen: "To read means not only to 'cipher' the scripted words but also to read the social, historical, and political codes in which they're written." Florens's voice infiltrating all the interior monologues and cutting directly into the structure of the master's house, the slave girl "ciphers from experience, reading signs (ciphers) and occupying 'ciphered' space itself—in the figural meaning of cipher as 'a person who or thing which fills a place but is of no importance; a nonentity'" (20). Her solace is ultimately her own narrative, carved in a talking room with invisible ink.

Manuela López Ramírez contends that Morrison tackles the multilayered "haunted-house" trope from a female perspective, her revenants historical, political, and cultural as well as individual. With the Gothic dwelling in *A Mercy* signifying a white patriarchal society that contains fragmented personal and familial identities, failed domestic ideology, and racist and colonial pasts, Morrison's transgressive rewriting emphasizes the destructive effects of racism and slavery and, consequently, the alienation of ethnic, especially black, females. As she articulates the unspeakable horrors of America's past, her revisitation of the haunted-house formula offering an alternative female critique, she simultaneously provides ways for the revision of American history by virtue of women's struggle for self-definition and empowerment.

Monalesia Earle draws on the work of a "a black heterosexual woman who has presumably been shaped by her cultural/racial background" (Toni Morrison) and "a white lesbian, whose private revelations about non-fictional events places her just as much on the margins of acceptable social constructions of the family as it does Morrison" (Alison Bechdel) to "explore how each author represents, and reflects back to us, the notion of family" (paragraph 11, Abstract). Declaring that images of belonging are just as valid for one person as another with a different lifestyle and that the meaning of "family" must be defined in context with the forces that influence our attitudes toward it, Earle maintains that Bechdel's graphic "*memtraunoir*" and Morrison's *A Mercy* ask a similar question: "How does the *idea* of family shape us?" Earle concludes that "women . . . have always been uniquely positioned to create a family where none may have existed before" (paragraphs 1, 34).

Alluding to pediatric psychoanalyst D. W. Winnicott's endorsement of a "good-enough mother," that is, that success in infant-care depends on devotion more than cleverness or education, Naomi Morgenstern notes that "Morrison's fiction recurrently explores the decisions of women who have little or no legal protection, characters who are always already located in the space of 'wilderness' (Morrison's term) or in the space of ethics" (Abstract). Morgenstern expands her focus on children and caregivers under extreme situations, including the degradation of slavery, into a book on the "wild child" in contemporary fiction, as texts like *A Mercy* grapple with anxieties about reproductive ethics and the future of humanity.

Susan Mayberry's "Visions and Revisions of American Masculinity in *A Mercy*" not only deals with the manifestations of New World masculinity in terms of power and class, but it addresses a broad spectrum of gender and sexuality: "Building upon *Can't I Love What I Criticize?* a monograph on masculinity in Morrison's earlier novels, [which affirms the balance between male and female], Mayberry argues that American masculinity originated in a patriarchal vision of ownership and enslavement" (128). She further asserts that *A Mercy* discloses Morrison's most developed "notions of homosexual masculinity . . ., associating its fluidity with sensitivity to women and children," and adds that Morrison "defines the free black man via his disruptive presence and the complex nature of freedom" (168). For Mar Gallego-Durán, the novel tests the limits of "hegemonic masculinity . . . by transgressing social and sexual boundaries," thereby signaling the threats posed by "an increasingly sexist, racist, and class-conscious value system," which defines the "people" as white, heterosexual, and male (Seward 251).

A Mercy and Psychoanalytic Criticism

Three chapters in *Toni Morrison's A Mercy: Critical Approaches* (Stave and Tally 2013) underscore the novel's psychological ramifications. Susana Vega-González examines its literal and figurative orphanhood, particularly with respect to the attacks on African American identity resulting from original displacement sustained by the institution of slavery. All orphaned in some way, the major characters succumb, survive, or prevail depending on their respective responses to their shared plight: European alienation from the natural world isolates Jacob and Rebekka, whereas Lina's connections with nature, Sorrow's affinity for motherhood, and Florens's instruction from her blacksmith/Yoruba guide allow them to transcend their orphaned status.

Shirley Stave is less optimistic. Relying on Lacanian theory to unpack *A Mercy*, specifically Lacan's concept of misrecognition as part of the Mirror Stage, Stave proposes that the American wilderness functions as the mirror, which reflects a false splendor and misleading unity to the "Europes" who gaze into it. She explains that all the immigrants end up like "children who have not yet entered the Symbolic Order." Deceived by the belief that they are "limitless and self-sufficient, requiring no community or familial connections," Rebekka replaces her dead husband with a mean-spirited God while a lost, dehumanized Florens turns destructively feral (4). Given that Florens becomes enslaved by both mother and lover, Jill Goad also despairs for Florens's misappropriation of self.

A Mercy: Critical Approaches's Mar Gallego-Durán joins other psychoanalytic critics who assess trauma (see Stave and Tally). Specifically, she scrutinizes the coping mechanisms used by *A Mercy*'s four major female characters to counter the trauma caused by an "overarching patriarchy," which limits their social, legal, and economic potential. An equitable community allows all to thrive; all rely on "rememory" to contain prior suffering. Compelled to engage with the implications of motherhood to construct a self-identity, some, like Sorrow, become complete; others, such as Florens, reject motherhood and community. Like Stave, Gallego-Durán construes Florens's solo voice as enabling her survival but ultimately "limited and unsound" (3–4).

If Eunsook Koo agrees that *A Mercy* extends the concepts of motherlove and its betrayal presented so poignantly in *Beloved*, this scholar is more positive about the success of Florens's reliance on the re-memories of being separated from her mother to reconstruct her fragmented past. Koo looks to the trauma theories of Freud, Cathy Caruth, Suzette Henke, and Judith Herman to apprehend Florens's recurring dream and self-journey along with Morrison's notions about memory, trauma, and subjectivity, specifically how confessional writing empowers the reclamation of pain and the possibility of healing by means of relocation in the narrative memory. Yi-jo Hsieh likewise incorporates the trauma studies described by Freud and Caruth to appraise the "abandoned child" and to explain how an understanding of trauma not only enables self-construction but enriches human experience. Hsieh additionally uses Frantz Fanon's theory of racism in *Black Skin, White Masks* to illustrate the effects of political ideology on personal identity. Drawing on neuroscience and social theories of trauma and memory, Evelyn Schreiber finds both personal and cultural memory at work in *A Mercy*, alleging that "attaining a positive sense of self occurs when personal memories can sustain subjectivity." Schreiber asserts that if cultural ritual conflicts with the expectations of the new environment, personal memory can protect dominion of the self, despite the pressures of the broader culture. *A Mercy*'s characters are unable to locate equilibrium, however, either through their bodily-stored memory or their inherited cultural demands (Seward 80–81).

Proposing that *A Mercy* uncovers the psychic damage inflicted by slavery as a series of failed messages between slave mother and slave daughter, Jean Wyatt turns to Jean Laplanche's theory of the enigmatic signifier, which similarly examines the effects of a parental message that cannot be understood, to clarify some baffling aspects of Florens's behavior and narrative style. Her misreading of a minha mãe's merciful arrangement of Florens's sale becoming the distorting lens through which Florens perceives the world, separation from her mother disables her ability to read the signs. Wyatt considers the novel's narrative structure to reproduce formally the consequences of mother-daughter separation.

López Ramírez acknowledges the familiarity of psychic trauma within Morrison's fiction, a trope which enables entry into a world inhabited by the victims of extraordinary social violence often left out of less expressive histories. Narrowing her focus to the particularly severe shattered identity prone to adolescents like Florens, López Ramírez concentrates on "Morrison's especially dramatic depiction of the destruction of the female teenager's self and her struggle for psychic wholeness in a hostile world. The adolescent's fragile identity embodies, better than any other, the terrible ordeal that the marginal self has to cope with to become a true human being outside the Western discourse" (75). Two criteria render the female teenager's split self more significant than the dementia of others: gender and age make this victim especially vulnerable and more apt to fall victim in adverse situations. Furthermore, the psychic disorders of teenagers predict a tragic future.

Addressing dismemberment more broadly in Morrison's fiction, Jaleel Akhtar's book investigates racism's debilitating effects on the psyche by way of history and culture in addition to psychology. Such multiple perspectives allow us, according to Akhtar, to liken "the impact of racism on individuals to the splitting of bodies, amputation, phantom limbs and traumatic memories, and in more concrete and visceral terms" (Abstract). In a monograph that engages contemporary reassessment of trauma extending beyond Freudian psychoanalysis, Laurie Vickroy theorizes trauma in the context of psychological, literary, and cultural criticism. She includes Morrison among writers who convey in narrative the relationship between individual traumas and the social forces of injustice, oppression, and objectification. Illustrating in *A Mercy* how the psychology of fear can be a driving force for individuals as well as for society, Vickroy believes that novels assist readers in understanding their own participation in systems of power and how they internalize the ideologies of those systems.

A Mercy and Ecocritical Theory

Morrison's novel about early America drew notice from another recent literary theory. James Peterson and Anissa Wardi's ecocritical ideas appear in *Toni Morrison's A Mercy: Critical Approaches* (ed. Stave and Tally). Although Peterson looks at the book through the lens of narratology, noting Morrison's attempt to focus reader attention on her characters' various interactions with their environments, he also shows how environmental value depends on cultural ideology. Contrasting what he deems the unconscious "ontological instability" of white owners with Florens's conscious devastation at being spatially separated from her mother, he believes that she abandons all human zones in favor of "wilderness." Wardi interrogates environmental issues via the idea of "home." Because white settlers fail to understand the inherent symbiosis between nature and human existence and because their assumption of ownership over the natural world precludes them from ever finding home, she interprets Vaark as prefiguring European exploitation of land and human beings, whereas Florens and Sorrow embody the African Diaspora. If Florens and Sorrow can claim no legal residence at the novel's conclusion, they nonetheless occupy Jacob's unfinished home and thereby assume New World birthright for themselves.

Fultz's 2013 collection includes Marc Conner's chapter on *A Mercy*'s language and landscapes. Shifting from Florens's ability to read and know herself to Morrison's appeal that we all pay attention to the landscape, Conner explores "ways in which the human urge to know is related to the earth and our responses to the land. Morrison's *need to understand how knowledge and geography speak to each other within narrative* form a defining concern of this novel" (148). Conner juxtaposes two attitudes that humans take toward the land: a desire to conquer or own it, or to live harmoniously with it.

Jennifer Terry's article treats *A Mercy* as a "counter-narrative" that both "exposes colonial relations to place and probes African American experiences of the natural world." It specifically redefines "wilderness" by highlighting the roles of women and nonwhites and challenges hegemonic settler and masculinist notions of the New World. As Florens's voice calls for an alternative engagement with landscape, Terry's article calls for attention to the intersections between ecocriticism and postcolonial theory. Similarly, Şemsettin Tabur includes *A Mercy* in a monograph that conceptualizes space as open, dynamic, and contested because socially and relationally produced. His study reads literature as a "cartographic practice charting the intricacies of the socio-spatiality of human life" and *A Mercy* as a map that represents and explores the real, contested, and imagined spaces of colonialism.

A Mercy and Intertextual Criticism

Three contributors to *A Mercy: Critical Approaches* accent the novel's complex intertextuality. Tessa Roynon traces its references to Miltonic journeys, noting especially its specific interfaces with *Paradise Lost* and *Comus*. She compares Satan's motivation for entering Paradise (to destroy the concord from which he is excluded) with that of Jacob Vaark (to renew Eden); she contrasts the masque's Lady, who is protected by an attendant spirit, with Florens, made raw to human and natural threats; she notes that Chaos is come again in *A Mercy* but with a difference—setting Milton's belief that humans either name chaos to control it or take arms against it to destroy it versus Morrison's third, more benevolent option: to quieten chaos by means of art. Roynon concludes that Morrison employs *A Mercy*'s Miltonic connections "to critique the European colonial enterprise and to underscore race, class, and gender in a way Milton did not take into account" (2).

Considering *A Mercy* as an allegory allows us, according to Justine Tally, to link it "not only with the Bible, but also with two other heavily allegorical canonical American works—Nathaniel Hawthorne's *The Scarlet Letter* and Arthur Miller's *The Crucible*." Tally insists that Morrison's novel challenges "the ethics of American foundational myths" and appraises "fundamentalist religious as well as post-9/11 political ideology" (3). Keren Omry likens *A Mercy* to another book that appeared after the 2001 World Trade Center bombing—Nalo Hopkinson's *The Salt Roads*. Whereas Omry agrees with Tally that Morrison joins other writers who understand the significance of retelling stories of origin to construct cultural identity, Omry identifies Vaark's journey as a quest for the American dream, which privileges financial success at the expense of domestic harmony. She maintains that both Hopkinson and Morrison foster literacy and art as positive negations of terrorism.

Sandy Alexandre allows that *A Mercy* follows the conventions of the archetypal quest narrative more closely than any of Morrison's other novels, except perhaps *Song of Solomon*. Its protagonist "goes on a treacherous journey filled with various obstacles and dangers while in search of something she is certain will ultimately prove salvific; encounters an unexpected yet helpful Samaritan along the way; and finally finds that much-sought-after thing." Because couching Florens's quest in the form of a slave narrative reduces a person (the blacksmith) to her "thing," *A Mercy* reveals that those who "have to accommodate themselves to the advent of chattel slavery must first prioritize their aspirations by foreclosing their desires for anything they could possibly consider as belonging to them, including a romantic partner" (223–25). As Florens's journey causes her to recognize that "she is actually an interpellated subject of US slavery's formation and inexorable institutionalizing," Morrison demonstrates how that peculiar institution's avaricious practices and repressive constraints shrink expansive human hope into diminishing slave desire. Josep Armengol contends that *A Mercy* may be interpreted as a "prequel" to Frederick Douglass's slave narrative. Both texts not only illustrate nineteenth-century America's increasing racialization of slavery but detail its class and gender biases—particularly the assertion by white male workers of their racial and gender supremacy over black men and black women that caused a class subjugation reducing them to virtual slaves.

We locate Ruth Anolik's piece on the textual elements of what she calls Morrison's American Gothic in a collection that gives the contemporary Gothic narrative its due. Anolik determines that *A Mercy* contains the genre's mandated tropes: "a fragmented narrative, destabilized identities, the image of the double, a haunted house, dangerous villains, endangered women, and anxious encounters with the Other and the self" (418). Although its central narrative exemplifies an exciting twenty-first-century feminized bildungsroman, it ultimately reverts to what Anolik deems "the antique Gothic," which reveals a modern cultural psychosis. As Florens's journey returns her to her desperate past and the inherited curse of slavery, we concede that the first decades of the twenty-first century were "no less dark and dangerous, no less Gothic, than the late seventeenth century in America when the horrors of slavery were about to commence" (431). Jami Carlacio explicates the narrative strategies that allow Florens to acquire the ability and agency to inscribe her bildungsroman on the walls and floor of her owner's abandoned Big House. These strategies not only enable Morrison's protagonist to uncover hidden knowledge via revelation and inquiry but also empower Morrison's readers.

Two academic journals that stress American multiculturalism provide articles written by British scholars with an intertextual interest in *A Mercy*. In *MELUS* Mark Sandy addresses Morrison as a legatee of the British Romantic movement, specifically that her "awareness of an integrated sense of community and her episodic encounters with nature and the sublime" remain indebted to the darker aspects of Wordsworth's rural poetics (35). Both artists view writing as an effort to interpret partial signs glimpsed through multiple reactions to a larger utterance.

Influenced by Emerson and Thoreau's "urbanized pastoral modes," Morrison translates Wordsworth's elegiac vision of the dispossessed and marginalized into her own version of the American pastoral.

In the *African American Review*, Roynon alludes once more to Milton to argue that *Paradise Lost* (1667) "significantly informs Morrison's representation of life in Virginia, Maryland and New England in the 1680s and '90s. The novel's engagement both with that poem and with its status in that specific time and locale is key to *A Mercy*'s central issues: the nature of freedom and oppression, of power and powerlessness, and of good and evil" (593). Roynon adds that Morrison's disruption of binaries, including the division between good and evil, probes the sharply defined morality of the Enlightenment. *A Mercy* confirms that "in its mutually constitutive relationship with both England and the American colonies of the late seventeenth century, the Enlightenment was always and already defined by paradox, moral ambiguity, and even chaos," and that "to wrest dominion" has always been a dangerous endeavor (604).

Two scholars emphasize the novel's biblical echoes. Geneva Moore notes that Morrison's prequel to *Beloved* references the sermon tradition to capture the colonial experience in Virginia and Maryland. As she excavates the neglected reality of the involvement of minority Americans, the novelist also "appropriates parody in her deconstruction and reconstruction of American history to query and restore truth to the narrative by 'reducing the lie [of the master discourse] to an absurdity'" (2). Katherine Bassard believes that contemporary African American authors who situate their fiction in the antebellum South perform important archival and hermeneutic work. Asserting that "neo-slave narratives frame their discussion of the past in order to define future debates about race, culture, and academic politics," Bassard points to the irony that in looking back these novels "carry forward the discussions of enslaved and free identities in biblical and extra-biblical contexts" (Abstract).

Two contributors to *Faulkner and Morrison* (ed. Hamblin and Rieger 2013) focus on *A Mercy*'s Faulknerian manifestations. In John Duvall's view, *A Mercy* joins *Jazz* and *Love* as responses to Faulkner's great novel on the dark house of race and family dynasty, *Absalom, Absalom!* Whereas Thomas Sutpen's story ends in violence and tragedy, however, Morrison's more hopeful treatment of Florens finds "an understanding of divine mercy made manifest through the small mercies enacted by flawed human beings" (34).[5] Theresa Towner relies on *Go Down, Moses* to compare Faulkner's "relentlessly masculine" bear Old Ben with Morrison's bear—"'a relentless female out to protect her young'"—as well as to associate Isaac McCaslin's opportunity to decipher his family history through his cousin's commissary ledgers with Florens's "talking room." Both novels depict societies in which masculinity is glorified and femininity underestimated; additionally,

---

5   As she highlights the power of language with respect to race and the social construction of identity, Doreen Fowler likewise looks to Faulkner's *Absalom, Absalom!* and Morrison's *A Mercy*.

Towner concludes, as Faulkner and Morrison record the dissolution of a family, they display "genealogies broken and dispersed by the ideology of whiteness in the process of crystalizing" (13). Maxine Montgomery's edited volume *Contested Boundaries: New Critical Essays on the Fiction of Toni Morrison* (2013) sets out to survey intertextuality within Morrison's oeuvre, particularly the relationship between her ninth novel and her previous works. Its topics range from "the conflicted mother-child relationship, the haunting legacy of slavery, the black female body as site of trauma, the thorny quest for an ideal home, and the perilous transatlantic journey" to "the desire for mercy," with *A Mercy* "serving as a locus for discussion of [Morrison's] re-figuration of concerns central to her narrative project" (2).

A Mercy and New Historical/Cultural Criticism

Two back-to-back articles in *MELUS* accent *A Mercy*'s new historical/cultural connections. Valerie Babb explains how the novel recasts the oft-repeated cultural origins narrative, capable of rendering a nation beloved as it glosses over the "forgetting" necessary for nation-building: in this case correcting "the epic of Englishmen who sailed to the 'vast and unpeopled countries of America' and created 'a citty [sic] upon a hill' that would be an example of God's grace toward the Chosen." In so doing, Morrison "re-places the racial, gender, and class complexities lost in the creation of a canonical narrative that sought to privilege the few over the many" (147).[6] Jessica Cantiello points out that reviewers of *A Mercy* generally do not separate the text from its publication date one week after President Barack Obama's election. She deems misleading the widespread tendency to associate Morrison's use of pre-racial to portray the novel's New World with the media's use of post-racial to capture Obama's America. Although many reviewers propose that *A Mercy* forecasts the "fluidity of race in contemporary America," the text poses a more flexible concept of race than do its collected reviews. Paradoxically, the reviews expose the persistence of racial construction in current society (165).

Libby Simon connects Morrison's novel to the reshuffling of racial, economic, and social categories that occurred after 9/11 and to the cultural adoption of domesticity to make sense of the calamity. Declaring this transitional moment to be multicultural, Simon examines similar anxieties about family, home, and community in *A Mercy* and explores "the ways in which the novel, set in the wilderness of seventeenth-century America, employs post-9/11 aesthetics of liminality and 'threshold' moments." Doing so causes it "to bear witness, promote marginalized voices, and in the vein of subversive post-9/11 novels, ultimately abandon the idea

---

6   Susan Strehle adds in an online article that *A Mercy* treats the American exceptionalist myth ironically, showing that the story of a "chosen people" rests on pernicious binary separations between an elect and its Others. If Florens pays the price of American exceptionalism, Morrison critiques the separation of Others by using a narrative form that deploys separation as a structural principle and perspective.

of a return to a reassuring domesticity only to warn against the dangers of zealous individualism and exceptionalism" (Abstract). Eugenia Bryan similarly confronts "afterimages" of slavery, noting that *A Mercy*, unlike the novelist's other works, illustrates that peculiar institution in various American forms, with the characters' only commonality their enslavement to the emerging socioeconomic culture.

Stephen Best questions whether "melancholy historicism," as modeled by Morrison's *Beloved*, is the sole approach to slave history, wondering if the "unforthcomingness" of the past may represent its deepest political, perhaps even human, significance. Best recommends the adoption of a history of discontinuity, again the archetype for which Morrison provides in *A Mercy*. The complicated textual effects of this later historical recovery reveal its author's apparent rejection of the effort she previously inspired to continue, resurrect, or complete the political projects of those who were defeated by history.

Hsiu-chuan Lee likewise believes that Morrison's attitude toward history in *A Mercy* is not simply a return to the past or a retrieval of the repressed. As she evokes a lost age and uncovers ideas that resist existing historical lines and racial categorizations, the novel forwards in its textual present an intermediary agency for negotiating the structure of history, thereby ushering in new systems for historical understanding. Anna Brickhouse's contribution to *The Oxford Handbook of Nineteenth-Century American Literature* treats *A Mercy* as Morrison's American rendition of Britain's Long Nineteenth Century; her twenty-first-century examination, by way of her commentary on Nathaniel Hawthorne and Herman Melville, entails three centuries of slavery in the Americas.

Agniesz Łobodziec analyzes the novel in terms of poetic realism, a concept coined by and usually associated with the French film movement of the 1930s. Striving more for truth of sensation and environment than for truth of fact, Morrison's literary poetic realism "juxtaposes detailed images of 17th-century Old Europe and the New World realms as well as the feelings that accompany the images" (150–51). In another collection that forwards analyses of fiction into other art forms, Philipp Löffler juxtaposes Morrison with Steven Spielberg to investigate postmodernism's influences on Morrison's historical fiction and Spielberg's films as they convey "the notion of the future . . . as an alien place." Löffler insists that seemingly disparate works such as *A Mercy* and *Saving Private Ryan* are united in their substitution of "the authenticity of historical experience" for historical "knowledge." They predict the ends of postmodernism as they challenge the "conventional aesthetic hierarchies" associated with postmodernism (17–18).

Nancy Peterson extends into a reading of *A Mercy* her observations about Louvre Museum guest-curator Toni Morrison's interest in nineteenth-century French painter Théodore Géricault: two artists who understand how to reanimate history by narrowing and deepening it. Garrett Stewart studies the novel in relation to three-dimensional sculpture, claiming that this approach may introduce a new postmodern and metafictional perspective vis-à-vis Morrison's ways of imagining from within her narratives their material conditions as books, that is, the political momentum and agency of their materiality.

Two scholars weigh the moral or religious implications of *A Mercy*. Mara Willard terms the book an example of what she calls the postsecular, where fiction breaks down the binary between religious and secular, exposing "implicit expectations of overcoming religion and realizing 'the secular' to be a constructed narrative that must begin to be historicized and contextualized" (468). Willard believes that, as Morrison portrays "human ambivalence about religious institutions, practices, beliefs, and history," she reflects the "richness of lived religion: loved, loathed, and ignored, variant across time, across populations, and even across a single actor" (469, 484). Thus *A Mercy*'s postsecularism is not at odds "with the literary depiction of a Christian's trust in the demands and promises of a faithful life" (469). Louis Ruprecht Jr. invites closer deliberation regarding the often-overlooked sexual intimacy of the plantation system. Using *A Mercy* to illustrate the life-threatening and frequently depraved nature of such intimacy, Ruprecht's article comes out of an American Academy of Religion roundtable, which addresses the appropriate tactics with which to engage in discussions of such delicate topics.

A Mercy and Pedagogical Criticism

Several scholars note *A Mercy*'s usefulness in the classroom. Aryn Bartley assigns it as her capstone project in a survey of American literature because its seventeenth-century setting requires students to review early American literature tropes even as it simultaneously raises questions fundamental to a survey course by foregrounding the processes of canonization and literary historiography: "By featuring the narration of a female African American writer—and by marking the uncertain future of her writings—the novel encourages students to consider how canonical literary histories are formed." They are challenged to recognize American literary histories "as being marked not only by the national visions they produce, but also by the ones they exclude" and urged "to think of their own reading as being both historically located and subject to history" (Abstract).

Early American Literature published four essays on teaching Morrison's seventeenth century in today's classroom that were originally part of a 2010 American Studies Association roundtable discussion. Professors of disciplines as diverse as first-year composition, American studies, gender studies, literary studies, and history opted to continue their conversation in print to share "the pedagogical strategies used to introduce students to challenging histories and literary texts, and to the changing academic and intellectual practices of [their] field." Lead presenter Chiara Cillerai assigns *A Mercy* in an introductory writing course to show beginning students how Morrison's reconstructed history connects colonial American writings to the present. Kristina Bross designates the novel as a capstone text for her "Living History" course, which reveals how memory, memorialization, and historical reenactment determine present-day American identities and recover voices repressed by traditional history. Susan Curtis explains how juxtaposing fiction with history allows graduate students to uncover the story in history and the fact of fiction. Finally, Lisa Logan responds to these teacher/scholars' collective effort to recollect the past via *A Mercy* (177–78).

Although Gabriella Friedman's essay does not provide specific strategies for teaching *A Mercy*, it does accord with Paula Moya's book chapter that close reading of literature remains a powerful tool in the ongoing struggle to imagine better ways of being free in the world. Friedman observes the link between colonial practices of interpretation and the Euro-American trope of wilderness: "By deploying the multilayered trope of wilderness, *A Mercy* highlights the way colonial epistemology is deeply embedded in conventional Euro-American ways of reading—whether the text be written document, land, or human body—that rely on notions of discrete selfhood, linear history, abstract logic, and the elimination of ambiguity. Through this same trope, the novel ultimately unsettles the colonized territory of the reading process, offering a mode of reading that ruptures colonial interpretation" (311).

Moya fits Morrison's oeuvre easily into a collection on the social imperative of literature that figures the relationship between reader and text as a kind of friendship, maintaining that it not only matters "which texts we read and teach, but also how we read them, and with whom." Because Morrison champions the kind of close reading that validates "how literature reflects, promotes, and contests pervasive sociocultural ideas about race, ethnicity, gender, and sexuality" (Abstract), *A Mercy*'s "twinned preoccupation with reading and responsibility" reflects its author's attempt "to do with race what she did with slavery in her magnum opus, *Beloved*: she wants to break it open to examine its origins and find what it does to those who are its victims as well as to those who benefit from its operations" (133).

Home (2012)

Home's introduction to the public occurred during the Toni Morrison Society's 2008 conference, "Toni Morrison and Modernism," where its author read the opening chapter from her tenth work (still in progress) at the College of Charleston's historic Sottile Theater. She shelved that half-finished project for months after the December 2010 death of her younger son, forty-five-year-old Slade, of, according to her, pancreatic cancer and a crazy proclivity for Chinese medicine. Inspired by her son and coauthor of several children's books, Morrison had already been thinking seriously about the concept of home in 2005 when she announced at a TMS conference that supercilious Louvre directors had requested she guest curate an exhibit, which she tentatively planned to call "Home." Dryly attributing the administrators' selection of an African American artist to the current unrest in Paris of former colonials, she also chuckled that it was Slade who half-jokingly suggested she incorporate a sample pyramid into her show since, outfitted by Egyptian royalty right down to the slaves deemed requisite to ensure civilized life after death, live burial of others certainly confirms the extremes to which people will go to get home. Fear of death and feelings of alienation inevitably accompanied by a mostly futile desire for safety have long been on Morrison's mind. Explaining at her Sottile reading that she had been wanting for some time to ponder the relationship between a brother and his sister, she allows that "Home is an idea rather than a place. It's where you feel safe" (Leve).[7]

We may find a good portion of *Home*'s absent foreword in the form of an original essay Morrison wrote for *The House That Race Built* (ed. Lubiano 1997), reprinted in a 1998 Vintage edition. If somewhat longer than her typical Vintage forewords, it reads in much the same way. Roynon notes:

> To some extent, the forewords can be said to follow a formula.... each begins either with a personal memory ... or with an observation about literary technique.... Morrison demonstrates the interconnectedness of the personal and public spheres; of aesthetic and political concerns; and of the distant past, the recent past and the present. Disclosures about her creative process sit next to analyses of other writers.... The tone is almost always engaging and conspiratorial; it is akin to the intimate manner of Claudia MacTeer's opening gambit in *The Bluest Eye*, "Quiet as it's kept".... ("Lobbying the Reader" 87)

The only formulaic foreword elements missing from the "Home" essay are "apparently indisputable interpretations of the text that is to follow [which] take their place among profoundly suggestive ambiguities" (Roynon, "Lobbying the Reader" 87).

Long aware of the presence of absences connected to racial matters and the longing for home, Morrison articulates in her essay "Home" themes that reappear in her novel *Home*:

> How to be both free and situated; how to convert a racist house into a race-specific yet nonracist home. How to enunciate race while depriving it of its lethal cling. They are questions of concept, of language, of trajectory, of habitation, of occupation, and, although my engagement with them has been fierce, fitful, and constantly (I think) evolving, they remain in my thoughts as aesthetically and politically unresolved. (5)

Home, dedicated to "Slade," takes as its foreword its epigraph, which is a poem Morrison wrote for André Previn's song cycle *Honey and Rue*, composed some

---

7 Morrison elaborates on her motivations for writing *Home* in an interview with novelist Christopher Bollen: "Another reason for *Home* is that I got very interested in the idea of when a man's relationship with a woman is pure—unsullied, not fraught. If it's his relationship with his mother or his girlfriend or his wife or his daughter, there's always another layer there. The only relationship I thought that would be minus that would be a brother and a sister. It could be masculine and protective without the baggage of sexuality. So the sort of Hansel and Gretel aspect really fascinated me. And his traveling back to save her would be transportation with violence all around him."

twenty years earlier and thus not originally intended for *Home*, but a sure indication of how long *Home*'s themes had haunted the author. Her lyric's atmosphere of alienation forwards her essay's unresolved ideas about home into her novel's anxiety of belonging:

> Whose house is this?
> Whose night keeps out the light
> In here?
> Say, who owns this house?
> It's not mine.
> I dreamed another, sweeter, brighter
> With a view of lakes crossed in painted boats;
> Of fields wide as arms open for me.
> This house is strange.
> Its shadows lie.
> Say, tell me, why does its lock fit my key?

Home's Initial Critical Reception History and Defining Critical Moments

Its defining critical moments the debate over a seemingly increasing reduction in the length of Morrison's novels, initial reaction to *Home* was mixed. *The Boston Globe*'s John Freeman pronounces the "short, swift, and luminescent book" to resemble nothing else Morrison has written. Whereas her robustly baroque storytelling has worked best in a large space, *Home* is not just "a short book by a writer who, at this point, could publish her collected recipes and earn accolades. It is in fact a remarkable thing: proof that Toni Morrison is at once America's most deliberate and flexible writer. She has almost entirely retooled her style to tell a story that demands speed, brevity, the threat of a looming curtain call."

The *Washington Post*'s Ron Charles applauds the artistic freedom declared in 145 calmly, unpretentiously profound pages by a writer who "doesn't have to prove anything anymore." Acknowledging that "this little book about a Korean War vet doesn't boast the Gothic swell of her masterpiece, *Beloved* (1987), or the luxurious surrealism of her most recent novel, *A Mercy* (2008)," Charles views *Home*'s "diminutive size and straightforward style" as surprisingly deceptive: "This scarily quiet tale packs all the thundering themes Morrison has explored before." Although she has never been more concise, the restraint in her prose poem "demonstrates the full range of her power" depicted in scenes "as quick and unexpected as a sniper's bullet" in which a few tightly presented details capture the ill health of mid-twentieth-century America.

The *New York Times* reviewer Leah Hager Cohen identifies *Home* "on the basis of its publisher's description a novel, on the basis of its length a novella, and on the basis of its stripped-down, symbol-laden plot something of an allegory." Maintaining that Morrison doubts the possibility of selfhood in a spiritually impoverished home as she probes the question both in Frank Money's specific circumstances and the broader sense of America's vicious inhospitality toward some of its own, Cohen praises the book's most provocative implication, "that there is no such thing as individual pathology."

Unlike *Ebony* reviewer Miles Marshall Lewis, however, who enthusiastically dubs Morrison "empress of literature . . . too long-in-the-tooth as a precise storyteller" not to know what she's doing," Cohen censures *Home*'s occasional lack of subtlety, insisting that it doesn't need revelations that read like "in-text SparkNotes." If Lewis concedes that merely describing the beats of this plot embodying the straightforward lyrical style of Morrison's twenty-first-century period could conceivably give away the entire book, Cohen amends: "Part of Morrison's longstanding greatness resides in her ability to animate specific stories about the black experience and simultaneously speak to all experience. . . . This work's accomplishment lies in its considerable capacity to make us feel that we are each not only resident but co-owner of, and collectively accountable for, this land we call home."

Cohen finds precedence from her esteemed colleague Michiko Kakutani. While this *New York Times* reviewer views *Home*'s "evil physician" and "monstrous grandmother" as verging on "fairy tale caricature," she praises an "economical tale" largely "free of the didactic writing that turned *Paradise* and *Love* into brittle, cartoonish exercises, pitting women against women, women against men, young against old." Kakutani appreciates Morrison's "new, angular voice and straight-ahead storytelling style that showcase her knowledge of her characters, and the ways in which violence and passion and regret are braided through their lives, the ways in which love and duty can redeem a blighted past."

United Kingdom reactions went back and forth as well. The *Telegraph*'s Nishia Lilia Diu also tags the novel as a "deft universal parable," granting that "a slip of a" Toni Morrison novel is always a "big book." Diu includes *Home* as part of Morrison's "ever more complete chronicling of the black American experience, from the beginnings of slavery in . . . *A Mercy*, to the Nineties closure of a chichi black holiday resort in *Love*," to the early fifties when the "end of legal segregation is approaching but Eugenics Boards still sit in at least a dozen states." Though Diu observes that this "swift-moving book bears many Morrison hallmarks: the conversational tone, the subtly circling structure, the shifting between narrators—and the violence," she encounters them "tipped so quietly and unexpectedly into the story that it winds you" and judges the siblings' psychological healing hurried. Nonetheless, "the horrors threaded through the narrative lose none of their power for being only hinted at and Morrison's writing is so deft that even barely sketched characters leap off the page."

The *Guardian*'s American reviewer disagreed. Sarah Churchwell answers the question she poses about *Home*, "Does Toni Morrison's latest novel stand up to her best?" by referring to John Updike's description of *A Mercy* as Morrison's last instalment of a worthy fictional project that discloses the shame of slavery and the adversity of being African American: "The nobility and necessity of the enterprise does not quite offset the sense of weariness that comes from that 'another instalment,' and Updike had a point: exposure of infamies and hardship is a fairly limited artistic ambition." If the pernicious effects of racism and sexism are Morrison's big themes, "her novels about them are getting smaller, in every sense; she seems to be losing patience with her own stories," which have come dangerously close to Aesopian fables. Churchwell concludes that "if Morrison had finished writing the novel she so carefully began, it might have been one of her best in years. But . . . *Home* barely begins before it ends; just when the reader expects the story to kick in to gear, as Frank arrives back in Georgia and finds Cee, Morrison seems to lose interest."

LA Times book critic David Ulin concurs that *Home*'s too-rapid happenings do not engage an author apparently detached from her fictional world. Though he confesses to greater respect for Morrison as a moral visionary than a fiction writer, Ulin admires what he considers to be her best work: *Song of Solomon, Beloved*, and *A Mercy*, three "masterpieces" more than most writers produce. Claiming that the Nobel laureate's charisma frequently hinders an honest critique of her writing flaws (specifically her tendency toward stylization, stentorian rhythms, biblical cadences, characters who function as archetypes), he deems *Home* "a thin book with some beautiful writing that ultimately comes off as insubstantial and contrived." That it is "a Toni Morrison novel" encapsulates Ulin's faint praise for *Home*, "which reads like a pastiche, a writer returning to the well once too often, operating less from narrative urgency than a kind of muscle memory."

Online response took the middle ground as well. Representing *themillions.com*, Malcolm Forbes alleges that for all its strengths, *Home* falls short. This is partly the result of Morrison trying to pack too much into a novel that, like Lotus, Georgia, is "much less than enough" (84), partly a secondary cast bursting with potential but with tales half-told, and partly character "mollycoddling" and a "saccharine bow-out." Nevertheless, Forbes believes the book leaves too lingering an impact— "the poignant depiction of a sundered family, the unflinching portrayal of war"— to "brusquely write the whole thing off." Like many, this critic opts for compromise: "We like Frank alive, but wish Morrison with her too-big heart had kept him in the shade. That, along with swapping her scattershot sketching for broader, splashier, and more daring brush strokes on a wider canvas, and *Home* would have been up there with Morrison's best."

Home Criticism

If the *MLA International Bibliography* identifies 25 citations issued on *Home* between 2014 and 2018, 16 of these appear in academic journals (15 of them peer-reviewed); 6 as book chapters/sections; and 3 as dissertation/thesis abstracts. Scholarly attention extends well beyond journals with an American multicultural emphasis; *MELUS* and *African American Review* provided only 1 article each. Foreign and online journals substantially increased their percentage of contributions: the *MLA Bibliography* lists 8 essays in venues from Brazil, Canada, China,

Denmark, Korea, and Spain, almost a third of the total MLA citations. Published articles and book chapters derive primarily from psychoanalytic; new historical/cultural; African American/postcolonial; intertextual; and feminist/womanist theoretical approaches.

Home and Psychoanalytic Criticism

This novel about a Korean War veteran's literal and metaphorical journey home drew its most immediate response from psychoanalytic critics, particularly those focused on trauma studies. Aitor Ibarrola defines the novel as "trauma fiction," or texts that attempt to resurrect previously neglected historical periods and reclaim forgotten stories untold by the unprivileged. Morrison's rendering of the genre relies on the staples of her narrative technique such as "the inclusion of multiple focalizers, the repetition of the same scenes from various viewpoints, intertextual references to earlier novels, and an intriguing dialogue going on between her main character and a kind of scribe—or implied author" (110). His primary question is whether Frank's journey affords him fully realized redemption; Ibarrola concludes that if *Home* confirms the probability of individual recovery from past trauma, it doubts the possibility of finding closure for the "insidious effects resulting from cultural and collective negation" (122). Contributing to a bilingual volume that fosters a reconsideration of the very notion of culture by examining the experiences and representations of nineteenth, twentieth, and twenty-first century people who changed cultures, Emmanuelle Andrès maintains that *Home*'s overwhelming sense of displacement is "not so much geographical and cultural as it is borne by an individual's grappling with time, memory and trauma" (109). Its pastoral ending becomes a natural setting for both healing the past and christening the future.

As she traces Frank Money's struggle to cope with his numbing childhood in Lotus, Georgia, and the post-traumatic stress of his stint in Korea, Jan Furman investigates Morrison's ideas about the ephemeral elusiveness of "truth." Her analysis reflecting Morrison's belief that "structure is meaning," Furman locates parallels among Frank's topographical journey, his dynamic dual-voiced narrative, and his determination to fix psychic coherence. The "story of Frank's maturation, rendered as a process of narrative integration," *Home* "moves beyond conventional assumptions of omniscient knowledge to expand the creative possibilities of rendering character as narrative identity" (Seward 231, 233, 241). López Ramírez compares *Home*'s exposé on the returning war veteran's madness with that of *Sula*'s Shadrack. By describing the homecoming of traumatized African American soldiers, whose symptoms and their consequences impair their lives, Morrison explores the tensions of a racially bigoted United States and the physical and psychological destruction that racism brings to blacks. *Home* joins *Sula* as an antiwar novel that portrays "anti-heroes, broken men, whose madness is associated with the war, but also with a racist America" ("Shell-Shocked" 129).

If David Coughlan includes a chapter on Morrison as his monograph surveys the figure of the ghost writer in contemporary American fiction, demonstrating how this theme connects to an ethics of writing that weighs personal and social responsibility, record and repetition, memory and forgetfulness, faithfulness and betrayal, Maxine Montgomery's essay approaches *Home* as a "cultural haunting" that bears not uncritical witness to forgotten wounds. Montgomery deems the final burial enacted by the brother/sister duo "a ritual performance rife with folkloric significance as the two pay tribute to a past that refuses to release its stranglehold on the present." Since nothing in Morrison's fictional world ever dies, with ancestral spirits from an Africanist belief system helping to make the invisible visible, the burial at *Home*'s ambiguous conclusion "points to the role of ghosts as enabling entities that allow traumatized individuals to mediate the psychologically fragmenting effects of anterior events" (14). Highlighting the profound influence of ghost stories on the art of the narrative, Morrison breathes new life into old legends, offering a vision "that is 'new' in the sense that it *revises* the past" as it allows "a fuller understanding of modern life and the individuals who both shape and are shaped by a complex history" (23).

Akhtar's multifaceted examination of dismemberment in Morrison's oeuvre unveils the improvisational dialogue between various voices that encourages us to "study her fiction from the interrelationship between or dialogization of different perspectives" (1). Acknowledging the interactive nature of all her novels, Akhtar insists that *Home* not only represents a "place of refuge from the social, historical and psychic dismemberment or traumas of racism which result in experiences of fragmentation, amputation and dismemberment," but its theme of burial connects it with the "larger writing project [Morrison] envisions as 'literary archaeology'" (10).

Home and New Historical/Cultural Criticism

Declaring that wartime killing has never made citizens of African Americans, nor has it brought them freedom, Lt. Col. Candice Pipes, head of English and Fine Arts at the United States Air Force Academy, relays the historical background out of which *Home* was born. Pipes explains that civil rights activists coined the term "Double V" during World War II, urging black troops to "win victory over both the foreign enemy and the enemy at 'home.'" This political campaign ultimately failed, however, "not because of any lack of bravery of black American soldiers, but because of a social system hell-bent on maintaining the status quo. The untold story is that even as black soldiers were fighting for the United States of America, for democracy, for their own respect and dignity, for their humanity, the roots of institutionalized racism were being dug in even deeper." Morrison's novel reflects this doubly complicated concept of home: "If home is belonging and safety and security, then African Americans are, by definition, always not at home" (1–2).

Pipes goes on to extend *Home*'s historical context into the Korean War. With established racism wearing away at African Americans' fighting spirit and another war looming, on July 26, 1948, President Truman issued Executive Order 9981, which called for "equality of opportunity" in the armed forces (2–3). Billed as an integrationist agenda, though couched in separate-but-equal language, the Order ironically triggered an upturn in beatings, burnings, rapes, murders, and false imprisonments of African Americans "almost in direct ratio to the surge towards war" (Phillips 10). Nonetheless, the supposedly integrated military afforded a new opportunity for black Americans to prove themselves: "As one Korean War veteran put it, 'the war was a better option than home'" (Phillips 114).

Confirming that US memory dismisses the Korean War as the "forgotten war,"[8] Joseph Darda notes that while commentators persist in characterizing the war on terror as an unparalleled era marked by permanent conflict, literary authors are returning to Korea to contest that narrative. Many look to 1945–53 for the material and rhetorical sources of the war on terror after the United States established a military government in Korea and during the Korean War itself. It was Korea, they remind us, "that provided the rationale for building a permanent standing military and a global network of more than seven hundred military installations throughout Europe and Asia." Listing Morrison among those authors mining that history, especially the war's contribution to racial-scientific violence at home, Darda includes *Home* among Korean War counternarratives: "Refusing the bracketed, three-year history of the war, they instead reveal the basis of an enduring warfare state in Korea and locate the war on terror in this legacy" (81–82).

Jae Eun Yoo adds that *Home* deserves closer scrutiny in light of the September 11, 2001, attack on the United States. She proposes that, since it challenges the official history of the Korean War that was part of the rhetoric recalled by the Bush-Cheney administration to justify its retaliatory and preemptive strikes following 9/11, Morrison's novel divulges how the brutality and repression "harbored in American society during the 1950s spill over onto foreign societies and, having been amplified on foreign battlefields, are brought back home—not only a historical observation but a productive response to 9/11" (Abstract).

Home and African American/Postcolonial Criticism

Two scholars explore the novel's diasporic nuances. Valorie Thomas coins the term "African diasporic vertigo" to decode *Home*'s method of decolonizing the psyche. Pointing out that two of Morrison's longstanding fictional values continue to anchor this book—black diasporic literacies and black vernacular culture as a site of knowledge and healing—Thomas describes *Home* as presenting a "psychogeography," or alternate imaginative landscape which "serves as a template for healing in the midst of trauma" via the "liminal space of the crossroads archetype" (Seward 194). Melissa Schindler analyzes how non-Anglophone women writers of African

---

8   Having reached adulthood in the 1950s, Morrison herself remembers that the Korean War "was called a 'police action' then—never a war—even though 53,000 soldiers died" (Bollen).

descent react to Paul Gilroy's notion of diaspora and modernism. Indicating that many black feminist authors privilege domestic sites, such as home and nation, over the masculinized space of the black Atlantic diaspora, Schindler investigates *Home*'s resistance to the romanticized nationalist home represented in Gilroy's *The Black Atlantic*, even as *Home*'s final passage suggests a possible resolution for the modernist split self.

Home and Intertextual Criticism

Several critics mention the intertextual implications of the novel. López Ramírez cites Morrison's oeuvre as renowned for its rich intertextuality, entwining black and white literary traditions, contemporary history, oral storytelling conventions, narrative, legends, myths, and fairytales. She asserts that *Home* re-envisions the fairytale genre, specifically "Hansel and Gretel," more intensely than Morrison's previous books to critique 1950s patriarchal postcolonial America and foreground the African American journey to selfhood. She additionally claims that Morrison not only employs fairy stories "to underpin her narrative, connecting them with many of the major motifs of the novel but also, for the first time, a fairy tale becomes the structural frame in which the characters' identity struggle takes place." In addition, Morrison's ability to universalize this black American bildungsroman is at least partially connected to her application of the role of fairytale ("Hansel" 145). Irene Visser connects its fairytale allusions to trauma intervention. Since *Home*'s "dark narratives of childhood abuse, war trauma, and racial discrimination . . . are offset by Morrison's use of motifs from the tale of 'Hansel and Gretel,'" Morrison "envisages ways toward the resolution of trauma that contribute to developments in literary trauma theory and presents a new and stronger sense of positive closure to the thematics of trauma than has so far been the case in her fiction" (148).

Erin Penner persists in scrutinizing the Morrison/Faulkner/Woolf connection. Remaining cautious about cross-racial and cross-cultural literary interpretation, Penner nevertheless believes that Morrison's *Home* both revives and rewrites elements of the literature that called out to her in graduate school. *Home*'s setting occupying the period when she wrote her 1955 Cornell University thesis on Faulkner and Woolf, Morrison links the war years in their novels to the Korean War in hers as she rejects American regard for the 1950s as a golden era: "The result is an allusive conversation that challenges critics to make room for both her scholarly and creative work as she serves up a cultural critique born of the past, but written to address the problems of the present." Morrison's scholarship on alienation in the works of Faulkner and Woolf enables her in *Home* to force an acknowledgment of racism and narrative control of the warfare state (McCarthyism) within the American chronicle. Most important, *Home* allows her to propose how an account framing the 1950s as an age of peace and prosperity "contributes to the neglect of soldiers returning from 'The Forgotten War' and to the increasing despair of individuals pressured to take the blame for what are deeply entrenched—but ignored— social ills" (343–44).

Shirley Stave attests to Morrison updating her own work, viewing *Home*'s Frank Money as *Tar Baby*'s Son revisited. In Stave's words: "... *Home* re-writes the characters in *Tar Baby* so as to allow the Son figure to achieve a maturity foreclosed in the original work and to encourage a re-reading of Jadine as an empowered woman" (Abstract). Susan Mayberry assesses *Home*'s intertextuality more broadly, elaborating on reviewer Michiko Kakutani's conclusion that the slim novel contains Morrison's major ideas. Reflecting Morrison's adroit ability to engage imaginatively with multiple subjects simultaneously, "*Home* encapsulates most of the themes that have fueled her fiction, establishing itself as 'a kind of tiny Rosetta Stone to [her] entire oeuvre' ("Soldier Is Defeated")." Motifs include Morrison's notions about masculinity that Mayberry outlined in *Can't I Love What I Criticize? The Masculine and Morrison* (2007). *Home* "continues to track such well-known paths as white male houses versus black male homes, the disruption of classical and popular masculine myths, the free black male, the traveling Ulysses scene, African American trauma, and the possibility of redemption via unmotivated respect." It explores some new directions as well, such as a brother/sister partnership and the fiction of gender unveiled by masculine sartorial performance ("Rosetta Stone" Abstract).

Home and Feminist/Womanist Criticism

Several scholars predicate their arguments on Patricia Hill Collins's description of "othermothering," a traditional West African practice in which "all the women in a household or village mothered all the children, regardless of biological ties" (Mayberry, "Masculine Othermothering" 14). Emphasizing that not only are women as capable as men of everyday violence against children, but men are equally as capable as women of nurturing children, Tosha Sampson-Choma interprets Collins's notion to include "brother-mother." She contends that Frank functions as Ycidra's primary nurturer, rewriting his own narrative "in the discourse of the brother-mother," while "their step-grandmother . . . demeans, demoralizes and emotionally abuses" them (Baxter 253–54).

In her feminist critique of Frank Money's masculinity, Mayberry particularizes and expands on reviewer Ron Charles's comment: "*Home* is unusual [for Morrison], not only in that it features a male protagonist but that it's so fiercely focused on the problem of manhood. The novel finally asks us to consider the manhood implicit in sacrifice, in laying down one's life." Mayberry bases her approach on Morrison's "womanist" insight that relationships between African American men and African American women must be understood in terms of the intersections of gender and race, and with respect to their participation in a larger, historically racist culture. *Home*'s re-view of Morrisonian masculinity indicates that not only have black men successfully retained their special vitality despite white male resistance, but their connections to black women have saved their lives.

Mayberry asserts, furthermore, that *Home* works to free mother love from unbalanced binaries—not by "lov[ing] nothing," but by helping both genders discern when an absence of love is "too much" along with "know[ing] when to stop" loving too much (*Beloved* 92; 86, 216; 104). Validating in many of her novels a range of maternal reactions to all sorts of others, Morrison endorses "'othermothering' as an 'acceptance of responsibility for a child not one's own, in an arrangement that may or may not be formal' (James 45)." In addition, Morrison "holds with community mothering, a related concept that encompasses women typically past childbearing years who have often previously othermothered and continue to care for adult community members." *Home* "extends these ideas to sanction what we may call 'masculine othermothering'—a symbiotic model in which Frank Money's learned bonding with the feminine allows him an African American manhood that enables him to become an effective othermother" ("Masculine Othermothering" 13).

Agreeing that, unlike Sethe's "too thick" love in *Beloved*, maternal love in *Home* is "much too thin—absent or even hateful," Rosanne Kennedy tallies the destructiveness of growing up in households that mirror "the dominant aesthetic, cultural, and economic values of white society." Kennedy scrutinizes the ways households in *Home* embody racist ideas resulting in "failed attempts at 'respectability'"... that forward "the (re) founding of a counter community" (Baxter 158).

God Help the Child (2015)

Like *A Mercy* and *Home*, *God Help the Child* has no foreword or afterword with the author's reflections on the novel's personal, historical, and/or literary content and context. Nonetheless, the book clearly has an unofficial foreword in *The Bluest Eye*, Morrison's first novel written in the late 1960s and published in 1970, where child abuse and parenting, especially mothering, are focal issues.[9] In her final work of fiction, Morrison appears to be surveying the progress—or lamenting the lack thereof—that the United States has made over the last half-century in protecting children from physical, sexual, and emotional/psychological mistreatment. Her particular focus is on African American girls, whom Morrison has long viewed as the most vulnerable members of American society because they are the most susceptible to "the damaging internalization of assumptions of immutable inferiority originating in an outside [white] gaze," the gaze that irretrievably damages Pecola in *The Bluest Eye* and wounds so many in *God Help the Child* (*BE* afterword 210).

---

9   *God Help the Child* has two unofficial forewords, *The Bluest Eye* and "Sweetness," the short story published in the *New Yorker* in February 2015, a first-person unreliable-narrator *tour de force* that Morrison created from the opening, middle, and closing monologues of *God Help the Child*. Because Morrison chose not to include in her elision the section of the novel where Sweetness pressures her daughter Bride to testify at Sofia's trial for sexual abuse, the short story does not address the sexual exploitation of children. Thus "Sweetness" is more limited as a foreword for *God Help the Child* than is *The Bluest Eye*, where Pecola's rape by her father is the shocking denouement of the novel.

Because Pecola's mother Pauline accepts absolutely the "white-gaze" view of non-white people as ugly and inferior, she physically beats this viewpoint into Pecola, essentially punishing her daughter for being black. Pecola's alcoholic father Cholly sets his daughter on the road to insanity by raping her when he is drunk. Pauline, however, is equally responsible for Pecola's tragedy: when Pecola identifies her father as the rapist, her mother refuses to believe the obvious truth, leaving Pecola completely unprotected from further sexual attack. When Pecola becomes pregnant, Pauline beats her daughter so severely that Pecola is seriously injured and the baby dies, brutality that helps push Pecola over the edge into insanity.

The Bluest Eye also demonstrates the importance especially for a black girl of a nurturing, protective Demeter-figure in her life through a sexual assault incident obviously meant to contrast with Pecola's rape. When Frieda MacTeer is groped by Mr. Henry, the boarder whose rent payment is a huge addition to the family budget, she immediately goes to find her mother to report the incident, though she risks punishment for breaking a strict rule to do so. Her mother tells her father, and both parents drop what they're doing, run home, and very publicly and loudly throw Mr. Henry out of their house. Because the MacTeer girls have a stern but loving and fiercely protective mother and a caring, supportive father, Frieda is not damaged by the groping incident, and Claudia, the narrator of *The Bluest Eye*, can [safely] become the knowledgeable witness-bearer for much-victimized Pecola, who by age twelve speaks only to her schizophrenic alter-ego.

God Help the Child extends Morrison's fictional survey of child abuse in the United States through the year 2015. Bride is raised by her mother, Sweetness, who proudly describes herself in the opening monologue as "high-yellow" . . . "with good hair," a woman so invested in her "skin privileges" that she has to stop herself from smothering her newborn daughter, whose "terrible color . . . Sudanese-black skin . . . was so black she scared [her]" (3). She bottle-feeds her baby because "nursing her was like having a pickaninny sucking [her] teat" (5), and she insists that her daughter call her "Sweetness" rather than Mother because "it was safer"—obviously only for Sweetness herself—for entirely racist reasons (6). Sweetness treats Bride like a house slave, screams at her for insignificant missteps, and, most damaging of all, never touches her daughter's skin, even when bathing her. In what has to be an ironic reference to Pauline's physical mistreatment of Pecola in *The Bluest Eye*, Bride disobeys Sweetness's rules deliberately to try to get her mother to hit or slap her just to feel her touch, but to no avail. To get Sweetness to hold her hand for the first and apparently last time, eight-year-old Bride lies during her testimony at a white kindergarten teacher's child molestation trial; twenty-year-old Sofia is unjustly convicted and imprisoned for fifteen years. The guilt Bride suffers for bearing false witness becomes just as damaging as Sweetness's refusal to touch her.

At the end of the novel, Bride is twenty-three, gorgeous in white clothes that set off her blue-black skin, extremely successful in the cosmetics industry (another connection to *The Bluest Eye*: Madam C. J. Walker, twentieth-century black cosmetics entrepreneur, was born Sarah Breedlove and like Pecola Breedlove was sexually abused at home as a child), and happily contemplating parenthood with Booker. However, Sweetness gets the last mean word: "Good luck and God help the child" (178).

In *The Bluest Eye*, Pecola is the only seriously afflicted child. In *God Help The Child*, Morrison's array of characters who are physically, emotionally, and/or psychologically affected by child abuse includes Bride, Booker, Booker's brother Adam, Booker's parents and siblings, Brooklyn, Sofia, Rain, Steve and Evelyn, Booker's aunt Queen, Queen's daughter Hannah, and Queen's other children. Morrison's fifty-year survey of child abuse in America unequivocally suggests that mistreatment of children in the United States is, if anything, much worse in 2015 than in 1970. Always interested in "who survives and who does not and why," however, she, rightly, refuses to blame those victims and connects that abuse to systemic racism even as she provides a tribute to the children who survive (Gates and Appiah 402).

Morrison inserts a bromide in the last paragraph of Sweetness's second monologue: "What you do to children matters. And they might never forget" (43). That Sweetness admits this is "a lesson I should have known all along" mitigates to some extent her defensive, self-serving explanations of why she has treated her dark-skinned daughter so badly. However, Morrison may well have inserted the bromide because she knew it would be both readily quotable and easily understandable to everyone across the globe—a final message on parenting from the world-famous writer who maintained that there were only two imperatives in her life: writing novels and mothering her children.

God Help the Child's Initial Critical Reception History and Defining Critical Moments

Defining critical moments for *God Help the Child* also resurrect nostalgia for *The Bluest Eye*. While virtually all the initial reaction to Morrison's last novel touches in some manner on her first, many reviewers find the latter less satisfying than the former. Writing for the *New York Times*, Kara Walker locates as "the still center of this furious novel" interactions between the "stark black" Bride and the "bone white" Rain—the first an adult, the second a child but "emotionally the same age"—both victimized as children. Walker applauds Morrison for paying attention to the jagged scar of child abuse that cuts through the sacrosanct social contract between adults and children. Walker praises this "brisk modern-day fairy tale with shades of the Brothers Grimm: imaginative cruelties visited on children; a journey into the woods; a handsome, vanished lover; witchy older women and a blunt moral—'What you do to children matters. And they might never forget.'" Walker laments, nonetheless, the book's disappointingly few surprises and the brevity of its scenes of transformation and healing.

This critic particularly appreciates Morrison's ear: her ability to write lovingly attuned to the textures and sounds of words. In addition, "the natural landscapes in her books have a way of erupting into lively play, giving richness and depth to her themes." Conversely, Walker argues, we get in *GHTC* "clipped first-person confessionals and unusually vague landscapes" along with characters who choose self-righteousness over compassion from a writer who herself "handles child abuse with a cautious disgust, not with the terrifying closeness of ... *The Bluest Eye*." Because the book "never struggles to answer the questions it poses," withholding information and keeping its characters at bay, Walker finds herself reading between the lines only to take away "the bitter supposition that childhood is the perfect condition to be manipulated by adult power because it is self-perpetuating." Though "every now and then" Morrison steps away from severe moralizing and "yields to the slow, tender, dangerous art of storytelling," she mostly yanks away possibilities of redemption so that instead of being lured by beauty inside terror and the messiness of human experience, we are faced with a "curt fable" more interested in "outrage than possibilities for empathy."

Central and west-coast big-city response was likewise mostly disenchanted. If Earle Ofari Hutchinson terms Morrison in the *Chicago Tribune* "an American literary treasure," he also accepts that "some treasures, no matter how valued or precious, can have blemishes that mar their luster." Reluctantly, he includes *GHTC* among that ilk. If its theme is "vintage Morrison," that is, an allegory about "a black woman on a near-mystical, tortuous journey of personal discovery set against the bitter hard knocks that come with being black and female in America," its method is "contrived." Like Walker, Hutchinson upbraids the author for taking the easy way out by peddling formulaic clichés and racial typecasting to shock the reader instead of fleshing out her characters and allowing her incisive prose to provide gradual insights into gender, race, and rebirth. Despite moments that remind us of "Morrison's magical wordcraft"—her natural affinity for saying so much with so few words—this critic confesses he'll have to hope for better from the next installment.

A *Los Angeles Times* reviewer highlights the lone center section in *GHTC*, which he considers to resonate with the power of Morrison's finest work. Illustrating that a single-minded search for justice can kill the soul, Booker's obsession with his brother's murder, according to David Ulin, deals sensitively with Morrison's signature issues: memory, family, the interplay between past and present. For all that, Booker's relationship with the "cipher" of a central character, Bride, "unfolds with little urgency or fire." If Ulin sympathizes with an author nearing the end of a long career who wants to look back on her beginnings, he insists that each book be judged on its own merits and deems *GHTC* not up to par. Reading like "a set of talking points, archetypes and illustrations," unconnected with the messiness of experience, *GHTC*, unlike Morrison's more challenging *The Bluest Eye*, does not resist easy resolution, relies on uninspired magical realism to make up for its lack of depth, and "rarely stirs into articulated life."

Walton Muyumba, on the other hand, includes Morrison among the greatest writers who expose childhood innocence as myth, acknowledging the painful truth that none of us enters adulthood unscathed. If he describes Morrison's fiction as filled with characters such as *The Bluest Eye*'s Pecola Breedlove "whose jacked-up childhoods hobble them like Oedipus on Mount Cithaeron," Muyumba claims that Morrison has nevertheless remained "more interested in the characters that manage to disengage from their psychological and physical damages in order to embrace the extant African-American experience as the human experience." Defining *GHTC* as "a tragicomic jazz opera played out in four parts," he pronounces it a solid example of Morrison's "late style," which originated with *Love*.

Distilled "to their atomic elements," driven by powerful narrative voices, and "paced for speed," these later fictions are, says Muyumba, not so much disappointingly curt as muscularly compressed, *GHTC*'s individual expressions intended not to enhance character but to "add dissonant timbre to Bride's narration and Morrison's themes." Like Ulin, the *Atlantic* critic is most impressed, however, with Booker's narrative: "Few writers, regardless of gender, can address the vagaries of black masculinity as sensitively, insightfully, and elegantly as Morrison." While she is famous for pitting lovers against each other, the contest in *GHTC*, Muyumba admits, is too easy; it lacks the requisite danger, details, or dark humor—which may account for some of the negative critique of Morrison's late style. Standing by "the beauty of her prose, her formal and imaginative risk-taking, her intellectual prowess [that is] founded on fiction about human devilishness and weakness, bodies crippled and in crisis, and the impact of our histories on our emotional faculties," this scholar views these strengths as perhaps somewhat constrained but "proudly on display" in *GHTC* and its author "fully capable of writing novels forever."

British newspapers basically concurred with the mixed reaction from their American counterparts. Writing for the *Guardian*, novelist Roxanne Gay despairs of *GHTC*, viewing it as "the kind of novel where you can feel the magnificence just beyond your reach. The writing and storytelling are utterly compelling, but so much is frustratingly flawed. The story carries the shape of a far grander book, where the characters are more fully explored and there is far more at stake." More specifically, Gay attributes the unfulfilled promise of "a magnificence, burning beneath the surface of every word" to undeveloped protagonists and figures like Brooklyn and Queen, who are temptingly presented and then ignored. Even so, Gay applauds the book's language, narrative shifts, and audacious premise from a writer who commands respect no matter her story. Too bad this is "a coming-of-age story for an adult woman in arrested development."

The *Independent*'s two reviewers are far less acerbic. Susan Elkin appreciates that, even as Morrison's novels have grown increasingly "svelte" over the years, they continue to retain their thematic connections to the American slave past and merge gritty realism with magical myth. This reviewer notices *GHTC*'s return to *The Bluest Eye*'s emphasis on racial self-hatred. Though Morrison originally intended her book to be called "The Wrath of Children," Elkin recognizes the note of hope at the end of a "compelling example of what you can achieve with skilled and sophisticated use of multiple narrators interspersed with third person sections." Morrison herself sometimes takes on the role of omniscient third-person narrator "able to skate effortlessly and invisibly among people, places and situations"; at other times she hands off that "clear voice" to her characters. Elkin encapsulates: "In less experienced hands it might be clumsy. Here it comes off beautifully, like a Picasso painting telling a story in a multi-dimensional series of superimposed snapshots as each character becomes ever more rounded and complete."

Reiterating its opening statement by light-skinned Sweetness, which reveals her horror at having given birth to blue-black Bride—"It's not my fault. So you can't blame me"— Razia Iqbal reminds us of the book's widespread import: "You sense that this could be a story whose very fibre is likely to interest anyone who cares about the building blocks of society: the family, and how we treat our children." Per her habit of introducing her intentions in the first few pages, following with the emotional weight of what we have learned, Morrison sets the potent words "fault" and "blame" in the context of a parent-child relationship, knowing full well the outcome will be "soaked in pain." Iqbal then tempers her compliments: "Some of the characters, though their stories have stayed in my mind, are too didactic on the page: prototypes for an idea rather than real people." However, after she reminds us that this last American laureate's Nobel Prize speech underscores language as "responsibility and redemption—personal and political," Iqbal appoints *GHTC* within the oeuvre of an author who clarifies things long obscured, in this case the consequence of reminding our children that they not only are important to us but are our immortality.

God Help the Child Criticism

The *MLA International Bibliography* provides a mere seventeen entries for *GHTC*; six of these can be found in foreign journals from Chile, Japan, Korea (2), Romania, and Spain, and one is a book chapter published by a German press. US contributions include two published editions, with *New Critical Essays on Toni Morrison's God Help the Child* (July 2020) accounting for nine MLA citations. The only Morrison novel to be set in our current moment, *GHTC* accrued 3,056 reviews on Goodreads and received a 3.74/5.00 from 21,650 ratings. Criticism relies upon psychoanalytic; feminist/womanist; new historical/cultural; and African American literary theories.

God Help the Child and Psychoanalytic Criticism

Preceding four trauma studies articles written in Korean (2017), Japanese (2019), and Spanish (2019), Manuela López Ramírez contributes a 2016 piece in English for a Spanish journal about the after-boom of child maltreatment in *God Help the Child*. Pointing out that Morrison revisits this, one of her primary thematic concerns in *The Bluest Eye* and elsewhere, López Ramírez explains that the last novel "weaves a tangled web of childhood trauma stories, in which all of the characters have suffered some kind of abuse: neglect, witnessing domestic violence, emotional and psychological abuse, molestation, sexual abuse, etc. [Morrison] shows how the child's exposure to traumatic experiences has dramatic far-reaching effects into adulthood, such as psychological, emotional, behavioral and social problems." As she illustrates ways in which the curse of past slavery maintains its hold on the present through "the phenomenon of colorism," she explores how racism and intra-racial discrimination result in various destructive coping mechanisms. If abuse victims often become future victimizers, *God Help the Child* also unveils the possibility of its characters' "restorative journeys towards redemption" (Abstract).

God Help the Child and Feminist/Womanist Criticism

Two feminist scholars focus on Bride. Stefanie Mueller observes that Morrison's previous novels depict female characters participating in economies that render their financial security and autonomy dependent on men. Prior novels additionally reveal Morrison more interested in the corrupting influence of wealth per se. Her most successful female professional, however, is *GHTC*'s Lula Ann Bridewell, a young executive who manages her own line of beauty products at a Los Angeles-based cosmetics company. Wearing only white clothes, she markets herself by "capitaliz[ing] on her dark skin" (*GHTC* 143). All the same, Mueller judges Morrison as condemning "a model of female entrepreneurship that follows the ideal of liberal individualism, in which ownership of the self is a value because it is the prerequisite for entering the capitalist system of exchange." *GHTC* rejects economic agency for black women by means of "radical self-reliance in which every woman is the CEO of her own life, responsible for herself alone and connecting with others only to exchange commodities" (160–61).

While Mueller's references to Madam C. J. Walker, Tyra Banks, and Morrison's own affiliations with the business of beauty rely heavily on cultural as well as feminist theory, Paula Martín-Salván's study is more narrowly black feminist. Claiming that *GHTC* is a quest narrative in which the protagonist questions her self-constructed adult identity as she confronts her past, Martín-Salván identifies Bride's body, as "privileged site for the construction of her identity," to encode "where the signs of an identity crisis will appear as symptoms of a childhood trauma." This scholar explores how the book's narrative structure "links the apparently unrelated transformations undergone by Bride's body into a single narrative of secrecy and trauma" (Abstract).

God Help the Child and New Historical/Cultural Criticism

Tamara Jovović's essay is more narrowly new historical/cultural. Considering *The Bluest Eye* and *GHTC* as bookends to Morrison's oeuvre and Morrison as repeatedly revisiting different historical epochs that illustrate a racially packed America, Jovović insists that Morrison not only "regards racism as one of the primary handicaps of American society," but that "we still need to talk about race in the post-racial era" (203–4). Jovović refers to Jeff Chang's account of recent American history to summarize Morrison's attitude: "In the United States of America, we still tend to begin each conversation about race as if it were new, from a willed presumption of what might be called racial innocence, as if we have lived nothing and learned nothing. Writing about race in America must always be a labor of recovery and faith and—yes—hope against the spectacle of fear and the twilight of forgetting" (28).

God Help the Child and African American Criticism

In their collection of essays about the black family in *GHTC*, editors Rhone Fraser and Natalie King-Pedroso incorporate insights about various conflicts in comradeship.[10] Divided into three parts that focus on aspects of the black family and relationships as they relate to the novel's protagonist, this 2020 collection first examines how Bride was socialized as a child. Part I includes essays on the significance of "the inner child/adult emotional development"; honoring family and fatherhood; and the crippling of community via race houses. Part II offers chapters that highlight the protagonist as a professional, examining Bride and Brooklyn as [dis]connected "sistahs from another mista"; ways in which professional women navigate space at work and at home; and Bride in the context of Yoruba deities and the "Sable Venus." Part III deals with Bride's journey as she leaves the workplace, including chapters on her potential partnership with Booker Starbern, according to Kobi Kambon's model of African self-consciousness; and how the Yoruba deity Oshun and Mary Jane Paul of BET's television series *Mary Jane* illuminate Bride's experiences.

A second full-length study on *GHTC* appeared in 2020. Editors Alice Eaton, Maxine Montgomery, and Shirley Stave note that Morrison's last novel returns her to signature themes explored in previous ones: racism and colorism; pernicious beauty standards particularly for African American women; mother-child relationships; and child sexual abuse. Morrison's only work set in the contemporary period, *GHTC*, like the rest of her oeuvre, transcends time to take on mythic attributes lending themselves to allegorical interpretation. The editors divide *New Critical Essays on God Help the Child* into three sections. The first addresses "how a subject overcomes the scarring left by a toxic childhood" and "the link between a dysfunctional childhood and a troubled adulthood." Acknowledging that Morrison's narratives "rely on intertextuality to enrich the readerly experience," section 2 examines her formal experimentation in *GHTC*, while the final section scrutinizes the novel's interplay with previous Morrison texts (ix–xii).

---

10   Morrison recalled her parents as more like comrades than the typical husband/wife couple.

CODA

The Critical Life of Toni Morrison ends not with the conclusion but with a coda: in ongoing memoriam of the writer, critic, teacher, editor, and public intellectual who died on August 5, 2019. Unlike Southern white male poet and New Critical theorist John Crowe Ransom, who, in defense of "l'art pour l'art," described the professional literary critic as "a man who, in dealing with a work of art, creates a little work of art in its honor," Toni Morrison defined great literature as socially astute and politically aware: "The best art is political and you ought to be able to make it unquestionably political and irrevocably beautiful at the same time" (Denard 64). Most of us who began our careers under the New Critical banner have come to engage with both schools of thought: blowing up the white male literary canon was certainly a result of the successful political assault by the feminist scholarship of men and women (black and white) on traditional literary discourse; literary critics are, indeed, men (and women) who, in dealing with a work of art, create art in its honor. Morrison has taught us "to expand articulation, rather than to close it, to open doors, sometimes not even closing the book—leaving the endings open for reinterpretation, re-visitation, a little ambiguity" (Jaffrey).

In his 2017 foreword to Morrison's *The Origin of Others*, author and activist Ta-Nehisi Coates honors the centrality of her work to America's present as well as its past. Although the book, derived from her 2016 Harvard University lecture series, "is not directly concerned with the rise of Donald Trump," it is "impossible to read her thoughts on belonging, on who fits under the umbrella of society and who does not, without considering our current moment." Coates sees yet another American cultural crisis resulting in our turning over the rocks on the field of American history to uncover the systemic racism writhing there from the beginning. As Morrison addresses "the oldest and most potent form of identity politics in American history—the identity politics of racism"—her oeuvre becomes politically for all time (ix–x).

The present moment also validates Morrison's belief in connections between the political and the personal as we bounce between one binary and another. A personal anecdote comes to mind. This book, begun in 2016, hit a road bump in July 2020 that affected the body politics of its author. At the height of the Black

Lives Matter protests over the murder of George Floyd, the Associated Press, the MLA, and the *New York Times*, encouraged by theorists such as Henry Louis Gates Jr., began to capitalize *Black* in regards to race while retaining the lower-case *white*. Other scholars took up the argument. Kwame Anthony Appiah and Nell Irvin Painter maintain that both terms should be capitalized: "Black and white are both historically created racial identities—and whatever rule applies to one should apply to the other" (Appiah).

Having used lower-case letters for black and white over three-quarters of the way through this book, I consulted with my editors. After perusing recently published material, my senior editor reported that he found some adopting *Black/white* while others opted for *black/white*: "By the time we get to copy-editing, it's quite possible that a new consensus will have emerged—or not." Self-described as "a stickler of a copyeditor," my press editor responded: "It bothers me to have terms that are formally analogous treated differently." Having already manually changed over a thousand *blacks* to *Black* in order to relieve such language matters, I managed to strain my body in my search for truth, complaining to my editors: "I've banged on this computer keypad so much that some of the letters have faded away, and I've clicked that blasted mouse so many times I've given myself carpel tunnel syndrome and tennis elbow. Thank God the ball's in ya'll's court!" Since "anything could appear to be something else, and probably was" (*Song of Solomon* 331–32) and "narrative is radical, creating us at the very moment it is being created" (*Nobel Lecture* 27), the ball, of course, is still bouncing. To my physical therapist's alarm and presumably Toni Morrison's delight, two versions of her *Critical Life* currently exist. My editors published this one; I'm in possession of the other.

This coda allows Morrison last words on ways in which language alters perception and becomes the measure of our lives. She often responded to critics who claimed she wrote about love that she wrote about its opposite: betrayal. She couched her speculations about race as an effect of power in her searches to embrace the Other. In other words, because writing is "really a way of thinking—not just feeling but thinking about things that are disparate, unresolved, mysterious, problematic or just sweet" (see Steinberg, *Writing for Your Life* 359), she rejected binaries for what might be in between.

Her 2002 essay "Grendel and His Mother," published in *The Source of Self-Regard*, assimilates these ideas beautifully. In it she compares the dilemma of *Beowulf*'s Grendel with that described in John Gardner's novel of the same name. Relying on the same plot and characters as the original, Garner asks us to enter the mind of the monster and examine his possibilities. Between Grendel's own suspicion that "noble language produces noble behavior" (and that the opposite is true as well) and advice from the dragon to get a pile of gold and sit on it, lies, according to Morrison, "the plane on which civic and intellectual life rests, rocks, and rolls." For Grendel and for us, this is the "space for as well as the act of thought"—the space that denies "easy answers, and violence committed because, in crisis, it is the only thing one knows how to do" (260–61).

The essay goes on to differentiate between *crisis*, which "demands 'final answers,' quick and definitive action," and *conflict*, which in the "clash of incompatible forces" calls for "adjustment, change, or compromise." Even when we recognize "legitimate oppositions, honest but different interpretations of data, contesting theories," conflict may occasionally have to be militarized—but never in the academy. The academy, in fact, must embrace oppositions if education is to occur. Because the mind has no purpose apart from trying to know, conflict is not only "a condition of intellectual life," but its pleasure. Maintaining that unruly democracy "is worth fighting for" while totalitarian fascism "is not," Morrison concludes: "I like to think that John Gardner's view will hold: that language—informed, shaped, reasoned, will become the hand that stays crisis and gives creative, constructive conflict air to breathe, startling our lives and rippling our intellect" (261–62). Whatever its expression—the artistic or the political; past or present; black or Black; in this world or of the next—Toni Morrison's critical life remains dedicated to ongoing inclusive, intelligent, nonviolent struggle. In her words, "Don't let anybody, anybody convince you this is the way the world is and therefore must be. It must be the way it ought to be" (*Source of Self-Regard* 72).

WORKS CITED

Abel, Elizabeth. "(E)Merging Identities: The Dynamics of Female Friendship in Contemporary Fiction by Women." *Signs* 6.3 (1981): 413–35.
———. "Black Writing, White Reading: Race and the Politics of Feminist Interpretation." *Critical Inquiry* 19.3 (Spring 1993): 470–98.
Adams, Tim. "Return of the Visionary." *Guardian*, Oct. 25, 2008. https://www.theguardian.com/books/2008/oct/26/mercy-toni-morrison.
Aguiar, Sarah Appleton. "Listening to the Mother's Voice in Toni Morrison's *Jazz*." *Journal of Contemporary Thought* 6 (1996): 51–65.
———. "'Passing On' Death: Stealing Life in Toni Morrison's *Paradise*." *African American Review* 38.3 (Fall 2004): 513–19.
Aithal, S. Krishnamoorthy. "Getting Out of One's Skin and Being the Only Person Inside: Toni Morrison's *Tar Baby*." *American Studies International* 34.2 (Oct. 1996): 76–85.
Akhtar, Jaleel. *Dismemberment in the Fiction of Toni Morrison*. Newcastle upon Tyne: Cambridge Scholars, 2014.
Akoma, Chiji. "The 'Trick of Narratives': History, Memory, and Performance in Toni Morrison's *Paradise*." *Oral Tradition* 15.1 (2000): 3–25.
Alexandre, Sandy. "From the Same Tree: Gender and Iconography in Representations of Violence in *Beloved*." *Signs* 36.4 (Summer 2011): 915–40.
———. "Lovesick in the Time of Smallpox: Romancing the State of Nature in Toni Morrison's *A Mercy*." *Criticism* 59.2 (Spring 2017): 223–46.
Allen, Alexander. "The Fourth Face: The Image of God in Toni Morrison's *The Bluest Eye*." *African American Review* 32.2 (Summer 1998): 293–303.
Als, Hilton. "Ghosts in the House: How Toni Morrison Fostered a Generation of Black Writers." *New Yorker*, Oct. 27, 2003. http://www.newyorker.com/magazine/2003/10/27/ghosts-in-the-house.
Alwes, Karla. "'The Evil of Fulfillment': Women and Violence in *The Bluest Eye*." In *Women and Violence in Literature: An Essay Collection*, 89–104. New York: Garland, 1990..
Amad, Soophia. "Women Who Make a Man: Female Protagonists in Toni Morrison's *Song of Solomon*." *Atenea* 28.2 (Dec. 2008): 59–73.
Anderson, Elliott. "Novels of America Past: Morrison's Black in 'the Bottom.'" *Chicago Tribune Book World*, Jan. 13, 1974: 3.
Anderson, Melanie R. "'What would be on the other side?': Spectrality and Spirit Work in Toni Morrison's *Paradise*." *African American Review* 42.2 (Summer 2008): 307–21.

WORKS CITED

Andrès, Emmanuelle. "From Korea to Lotus, Georgia: Home, Displacement and the Making of Self in Toni Morrison's *Home*." In *Cultures in Movement*, edited and with an introduction by Martine Raibaud, Micéala Symington, Ionut Untea, and David Waterman, 109–22. Newcastle upon Tyne: Cambridge Scholars, 2015.

Andrews, Jennifer. "Reading Toni Morrison's *Jazz*: Rewriting the Tall Tale and Playing the Trickster in the White American and African-American Humour Traditions." *Canadian Review of American Studies* 29.1 (1999): 87–107.

Andrews, William L. "Toni Morrison's *Beloved* and the Traditions of the African American Slave Narrative." *GRAAT* 14 (1996): 115–24.

Androne, Helane Adams. "Revised Memories and Colliding Identities: Absence and Presence in Morrison's 'Recitatif' and Viramontes's 'Tears on My Pillow.'" *MELUS* 32.2 (Summer 2007): 133–50.

Angelo, Bonnie. "The Pain of Being Black." *Time* (May 22, 1989): 68–70.

Anolik, Ruth Bienstock. "Haunting Voices, Haunted Text: Toni Morrison's *A Mercy*." In *21st Century Gothic: Great Gothic Novels since 2000*, edited by Daniel Olson, 418–31. Lanham, MD: Scarecrow, 2011.

Appel, Sara. "A Turn of the Sphere: The Place of Class in Intersectional Analysis." In *A History of American Working-Class Literature*, edited by Nicholas Coles and Paul Lauter, 406–23. Cambridge: Cambridge University Press, 2017.

Appiah, K. A. "The Case for Capitalizing the *B* in Black." *Atlantic*, June 18, 2020. https://www.theatlantic.com/ideas/archive/2020/06/time-to-capitalize-blackand-white/613159/.

Aristodemou, Maria. "Language, Ethics, and Imagination: Narratives of the [M]other in Law and Literature." *New Formations* 32 (Autumn-Winter 1997): 34–48.

Armengol, Josep M. "Slavery in Black and White: The Racialisation of (Male) Slavery in Frederick Douglass's *Narrative* and/vs. Toni Morrison's *A Mercy*." *Postcolonial Studies* 20.4 (Dec. 2017): 479–93.

Armstrong, Nancy. "Why Daughters Die: The Racial Logic of American Sentimentalism." *Yale Journal of Criticism* 7.2 (1994): 1–24.

Armstrong, Piers. "Afro-Latin Carnival and the Carnivalesque in the African American Novel." *Latin American and Caribbean Ethnic Studies* 7.3 (Nov. 2012): 295–320.

Ashe, Bertram D. "'Why Don't He Like My Hair?': Constructing African-American Standards of Beauty in Toni Morrison's *Song of Solomon* and Zora Neale Hurston's *Their Eyes Were Watching God*." *African American Review* 29.4 (Winter 1995): 579–92.

Askeland, Lori. "Remodeling the Model Home in *Uncle Tom's Cabin* and *Beloved*." *American Literature* 64.4 (1992): 785–805.

Atieh, Majda. "The Revelation of the Veiled in Toni Morrison's *Paradise*: The Whirling Dervishes in the Harem of the Convent" *MELUS* 3.2 (Summer 2011): 89–107.

Atkinson, Yvonne. "Language That Bears Witness: The Black English Oral Tradition in the Works of Toni Morrison." In *The Aesthetics of Toni Morrison: Speaking the Unspeakable*, edited by Marc Conner, 12–30. Jackson: University Press of Mississippi, 2000.

Atlas, Marilyn Judith. "Cracked Psyches and Verbal Putty: Geography and Integrity in Toni Morrison's *Jazz*." *Midwestern Miscellany* 24 (1996): 63–76.

———. "The Issue of Literacy in America: Slave Narratives and Toni Morrison's *The Bluest Eye*." *Midamerica* 27 (2000): 106–18.

———. "Toni Morrison's *Beloved* and the Reviewers." *Midwestern Miscellany* 18 (1990): 45–57.

Atwood, Margaret. "Haunted by Their Nightmare." *New York Times Book Review* (Sept. 13, 1987): 7.1.
———. "That Certain Thing Called the Girlfriend." *New York Times Books*, May 11, 1986. http://www.nytimes.com/books/00/09/03/specials/atwood-girlfriend.html.
Aubry, Timothy. "Beware the Furrow of the Middlebrow: Searching for *Paradise* on *The Oprah Winfrey Show*." *Modern Fiction Studies* 52.2 (Summer 2006): 350–73.
———. "Why Is *Beloved* So Universally Beloved? Uncovering Our Hidden Aesthetic Criteria." *Criticism* 58.3 (Summer 2016): 483–506.
Awkward, Michael. "'Unruly and Let Loose': Myth, Ideology, and Gender in *Song of Solomon*." *Callaloo* 13.3 (Summer 1990): 482–98.
Azouz, Samy "Cinema and Ideology in *The Bluest Eye* by Toni Morrison." *Americana* 4.2 (Fall 2008): n.p.
Azumurana, Solomon Omatsola. "The Dilemma of Western Education in Aidoo's *Changes: A Love Story*, Naylor's *The Women of Brewster Place*, and Morrison's *Beloved*. *Comparative Literature and Culture* 15.1 (Mar. 2013): 1–10.
Babb, Valerie. "*E Pluribus Unum*? The American Origins Narrative in Toni Morrison's *A Mercy*." *MELUS* 36.2 (Summer 2011): 147–64.
Babbitt, Susan. "Identity, Knowledge, and Toni Morrison's *Beloved*: Questions about Understanding Racism." *Hypatia* 9.3 (Summer 1994): 1–18.
Backes, Nancy. "Growing Up Desperately: The Adolescent 'Other' in the Novels of Paule Marshall, Toni Morrison, and Michelle Cliff." In *Women of Color: Defining the Issues, Hearing the Voices*, edited by Diane Long Hoeveler, Janet K. Boles, and Toni-Michelle Travis, 147–57. Westport, CN: Greenwood, 2001.
Backus, Margot Gayle. "'Looking for That Dead Girl': Incest, Pornography, and the Capitalist Family Romance in *Nightwood*, *The Years* and *Tar Baby*." *American Imago* 51.4 (1994): 521–45.
Badode, R. M. "American Society as Reflected in Toni Morrison's *The Bluest Eye*." In *Indian Views on American Literature*, edited by A. A. Mutalik-Desai. Prestige Books, 1998. 84–94.
Bailin, Deborah. "Natural History as National History in Toni Morrison's *Beloved*." *LATCH* 4 (2011): 32–62.
Baillie, Justine. "Contesting Ideologies: Deconstructing Racism in African-American Fiction." *Women: A Cultural Review* 14.1 (Spring 2003): 20–37.
———. "'Dread and Love': Postcolonial Theory and Practice in Toni Morrison's *Playing in the Dark* and *Song of Solomon* and William Faulkner's *Go Down, Moses*." *Critical Engagements* 1.1 (2007): 166–87.
Baker, Houston A., Jr. "Knowing Our Place: Psychoanalysis and *Sula*. In *Toni Morrison*, edited by Linden Peach, 103–9. New York: St. Martin's, 1997.
———. "The Point of Entanglement: Modernism, Diaspora, and Toni Morrison's *Love*." In *Contemporary African American Literature: The Living Canon*, edited by Lovalerie King and Shirley Moody-Turner, 17–40. Bloomington: Indiana University Press, 2013.
Bakerman, Jane S. "Failures of Love: Female Initiation in the Novels of Toni Morrison." *American Literature* 52.4 (Jan. 1981): 541–63.
———. "*Song of Solomon*." *College Language Association Journal* 21.3 (Mar. 1978): 446–47.
Balestra, Alisa A. "Racial and Cultural Rootedness: The Effect of Intraracial Oppression in *The Bluest Eye*." *49th Parallel* 16 (Autumn 2005): n.p.

Balon, Rebecca. "Kinless or Queer: The Unthinkable Queer Slave in Toni Morrison's *Beloved* and Robert O'Hara's *Insurrection: Holding History*." *African American Review* 48.1–2 (Spring–Summer 2015): 141–55.

Banyiwa-Horne, Naana. "The Scary Face of the Self: An Analysis of the Character of *Sula* in Toni Morrison's *Sula*. *SAGE* 2.1 (1985): 28–31.

Barksdale, Richard K. "Castration Symbolism in Recent Black American Fiction." *College Language Association Journal* 29.4 (1986): 400–413.

Barnes, Deborah. "Movin' On Up: The Madness of Migration in Toni Morrison's *Jazz*." In *Toni Morrison's Fiction: Contemporary Criticism*, edited by David L. Middleton, 283–95. New York: Garland, 1997.

Barnett, Pamela E. "Figurations of Rape and the Supernatural in *Beloved*." *PMLA* 112.3 (May 1997): 418–27.

Barr, Jason. "Viewing Toni Morrison's *Paradise* as a Response to William Carlos Williams's *Paterson*." *African American Review* 44.3 (Fall 2011): 421–33.

Bartley, Aryn. "'My Telling Can't Hurt You': Teaching Toni Morrison's *A Mercy* in a Survey of American Literature." *Teaching American Literature* 5.3–4 (Spring–Summer 2012): 16–28.

Bartold, Bonnie J. *Black Time: Fiction of Africa, the Caribbean and the United States*. New Haven, CT: Yale University Press, 1981.

Bassard, Katherine Clay. "The Race for Faith: Justice, Mercy and the Sign of the Cross in African American Literature." *Religion & Literature* 38.1 (Spring 2006): 95–114.

———. "Reading between the Lines: Neo-Slave Narrative and the KJV." In *The King James Bible across Borders and Centuries*, 195–214. Pittsburgh: Duquesne University Press, 2014.

Bast, Florian. "Reading Red: The Troping of Trauma in Toni Morrison's *Beloved*." *Callaloo* 34.4 (Fall 2011): 1069–87.

Bastien, David T., and Todd J. Hostager. "Jazz as Social Structure, Process, and Outcome." In *Jazz in Mind: Essays on the History and Meanings of Jazz*, edited by Reginald T. Backner and Steven Weiland, 149–65. Detroit, MI: Wayne State University Press, 1991.

Basu, Biman. "The Black Voice and the Language of the Text: Toni Morrison's *Sula*." *College Literature* 23.3 (Oct. 1996): 88–103.

———. "Postcolonial World Literature: Forster-Roy-Morrison." *The Comparatist* 38 (Oct. 2014): 158–87.

Baum, Rosalie Murphey. "Alcoholism and Family Abuse in *Maggie* and *The Bluest Eye*." *Mosaic* 19.3 (Summer 1986): 91–105.

Bawer, Bruce. "All That Jazz." *New Criterion* 10.9 (May 1992): 10–17. https://www.newcriterion.com/issues/1992/5/all-that-jazz.

Baxter, Lee. "Rethinking, Rewriting Self and Other in Toni Morrison's *Love*." In Baxter and Satz, *Toni Morrison on Mothers and Motherhood*, 88–104.

Baxter, Lee, and Martha Satz, eds. *Toni Morrison on Mothers and Motherhood*. Bradford, ON, Canada: Demeter, 2017.

Beaulieu, Elizabeth Ann. *The Toni Morrison Encyclopedia*. Westport, CT: Greenwood, 2003.

Beaver, Harold. "Black Gothic." *Times Literary Supplement*, Nov. 24, 1977, 1359.

Beliveau, Laura Bolf. "Challenging Texts: Challenging Students to Critically Connect Literature and History." *English Journal* 99.1 (Sept. 2009): 106–9.

Bell, Bernard W. *The Afro-American Novel and Its Tradition*. Amherst: University of Massachusetts Press, 1987.

———. "*Beloved*: A Womanist Neo-Slave Narrative; Or Multivocal Remembrances of Things Past." *African American Review* 26.1 (Spring 1992): 7–15.

Bell, Pearl K. "Fiction." *Commentary* 72 (Aug.1981): 56–58.

Bell, Roseann P., Bettye J. Parker, and Beverly Guy-Sheftall, eds. *Sturdy Black Bridges: Visions of Black Women in Literature*. New York: Doubleday Anchor, 1979.

Benjamin, Shanna Greene. "The Space that Race Creates: An Interstitial Analysis of Toni Morrison's 'Recitatif.'" *Studies in American Fiction* 40.1 (Spring 2013): 87–106.

Bennett, Juda. *Toni Morrison and the Queer Pleasure of Ghosts*. Albany: SUNY Press, 2015.

Bennett, Michael, and Vanessa D. Dickerson, eds. *Recovering the Black Female Body: Self-Representations by African American Women*. New Brunswick, NJ: Rutgers University Press, 2000.

Bennett, Paula. "The Mother's Part: Incest and Maternal Deprivation in Woolf and Morrison." In *Narrating Mothers: Theorizing Maternal Subjectivities*, edited by Brenda O. Daly and Maureen T. Reddy, 125–38. Knoxville: University of Tennessee Press, 1991.

Benston, Kimberly W. "Late Coltrane: A Re-membering of Orpheus." In *Chant of Saints*, edited by Michael S. Harper and Robert B. Stepto, 413–24. Chicago: University of Illinois Press, 1979.

Berben-Masi, Jacqueline. "Justice in Toni Morrison's *Love*." *GRAAT Online* 7 (Jan. 2010): 152–67.

Bergenholtz, Rita A. "Toni Morrison's *Sula*: A Satire on Binary Thinking." *African American Review* 30.1 (Spring 1996): 89–98.

Berger, James. "Ghosts of Liberalism: Morrison's *Beloved* and the Moynihan Report." *PMLA* 111.3 (May 1996): 408–20.

Berlant, Lauren. "Poor Eliza." *American Literature* 70.3 (Sept. 1998): 635–68.

Berret, Anthony J. "Toni Morrison's Literary Jazz." *CLA Journal* 32.3 (Mar. 1989): 267–83.

Bergthaller, Hannes. "Dis(re)membering History's Revenants: Trauma, Writing, and Simulated Orality in Toni Morrison's *Beloved*." *Connotations* 16.1–3 (2006–7): 116–36.

———. "Written Sounds and Spoken Letters, but All in Print: An Answer to Bärbel Höttges." *Connotations* 20.2–3 (2010–11): 289–92.

Best, Stephen. "On Failing to Make the Past Present." *Modern Language Quarterly* 73.3 (Sept. 2012): 453–74.

Bidney, Martin. "Creating a Feminist-Communitarian Romanticism in *Beloved*: Toni Morrison's New Uses for Blake, Keats, and Wordsworth." *Papers on Language and Literature* 36.3 (Summer 2000): 271–301.

"Bill Cosby's wife breaks her silence, compares him to lynching victim Emmett Till." *CBS News* (May 3, 2018). https://www.cbsnews.com/news/bill-cosby-wife-camille-cosby-breaks-her-silence-after-guilty-verdict/.

Billingslea-Brown, Alma Jean. *Crossing Borders through Folklore: African American Women's Fiction and Art*. Columbia: University of Missouri Press, 1999. 67–83.

Bisla, Sundeep. "Reading the Native Informant Reading: The Art of Passing on Empathy in *Beloved*." *Cultural Critique* 42 (Spring 1999): 104–36.

"Black Writers in Praise of Toni Morrison." *New York Times Book Review*, Jan. 24, 1988. Web. Aug. 3, 2019.

Blackburn, Sara. "Review of *Sula*, by Toni Morrison." *New York Times Book Review*, Dec. 30, 1973, 3.

Blake, Susan. "Folklore and Community in *Song of Solomon*." *MELUS* 7.3 (1980): 77–82.

Bloom, Harold. "Two African-American Masters of the American Novel." *Journal of Blacks in Higher Education* 28 (Summer 2000): 89–93.
Blyn, Robin. "Memory under Reconstruction: *Beloved* and the Fugitive Past." *Arizona Quarterly* 54.4 (Winter 1998): 111–40.
Bollen, Christopher "Toni Morrison." *Interview*, May 1, 2012. Retrieved from https://www.interviewmagazine.com/culture/toni-morrison.
Bonnet, Michèle. "'To Take the Sin Out of Slicing Trees . . .': The Law of the Tree in *Beloved*." *African American Review* 31.1 (Spring 1997): 41–54.
Boswell, Maia. "'Ladies,' 'Gentlemen,' and 'Colored': 'The Agency of (Lacan's Black) Letter' in the Outhouse." *Cultural Critique* 41 (Winter 1999): 108–38.
Boudreau, Kristin. "Pain and the Unmaking of Self in Toni Morrison's *Beloved*." *Contemporary Literature* 36.3 (Fall 1995): 447–65.
Bouson, Brooks J. "'Quiet as It's Kept': Shame and Trauma in Toni Morrison's *The Bluest Eye*." In *Scenes of Shame: Psychoanalysis, Shame, and Writing*, edited by Joseph Adamson and Hilary Clark, 207–36. Albany: SUNY Press, 1999.
———. "Uncovering the 'Beloved' in the Warring and Lawless Women in Toni Morrison's *Love*." *Midwest Quarterly* 49.4 (Summer 2008): 358–73.
Boutry, Katherine. "Black and Blue: The Female Body of Blues Writing in Jean Toomer, Toni Morrison, and Gayl Jones." In *Black Orpheus: Music in African American Fiction from the Harlem Renaissance to Toni Morrison*, edited by Saadi A. Simawe and Daniel Albright, 91–118. New York: Garland, 2000.
Bowers, Maggie Ann. "Acknowledging Ambivalence: The Creation of Communal Memory in the Writing of Toni Morrison." *Wasafiri* 27 (Spring 1998): 19–23.
Bowman, Diane Kim. "Flying High: The American Icarus in Morrison, Roth, and Updike." *Perspectives on Contemporary Literature* (1982): 810–17.
Branch, Eleanor. "Through the Maze of the Oedipal: Milkman's Search for Self in *Song of Solomon*." *Literature and Psychology* 41.1–2 (1995): 52–84.
Bredella, Lothar. "Decolonizing the Mind: Toni Morrison's *The Bluest Eye* and *Tar Baby*. In *Intercultural Encounters—Studies in English Literatures*, edited by Heinz Antor and Kevin L. Cope, 363–84. Heidelberg: Universitätsverlag C. Winter, 1999.
Brenkman, John. "Politics and Form in *Song of Solomon*." *Social Text* 39 (Summer 1994): 57–82.
Brenner, Gerry. "*Song of Solomon*: Morrison's Rejection of Rank's Monomyth and Feminism." *Studies in American Fiction* 15.1 (Spring 1987): 13–24.
Brickhouse, Anna. "Transatlantic vs. Hemispheric: Toni Morrison's Long Nineteenth Century." In *The Oxford Handbook of Nineteenth-Century American Literature*, edited by Russ Castronovo, 137–59. Oxford: Oxford University Press, 2012.
Britton, Wesley. "The Puritan Past and Black Gothic: The Haunting of Toni Morrison's *Beloved* in Light of Hawthorne's *The House of the Seven Gables*." *Nathaniel Hawthorne Review* 21.2 (Fall 1995): 7–23.
Broad, Robert L. "Giving Blood to the Scraps: Haints, History, and Hosea in *Beloved*." *African American Review* 28.2 (Summer 1994): 189–96.
Brophy-Warren, Jamin. "A Writer's Vote." *Wall Street Journal*, Nov. 7, 2008, W5.
Brown, Bill. "How to Do Things with Things (A Toy Story)." *Critical Inquiry* 24.4 (Summer 1998): 935–64.

Brown, Caroline. "Golden Gray and the Talking Book: Identity as a Site of Artful Construction in Toni Morrison's *Jazz*." *African American Review* 36.4 (Winter 2002): 629–42.
Brown, Cecil. "Interview with Toni Morrison." *Massachusetts Review* 36 (1995–96): 455–73.
Brown, Joseph. "To Cheer the Weary Traveler: Toni Morrison, William Faulkner, and History." *Mississippi Quarterly* 49.4 (Fall 1996): 709–26.
Brown, Rosellen. "The Pleasure of Enchantment." *Nation*, Oct. 17, 1987, 418.
Broyard, Anatole. "Two-Way Protest: *Tar Baby* by Toni Morrison." *New York Times*, Mar. 21, 1981. http://www.nytimes.com/1981/03/21/books/books-of-the-times-049574.html.
Bruck, Peter, and Wolfgang Karrer, eds. *The Afro-American Novel since 1960*. New York: B. R. Grüner, 1982.
Bryan, Eugenia P. "Written on the Walls: Reflections of Shifting Definitions of Slavery and Self in Toni Morrison's *A Mercy*." In *Afterimages of Slavery: Essays on Appearances in Recent American Films, Literature, Television and Other Media*, edited by Marlene D. Allen and Seretha D. Williams, 89–109. Jefferson, NC: McFarland, 2012.
Bryant, Cedric Gael. "'Every Goodbye Ain't Gone': The Semiotics of Death, Mourning, and Closural Practice in Toni Morrison's *Song of Solomon*." *MELUS* 24.3 (Fall 1999): 97–110.
———. "The Orderliness of Disorder: Madness and Evil in Toni Morrison's *Sula*." *Black American Literature Forum* 24.4 (Winter 1990): 731–45.
———. "'The Soul Has Bandaged Moments': Reading the African American Gothic in Wright's 'Big Boy Leaves Home,' Morrison's *Beloved*, and Gomez's *Gilda*." *African American Review* 39.4 (Winter 2005): 541–53.
Bryant, Ceron L. "Seeking Peace: The Application of Third Space Theory in Toni Morrison's *Sula*." *CLA Journal* 56.3 (2013): 251–66.
Bryant, Jerry H. "Something Ominous Here." *Nation* 219, July 6, 1974, 23–24.
Buchanan, Jeffrey M. "'A Productive and Fructifying Pain': Storytelling as Teaching in *The Bluest Eye*." *Reader* 50 (Spring 2004): 59–75.
Budic, Emily Miller. "Absence, Loss, and the Space of History in Toni Morrison's *Beloved*." *Arizona Quarterly* 48.2 (Summer 1992): 117–38.
Buehrer, David. "*American History X*, Morrison's *Song of Solomon*, and the Psychological Intersections of Race, Class, and Place in Contemporary America." *Journal of Evolutionary Psychology* 25.1–2 (Mar. 2004): 18–23.
———. "Fragmentation and Beyond: Characterization in Toni Morrison's *Song of Solomon*." *Journal of Evolutionary Psychology* 16.1–2 (Mar. 1995): 2–8.
Buisson, Françoise. "*The Bluest Eye*, *The Sound and the Fury*, and the Grecian Urn: Faulkner's and Morrison's Quest for Beauty." In *Faulkner and Morrison*, edited by Robert W. Hamblin and Christopher Rieger, 97–115. Cape Girardeau: Southeast Missouri State University Press, 2013.
Bulsterbaum, Allison A. "'Sugarman Gone Home': Folksong in Toni Morrison's *Song of Solomon*." *Publications of the Arkansas Philological Association* 10.1 (Spring 1984): 15–28.
Bump, Jerome. "Family Systems Therapy and Narrative in Toni Morrison's *The Bluest Eye*." In *Reading the Family Dance: Family Systems Therapy and Literary Study*, edited by John V. Knapp and Kenneth Womack, 151–70. Newark: University of Delaware Press, 2003.

———. "Racism and Appearance in *The Bluest Eye*: A Template for an Ethical Emotive Criticism." *College Literature* 37.2 (Spring 2010): 147–70.

Burgess, Françoise. "The White Woman: The Black Woman's Nemesis." *Revue Française d'Etudes Américaines* 67 (Jan. 1996): 99–107.

Burkhalter, Cindy. "Surrendering to the Air: Metaphors for Traditional African-American Wisdom in Toni Morrison's *Song of Solomon*." *JASAT* 26 (Oct. 1995): 55–65.

Burrell, Vernita. "Keep Your Hands off My Ethics: The Ethics of Reading in *The Bluest Eye* and 'Sonny's Blues.'" *ASEBL Journal* 7.1 (Spring 2011): 1–4.

Burton, Angela. "Signifyin(g) Abjection: Narrative Strategies in Toni Morrison's *Jazz*." In *Toni Morrison*, ed. Linden Peach, 154–69. New York: St. Martin's, 1997.

Busby, Margaret. "Toni Morrison: beloved and all that jazz: Margaret Busby on the new Nobel laureate, whose wisdom can nourish us all" (Oct. 8, 1993). http://www.independent.co.uk/arts-entertainment/books/books-toni-morrison-beloved-and-all-that-jazz-margaret-busby-on-the-new-nobel-laureate-whose-wisdom-1509591.html.

Butler, Robert James. "Open Movement and Selfhood in Toni Morrison's *Song of Solomon*." *Centennial Review* 28/29.4/1 (Fall–Winter 1984–85): 58–75.

Byerman, Keith E. *Fingering the Jagged Grain: Tradition and Form in Recent Black Fiction*. Athens: University of Georgia Press, 1985.

———. "Intense Behaviors: The Use of the Grotesque in *The Bluest Eye* and *Eva's Man*." *CLA Journal* 25.4 (June 1982): 447–57.

Byrne, Dara. "'Yonder they do not love your flesh': Community in Toni Morrison's *Beloved*; The Limitations of Citizenship and Property in the American Public Sphere." *Canadian Review of American Studies* 29.2 (1999): 25–59.

Campbell, Jan. "Images of the Real: Reading History and Psychoanalysis in Toni Morrison's *Beloved*." *Women* 7.2 (Autumn 1996): 136–49.

Campbell, Jane. *Mythic Black Fiction: The Transformation of History*. Knoxville: University of Tennessee Press, 1986.

Campbell, Joseph. *The Hero with a Thousand Faces*. New York: Pantheon, 1949.

Campbell, Josie P. "To Sing the Song, To Tell the Tale: A Study of Toni Morrison and Simone Schwarz-Bart." *Comparative Literature Studies* 22.3 (Fall 1985): 394–412.

Candel Bormann, Daniel. "The Material Bodily Principle in Mikhail Bakhtin's *Rabelais and His World* and Toni Morrison's *The Bluest Eye*." In *Proceedings of the 20th International AEDEAN Conference*, edited by P. Guardia and J. Stone, 389–94. Universitat de Barcelona, 1997.

Cannon, Elizabeth M. "Following the Traces of Female Desire in Toni Morrison's *Jazz*." *African American Review* 31.2 (Summer 1997): 235–47.

Cantiello, Jessica. "From Pre-Racial to Post-Racial? Reading and Reviewing *A Mercy* in the Age of Obama." *MELUS* 36.2 (Summer 2011): 165–83.

Capuano, Peter J. "Truth in Timbre: Morrison's Extension of Slave Narrative Song in *Beloved*." *African American Review* 37.1 (Spring 2003): 95–103.

Carden, Mary Paniccia. "Models of Memory and Romance: The Dual Endings of Toni Morrison's *Beloved*." *Twentieth Century Literature* 45.4 (Winter 1999): 401–27.

———. "'Trying to find a place when the streets don't go there': Fatherhood, Family, and American Racial Politics in Toni Morrison's *Love*." *African American Review* 44.1–2 (Spring 2011): 131–47.

Carlacio, Jami. "Narrative Epistemology: Storytelling as Agency in *A Mercy*." In *Toni Morrison: Paradise/Love/A Mercy*, edited by Lucille P. Fultz, 129–46. London: Bloomsbury, 2013.

Carpenter, Faedra Chatard. "Spectacles of Whiteness from Adrienne Kennedy to Suzan-Lori Parks." In *The Cambridge Companion to African American Theatre*, edited by Harvey Young, 174–95. Cambridge: Cambridge University Press, 2013.

Carruth, Allison. "'The Chocolate Eater': Food Traffic and Environmental Justice in Toni Morrison's *Tar Baby*." *Modern Fiction Studies* 55.3 (2009): 596–619.

Casler, Jeanine. "Monstrous Motherhood across Cultures: The Rejection of the Maternal." *JAISA* 5.1 (Fall 1999): 43–54.

Chang, Jeff. *Who We Be: The Colorization of America*. New York: St. Martin's, 2014.

Chang, Shu-li. "Daughterly Haunting and Historical Traumas: Toni Morrison's *Beloved* and Jamaica Kincaid's *The Autobiography of My Mother*." *Concentric* 30.2 (July 2004): 105–27.

Charles, Ron. "Toni Morrison's Feminist Portrayal of Racism." *The Christian Science Monitor*, Jan. 29, 1998. https://www.csmonitor.com/1998/0129/012998.feat.books.1.html.

———. "Toni Morrison's *Home*, a Restrained but Powerful Novel." *Washington Post*, Apr. 30, 2012. Retrieved from https://www.washingtonpost.com/entertainment/books/book-review-toni-morrisons-home-a-restrained-but-powerful-novel/2012/04/30/gIQAKiWSsT_story.html?utm_term=.2b3a2925ba6b.

Chen, Chang-fang. "Bakhtinian Strategies and Ethnic Writers: A Comparative Study of the Novels of Toni Morrison and Maxine Hong Kingston." In *The Force of Vision, III: Powers of Narration; Literary Theory*, edited by Earl Miner, Toru Haga, Gerald Gillespie, André Lorant, Will van Peer, and Elrud Ibsch, 221-28. International Comparative Literature Association, 1995.

Cheng, Anne Anlin. "Wounded Beauty: An Exploratory Essay on Race, Feminism, and the Aesthetic Question." *Tulsa Studies in Women's Literature* 19.2 (Fall 2000): 191–217.

Choice (Jan. 1988): 768.

Christian, Barbara. *Black Feminist Criticism: Perspectives on Black Women Writers*. New York: Pergamon, 1985.

———. *Black Women Novelists: The Development of a Tradition, 1891–1976*. Westport, CT: Greenwood, 1980.

———. "Community and Nature: The Novels of Toni Morrison." *Journal of Ethnic Studies* 7.4 (Winter 1980): 65–78.

———. "Fixing Methodologies: *Beloved*." *Cultural Critique* 24 (Spring 1993): 5–15.

———. "Testing the Strength of the Black Cultural Bond: Review of Toni Morrison's *Tar Baby*." *In These Times*, July 14, 1981, 19.

Churchwell, Sarah. "*Home* by Toni Morrison." *Guardian*, Apr. 27, 2012. Retrieved from https://www.theguardian.com/books/2012/apr/27/toni-morrison-sarah-churchwell-home.

Cillerai, Chiara. "Roundtable: Remembering the Past; Toni Morrison's Seventeenth Century in Today's Classroom [Special Section]" *Early American Literature* 48.1 (2013): 177–99.

Clark, Norris. "Flying Black: Toni Morrison's *The Bluest Eye*, *Sula*, and *Song of Solomon*." *Minority Voices* 4.2 (Fall 1980): 51–63.

Clary, Françoise. "Fractures Identitaires dans *The Bluest Eye* de Toni Morrison." *Annales du Centre de Recherches sur l'Amérique Anglophone* 20 (1995): 55–65.

Clemons, Walter. "A Gravestone of Memories." *Newsweek*, Sept. 28, 1987, 74.

Cohen, Leah Hager. "Point of Return: *Home*, a Novel by Toni Morrison." *New York Times*, May 17, 2012. Retrieved from https://www.nytimes.com/2012/05/20/books/review/home-a-novel-by-toni-morrison.html.
Coleman, James W. "Beyond the Reach of Love and Caring: Black Life in Toni Morrison's *Song of Solomon*." *Obsidian II* 1.3 (Winter 1986): 151–61.
———. "The Quest for Wholeness in Toni Morrison's *Tar Baby*." *Black American Literature Forum* 20.1/2 (Spring–Summer 1986): 63–73.
Conner, Marc C., ed. *The Aesthetics of Toni Morrison: Speaking the Unspeakable*. Jackson: University Press of Mississippi, 2000.
———. "Wild Women and Graceful Girls: Toni Morrison's Winter's Tale." In *Nature, Woman, and the Art of Politics*, edited by Eduardo A. Velasquez, 341–69. Lanham, MD: Roman & Littlefield, 2000.
Coonradt, Nicole M. "To Be Loved: Amy Denver and Human Need—Bridges to Understanding in Toni Morrison's *Beloved*." *College Literature* 32.4 (Fall 2005): 168–87.
Cooper, Brittney. "'Maybe I'll Be a Poet, Rapper': Hip-Hop Feminism and Literary Aesthetics in *Push*." *African American Review* 46.1 (Spring 2013): 55–69.
Cornell, Drucilla. "The Wild Woman and All That Jazz." In *Feminism beside Itself*, edited by Diane Elam and Robyn Wiegman, 313–21. New York: Routledge, 1995.
Cosca, David. "Is 'Hell a Pretty Place'? A White Supremacist Eden in Toni Morrison's *Beloved*." *Interdisciplinary Humanities* 30.2 (Summer 2013): 9–23.
Coughlan, David. *Ghost Writing in Contemporary American Fiction*. New York: Palgrave Macmillan, 2016.
Cowart, David. "Faulkner and Joyce in Morrison's *Song of Solomon*." *American Literature* 62.1 (Mar. 1990): 87–100.
Crabtree, Claire. "Interior Frontiers in Faulkner's *The Bear* and Toni Morrison's *Beloved*." *British and American Studies* (1997): 132–38.
Crouch, Stanley. "Aunt Medea." *New Republic* 197 (Oct. 19, 1987): 38–43.
Cullinan, Colleen Carpenter. "A Maternal Discourse of Redemption: Speech and Suffering in Morrison's *Beloved*." *Religion and Literature* 34.2 (Summer 2002): 77–104.
Cutter, Martha J. "The Story Must Go On and On: The Fantastic, Narration, and Intertextuality in Toni Morrison's *Beloved* and *Jazz*." *African American Review* 34.1 (Spring 2000): 61–75.
Dahill-Baue, William. "Insignificant Monkeys: Preaching Black English in Faulkner's *The Sound and the Fury* and Morrison's *The Bluest Eye* and *Beloved*." *Mississippi Quarterly* 49.3 (Summer 1996): 457–73.
Dalsgård, Katrine. "The One All-Black Town Worth the Pain: (African) American Exceptionalism, Historical Narration, and the Critique of Nationhood in Toni Morrison's *Paradise*." *African American Review* 35.2 (Summer 2001): 233–48.
Daly, Brenda. "Taking Whiteness Personally: Learning to Teach Testimonial Reading and Writing in the College Literature Classroom." *Pedagogy* 5.2 (Spring 2005): 213–46.
Daniel, Janice Bares. "Function or Frill: The Quilt as Storyteller in Toni Morrison's *Beloved*." *Midwest Quarterly* 41.3 (Spring 2000): 321–29.
Daniels, Jean. "The Call of Baby Suggs in *Beloved*: Imagining Freedom in Resistance and Struggle." *Griot* 21.2 (Fall 2002): 1–7.
Daniels, Steven V. "Putting 'His Story next to Hers': Choice, Agency, and the Structure of *Beloved*." *Texas Studies in Literature and Language* 44.4 (Winter 2002): 349–67.

Darda, Joseph. "The Literary Afterlife of the Korean War." *American Literature* 87.1 (Mar. 2015): 79–105.
Darling, Marsha Jean. "Ties That Bind." *Women's Review of Books* 5.6 (Mar. 1988): 4–5.
Dauterich, Edward. "Hybrid Expression: Orality and Literacy in *Beloved*." *Midwest Quarterly* 47.1 (Autumn 2005): 26–39.
Davidson, Rob. "Racial Stock and 8-Rocks: Communal Historiography in Toni Morrison's *Paradise*." *Twentieth Century Literature* 47.3 (Fall 2001): 355–73.
Davis, Arthur P. "Novels of the New Black Renaissance." *College Language Association Journal* 21 (June 1978): 475–77.
Davis, Christina. "*Beloved*: A Question of Identity." *Présence Africaine*, Nouvelle Série. no. 145 (1988): 151–56. Accessed May 20, 2021. http://www.jstor.org/stable/24351592.
De Angelis, Rose. "Rewriting the Black Matriarch: Eva in Toni Morrison's *Sula*." *MAWA Review* 16.1–2 (2001): 52–59.
De Arman, Charles. "Milkman as the Archetypal Hero: 'Thursday's Child Has Far to Go.'" *Obsidian* 6.3 (Winter 1980): 56–59.
Dee, Ruby. "Black Family Search for Identity." *Freedomways* 11 (Third Quarter 1971): 319–20.
Degler, Rebecca. "Ritual and 'Other' Religions in *The Bluest Eye*." In *Toni Morrison and the Bible*, edited by Shirley A. Stave, 232–55. New York: Peter Lang, 2006.
DeLancey, Dayle B. "Motherlove Is a Killer: *Sula*, *Beloved*, and the Deadly Trinity of Motherlove." *SAGE* 7.2 (1990): 15–18.
Delashmit, Margaret. "*The Bluest Eye*: An Indictment." *Griot* 20.1 (Spring 2001): 12–18.
Delazari, Ivan. "Voicing the Split Narrator: Readers' Chores in Toni Morrison's 'Recitatif.'" In *Audionarratology: Interfaces of Sound and Narrative*, edited by Jarmila Mildorf and Till Kinzel, 199–215. Berlin: De Gruyter, 2016.
Demetrakapoulos, Stephanie. "Maternal Bonds as Devourers of Women's Individuation in Toni Morrison's *Beloved*." *African American Review* 26.1 (Spring 1992): 51–59.
———. "The Nursing Mother and Feminine Metaphysics: An Essay on Embodiment." *Soundings* 65.4 (Winter 1982): 430–43.
Demetrakapoulos, Stephanie, and Karla Holloway. *New Dimensions of Spirituality*. Westport, CT: Greenwood, 1987.
Denard, Carolyn, ed. *Toni Morrison: Conversations*. Jackson: University Press of Mississippi, 2008.
———, ed. *Toni Morrison: What Moves at the Margin: Selected Nonfiction*. Jackson: University Press of Mississippi, 2008.
Depci, Aytemis, and Bülent Tanritanir. "Triple Oppression on Women in Toni Morrison's *Tar Baby* and *The Bluest Eye*." *Journal of Academic Social Science Studies* 6.6 (2013): 455–73.
Deusner, Stephen M. "*Love* by Toni Morrison." *Reading Group Guides* (Jan. 22, 2011). https://www.readinggroupguides.com/reviews/love.
DeVita, Alexis Brooks. "Not Passing On *Beloved*: The Sacrificial Child and the Circle of Redemption." *Griot* 19.1 (Spring 2000): 1–12.
De Weever, Jacqueline. "Toni Morrison's Use of Fairy Tale, Folk Tale and Myth in The *Song of Solomon*." *Southern Folklore Quarterly* 44 (1980): 131–44.
Dickerson, Vanessa D. "The Naked Father in Toni Morrison's *The Bluest Eye*." In *Refiguring the Father: New Feminist Readings of Patriarchy*, edited by Patricia Yaeger and Beth Kowaleski-Wallace, 108–27. Carbondale: Southern Illinois University Press, 1989.

———. "Summoning SomeBody: The Flesh Made Word in Toni Morrison's Fiction." In *Recovering the Black Female Body: Self-Representations by African American Women*, edited by Michael Bennett, Vanessa Dickerson, and Carla Peterson, 195–216. New Brunswick, NJ: Rutgers University Press, 2001.

Dickson-Carr, Darryl. "The Projection of the Beast: Subverting Mythologies in Toni Morrison's *Jazz*." *CLA Journal* 49.2 (Dec. 2005): 168–83.

Diedrich, Maria. "'Things Fall Apart?' The Black Critical Controversy over Toni Morrison's *Beloved*." *American Studies* 34.2 (1989): 175–86.

Ding, Yang, and Xiangguo Kong. "Tragedy of the Self-Splitting—A Psychological Reading of Toni Morrison's *The Bluest Eye*." *Frontiers of Literary Studies in China* 4.2 (June 2010): 298–320.

Distel, Kristin. "'Are You Sure She Was Your Sister?' Sororal Love and Maternal Failure in Toni Morrison's *Paradise*." In Baxter and Satz, *Toni Morrison on Mothers and Motherhood*, 122–39.

Dittmar, Linda. "'Will the Circle Be Unbroken?' The Politics of Form in *The Bluest Eye*." *Novel* 23.2 (Winter 1990): 137–55.

Diu, Nisha Lilia. "*Home* by Toni Morrison." *Telegraph*, May 10, 2012. Retrieved from https://www.telegraph.co.uk/culture/books/fictionreviews/9246047/Home-by-Toni-Morrison-review.html.

Dobbs, Cynthia. "Diasporic Designs of House, Home, and Haven in Toni Morrison's *Paradise*." *MELUS* 36.2 (Summer 2011): 109–26.

———. "Toni Morrison's *Beloved*: Bodies Returned, Modernism Revisited." *African American Review* 32.4 (Winter 1998): 563–78.

Dodman, Trevor: "'Belated Impress': *River George* and the African American Shell Shock Narrative." *African American Review* 44:1–2 (Spring–Summer 2011): 149–66.

Doughty, Peter. "A Fiction for the Tribe: Toni Morrison's *The Bluest Eye*." In *The New American Writing: Essays on American Literature since 1970*, edited by Graham Clarke, 29–50. New York: St. Martin's, 1990.

Douglas, Christopher. "What *The Bluest Eye* Knows about Them: Culture, Race, Identity." *American Literature* 78.1 (Mar. 2006): 141–68.

Dowling, Collette. "The Song of Toni Morrison." *New York Times*, May 20, 1979, 110.

Doyle, Laura. "Bodies Inside/Out: Violation and Resistance from the Prison Cell to *The Bluest Eye*." In *Feminist Interpretations of Maurice Merleau-Ponty*, edited by Dorothea Olkowski, Gail Weiss, and Nancy Tuana, 183–208. State College: Pennsylvania State University Press, 2006.

Doyle, Mary Ann. "'You Are Your Own Best Thing': Teaching Toni Morrison's *Beloved* Using Question-Hypothesis-Questions." *Cultural Studies* 9.2 (May 1995): 364–80.

Drake, Kimberly. "Rape and Resignation: Silencing the Victim in the Novels of Morrison and Wright." *Literature Interpretation Theory* 6.1–2 (Apr. 1995): 63–72.

Dubek, Laura. "'Pass It On!': Legacy and the Freedom Struggle in Toni Morrison's *Song of Solomon*." *Southern Quarterly* 52.2 (Winter 2015): 90–109.

Dubey, Madhu. *Black Women Novelists and the Nationalist Aesthetic*. Bloomington: Indiana University Press, 1994.

———. "Narration and Migration: *Jazz* and Vernacular Theories of Black Women's Fiction." *American Literary History* 10.2 (Summer 1998): 291–316.

———. "The Politics of Genre in *Beloved*." *Novel* 32.2 (Spring 1999): 187–206.

Dudar, Helen. "Toni Morrison: Finally Just a Writer." *Wall Street Journal*, Sept. 30, 1987, 34.

Durkin, Anita. "Object Written, Written Object: Slavery, Scarring, and Complications of Authorship in *Beloved*." *African American Review* 41.3 (Fall 2007): 541–56.

Durrans, Stéphanie, ed. *Thy Truth Then Be Thy Dowry: Questions of Inheritance in American Women's Literature*. Newcastle upon Tyne: Cambridge Scholars, 2014.

Duvall, John. "Authentic Ghost Stories: *Uncle Tom's Cabin, Absalom, Absalom!*, and *Beloved*." *Faulkner Journal* 4.1–2 (Fall 1988–Spring 1989): 83–97.

———. "Descent in the 'House of Chloe': Race, Rape, and Identity in Toni Morrison's *Tar Baby*." *Contemporary Literature* 38.2 (Summer 1997): 325–49.

———. "Doe Hunting and Masculinity: *Song of Solomon* and *Go Down, Moses*." *Arizona Quarterly* 47.1 (Spring 1991): 95–115.

———. "Naming Invisible Authority: Toni Morrison's Covert Letter to Ralph Ellison." *Studies in American Fiction* 25.2 (Autumn 1997): 241–53.

———. "Parody or Pastiche? Kathy Acker, Toni Morrison, and the Critical Appropriation of Faulknerian Masculinity." *Faulkner Journal* 15.1/2 (Fall 1999/2000): 169–84.

Earle, Monalesia. "Does 21st Century Feminist Fiction Challenge or Uphold Conventional Notions of the Family? A Critique of *A Mercy* and *Fun Home*." *ImageTexT: Interdisciplinary Comics Studies* 7.4 (2014): 34 paragraphs.

Eckard, Paula Gallant. "The Interplay of Music, Language, and Narrative in Toni Morrison's *Jazz*." *CLA Journal* 28.1 (1994): 11–19.

Eckstein, Lars. "A Love Supreme: Jazzthetic Strategies in Toni Morrison's *Beloved*." *African American Review* 40.2 (Summer 2006): 271–83.

Edelberg, Cynthia Dubin. "Morrison's Voice: Formal Education, the Work Ethic, and the Bible." *American Literature* 58 (May 1986): 236–37.

Edmunds, Susan. "Houses of Contention: *Tar Baby* and *Essence*." *American Literature* 90.3 (Sept. 2018): 613–41.

Edwards, Thomas R. "Ghost Story." *New York Review of Books* 34, Nov. 5, 1987, 18.

Eke, Maureen N., ed. *Beloved: Critical Insights*. Ipswich, MA: Salem, 2015.

Elia, Nada. "'Kum Buba Yali Kum Buba Tambe, Ameen, Ameen, Ameen' Did Some Flying Africans Bow to Allah?" *Callaloo* 26.1 (Winter 2003): 182–202.

———. *Trances, Dances, and Vociferations: Agency and Resistance in Africana Women's Narratives*. New York: Garland, 2001.

Elkin, Susan. "*God Help the Child* by Toni Morrison." *Independent*, Apr. 18, 2015. Retrieved from https://www.independent.co.uk/arts-entertainment/books/reviews/god-help-the-child-by-toni-morrison-book-review-the-tyranny-of-memory-can-make-a-destructive-10182633.html.

Elliot, Mary Jane Suero. "Postcolonial Experience in a Domestic Context: Commodified Subjectivity in Toni Morrison's *Beloved*." *MELUS* 25.3–4 (Fall–Winter 2000): 181–202.

Elliott, Mary Grace. "'Remembering How to Be Me': The Inherent Schism of Motherhood in Twentieth-Century American Literature." *quint* 4.4 (Sept. 2012): 67–80.

Ellis, Kate. "Text and Undertext: Myth and Politics in Toni Morrison's *Song of Solomon*." *Literature Interpretation Theory* 6.1–2 (Apr. 1995): 35–45.

Ellison, Ralph. "Richard Wright's Blues." 1945. In *The Collected Essays*, edited by John F. Callahan. New York: Modern Library, 1995.

Emberley, Julia. "Material Fictions of Desire: Transactional Readings, Fashion, and the 'Worlding' of Everyday Life in Contemporary Women's Writing." *Fashion Theory* 11.4 (2007): 463–82.

WORKS CITED

Emerson, Cheryl. "'My Skin Is Black Upon Me': Toni Morrison's *A Mercy* and the Question of a Female Job." *South Atlantic Review* 82.2 (Summer 2017): 12–23.

Eppert, Claudia. "Histories Re-imagined, Forgotten and Forgiven: Student Responses to Toni Morrison's *Beloved*." *Changing English* 10.2 (Oct. 2003): 185–94.

Erickson, Peter B. "Images on Nurturance in Toni Morrison's *Tar Baby*." *College Language Association Journal* 28 (Sept. 1981): 11–31.

Escoda Agusti, Clara. "Strategies of Subversion: The Deconstruction of Madness in *Eva's Man*, *Corregidora*, and *Beloved*." *Atlantis* 27.1 (June 2005): 29–38.

Evans, Mari, ed. *Black Women Writers (1950–1980): A Critical Evaluation*. New York: Anchor-Doubleday, 1984.

Evans, Shari. "Programmed Space, Themed Space and the Ethics of Home in Toni Morrison's *Paradise*." *African American Review* 46.2–3 (Summer–Fall 2013): 381–96.

Farrell, Susan. "'Who'd He Leave Behind?': Gender and History in Toni Morrison's *Song of Solomon*." *Bucknell Review* 39.1 (1995): 131–50.

Feng, Pin-chia. *The Female Bildungsroman by Toni Morrison and Maxine Kong Kingston: A Postmodern Reading*. New York: Peter Lang, 1997.

Ferrier, Carole. "Teaching African American Women's Literature in Australia: Reading Toni Morrison in the Deep North." In *Teaching African American Women's Writing*, edited by Gina Wisker, 137–56. London: Palgrave Macmillan, 2010.

Fick, Thomas H. "Toni Morrison's 'Allegory of the Cave': Movies, Consumption, and Platonic Realism in *The Bluest Eye*." *Journal of the Midwest Modern Language Association* 22.1 (Spring 1989): 10–22.

Fils-Aimé, Holly. "The Living Dead Learn to Fly: Themes of Spiritual Death, Initiation and Empowerment in *Praisesong for the Widow* and *Song of Solomon*." *MAWA Review* 10.1 (June 1995): 3–12.

———. "The Sweet Scent of Ginger: Understanding the Roots of *Song of Solomon* and *Mama Day*." *Griot* 15.1 (Spring 1996): 27–33.

Fisher, Ann H. "Review of *Beloved*, by Toni Morrison." *Library Journal* 112 (Sept. 1, 1987): 201.

Fishman, Charles. "Naming Names: Three Recent Novels by Women Writers." *Names* 32.1 (1984): 33–44.

FitzGerald, Jennifer. "Selfhood and Community: Psychoanalysis and Discourse in *Beloved*." *Modern Fiction Studies* 39.3–4 (Fall–Winter 1993): 669–87.

Flanagan, Joseph. "The Seduction of History: Trauma, Re-Memory, and the Ethics of the Real." *CLIO* 31.4 (Summer 2002): 387–402.

Fletcher, Judith. "Signifying Circe in Toni Morrison's *Song of Solomon*." *Classical World* 99.4 (2006): 405–18.

Flint, Holly. "Toni Morrison's *Paradise*: Black Cultural Citizenship in the American Empire." *American Literature* 78.3 (2006): 585–612.

Forbes, Malcolm. "Where the Heart Is: Toni Morrison's *Home*." *Millions*, May 24, 2012. Retrieved from https://themillions.com/2012/05/where-the-heart-is-on-toni-morrisons-home.html.

Foreman, P. Gabrielle. "Past-On Stories: History and the Magically Real, Morrison and Allende on Call." *Feminist Studies* 18.2 (Summer 1992): 368–88.

Fowler, Doreen. "Morrison's Return to Faulkner: *A Mercy* and *Absalom, Absalom!*" In *Faulkner and the Black Literature of the Americas: Faulkner and Yoknapatawpha*, edited by Jay Watson and James G. Thomas Jr., 233–44. Jackson: University Press of Mississippi, 2013.

———. "'Nobody Could Make It Alone': Fathers and Boundaries in Toni Morrison's *Beloved*." *MELUS* 36.2 (Summer 2011): 13–33.

Fraile-Marcos, Ana María. "Hybridizing the 'City upon a Hill' in Toni Morrison's *Paradise*." *MELUS* 28.4 (Winter 2003): 3–33.

Frampton, Edith. "'You Just Can't Fly On Off and Leave a Body': The Intercorporeal Breastfeeding Subject of Toni Morrison's Fiction." *Women* 16.2 (Summer 2005): 141–63.

Franco, Dean. "What We Talk about When We Talk about *Beloved*." *Modern Fiction Studies* 52.2 (Summer 2006): 415–39.

Frankel, Haskel. "The Bluest Eye." *New York Times Book Review*, Nov. 1, 1970, 46.

Fraser, Rhone, and Natalie King-Pedroso, eds. *Critical Responses about the Black Family in Toni Morrison's God Help the Child*. Lanham, MD: Lexington Books, 2020.

Freeman, John. "*Home: A Novel* by Toni Morrison." *Boston Globe*, May 13, 2012. Retrieved from https://www.bostonglobe.com/arts/books/2012/05/12/review-home-novel-toni-morrison/qG7a2XVE93i9BdbzoCfjKO/story.html.

Frever, Trinna S. "'Oh! You Beautiful Doll!': Icon, Image, and Culture in Works by Alvarez, Cisneros, and Morrison." *Tulsa Studies in Women's Literature* 28.1 (Spring 2009): 121–39.

Friedman, Gabriella. "Cultivating America: Colonial History in the Morrisonian Wilderness." *Modern Fiction Studies* 64.2 (Summer 2018): 311–33.

Frye, Joanne S. *Living Stories, Telling Lives: Women and the Novel in Contemporary Experience*. Ann Arbor: University of Michigan Press, 1986.

Fulton, Lorie Watkins. "Hiding Fire and Brimstone in Lacy Groves: The Twinned Trees of *Beloved*." *African American Review* 39.1–2 (Spring–Summer 2005): 189–99.

———. "William Faulkner Reprised: Isolation in Toni Morrison's *Song of Solomon*." *Mississippi Quarterly* 58.1–2 (Winter/Spring 2004–5): 7–24.

Fultz, Lucille P. "*Love*: An Elegy for the African American Community, or The Unintended Consequences of Desegregation/Integration." In *Toni Morrison: Memory and Meaning*, ed. Adrienne Lanier Seward and Justine Tally, 93–104. Jackson: University Press of Mississippi, 2014.

———. "Southern Ethos/Black Ethics in Toni Morrison's Fiction." *Studies in the Literary Imagination* 31.2 (Fall 1998): 79–95.

———. "To Make Herself: Mother-Daughter Conflicts in Toni Morrison's *Sula* and *Tar Baby*." In *Women of Color: Mother-Daughter Relationships in 20th-Century Literature*, edited by Elizabeth Brown-Guillory, 228–43. Austin: University of Texas Press, 1996.

———, ed. *Toni Morrison: Paradise, Love, A Mercy*. London: Bloomsbury, 2013.

———. *Toni Morrison: Playing with Difference*. Urbana: University of Illinois Press, 2003.

Fulweiler, Howard. "Belonging and Freedom in Morrison's *Beloved*: Slavery, Sentimentality, and the Evolution of Consciousness." *Centennial Review* 40.2 (Spring 1996): 331–58.

Furman, Jan. *Toni Morrison's Song of Solomon: A Casebook*. Oxford: Oxford University Press, 2003.

Fuston-White, Jeanna. "'From the Seen to the Told': The Construction of Subjectivity in Toni Morrison's *Beloved*." *African American Review* 36.3 (Fall 2002): 461–73.

Gant, Liz. "Books Noted." *Black World*, May 1971, 51.

Garabedian, Deanna M. "Toni Morrison and the Language of Music." *CLA Journal* 41.3 (Mar. 1998): 303–18.

Garbus, Lisa. "The Unspeakable Stories of *Shoah* and *Beloved*." *College Literature* 26.1 (Winter 1999): 52–68.

Gardner, Renee Lee. "Subverting Patriarchy with Vulnerability: Dismantling the Motherhood Mandate in Toni Morrison's *Beloved*." *Women's Studies* 45.1–4 (Jan.–June 2016): 203–14.

Garner, John. *Grendel*. 1971. New York: Vintage, 1989.

Gates, David. "Original Sins." *New York Times*, Nov. 28, 2008. Retrieved from https://www.nytimes.com/2008/11/30/books/review/Gates-t.html.

Gates, Henry Louis, Jr.. *Thirteen Ways of Looking at a Black Man*. 1997. New York: First Vintage Books, 1998.

Gates, Henry Louis, Jr. and K. A. Appiah, eds. *Toni Morrison: Critical Perspectives Past and Present*. New York: Amistad, 1993.

Gauthier, Marni. "The Other Side of *Paradise*: Toni Morrison's (Un)Making of Mythic History." *African American Review* 39.3 (Fall 2005): 395–414.

Gay, Roxanne. "*God Help the Child* by Toni Morrison." *Guardian*, Apr. 29, 2015. Retrieved from https://www.theguardian.com/books/2015/apr/29/god-help-the-child-toni-morrison-review-nov.

George, Sheldon. "Approaching the Thing of Slavery: A Lacanian Analysis of Toni Morrison's *Beloved*." *African American Review* 45.1–2 (Spring–Summer 2012): 115–30.

Gerster, Carole J. "From Film Margin to Novel Center: Toni Morrison's *The Bluest Eye*." *West Virginia University Philological Papers* 38 (1992): 191–200.

Gibson, Donald B. "Text and Countertext in Toni Morrison's *The Bluest Eye*." *Lit* 1.1–2 (Dec. 1989): 19–32.

Gilbert, Katherine. "'The Best Hiding Place': Internalization and Coping Mechanisms in Toni Morrison's *The Bluest Eye*." *MAWA Review* 8.2 (Dec. 1993): 48–52.

Gillan, Jennifer. "Focusing on the Wrong Front: Historical Displacement, the Maginot Line, and *The Bluest Eye*." *African American Review* 36.2 (Summer 2002): 283–98.

Gillespie, Carmen, ed. *Toni Morrison: Forty Years in the Clearing*. Lewisburg, PA: Bucknell University Press, 2012.

Gillespie, Diane, and Missy Dehn Kubitschek. "Who Cares? Women-Centered Psychology in *Sula*." *Black American Literature Forum* 24.1 (Spring 1990): 21–48. Rpt. in *Toni Morrison's Fiction: Contemporary Criticism*, edited by David L. Middleton, 61–91. New York: Garland, 1997. Rpt. in *Understanding Toni Morrison's Beloved and Sula*, edited by Solomon O. and Marla W. Lyasere, 19–48. Troy, NY: Whitston, 2000.

Gillespie, Marcia Ann. "Toni Morrison." *Ms*, Jan. 1988, 60–61.

Ginsburg, Ruth, and Shlomith Rimmon-Kenan. "Is There a Life after Death? Theorizing Authors and Reading *Jazz*." In *Narratologies: New Perspectives on Narrative Analysis*, edited by David Herman, 66–87. Columbus: Ohio State University Press, 1999.

Giovanni, Nikki. "*Song of Solomon*." *Encore* 6, Nov. 7, 1977, 39–40.

Girshin, Thomas. "Preserving the Body of Earth: An Ethic of Intercorporeality in Morrison's *Beloved*." *Atenea* 26.1 (June 2006): 151–63.

Gladys, P. V. Annie, and Edwinsingh Jeyachandra. "The Danger Lurking Within: The African American Woman in Toni Morrison's *The Bluest Eye*." *Language in India* 10.1 (Jan. 2010): n.p.

Glover, Toni. "Morrison, Music, and Metaphor." *Journal of the Georgia Philological Association* 1 (2006): 66-76.
Goad, Jill. "Enslaved by Mother and Lover: Florens' Impossible Search for Self-Love in Toni Morrison's *A Mercy*." *New Academia* 3.2 (Apr. 2014): 1-6.
Goldman, Anne E. "'I Made the Ink'; (Literary) Production and Reproduction in *Dessa Rose* and *Beloved*." *Feminist Studies* 16.2 (Summer 1990): 313-30.
Goldstein, Philip. "The Modernist Fiction of Ellison and Morrison: Between Communism and Black Art." In *Black Writers and the Left*, edited by Kristin Moriah, 33-44. Newcastle upon Tyne: Cambridge Scholars, 2013.
Goldstein-Shirley, David. "Race/[Gender]: Toni Morrison's 'Recitatif.'" *Journal of the Short Story in English* 27 (1996): 83-95.
Goodburn, Amy. "Racing (Erasing) White Privilege in Teacher/Research Writing about Race." In *Race, Rhetoric, and Composition,* ed. Keith Gilyard, 67-86. Portsmouth, NH: Heinemann Books, 1999.
Goodman, Walter. "The Lobbying for Literary Prizes." *New York Times*, Jan. 28, 1988, C26.
Gornick, Vivian. "Into the Dark Heart of Childhood." *Village Voice*, Aug. 29, 1977, 41.
Gourdine, Angeletta K. M. "Colored *Readings*; or, Interpretation and the Raciogendered Body." In *Reading Sites: Social Difference and Reader Response*, edited by Patrocinio P. Schweickart and Elizabeth A. Flynn, 60-82. New York: MLA, 2004.
———. "Hearing Reading and Being *Read* by Beloved." *NWSA Journal* 10.2 (Summer 1998): 13-31.
Gowda, H. H. Anniah. "Feminine Black Voice." *Literary Half-Yearly* 35.1 (Jan. 1994): 28-50.
Goyal, Yogita. "The Gender of Diaspora in Toni Morrison's *Tar Baby*." *Modern Fiction Studies* 52.2 (Summer 2006): 393-414.
Grandt, Jürgen. "Kinds of Blue: Toni Morrison, Hans Janowitz, and the Jazz Aesthetic." *African American Review* 38.2 (Summer 2004): 303-22.
Grant, Robert. "Absence into Presence: The Thematics of Memory and 'Missing' Subjects in Toni Morrison's *Sula*." In *Critical Essays on Toni Morrison*, edited by Nellie Y. McKay, 90-103. Boston: Hall, 1988.
Grausam, Daniel. "On the Idea of In(ter)dependence: *Paradise* and Foreign Policy." *MELUS* 36.2 (Summer 2011): 127-45.
Gravett, Sharon L. "Toni Morrison's *The Bluest Eye*: An Inverted *Walden*?" *West Virginia University Philological Papers* 38 (1992): 201-11.
Gray, Paul. "Something Terrible Happened." *Time*, Sept. 21, 1987, 75.
Greenbaum, Vicky. "Teaching *Beloved*: Images of Transcendence." *English Journal* 91.6 (July 2002): 83-87.
Greenfield-Sanders, Timothy, dir. *Toni Morrison: The Pieces I Am*. Perfect Day Films, 2019.
Greenway, Gina Nicole. "Into the Wood: The Image of the Chokecherry Tree in Toni Morrison's *Beloved*." *Proteus* 21.2 (Fall 2004): 3-7.
Grewal, Gurleen. *Circles of Sorrow, Lines of Struggle: The Novels of Toni Morrison*. Baton Rouge: Louisiana State University Press, 1998.
Griesinger, Emily. "Why Baby Suggs, Holy, Quit Preaching the Word: Redemption and Holiness in Toni Morrison's *Beloved*." *Christianity and Literature* 50.4 (Summer 2001): 689-702.
Griffith, Johnny R. "In the End is the Beginning: Toni Morrison's Post-Modern, Post-Ethical Vision of *Paradise*." *Christianity and Literature* 60.4 (Summer 2011): 581-610.

WORKS CITED

Griffith, Paul. *Art and Ritual in the Black Diaspora: Archetypes of Transition*. Lanham, MD: Lexington Books, 2017.

Grobman, Laurie. "Postpositivist Realism in the Multicultural Writing Classroom: Beyond the Paralysis of Cultural Relativism." *Pedagogy* 3.2 (Spring 2003): 205–25.

Groover, Kristina K. "The Wilderness Within: Home as Sacred Space in American Women's Writing—Jewett's *The Country of the Pointed Firs*, Morrison's *The Bluest Eye* and Gibbons' *Ellen Foster*." *MAWA Review* 12.1 (June 1997): 13–29.

Gruber, Elizabeth. "Back to the Future: Ecological Crisis and Recalcitrant Memory in *The Tempest* and *Tar Baby*." *Literature Interpretation Theory* 21.4 (2010): 223–41.

Guth, Deborah. "A Blessing and a Burden: The Relation to the Past in *Sula*, *Song of Solomon* and *Beloved*." *Modern Fiction Studies* 39.3–4 (Fall–Winter 1993): 575–96.

Gwin, Minrose C. "'Hereisthehouse': Cultural Spaces of Incest in *The Bluest Eye*." In *Incest and the Literary Imagination*, edited by Elizabeth Barnes, 316–28. Gainesville: University Press of Florida, 2002.

Hall, Cheryl. "Beyond the 'Literary Habit': Oral Tradition and Jazz in *Beloved*." *MELUS* 19.1 (Spring 1994): 89–95.

Hall, Molly Volanth. "*Beloved* as Ecological Testimony: The Displaced Subject of American Slavery." *Isle* 25.3 (Summer 2018): 549–65.

Hamblin, Robert W. and Christopher Rieger, eds. *Faulkner and Morrison*. Cape Girardeau: Southeast Missouri State University Press, 2013.

Hamilton, Cynthia. "Revisions, Rememories and Exorcisms: Toni Morrison and the Slave Narrative." *Journal of American Studies* 30.3 (Dec. 1996): 429–45.

Handley, William R. "The House a Ghost Built: Nommo, Allegory, and the Ethics of Reading in Toni Morrison's *Beloved*." *Contemporary Literature* 36.4 (Winter 1995): 676–701.

Hansen, Morten. "I Am Become Wilderness: Toni Morrison's *A Mercy* and Global American Space." *Literature Interpretation Theory* 29.3 (2018): 210–27.

Harack, Katrina. "'Not Even in the Language They Had Invented for Secrets': Trauma, Memory, and Re-witnessing in Toni Morrison's *Love*." *Mississippi Quarterly* 66.2 (Spring 2013): 255–78.

Hardack, Richard. "'A Music Seeking Its Own Words': Double-Timing and Double Consciousness in Toni Morrison's *Jazz*." *Callaloo* 18.2 (Spring 1995): 451–71.

Hardin, Tayana L. "The I Who Arrives: A Meditation on History as Inheritance." *Pedagogy* 18.3 (Oct. 2018): 531–40.

Harding, Wendy, and Jacky Martin. "Reading at the Cultural Interface: The Corn Symbolism of *Beloved*." *MELUS* 19.2 (Summer 1994): 85–97.

Harris, A. Leslie. "Myth as Structure in Toni Morrison's *Song of Solomon*." *MELUS* 7 (1980): 69–76.

Harris, Middleton A., ed. *The Black Book*. 1974. New York: Random House, 2009.

Harris, Middleton A., Ernest Smith, Morris Levitt, and Roger Furman, eds. *The Black Book*. 1974. 35th anniversary ed., with a new foreword by Toni Morrison. New York: Random House, 2009.

Harris, Trudier. *Fiction and Folklore: The Novels of Toni Morrison*. Knoxville: University of Tennessee Press, 1991.

———. "Of Mother Love and Demons." *Callaloo* 11 (Spring 1988): 387–89.

———. "Watchers Watching Watchers: Positioning Characters and Readers in Baldwin's 'Sonny's Blues' and Morrison's 'Recitatif.'" In King and Scott, *James Baldwin and Toni Morrison: Comparative Critical and Theoretical Essays*, 103–20.

Härting, Heike. "'Chokecherry Tree(s)': Operative Modes of Metaphor in Toni Morrison's *Beloved*." *ARIEL* 29.4 (Oct. 1998): 23–51.
Hassan Khan, Reza, and Shafiqur Rahman. "The Framework of Racism in Toni Morrison's *The Bluest Eye*: A Psychosocial Interpretation." *Advances in Language and Literary Studies* 5.2 (2014): 25–28.
Hastings, Phyllis. "*The Bluest Eye* and the American Dream." In *Literature and Black Aesthetics*, edited by Dele Orisawayi, Ernest N. Emenyonu, Ebele Eko, Julius Ogu, Emilia Oku, and Agantiem Abang, 58–66. Ibidan, Nigeria: Heinemann Books, 1990.
Hausknecht, Gina. "Self-Possession, Dolls, Beatlemania, Loss: Telling the Girl's Own Story." In *The Girl: Construction of the Girl in Contemporary Fiction by Women*, edited by Ruth O. Saxton, 21–42. New York: St. Martin's, 1998.
Hawthorne, Evelyn. "On Gaining the Double-Vision: *Tar Baby* as Diasporean Novel." *Black American Literature Forum* 22.1 (Spring 1988): 97–107.
Hayes, Elizabeth T. "'Like Seeing You Buried': Persephone in *The Bluest Eye*, *Their Eyes Were Watching God*, and *The Color Purple*." In *Images of Persephone: Feminist Readings in Western Literature*, edited by Elizabeth T. Hayes, 170–94. Gainesville: University Press of Florida, 1994.
———. "The Named and the Nameless: Morrison's 124 and Naylor's 'the Other Place' as Semiotic Chorae." *African American Review* 38.4 (Winter 2004): 669–81.
Hébert, Kimberly G. "Acting the Nigger: Topsy, Shirley Temple, and Toni Morrison's Pecola." In *Approaches to Teaching Stowe's Uncle Tom's Cabin*," edited by Elizabeth Ammons and Susan Belasco, 184–998. New York: MLA, 2000.
Heffernan, Theresa. "*Beloved* and the Problem of Mourning." *Studies in the Novel* 30.4 (Winter 1998): 558–73.
Heller, Dana. "Reconstructing Kin: Family, History, and Narrative in Toni Morrison's *Beloved*." *College Literature* 21.2 (June 1994): 105–17.
Heller, Zoë. "Feathered Wombs." *London Review of Books* 20.9, May 7, 1998, 25.
Henderson, Mae Gwendolyn. "Speaking in Tongues: Dialogics, Dialectics, and the Black Woman Writer's Literary Tradition." In *African American Literary Theory: A Reader*, edited by Winston Napier, 348–68. New York: New York University Press, 2000.
Henton, Jennifer E. "*Sula*'s Joke on Psychoanalysis." *African American Review* 45.1–2 (Spring/Summer 2012): 99–113.
Heyman, Richard. "Universalization and Its Discontents: Morrison's *Song of Solomon*—A (W)hol(e)y Black Text." *African American Review* 29.3 (Fall 1995): 381–92.
Hichri, Asma "Hunger 'Beyond Appetite': Nurture Dialectics in Toni Morrison's *Beloved*." *ARIEL* 44.2–3 (Apr.–July 2013): 195–220.
Hilfrich, Carola. "Anti-Exodus: Countermemory, Gender, Race, and Everyday Life in Toni Morrison's *Paradise*." *Modern Fiction Studies* 52.2 (Summer 2006): 321–49.
Hindman, Jane E. "'A Little Space, a Little Time, Some Way to Hold Off Eventfulness': African American Quiltmaking as Metaphor in Toni Morrison's *Beloved*." *Literature Interpretation Theory* 6.1–2 (Apr. 1995): 101–20.
Ho, Wen-ching. "In Search of a Female Self: Toni Morrison's *The Bluest Eye* and Maxine Hong Kingston's *The Woman Warrior*." *American Studies* 17.3 (Sept. 1987): 1–44.
Hobby, Blake, ed. *Exploration and Colonization*. New York: Bloom's Literary Criticism, 2010.
———, ed. *The Trickster*. New York: Bloom's Literary Criticism, 2010.

Hogue, Bev. "Naming the Bones: Bodies of Knowledge in Contemporary Fiction." *Modern Fiction Studies* 52.1 (Spring 2006): 121–42.
Holden-Kirwan, Jennifer L. "Looking into the Self That Is No Self: An Examination of Subjectivity in *Beloved*." *African American Review* 32.3 (Fall 1998): 415–26.
Holland, Sharon P. "Bakulu Discourse: The Language of the Margin in Toni Morrison's *Beloved*." *Literature Interpretation Theory* 6.1–2 (Apr. 1995): 89–100.
Hollis, Burney J., ed. *Amid Visions and Revisions: Poetry and Criticism on Literature and the Arts*. Baltimore, MD: Morgan State University Press, 1985.
Holloway, Karla F. C. "*Beloved*: America's Grammar Book." *Daedalus* 143.1 (Winter 2014): 107–14.
———. "*Beloved*: A Spiritual." *Callaloo* 13.3 (Summer 1990): 516–25.
Holloway, Karla F. C., and Stephanie A. Demetrakopoulos. *New Dimensions of Spirituality: A Biracial and Bicultural Reading of the Novels of Toni Morrison*. Westport, CT: Greenwood, 1987.
Holmes, Kristine. "'This Is Flesh I'm Talking about Here': Embodiment in Toni Morrison's *Beloved* and Sherley Anne Williams' *Dessa Rose*." *Literature Interpretation Theory* 6.1–2 (Apr. 1995): 121–32.
Holton, Robert. "Bearing Witness: Toni Morrison's *Song of Solomon* and *Beloved*." *English Studies in Canada* 20.1 (Mar. 1994): 79–90.
Homans, Margaret. "'Her Very Own Howl': The Ambiguities of Representation in Recent Women's Fiction." *Signs* 9.2 (1983): 186–205.
hooks, bell. "Touching the Earth." In *At Home on the Earth: Becoming Native to Our Place*, edited by David Landis Barnhill, 51–56. Berkeley: University of California Press, 1999.
Hooper, Lita. "A Black Feminist Critique of *The Bride Price* and *The Bluest Eye*." *Journal of African Children's and Youth Literature* 6 (1994–95): 74–81.
Horn, Miriam. "Five Years of Terror." *U.S. News & World Report* 19 (Oct. 1987): 75.
Horvitz, Deborah. "Nameless Ghosts: Possession and Dispossession in *Beloved*." *Studies in American Fiction* 17.2 (Autumn 1989): 157–67.
Höttges, Bärbel. "Written Sounds and Spoken Letters: Orality and Literacy in Toni Morrison's *Beloved*." *Connotations* 19.1–3 (2009–10): 147–60.
House, Elizabeth B. "The Sweet Life in Toni Morrison's Fiction." *American Literature* 56 (May 1984): 195–200.
———. "Toni Morrison's Ghost: The Beloved Who Is Not Beloved." *Studies in American Fiction* 18.1 (Spring 1990): 17–26.
Hovet, Grace Ann, and Barbara Lounsberry. "Flying as Symbol and Legend in Toni Morrison's *The Bluest Eye*, *Sula*, and *Song of Solomon*." *CLA Journal* 27.2 (Dec. 1983): 119–40.
Hsieh, Yi-jo. "Trauma and Healing: A Psychoanalytic Reading of Florens' Confession in Toni Morrison's *A Mercy*." *New Academic* 2.4 (Oct. 2013): 1–11.
Huang, Hsin-ya. "Three Women's Texts and the Healing Power of the Other Woman." *Concentric* 28.1 (Jan. 2003): 153–80.
Hubbard, Dolan. "In Quest of Authority: Toni Morrison's *Song of Solomon* and the Rhetoric of the Black Preacher." *CLA Journal* 35.3 (1992): 288–302.
Hull, Akasha Gloria, Barbara Smith, and Patricia Bell-Scott, eds. *All the Women Are White, All the Blacks Are Men, But Some of Us Are Brave*. New York: Feminist, 1982.
Humann, Heather Duerre. "Family and Violence in *Love*." *Women's Studies* 43.2 (Feb. 2014): 246–62.

Hunt, Michelle. "Women as Commodities in Danticat's *Breath, Eyes, Memory* and Morrison's *The Bluest Eye*." *Pennsylvania Literary Journal* 8.2 (Summer 2016): 120–49.
Hurston, Zora Neale. *Their Eyes Were Watching God*. Afterword by Henry Louis Gates Jr. and foreword by Mary Helen Washington. New York: Harper Perennial, 2003.
Hutch, Angela. "Electric Rubens." *Listener* (Dec. 17 and 24, 1981): 793.
Hutchinson, Earle Ofari. "Review: God Help the Child by Toni Morrison." *Chicago Tribune*, Apr. 16, 2015. Retrieved from https://www.chicagotribune.com/entertainment/books/ct-prj-toni-morrison-god-help-the-childe-20150416-story.html.
Iannone, Carol. "Toni Morrison's Career." *Commentary* 84.6 (Dec. 1987): 59–63.
Ibarrola, Aitor. "The Challenges of Recovering from Individual and Cultural Trauma in Toni Morrison's *Home*." *International Journal of English Studies* 14.1 (2014): 109–24.
Ikuenobe, Polycarp. "Flying and Myth in *Song of Solomon*'s African Cultural and Philosophical Foundation." *International Journal of African Studies* 2.2 (Spring 2001): 49–78.
Imbrie, Ann. "'What Shalimar Knew': Toni Morrison's *Song of Solomon* as a Pastoral Novel." *College English* 55.5 (Sept. 1993): 473–90.
Insko, Jeffrey. "Literary Popularity: *Beloved* and Pop Culture." *Literature Interpretation Theory* 12.4 (Dec. 2001): 427–47.
Insoo, Lee. "Adrienne Kennedy's *A Lesson in Dead Language*: A Narrative Battle over the Meaning of Women's Bleeding." *Journal of Modern English Drama* 25.2 (Aug. 2012): 215–42.
Iqbal, Razia. "Review of *God Help the Child* by Toni Morrison," Apr. 9, 2015. Retrieved from https://www.independent.co.uk/arts-entertainment/books/reviews/god-help-the-child-by-toni-morrison-book-review-pain-and-trauma-live-just-under-the-skin-10164870.html.
Irving, John. "Morrison's Black Fable." *New York Times Books*, Mar. 29, 1981. http://www.nytimes.com/books/97/06/15/lifetimes/irving-tar.html.
Izgarjan, Aleksandra. "BREAthtaKING Beauty: Gender and Race Conventions in Toni Morrison's *The Bluest Eye*." In *The Beauty of Convention: Essays in Literature and Culture*, edited by Marija Krivokapić-Knežević and Aleksandra Nikčević-Batrićvić, 137–53. Newcastle upon Tyne, UK: Cambridge Scholars, 2014.
———. "On the 'Untranslatability' of African American Vernacular English." *B. A. S.* 4.1 (1999): 156–67.
Jablon, Madelyn. "Rememory, Dream History, and Revision in Toni Morrison's *Beloved* and Alice Walker's *The Temple of My Familiar*." *CLA Journal* 37.2 (Dec. 1993): 136–44.
Jackson, Chuck. "A 'Headless Display': *Sula*, Soldiers, and Lynching. *Modern Fiction Studies* 52.2 (2006): 374–92.
Jaffrey, Zia. "The *Salon* Interview—Toni Morrison." *Salon*, Feb. 3, 1998: http://www.salon.com/1998/02/02/cov_si_02int/.
James, Stanlie. "Mothering: A Possible Black Feminist Link to Social Transformations." In *Theorizing Black Feminism: The Visionary Pragmatism of Black Women*, edited by Stanlie James and A. P. Busia, 44–54. New York: Routledge, 1993.
Janowitz, Hans. *Jazz*., edited by Rolf Riess. 1927. Bonn: Weidle, 1999.
Jarrett, Gene. "'Couldn't Find Them Anywhere': Thomas Glave's *Whose Song?* (Post) Modernist Literary Queerings, and the Trauma of Witnessing, Memory, and Testimony." *Callaloo* 23.4 (Fall 2000): 1241–58.

"Jazz." *Kirkus Reviews* (Feb. 15, 1992). https://www.kirkusreviews.com/book-reviews/toni-morrison/jazz/.

"Jazz." *Publisher's Weekly* (Apr. 1993). https://www.publishersweekly.com/978-0-452-26965-1.

Jefferson, Margo. "Black Gold." *Newsweek*, Sept. 12, 1977, 93, 96, 100.

———. "Toni Morrison: Passionate and Precise." *Ms.* 3 (Dec. 1974): 34–35, 37, 39.

Jenkins, Candice M. "Pure Black: Class, Color, and Intraracial Politics in Toni Morrison's *Paradise*." *Modern Fiction Studies* 52.2 (Summer 2006): 270–96.

Jennings, La Vinia Delois. *Margaret Garner*. Charlottesville: University of Virginia Press, 2016.

———. *Toni Morrison and the Idea of Africa*. Cambridge: Cambridge University Press, 2008.

Jessee, Sharon. "The Contrapuntal Historiography of Toni Morrison's *Paradise*: Unpacking the Legacies of the Kansas and Oklahoma All-Black Towns." *American Studies* 47.1 (Spring 2006): 81–112.

Jesser, Nancy. "Violence, Home, and Community in Toni Morrison's *Beloved*." *African American Review* 33.2 (Summer 1999): 325–45.

Jewett, Chad. "The Modality of Toni Morrison's *Jazz*." *African American Review* 48.4 (Winter 2015): 445–56.

John, Eileen. "Subtlety and Moral Vision in Fiction." *Philosophy and Literature* 19.2 (Oct. 1995): 308–19.

Johnson, Diane. *Terrorists and Novelists*. New York: Knopf, 1982.

Joiner, Jennie J. "The Slow Burn of Masculinity in Faulkner's Hearth and Morrison's Oven." *Faulkner Journal* 25.2 (Spring 2010): 53–68.

Jones, Bessie W., and Audrey L. Vinson. *The World of Toni Morrison: Explorations in Literary Criticism*. Dubuque, IA: Kendall Hunt, 1985.

Jones, Carolyn M. "Southern Landscape as Psychic Landscape in Toni Morrison's Fiction." *Studies in the Literary Imagination* 31.2 (Fall 1998): 37–48.

———. "*Sula* and *Beloved*: Images of Cain in the Novels of Toni Morrison." *African American Review* 27.4 (Winter 1993): 615–26.

———. "Traces and Cracks: Identity and Narrative in Toni Morrison's *Jazz*." *African American Review* 31.3 (Fall 1997): 481–95.

Jones, Jill C. "The Eye of a Needle: Morrison's *Paradise*, Faulkner's *Absalom, Absalom!*, and the American Jeremiad." *Faulkner Journal* 17.2 (Spring 2002): 3–23.

Jordan, Margaret I. *African American Servitude and Historical Imaginings: Retrospective Fiction and Representation*. London: Palgrave Macmillan, 2004.

Jovović, Tamara. "Rethinking Race: Toni Morrison's *The Bluest Eye* and *God Help the Child*." *British and American Studies* 25 (2019): 199–204.

Joyce, Joyce Ann. "Structural and Thematic Unity in Toni Morrison's *Song of Solomon*." *CEA Critic* 49.2–4 (Winter–Summer 1986–87): 185–98.

Jurecic, Ann. "Empathy and the Critic." *College English* 74.1 (Sept. 2011): 10–27.

Kakutani, Michiko. "Bonds That Seem Cruel Can Be Kind." *New York Times*, Nov. 3, 2008. Retrieved from https://www.nytimes.com/2008/11/04/books/04kaku.html.

———. "Books of the Times." *New York Times*, Sept. 2, 1987, C24.

———. "*Paradise*: Worthy Women, Unredeemable Men." *New York Times*, Jan. 6, 1998.

———. "Soldier Is Defeated by War Abroad, Then Welcomed Back by Racism." *New York Times*, May 7, 2012. Retrieved from https://www.nytimes.com/2012/05/08/books/home-a-novel-by-toni-morrison.html.

Kang, Nancy. "To Love and Be Loved: Considering Black Masculinity and the Misandric Impulse in Toni Morrison's *Beloved*." *Callaloo* 26.3 (Summer 2003): 836–54.
Kaplan, Sara Clarke. "A Response to Maurice Wallace." *American Literary History* 20.4 (Winter 2008): 807–13.
Karavanta, Mina. "Toni Morrison's *A Mercy* and the Counterwriting of Negative Communities: A Postnational Novel." *Modern Fiction Studies* 58.4 (Winter 2012): 723–46.
Katawal, Ubaraj. "An Administered Life in 'Paradise.'" *South Central Review* 34.1 (Spring 2017): 32–52.
Kawash, Samira. "Haunted Houses, Sinking Ships: Race, Architecture, and Identity in *Beloved* and *Middle Passage*." *New Centennial Review* 1.3 (Winter 2001): 67–86.
Kearly, Peter R. "Toni Morrison's *Paradise* and the Politics of Community." *Journal of American and Comparative Cultures* 23.2 (Summer 2000): 9–16.
Keizer, Arlene R. "*Beloved*: Ideologies in Conflict, Improvised Subjects." *African American Review* 33.1 (Spring 1999): 105–23.
Kérchy, Anna. "Narrating the Beat of the Heart, Jazzing the Text of Desire: A Comparative Interface of James Baldwin's *Another Country* and Toni Morrison's *Jazz*." In King and Scott, *James Baldwin and Toni Morrison: Comparative Critical and Theoretical Essays*, 37–62.
Khaleghi, Mahboobeh. "Narration and Intertextuality in Toni Morrison's *Jazz*." *Criterion* 2.1 (Apr. 2011): 1–10.
Khawaja, Mabel, Jon-Christian Suggs, and James Berger (rejoinder). "Toni Morrison's *Beloved*." *PMLA* 112.1 (Jan. 1997): 115–18.
Khayati, Abdellatif. "Representation, Race, and the 'Language' of the Ineffable in Toni Morrison's Narrative." *African American Review* 33.2 (Summer 1999): 313–24.
Khushu-Lahiri, Rajyashree. "Matrilineage, Migrancy and Morrison's *The Bluest Eye*." In *New Waves in American Literature*, edited by A. A. Mutalik-Desai, V. K. Malhotra, T. S. Anand, and Prashant K. Sinha, 17–22. Creative Publishing, 1999.
Kim, Aeju. "Deconstructive Mythmaking in Toni Morrison's *Song of Solomon* and *Tar Baby*." *Journal of English Language and Literature* 42.2 (1995): 381–95.
———. "The Psychological Effects of Migration and Narrative Strategies in *The Bluest Eye*, *Song of Solomon*, and *Jazz*." *Journal of English Language and Literature* 45.4 (Winter 1999): 1021–32.
Kim, Kwangsoon. "Playing in the Marginal Space: Unlearning and Queering the Master's Narrative in Toni Morrison's *Sula*." *Journal of English Language and Literature* 59.6 (2013): 1021–34.
Kim, Miehyeon. "Sympathy and Indeterminacy in Toni Morrison's 'Recitatif.'" *Feminist Studies in English Literature* 23.1 (2015): 133–66.
Kim, Myung Ja. "Literature as Engagement: Teaching African American Literature to Korean Students." *MELUS* 29.3–4 (Fall–Winter 2004): 103–20.
Kim, Sun-ok. "The Origin of American Racism and the Construction of Multiracial Subjects in Toni Morrison's *A Mercy*." *Journal of English Language and Literature* 62.4 (Dec. 2016): 627–47.
King, Lovalerie, and Lynn Orilla Scott, eds. *James Baldwin and Toni Morrison: Comparative Critical and Theoretical Essays*. London: Palgrave Macmillan, 2006.

King, Nicole. "'You Think Like You White': Questioning Race and Racial Community through the Lens of Middle-Class Desire(s)." *Novel* 35.2-3 (Spring-Summer 2002): 211-30.
Kitts, Lenore. "Toni Morrison and 'Sis Joe': The Musical Heritage of Paul D." *Modern Fiction Studies* 52.2 (Summer 2006): 495-523.
Klotman, Phyllis R. "Dick-and-Jane and the Shirley Temple Sensibility in *The Bluest Eye*." *Black American Literature Forum* 13.4 (Winter 1979): 123-25.
Knadler, Stephen. "Domestic Violence in the Harlem Renaissance: Remaking the Record in Nella Larsen's *Passing* and Toni Morison's *Jazz*." *African American Review* 38.1 (Spring 2004): 99-118.
Knoflíčková, Marie. "Racial Identities Revisited: Toni Morrison's 'Recitatif.'" *Litteraria Pragensia* 21.41 (July 2011): 22-33.
Kodat, Catherine Gunther. "Margaret Garner and the Second Tear." *American Quarterly* 60.1 (Mar. 2008): 159-71.
Kolmerten, Carol A., Stephen M. Ross, and Judith Bryant Wittenberg, eds. *Unflinching Gaze: Morrison and Faulkner Re-Envisioned*. Jackson: University Press of Mississippi, 1997.
Koo, Eunsook. "The Betrayal of Love, Trauma Narrative and Subjectivity Formation: Toni Morrison's *A Mercy*." *Journal of English Language and Literature* 57.5 (2011): 813-39.
Koolish, Lynda. "Fictive Strategies and Cinematic Representations in Toni Morrison's *Beloved*: Postcolonial Theory/Postcolonial Text." *African American Review* 29.3 (Fall 1995): 421-38.
Koopman, Emy. "Incestuous Rape, Abjection, and the Colonization of Psychic Space in Toni Morrison's *The Bluest Eye* and Shani Mootoo's *Cereus Blooms at Night*." *Journal of Postcolonial Writing* 49.3 (July 2013): 303-15.
Kreyling, Michael. "'Slave Life, Freed Life—Everyday Was a Test and Trial': Identity and Memory in *Beloved*." *Arizona Quarterly* 63.1 (Spring 2007): 109-36.
Krumholz, Linda. "Blackness and Art in Toni Morrison's *Tar Baby*." *Contemporary Literature* 49.2 (2008): 263-92.
———. "The Ghosts of Slavery: Historical Recovery in Toni Morrison's *Beloved*." *African American Review* 26.3 (Fall 1992): 395-408.
———. "Reading and Insight in Toni Morrison's *Paradise*." *African American Review* 36.1 (Spring 2002): 21-34.
———. "Rituals of Manhood and Rituals of Reading in *Song of Solomon*." *Modern Fiction Studies* 39.3-4 (Fall-Winter 1993): 551-74.
Kuehl, Linda. *Saturday Review* 4, Sept. 17, 1977, 41.
Kuenz, Jane. "*The Bluest Eye*: Notes on History, Community, and Black Female Subjectivity." *African American Review* 27.3 (Fall 1993): 421-31.
Kulkarni, Harihar. "Mirrors, Reflections, and Images: Malady of Generational Relationship and Girlhood in Toni Morrison's *The Bluest Eye*." *Indian Journal of American Studies* 23.2 (Summer 1993): 1-6.
Lake, Christina Bieber. "The Demonic in Service of the Divine: Toni Morrison's *Beloved*." *South Atlantic Review* 69.3-4 (Fall 2004): 51-80.
Lange, Bonnie Shipman. "Toni Morrison's Rainbow Code." *Critique* (Spring 1983): 173-82.
Larson, Charles R. "Hymning the Black Past." *Washington Post Book World*, Sept. 4, 1977, 37.

Lawrence, David. "Fleshly Ghosts and Ghostly Flesh: The Word and the Body in *Beloved*." *Studies in American Fiction* 19.2 (Autumn 1991): 189–201.
Lawson, Charles. "Our Heart of Darkness." *Chicago Tribune* 14, Aug. 30, 1987, 1.
Le Clair, Thomas. "'The Language Must Not Sweat': A Conversation with Toni Morrison." *New Republic* 184 (Mar. 21, 1981): 25–29. Rpt. in Gates and Appiah, *Toni Morrison: Critical Perspectives Past and Present*, 369–77.
Ledbetter, Mark. "Through the Eyes of a Child: Looking for Victims in Toni Morrison's *The Bluest Eye*." In *Literature and Theology at Century's End*, edited by Gregory Salyer and Robert Detweiler, 177–88. Scholars' Press, 1995.
Lee, Catherine Carr. "The South in Toni Morrison's *Song of Solomon*: Initiation, Healing, and Home." *Studies in the Literary Imagination* 31.2 (Fall 1998): 109–23.
Lee, Dorothy H. "*Song of Solomon*: To Ride the Air." *Black American Literature Forum* 16.2 (Summer 1982): 64–70.
Lee, Hsiu-chaun. "Historical Distance and Textual Intimacy: How Newness Enters Toni Morrison's *A Mercy*." *Concentric* 37.2 (Sept. 2011): 135–55.
Lee, Kun Jong: "An Overview of Korean/Asian American Literary Studies in Korea, 1964–2009." *Inter-Asia Cultural Studies* 13.2 (2012). http://www.tandfonline.com/doi/abs/10.1080/14649373.2012.659813?src=recsys&journalCode=riac20.
Lee, Madeline. *Ms.* (July 1981): 26.
Lee, Rachel. "Missing Peace in Toni Morrison's *Sula* and *Beloved*." *African American Review* 28.4 (Winter 1994): 571–83.
Lee, Soo-Hyun. "*The Bluest Eye*: Tragic Aspects of Black Consciousness of the Self." *Studies in Modern Fiction* 9.1 (Summer 2002): 195–217.
Lee, Suk-Hee. "The Internalization of Colonial Discourse in *The Bluest Eye*." *Journal of English Language and Literature* 45.3 (1999): 629–45.
Lehmann-Haupt, Christopher. "Underwritten and Overwritten." *New York Times*, Jan. 7, 1974, 29.
Lei, Lily Wang. "Troublesome Tricksters: Memory, *Objet a*, Foreignness, Abjection and Healing in Morrison's *Beloved* and *Love*." In *The Search for Wholeness and Diaspora Literacy in Contemporary African American Literature*, edited by Silvia Pilar Castro-Borrego and Johnnella E. Butler, 83–103. Newcastle upon Tyne: Cambridge Scholars, 2011.
Leonard, John. "Three First Novels on Race." *New York Times*, Nov. 13, 1970, 46.
———. "To Ride the Air to Africa." *New York Times*, Sept. 6, 1977, 37.
Lepow, Lauren. "Paradise Lost and Found: Dualism and Edenic Myth in Toni Morrison's *Tar Baby*." *Contemporary Literature* 28.3 (1987): 363–77.
Lesoinne, Veronique. "Answer Jazz's Call: Experiencing Toni Morrison's *Jazz*." *MELUS* 22.3 (Fall 1997): 151–66.
Leve, A. (). "Toni Morrison on Love, Loss and Modernity." *Telegraph*, July 17, 2012. Retrieved from http://www.telegraph.co.uk/culture/books/authorinterviews/9395051/Toni-Morrison-on-love-loss-and-modernity.html.
Levy, Andrew. "Telling *Beloved*." *Texas Studies in Literature and Language* 33.1 (Spring 1991): 114–23.
Lewis, Barbara Williams. "The Function of Jazz in Toni Morrison's *Jazz*." In *Toni Morrison's Fiction: Contemporary Criticism*, edited by David L. Middleton, 271–81. New York: Garland, 1997.

Lewis, Charles. "The Ironic Romance of New Historicism: *The Scarlet Letter* and *Beloved* Standing in Side by Side." *Arizona Quarterly* 51.1 (Spring 1995): 32–60.

Lewis, Miles Marshall. "Toni Morrison's Stunning Home." *Ebony*, May 8, 2012. Retrieved from https://www.ebony.com/entertainment-culture/review-toni-morrisons-stunning-home/.

Lewis, Vashti Crutcher. "African Tradition in Toni Morrison's *Sula*." *Phylon* 48.1 (1987): 91–97.

Li, Stephanie. "Paradise Lost: Reconciling the Semiotic and Symbolic in Toni Morrison's *Love*." *Studies in the Literary Imagination* 47.1 (Spring 2014): 27–47.

Lilienfeld, Jane. "'To Have the Reader Work with the Author': The Circulation of Knowledge in Virginia Woolf's *To the Lighthouse* and Toni Morrison's *Jazz*." *Modern Fiction Studies* 52.1 (Spring 2006): 42–65.

Lillvis, Kristen. "Becoming Self and Mother: Posthuman Liminality in Toni Morrison's *Beloved*." *Critique* 54.4 (2013): 452–64.

Linehan, Thomas M. "Narrating the Self: Aspects of Moral Psychology in Toni Morrison's *Beloved*." *Centennial Review* 41.2 (Spring 1997): 301–30.

Liscio, Lorraine. "*Beloved*'s Narrative: Writing Mother's Milk." *Tulsa Studies in Women's Literature* 11.1 (Spring 1992): 31–46.

Łobodziec, Agnieszka. "Poetically Realistic Juxtapositions of Anglo-American Old and New World Experiences Portrayed in Toni Morrison's *A Mercy*." In *Ex-changes: Comparative Studies in British and American Cultures*, edited by Edyta Lorek-Jezinska and Katarzyna Wieckowska, 150–66. Newcastle upon Tyne: Cambridge Scholars, 2012.

Lock, Helen. "'Building up from Fragments': The Oral Memory Process in Some Recent African-American Written Narratives." *College Literature* 22.3 (Oct. 1995): 109–20.

Lockhurst, Roger. "'Impossible Mourning' in Toni Morrison's *Beloved* and Michele Roberts's *Daughters of the House*." *Critique* 37.4 (Summer 1996): 243–60.

Löffler, Philipp. "Aliens in America: Toni Morrison, Steven Spielberg, and the Ends of Postmodernism." In *The Poetics of Genre in the Contemporary Novel*, edited by Tim Lanzendörfer, 17–33. Lanham, MD: Lexington, 2016.

Loichot, Valérie. *Orphan Narratives: The Postplantation Literature of Faulkner, Glissant, Morrison, and Saint-John Perse*. Charlottesville: University of Virginia Press, 2007.

Long, Lisa A. "A New Midwesternism in Toni Morrison's *The Bluest Eye*." *Twentieth Century Literature* 59.1 (Spring 2013): 104–25.

López Ramírez, Manuela. "Childhood Cuts Festered and Never Scabbed Over: Child Abuse in Toni Morrison's *God Help the Child*." *Revista Alicantina de Estudios Ingleses* 29 (Nov. 2016): 145–64.

———. "'Hansel and Gretel' in Toni Morrison's *Home*." *49th Parallel* 34 (Autumn 2014): 143–68.

———. "The Haunted House in Toni Morrison's *A Mercy*." *Revista de Estudios Norteamericanos* 19 (2015): 99–113.

———. "Icarus and Daedalus in Toni Morrison's *Song of Solomon*." *Journal of English Studies* 10 (2012): 105–29.

———. "The Shell-Shocked Veteran in Toni Morrison's *Sula* and *Home*." *Atlantis* 38.1 (2016): 129–47.

———. "The Theme of the Shattered Self in Toni Morrison's *The Bluest Eye* and *A Mercy*." *Miscelánea* 48 (2013): 75–91.

Lounsberry, Barbara, and Grace Ann Hovet. "Principles of Perception in Toni Morrison's *Sula*." *Black American Literature Forum* 13.4 (Winter 1979): 126–29.
"'Love is never any better than the lover': Toni Morrison—a Life in Quotes." https://www.theguardian.com/books/2019/aug/06/toni-morrison-author-life-in-quotes.
"*Love* by Toni Morrison." *Kirkus Reviews*, Aug. 1, 2003. https://www.kirkusreviews.com/book-reviews/toni-morrison/love-2/.
Lubiano, Wahneema, ed. *The House That Race Built*. 1997. New York: Vintage, 1998.
Lucky, Crystal J. "Ancestral Wisdom in Toni Morrison's *The Bluest Eye*." *Proteus* 21.2 (Fall 2004): 21–26.
Luebke, Steven R. "The Portrayal of Sexuality in Toni Morrison's *The Bluest Eye*." In *Censored Books, II: Critical Viewpoints*," edited by Nicholas J. Karolides, 87–94. Lanham, MD: Scarecrow, 2002.
Lutz, John. "Sealskins and Original Dimes: Exploitation, Class, and Commodity Fetishism in Toni Morrison's *Tar Baby*." *Critique* 54.1 (2013): 56–69.
Lyles, Lois. "Let My Daughter Go: The Jewish Mother and the Black Mother in Novels about Catastrophe and Bondage." *Shofar* 17.2 (Winter 1999): 102–9.
MacKethan, Lucinda H. "Names to Bear Witness: The Theme and Tradition of Naming in Toni Morrison's *Song of Solomon*." *CEA Critic* 49.2-4 (Winter–Summer 1986–87): 199–207.
Magness, Patricia. "'The Knight and the Princess': The Structure of Courtly Love in Toni Morrison's *Tar Baby*." *South Atlantic Review* 54.4 (1989): 85–99.
Magras, Lydia. "Popular Reception of Toni Morrison's *Beloved*: Reading the Text through Time." *Reception* 7 (2015): 29–44.
Mahaffey, Paul. "Rethinking Biracial Female Sexuality in Toni Morrison's *Tar Baby*." *Proteus* 21.2 (2004): 38–42.
Maher, Rob. "*Jazz*." Feb. 25, 2014. http://eponymistuk.blogspot.com/2014/02/another-day-anotherbook-review-review.html.
Makino, Rie. "The World without Fathers: Reconstructing Faulknerian Masculinities in Toni Morrison's *Beloved*." *Journal of English Language and Literature* 52.5 (Winter 2006): 1201–24.
Malcolm, Cheryl Alexander. "Family Values? Father/Daughter Seduction in Toni Morrison's *The Bluest Eye* and Milcha Sanchez-Scott's *Roosters*." In *Reflections on Ethical Values in Post (?) Modern American Literature*, edited by Teresa Pyzik, 115–24. Katowice, Poland: University of Silesia Press, 2000.
Malmgren, Carl D. "Mixed Genres and the Logic of Slavery in Toni Morrison's *Beloved*." *Critique* 36.2 (Winter 1995): 96–106.
———. "Texts, Primers, and Voices in Toni Morrison's *The Bluest Eye*." *Critique* 41.3 (Spring 2000): 251–62.
Mandel, Naomi. "'I Made the Ink': Identity, Complicity, 60 Million, and More." *Modern Fiction Studies* 48.3 (Fall 2002): 581–613.
Mantel, Hillary. "How Sorrow Became Complete." *Guardian*, Nov. 7, 2008. Retrieved from https://www.theguardian.com/books/2008/nov/08/a-mercy-toni-morrison.
Margaronis, Maria. "The Anxiety of Authenticity: Writing Historical Fiction at the End of the Twentieth Century." *History Workshop Journal* 65 (Spring 2008): 138–60.
Marks, Kathleen Kelly. *Toni Morrison's Beloved and the Apotropaic Imagination*. Columbia: University of Missouri Press, 2002.

———. "Melancholy and the Unyielding Earth in *The Bluest Eye*." In *Toni Morrison: Forty Years in the Clearing*, edited by Carmen Gillespie, 175-94. Lewisburg, PA: Bucknell University Press, 2012.
Martindale, Kym. "Response to 'Feathered Wombs.'" *London Review of Books* 20.15, July 30, 1998.
Martins, José Endoença. "Black Women's 'Two-ness' in African-American Literature: Can Black and White Worlds Join Together?" *Acta Scientiarum: Language and Culture* 32.1 (Jan.-June 2010): 27-34.
Martín-Salván, Paula. "The Secret of Bride's Body in Toni Morrison's *God Help the Child*." *Critique* 59.5 (2018): 609-23.
Marvin, Patricia H. "Toni Morrison: *The Bluest Eye*." *Library Journal* 95 (Nov. 1, 1970): 3806.
Mason, Theodore O., Jr. "The Novelist as Conservator: Stories and Comprehension in Toni Morrison's *Song of Solomon*." *Contemporary Literature* 29.4 (Winter 1988): 564-81.
Mathieson, Barbara Offut. "Memory and Motherlove in Morrison's *Beloved*." *American Imago* 47.1 (Spring 1990): 1-21.
Mayberry, Katherine J. "The Problem of Narrative in Toni Morrison's *Jazz*." In *Toni Morrison's Fiction: Contemporary Criticism*, edited by David Middleton, 297-309. New York: Garland, 1997.
Mayberry, Susan Neal. *Can't I Love What I Criticize? The Masculine and Morrison*. Athens: University of Georgia Press, 2007.
———. "'Everything about her had two sides to it': The Foreigner's Home in Toni Morrison's *Paradise*." *African American Review* 42.3-4 (Fall-Winter 2008): 565-78.
———. "Guess Who's Coming to Dinner? Food, Race, and [En]countering the Modern in Toni Morrison's *Tar Baby*." In *Toni Morrison: Forty Years in the Clearing*, edited by Carmen Gillespie, 211-35. Lewisburg, PA: Bucknell University Press, 2012.
———. "*Home* as a Rosetta Stone for Toni Morrison's Decryptions of the Masculine." *US-China Foreign Language* 15.5 (May 2017): 315-29.
———. "Masculine Othermothering in Toni Morrison's *Home*." In Baxter and Satz, *Toni Morrison on Mothers and Motherhood*, 13-37.
———. "Putting Down Parking Lots Out There in Unpaved *Paradise*: Toni Morrison [En]Counters American Cowboy Culture." *South Atlantic Review* 75.3 (Summer 2010): 83-108.
———. "Something Other Than a Family Quarrel: The Beautiful Boys in Morrison's *Sula*." *African American Review* 37.4 (Winter 2003): 517-33.
———. "Visions and Revisions of American Masculinity in *A Mercy*." In *Toni Morrison: Paradise/Love/A Mercy*, edited by Lucille P. Fultz, 166-84. London: Bloomsbury, 2013.
Mbalia, Doreatha Drummond. "*Tar Baby*: A Reflection of Morrison's Developed Class Consciousness." In *Toni Morrison*, edited by Linden Peach, 89-102. New York: St. Martin's, 1997.
———. "Women Who Run with Wild: The Need for Sisterhoods in *Jazz*." *Modern Fiction Studies* 39.3-4 (Fall-Winter 1993): 623-46.
McClain, Ruth Rambo. "Review of *Sula*, by Toni Morrison." *Black World* 23 (June 1974): 51-52, 85.
McClaren, James. "Song of Solomon." *Cross Currents* (Fall 1978): 369-72.
McDonald, Paul Penrith. *Reading Toni Morrison's Beloved: A Literature Insight*. England: Humanities Ebooks (HEB), 2013.

McDowell, Deborah E. "'The Self and the Other': Reading Toni Morrison's *Sula* and the Black Female Text." In *Critical Essays on Toni Morrison*, edited by Nellie Y. McKay, 77–90. Boston: Hall, 1988.
McKay, Nellie Y., ed. *Critical Essays on Toni Morrison*. Boston: G. K. Hall, 1988.
———. "An Interview with Toni Morrison." 1983. Rpt. in Gates and Appiah, *Toni Morrison: Critical Perspectives Past and Present*, 396–411.
McKay, Nellie Y., and Kathryn Earle, eds. *Approaches to Teaching the Novels of Toni Morrison*. New York: The Modern Language Association of America, 1997.
McKee, Patricia. "Geographies of *Paradise*." *New Centennial Review* 3.1 (2003): 197–223.
———. *Producing American Races: Henry James, William Faulkner, Toni Morrison*. Durham, NC: Duke University Press, 1999.
———. "Spacing and Placing Experience in Toni Morrison's *Sula*." *Modern Fiction Studies* 42.1 (Spring 1996): 1–30.
McKible, Adam. "'These Are the Facts of the Darky's History': Thinking History and Reading Names in Four African American Texts" *African American Review* 28.2 (Summer 1994): 223–35.
McMillan, Terry. "*Beloved* Blends Myth, Surrealism in Slave's Tale." *Atlanta Journal/Constitution*, Oct. 21, 1987, J10.
McNamara, Marygai, Maria Simms, and Pat Skinner. "Toni Morrison's *Beloved*: Post-Colonial Writing and the Discourse of Aboriginal Australians." *LiNQ* 25.1 (May 1998): 9–35.
McWilliams, Mark B. "The Human Face of the Age: The Physical Cruelty of Slavery and the Modern American Novel." *Mississippi Quarterly* 56.3 (Summer 2003): 353–71.
Medoro, Dana. "Justice and Citizenship in Toni Morrison's *Song of Solomon*." *Canadian Review of American Studies* 32.1 (2002): 1–15.
Mellard, James M. "'Families Make the Best Enemies': Paradoxes of Narcissistic Identification in Toni Morrison's *Love*." *African American Review* 43.4 (Winter 2009): 699–712.
———. "The Jews of Ruby, Oklahoma: Politics, Parallax, and Ideological Fantasy in Toni Morrison's *Paradise*." *Modern Fiction Studies* 56.2 (Summer 2010): 349–77.
———. "Unimaginable Acts Imagined: Fathers, Family Myth, and the Postmodern Crisis of Paternal Authority in Toni Morrison's *Love*." *Mississippi Quarterly*: 63.1–2 (Winter–Spring 2010): 233–67.
———. "Žižekian Reading: Sex, Politics, and Traversing (the) Fantasy in Toni Morrison's *Paradise*." *Studies in the Novel* 40.4 (Winter 2008): 465–91.
Menand, Louis. "The War between Men and Women." *New Yorker*, Jan. 12, 1998. https://www.newyorker.com/magazine/1998/01/12/the-war-between-men-and-women.
Mendelsohn, Jane. "Harlem on Her Mind: Toni Morrison's Language of Love." *Village Voice Literary Supplement* 105 (May 1992): 25–26. http://www.janemendelsohn.com/on-toni-morrison/.
Mermann-Jozwiak, Elisabeth. "Re-Membering the Body: Body Politics in Toni Morrison's *The Bluest Eye*." *Literature Interpretation Theory* 12.2 (June 2001); 189–203.
Metting, Fred. "The Possibilities of Flight: The Celebration of Our Wings in *Song of Solomon*, *Praisesong for the Widow*, and *Mama Day*." *Southern Folklore* 55.2 (1998): 145–68.
Michael, Magali Cornier. "Re-Imagining Agency: Toni Morrison's *Paradise*." *African American Review* 36.4 (Winter 2002): 643–61.
Michlin, Monica. "Narrative as Empowerment: *Push* and the Signifying on Prior African-American Novels on Incest." *Etudes Anglaises* 59.2 (Apr.–June 2006): 170–85.

Mickelson, Anne Z. *Reaching Out: Sensitivity and Order in Recent American Fiction by Women.* Metuchen, NJ: Scarecrow, 1979.

Middleton, Joyce Irene. "Confronting the 'Master Narrative': The Privilege of Orality in Toni Morrison's *The Bluest Eye*." *Cultural Studies* 9.2 (May 1995): 301–17.

———. "Orality, Literacy, and Memory in Toni Morrison's *Song of Solomon*." *College English* 55.1 (Jan. 1993): 64–75.

Mikkelsen, Nina. "Diamonds within Diamonds within Diamonds: Ethnic Literature and the Fractal Aesthetic." *MELUS* 27.2 (Summer 2002): 95–116.

Millar, Neil. "Toni Morrison's Brilliant Black Novel." *Christian Science Monitor*, Oct. 20, 1977, 25.

Miller, Adam David. "Breedlove, Peace and the Dead: Some Observations on the World of Toni Morrison." *Black Scholar* (Mar. 1978): 47–50.

Miller, Laura. "The Last Resort." *New York Times*, Nov. 2, 2003. https://www.nytimes.com/2003/11/02/books/the-last-resort.html.

Milne, Leah. "Choosing Africa: The Importance of Naming in *Beloved* and *The Poisonwood Bible*." *CLA Journal* 55.4 (June 2012): 352–96.

Milton, Edith. *Yale Review* (Winter 1982): 259–60.

Miner, Madonne M. "Lady No Longer Sings the Blues: Rape, Madness, and Silence in *The Bluest Eye*." In *Conjuring: Black Women, Fiction, and Literary Tradition*, edited by Marjorie Pryse and Hortense J. Spillers, 176–91. Bloomington: Indiana University Press, 1985.

Mitchell, Angelyn. "'Sth, I Know that Woman': History, Gender, and the South in Toni Morrison's *Jazz*." *Studies in the Literary Imagination* 31.2 (Fall 1998): 49–60.

Mitchell, Carolyn. "'I Love to Tell the Story': Biblical Revisions in *Beloved*." *Religion and Literature* 23.3 (Autumn 1991): 27–42.

Mix, Deborah. "Enspirited Bodies and Embodied Spirits in Toni Morrison's *Paradise*." *Studies in the Humanities* 41.1–2 (Mar. 2015): 165–91.

Mobley, Marilyn E. "Narrative Dilemma: Jadine as Cultural Orphan in Toni Morrison's *Tar Baby*." *Southern Review* 23.4 (1987): 761–70.

Mobley, Marilyn Sanders. *Folk Roots and Mythic Wings in Sarah Orne Jewett and Toni Morrison.* Baton Rouge: Louisiana State University Press, 1994.

Mock, Michele. "Spitting Out the Seed: Ownership of Mother, Child, Breasts, Milk, and Voice in Toni Morrison's *Beloved*." *College Literature* 23.3 (Oct. 1996): 117–26.

Moglene, Helene. "Redeeming History: Toni Morrison's *Beloved*." *Cultural Critique* 24 (Spring 1993): 17–40.

Mohanty, Satya P. "The Epistemic Status of Cultural Identity: On *Beloved* and the Postcolonial Condition." *Cultural Critique* 24 (Spring 1993): 41–80.

Montgomery, Maxine. "Bearing Witness to Forgotten Wounds: Toni Morrison's *Home* and the Spectral Presence." *South Carolina Review* 47.2 (Spring 2015): 14–24.

———, ed. *Contested Boundaries: New Critical Essays on the Fiction of Toni Morrison.* Newcastle upon Tyne: Cambridge Scholars, 2013.

Moon, Set Byul. "A Possibility of Black Manhood through Re-Reading Black Veterans in Toni Morrison's *Sula*." *British and American Fiction* 22.3 (2015): 57–91.

Moore, Caroline. "*A Mercy* by Toni Morrison." *Telegraph*, Nov. 14, 2008. Retrieved from https://www.telegraph.co.uk/culture/books/fictionreviews/3563259/A-Mercy-by-Toni-Morrison-review.html.

Moore, Geneva Cobb. "A Demonic Parody: Toni Morrison's *A Mercy*." *Southern Literary Journal* 44.1 (Fall 2011): 1–18.
Mootry, Maria K. "One Man's Quest for a Usable Past." *Chicago Tribune Book World* (Sept. 11, 1977): 8.
Moqbel Al Areqi, Rashad Mohammed. "Thorny Journey from Slavery to Salvation." *Theory and Practice in Language Studies* 4.3 (Mar. 2014): 466–72.
Moraru, Christian. "Reading the Onomastic Text: 'The Politics of the Proper Name' in Toni Morrison's *Song of Solomon*." *Names* 44.3 (Sept. 1996): 189–204.
Moreland, Richard C. "'He Wants to Put His Story Next to Hers': Putting Twain's Story Next to Hers in Morrison's *Beloved*." *Modern Fiction Studies* 39.3–4 (Fall–Winter 1993): 501–25.
Morgan, Kathleen. "The Homeric Cyclops Episode and 'Otherness' in Toni Morrison's *Jazz*." *Classical and Modern Literature* 18.3 (Spring 1998): 219–29.
Morgenstern, Naomi. "Literature Reads Theory: Remarks on Teaching with Toni Morrison." *University of Toronto Quarterly* 74.3 (Summer 2005): 816–28.
———. "Maternal Love/Maternal Violence: Inventing Ethics in Toni Morrison's *A Mercy*." *MELUS* 39.1 (Spring 2014): 7–29.
———. "Mother's Milk and Sister's Blood: Trauma and the Neoslave Narrative." *Differences* 8.2 (Summer 1996): 101–26.
———. *Wild Child: Intensive Parenting and Posthumanist Ethics*. Minneapolis: University of Minnesota Press, 2018.
Mori, Aoi. "Embracing Jazz: Healing of Armed Women and Motherless Children in Toni Morrison's *Jazz*." *CLA Journal* 42.3 (Mar. 1999): 320–30.
Morris, Susana M. "A Past Not Pure But Stifled: Vexed Legacies of Leadership in Toni Morrison's *Love*." *South Atlantic Quarterly* 112.2 (Spring 2013): 319–38.
———. "'Sisters separated for much too long': Women's Friendship and Power in Toni Morrison's 'Recitatif.'" *Tulsa Studies in Women's Literature* 32.1 (Spring 2013): 159–80.
"Morrison Gets Personal with 'Moms.'" *TODAY.com*, Nov. 6, 2003. https://www.today.com/popculture/morrison-gets-personal-moms-wbna3341544.
Morrison, Toni. *Beloved*. 1987. New York: Knopf, 1988.
———. *Beloved*. 1987. New York: Vintage, 2004.
———. *The Bluest Eye*. 1970. New York: Knopf, 2000.
———. *The Bluest Eye*. 1970. New York: Plume, 1994. Afterword 1993.
———. *The Dancing Mind*. 1996. New York: Knopf, 2003.
———. *God Help the Child*. New York: Knopf, 2015.
———. *Home*. 2012. New York: Vintage, 2013.
———. *Jazz*. 1992. New York: Vintage, 2004.
———. Jeanette K. Watson Distinguished Professor Lecture Series, Syracuse University. *The Bluest Eye* Seminar Session, Oct. 5, 1988.
———. *Love*. 2003. New York: Vintage, 2005.
———. *A Mercy*. 2008. New York: Vintage, 2009.
———. *The Nobel Lecture in Literature, 1993*. New York: Knopf, 2002.
———. *The Origin of Others*. Cambridge: Harvard University Press, 2017.
———. *Paradise*. 1997. New York: Vintage, 2014.
———. *Playing in the Dark: Whiteness and the Literary Imagination*. 1992. New York: Vintage, 1993.

———. "Recitatif." 1983. *Calling the Wind: Twentieth-Century African-American Short Stories*, edited by Clarence Major, 438–53. New York: HarperPerennial, 1993.

———. "Rootedness: The Ancestor as Foundation." In *Black Women Writers (1950–1980): A Critical Evaluation*, edited by Mari Evans, 339–45. New York: Anchor Books, 1984.

———. *Song of Solomon*. 1977. New York: Vintage, 2004.

———. *The Source of Self-Regard: Selected Essays, Speeches, and Meditations*. New York: Knopf, 2019.

———. *Sula*. 1973. New York: Vintage, 2004.

———. "Sweetness." *New Yorker*, Feb. 9, 2015. Retrieved from https://www.newyorker.com/magazine/2015/02/09/sweetness-2.

———. *Tar Baby*. 1981. New York: Vintage, 2004.

———. "Unspeakable Things Unspoken: The Afro-American Presence in American Literature." *The Tanner Lectures on Human Values*, delivered at the University of Michigan, Oct. 7, 1988. *Michigan Quarterly Review* 28.1 (1989): 1–34. http://tanner-lectures.utah.edu/_documents/a-to-z/m/morrison90.pdf.

———. *What Moves at the Margin: Selected Nonfiction*. Jackson: University Press of Mississippi, 2008.

———. "What the Black Woman Thinks about Women's Lib." *New York Times Magazine*, Aug. 22, 1971, 14.

Morrison, Toni, and Slade Morrison. *Who's Got Game? The Ant or the Grasshopper?* New York: Scribner, 2003.

Moses, Cat. "The Blues Aesthetic in Toni Morrison's *The Bluest Eye*." *African American Review* 33.4 (Winter 1999): 623–37.

Moya, Paula. "The Misprison of Mercy: Race and Responsible Reading in Toni Morrison's *A Mercy*." In *The Social Imperative: Race, Close Reading, and Contemporary Literary Criticism*, 133–62. Stanford, CA: Stanford University Press, 2015.

Moyers, Bill. "Toni Morrison: A Writer's Work." In *The Moyers Collection: A World of Ideas*. Princeton, NJ: Films for the Humanities and Sciences, 1994.

Mueller, Stefanie. "Black Women's Business: Female Entrepreneurship and Economic Agency in Toni Morrison's *God Help the Child*." In *Power Relations in Black Lives: Reading African American Literature and Culture with Bourdieu and Elias*, edited by Christa Buschendorf, 145–64. American Culture Series 17.1. Transcipt Verlag, 2017.

Munafo, Giavanna. "'No Sign of Life': Marble-Blue Eyes and Lakefront Houses in *The Bluest Eye*." *Literature Interpretation Theory* 6.1–2 (Apr. 1995): 1–19.

Murline, Anna. "This Side of 'Paradise.'" *U.S. News & World Report*, Jan. 19, 1998, 71.

Murray, Robin. "Textual Authority, Reader Authority, and Social Authority: Reconfiguring Literature and Experience in a Reader-Response Context." *Readerly/Writerly Texts: Essays on Literature, Literary/Textual Criticism, and Pedagogy* 8.1–2 (Spring-Winter 2000): 9–21.

Murray, Rolland. "The Long Strut: *Song of Solomon* and the Emancipatory Limits of Black Patriarchy." *Callaloo* 22.1 (Winter 1999): 121–33.

Muyumba, Walton. "Lady Sings the Blues." *Atlantic*, Apr. 23, 2015. Retrieved from https://www.theatlantic.com/entertainment/archive/2015/04/morrison-review-god-help-the-child/391197/.

Nance, Kevin. "The Spirit and the Strength." *Poets and Writers Magazine* 36.6 (Nov.–Dec. 2008): 47–54.

Naylor, Carolyn A. "Cross-Gender Significance of the Journey Motif in Selected Afro-American Fiction." *Colby Library Quarterly* 18.1 (Mar. 1982): 26–38.

Neelakantan, G., and Sathyaraj Venkatesan. "Toni Morrison's Quarrel with the Civil Rights Ideology in *Love*." *International Fiction Review* 34.1–2 (Jan. 2007): 139–46.

Nevins, Jake. "The Literary Life of Michiko Kakutani: The Book Critic's Best Feuds and Reviews." *Guardian*, July 28, 2017. https://www.theguardian.com/media/2017/jul/28/the-literary-life-of-michiko-kakutani-the-book-critics-best-feuds-and-reviews.

Ng, Andrew Hock Soon. "Toni Morrison's *Beloved*: Space, Architecture, Trauma." *Symplokē* 19.1–2 (2011): 231–45.

Ng, Lay Sion, and Ruzbeh Babaee. "Exploding and Being Swallowed: Cannibalism in Toni Morrison's *Beloved*." *International Journal of Comparative Literature and Translation Studies* 5.1 (2017): 11–15.

Nicholson, David. "Toni Morrison's Rhapsody in Blues," Apr. 19, 1992. https://www.washingtonpost.com/archive/entertainment/books/1992/04/19/toni-morrisons-rhapsody-in-blues/b4ea0391-15fe-4cfd-98c0-f49720ca32df/?utm_term=.706d16c2e920.

Nicol, Kathryn. "Visible Differences: Viewing Racial Identity in Toni Morrison's *Paradise* and 'Recitatif.'" In *Literature and Racial Ambiguity*, edited by Teresa Hubel and Neil Brooks, 209–31. Amsterdam: Editions Rodopi B.V., 2002.

Nodelman, Perry. "The Limits of Structures: A Shorter Version of a Comparison between Toni Morrison's *Song of Solomon* and Virginia Hamilton's *M. C. Higgins the Great*." *Children's Literature Association Quarterly* 7.3 (Fall 1982): 45–48.

Novak, Phillip. "'Circles and Circles of Sorrow': In the Wake of Morrison's *Sula*." *PMLA* 114.2 (1999): 184–93.

Nowlin, Michael. "Toni Morrison's *Jazz* and the Racial Dreams of the American Writer." *American Literature* 71.1 (Mar. 1999): 151–74.

O'Brien, Edna. "The Clearest Eye." *New York Times*, Apr. 5, 1992. http://www.nytimes.com/books/98/01/11/home/14425.html.

O'Connor, Douglas. "Review of *Sula*, by Toni Morrison." *Black Creation* 6 (Annual 1974–75): 65–66.

Oforlea, Aaron Ngozi. *James Baldwin, Toni Morrison, and the Rhetorics of Black Male Subjectivity*. Columbus: Ohio State University Press, 2017.

Ogunyemi, Chikwenye Okonjo. "An Abiki-Ogbanje Atlas: A Pre-Text for Rereading Soyinka's *Aké* and Morrison's *Beloved*." *African American Review* 36.4 (Winter 2002): 663–78.

———. "*Sula*: 'A Nigger Joke.'" *Black American Literature Forum* 13.4 (Winter 1979): 130–33.

O'Keefe, Vincent A. "From 'Other' Sides of the Realist Tracks: (A)Gnostic Narratives in Toni Morrison's *Jazz*." *Centennial Review* 41.2 (Spring 1997): 331–49.

———. "Reading Rigor Mortis: Offstage Violence and Excluded Middles 'in' Johnson's *Middle Passage* and Morrison's *Beloved*." *African American Review* 30.4 (Winter 1996): 635–47.

Omry, Keren. "Baldwin's Bop 'N' Morrison's Mood: Bebop and Race in James Baldwin's *Another Country* and Toni Morrison's *Jazz*." In King and Scott, *James Baldwin and Toni Morrison: Comparative Critical and Theoretical Essays*, 11–35.

———. "Literary Free Jazz? *Mumbo Jumbo* and *Paradise*: Language and Meaning." *African American Review* 41.1 (Spring 2007): 127–41.

O'Neill, Caitlin. "'The Shape of Mystery': The Visionary Resonance of Harriet Jacobs's *Incidents in the Life of a Slave Girl*." *Journal of American Culture* 41.1 (Mar. 2018): 56–67.

Oprah.com. http://www.oprah.com/oprahsbookclub/about-paradise-by-toni-morrison/all.

O'Reilly, Andrea. "In Search of My Mother's Garden, I Found My Own: Mother-Love, Healing, and Identity in Toni Morrison's *Jazz*." *African American Review* 30.3 (Fall 1996): 367–79.

———. "Maternal Conceptions in Toni Morrison's *The Bluest Eye* and *Tar Baby*: 'A Woman Has to Be a Daughter before She Can Be Any Kind of Woman.'" In *This Giving Birth: Pregnancy and Childbirth in American Women's Writing*," edited by Julie Tharp and Susan MacCallum-Whitcomb, 83–102. Madison, WI: Popular, 2000.

———. *Toni Morrison and Motherhood: A Politics of the Heart*. Albany: SUNY Press, 2004.

Orr, Elaine Neil. *Subject to Negotiation: Reading Feminist Criticism and American Women's Fictions*. Charlottesville: University of Virginia Press, 2007.

Ortega, Gemma. "The First of Many Heroines: Claudia's Dialogic Escape in Toni Morrison's *The Bluest Eye*." *South Atlantic Review* 83.2 (Summer 2018): 126–44.

Osagie, Iyunolu. "Is Morrison Also among the Prophets?: 'Psychoanalytic' Strategies in *Beloved*." *African American Review* 28.3 (Fall 1994): 423–40.

Osucha, Eden. "Race and the Regulation of Intimacy in the Moynihan Report, the Griswold Decision, and Morrison's *Paradise*." *American Literary History* 27.2 (Summer 2015): 256–84.

Otten, Terry. "The Crime of Innocence in Toni Morrison's *Tar Baby*." *Studies in American Fiction* 14 (Autumn 1986): 153–63.

Pacquet-Deyris, Anne-Marie. "Scènes d'esprit: *Beloved* [Jonathan Demme, 1998; Toni Morrison, 1987]." *Revue Française d'Etudes Américaines* 101 (Sept. 2004): 96–106.

Page, Philip. "Circularity in Toni Morrison's *Beloved*." *African American Review* 26.1 (Spring 1992): 31–39.

———. *Dangerous Freedom: Fusion and Fragmentation in Toni Morrison's Novels*. Jackson: University Press of Mississippi, 1995.

———. "Furrowing All the Brows: Interpretation and the Transcendent in Toni Morrison's *Paradise*." *African American Review* 35.4 (Winter 2001): 637–51.

———. "Traces of Derrida in Toni Morrison's *Jazz*." *African American Review* 29.1 (Spring 1995): 55–66.

Painter, Nell Irvin. "Why 'White' should be capitalized, too." *Washington Post*, July 22, 2020. https://www.washingtonpost.com/opinions/2020/07/22/why-white-should-be-capitalized/.

Pal, Payel, and Gurumurthy Neelakantan. "Morrison's Prostitutes in *The Bluest Eye*." *Notes on Contemporary Literature* 44.2 (Mar. 2014): 4–7.

Palladino, Mariangela. "Aphrodite's Faces: Toni Morrison's *Love* and Ethics." *Modern Fiction Studies* 58.2 (Summer 2012): 334–52.

Paquet, Sandra Pouchet. "The Ancestor as Foundation in *Their Eyes Were Watching God* and *Tar Baby*." *Callaloo* 13.3 (Summer 1990): 499–515.

Paquet-Deyris, Anne-Marie. "Toni Morrison's *Jazz* and the City." *African American Review* 35.2 (Summer 2001): 219–31.

"*Paradise* by Toni Morrison." *Kirkus Reviews*. https://www.kirkusreviews.com/book-review/toni-morrison/paradise-morrison/?utm_source=google&utm_medium=cpc&utm_term=&utm_campaign=DSA.

"'Paradise': Worthy Women, Unredeemable Men." Review of *Paradise* by Toni Morrison. *New York Times*, January 6, 1998. https://archive.nytimes.com/www.nytimes.com/books/98/01/04/daily/morrison-book-review-art.html?scp=17&sq=History:%2520A%2520Novel&st=cse.

Parker, Emma. "A New Hysteria in Toni Morrison's *Beloved*." *Twentieth Century Literature* 47.1 (Spring 2001): 1–19.

Parrish, Timothy L. "Imagining Slavery: Toni Morrison and Charles Johnson." *Studies in American Fiction* 25.1 (Spring 1997): 81–100.

Pass, Olivia McNeely. "Toni Morrison's *Beloved*: A Journey through the Pain of Grief." *Journal of Medical Humanities* 27.2 (Summer 2006): 117–24.

Pattison, Dale. "Building Intimacy: The Erotic Architectures of Toni Morrison's *Jazz*." *Critique* 58.2 (2017): 129–45.

Peach, Linden. "Body Difference in Toni Morrison's Fiction." In *Toni Morrison: Forty Years in the Clearing*, edited by Carmen Gillespie, 273–85. Lewisburg, PA: Bucknell University Press, 2012.

Pearce, Richard. "Toni Morrison's *Jazz*: Negotiations of the African American Beauty Culture." *Narrative* 6.3 (Oct. 1998): 307–24.

Penner, Erin. "For Those 'Who Could Not Bear to Look Directly at the Slaughter': Morrison's *Home* and the Novels of Faulkner and Woolf." *African American Review* 49.4 (Winter 2016): 343–59.

Peoples, Tim. "Meditation and Artistry in *The Bluest Eye* by Toni Morrison and *Their Eyes Were Watching God* by Zora Neale Hurston." *Midwest Quarterly* 53.2 (Winter 2012): 177–92.

Pereira, Malin Walther. "Periodizing Toni Morrison's Work from *The Bluest Eye* to *Jazz*: The Importance of *Tar Baby*." *MELUS* 22.3 (Fall 1997): 71–82.

Perry, Imani. *Vexy Thing: On Gender and Liberation*. Durham, NC: Duke University Press, 2018.

Pessoni, Michele. "'She Was Laughing at Their God': Discovering the Goddess within in *Sula*." *African American Review* 29.3 (Fall 1995): 439–51.

Peterson, Christopher. "*Beloved*'s Claim." *Modern Fiction Studies* 52.3 (Fall 2006): 548–69.

Peterson, Nancy J. *Beloved: Character Studies*. England: Continuum, 2008.

———. "Théodore Géricault, and Incendiary Art." In *Toni Morrison: Forty Years in the Clearing*, edited by Carmen R. Gillespie, 287–99. Lewisburg, PA: Bucknell University Press, 2012.

———, ed. *Toni Morrison: Critical and Theoretical Approaches*. Baltimore: Johns Hopkins University Press, 1997.

Pettis, Joyce. "Difficult Survival: Mothers and Daughters in *The Bluest Eye*." *SAGE* 4.2 (Fall 1987): 26–29.

Phelan, James. "Rhetorical Theory, Cognitive Theory, and Morrison's '"Recitatif"': From Parallel Play to Productive Collaboration." In *The Oxford Handbook of Cognitive Literary Studies*, edited by Lisa Zunshine. Oxford: Oxford University Press, 2015.

Phillips, Kimberley L. *War! What Is It Good For?: Black Freedom Struggles and the U.S. Military from World War II to Iraq*. Chapel Hill: University of North Carolina Press, 2012.

Phipps, Keith. "Toni Morrison: *Love*." *The A.V. Club*, Nov. 18, 2003. https://aux.avclub.com/toni-morrison-love-1798199083.

———. "Toni Morrison: *Paradise*." Accessed March 29, 2002. https://aux.avclub.com/toni-morrison-paradise-1798193089.

"Phylicia Rashad Breaks Silence on Bill Cosby Allegations." *ABC News*, Jan. 7, 2015. https://abcnews.go.com/Entertainment/phylicia-rashad-finally-speaks-bill-cosby-allegations/story?id=28055944.

Pici, Nicholas F. "Trading Meanings: The Breath of Music in Toni Morrison's *Jazz*." *Connotations: A Journal for Critical Debate* 7.3 (1997–98): 372–98.

Pickney, Darryl. "Hate." *New York Review of Books*, Dec. 4, 2003. https://www.nybooks.com/articles/2003/12/04/hate/.

Pipes, Candice L. "The Impossibility of *Home*." *War, Literature, and the Arts: An International Journal of the Humanities* 26 (Jan. 1, 2014): 1–15.

Plasa, Carl, ed. *Toni Morrison: Beloved*. New York: Columbia University Press, 1998.

Pocock, Judy. "'Through a Glass Darkly': Typology in Toni Morrison's *Song of Solomon*." *Canadian Review of American Studies* 35.3 (2005): 281–98.

Podolsky, Marjorie. "Black Women Writers Playing the 'Dozens.'" *Pennsylvania English* 20.2 (Spring 1996): 3–11.

Portales, Marco. "Toni Morrison's *The Bluest Eye*: Shirley Temple and Cholly." *Centennial Review* 30.4 (Fall 1986): 496–506.

Potter, George. "Forced Domination: Intersections of Sex, Race and Power in *Light in August* and *The Bluest Eye*." *Proteus* 21.2 (Fall 2004): 43–48.

Powell, Betty Jane. "'Will the Parts Hold?': The Journey toward a Coherent Self in *Beloved*." *Colby Quarterly* 31.2 (June 1995): 105–13.

Powell, Timothy B. "Toni Morrison: The Struggle to Depict the Black Figure on the White Page." *Black American Literature Forum* 24.4 (Winter 1990): 747–60.

Prescott, Peter S. "Dangerous Witness." *Newsweek* 83, Jan. 7, 1974, 63.

Price, Reynolds. "Black Family Chronicle." *New York Times Book Review*, Sept. 11, 1977, 1, 48.

Pringle, Mary Beth. "On a Jet Plane: Jadine's Search for Identity through Place in Toni Morrison's *Tar Baby*." *Midwestern Miscellany* 24 (1996): 37–50.

Pryce, Marjorie Lee, and Hortense J. Spillers. *Conjuring: Black Women, Fiction, and Literary Tradition*. Bloomington: Indiana University Press, 1985.

Pryse, Marjorie. "Signifyin(g) on Reparation in Toni Morrison's *Jazz*." *American Literature* 80.3 (Sept. 2008): 583–609.

Qasim, Khamsa, Mazhar Hayat, and Uzma Asmat. "Black Women and Racial Stereotypes: A Black Feminist Reading of Morrison's Novels." *Language in India* 12.5 (May 2012): 211–25.

Ragaišienė, Irena. "Black Self, Racial World: Toni Morrison's *The Bluest Eye* as a Terminated Bildungsroman." *Darbai ir Dienos* 32 (2002): 219–40.

Rainwater, Catherine, and William J. Scheick. *Contemporary American Women Writers: Narrative Strategies*. Lexington: University Press of Kentucky, 1985.

Ramadanovic, Petar. "'You Your Best Thing, Sethe': Trauma's Narcissism." *Studies in the Novel* 40.1–2 (Spring–Summer 2008): 178–88.

Ramey, Deanna. "A Comparison of the Triads of Women in Toni Morrison's *Sula* and *Song of Solomon*." *Mount Olive Review* 6 (Spring 1992): 104–9.

Ramos, Peter. "Beyond Silence and Realism: Trauma and the Function of Ghosts in *Absalom, Absalom!* and *Beloved*." *Faulkner Journal* 23.2 (Spring 2008): 47–66.

Ramsey, William. "An End of Southern History: The Down-Home Quests of Toni Morrison and Colson Whitehead." *African American Review* 41.4 (Winter 2007): 769–85.
Rand, Lizabeth A. "Female Discourse in *The Bluest Eye*—The Quest for Voice and Vision" *MAWA Review* 12.2 (Dec. 1997): 69–79.
Rand, Naomi R. *Silko, Morrison, and Roth: Studies in Survival*. New York: Peter Lang, 1999.
Randle, Gloria T. "'Knowing When to Stop': Loving and Living Small in the Slave World of *Beloved*." *CLA Journal* 41.3 (Mar. 1998): 279–302.
Randolph, Laura B. "The Magic of Toni Morrison." *Ebony* 43.9 (1988): 100–106.
Ravell-Pinto, Thelma M. "Comparative Aesthetic: Buchi Emecheta and Toni Morrison." In *The Growth of African Literature: Twenty-Five Years after Dakar and Fourah Bay*, edited by Edris Makward, Thelma Ravell-Pinto, and Aliko Songolo, 225–35. Trenton, NJ: Africa World Press, 1998.
Rayson, Ann. "Decoding for Race: Toni Morrison's 'Recitatif' and Being White, Teaching Black." In *Changing Representations of Minorities East and West*, edited by Larry E. Smith and John Rieder, 41–46. Honolulu: University of Hawaii Press, 1996.
———. "Foreign Exotic or Domestic Drudge? The African American Woman in *Quicksand* and *Tar Baby*." *MELUS* 23.2 (1998): 87–100.
Read, Andrew. "'As if word magic had anything to do with the courage it took to be a man': Black Masculinity in Toni Morrison's *Paradise*." *African American Review* 39.4 (Winter 2005): 527–40.
Reed, Harry. "Toni Morrison, *Song of Solomon*, and Black Cultural Nationalism." *Centennial Review* 32.1 (Winter 1988): 50–64.
Reed, Roxanne R. "The Restorative Power of Sound: A Case for Communal Catharsis in Toni Morrison's *Beloved*." *Journal of Feminist Studies in Religion* 23.1 (Spring 2007): 55–71.
Reneau, Ingrid. "Dancing the Clearing in Academia Struggle." *Western Journal of Black Studies* 27.4 (Winter 2003): 258–62.
Reyes, Angelita. "Ancient Properties in the New World: The Paradox of the 'Other' in Toni Morrison's *Tar Baby*." *Black Scholar* 17.2 (Mar./Apr. 1986): 19–25.
———. "Politics and Metaphors of Materialism in Paule Marshall's *Praisesong for the Widow* and Toni Morrison's *Tar Baby*." In *Politics and the Muse: Studies in the Politics of Recent American Literature*, edited by Adam J. Sorkin, 179–205. Bowling Green, OH: Popular, 1989.
Rice, Alan. "Erupting Funk: The Political Style of Toni Morrison's *Tar Baby* and *The Bluest Eye*." In *Postcolonial Literatures: Expanding the Canon*, edited by Deborah L. Madsen, 133–47. London: Pluto Press, 1999.
———. "'It Don't Mean a Thing If It Ain't Got That Swing': Jazz's Many Uses for Toni Morrison." In *Black Orpheus: Music in African American Fiction from the Harlem Renaissance to Toni Morrison*, edited by Saadi Simawe and Daniel Albright, 153–80. New York: Garland, 2000.
———. "Jazzing It Up a Storm: The Execution and Meaning of Toni Morrison's Jazzy Prose Style." *Journal of American Studies* 28.3 (Dec. 1994): 423–32.
———. "'Who's Eating Whom': The Discourse of Cannibalism in the Literature of the Black Atlantic from Equiano's *Travels* to Toni Morrison's *Beloved*." *Research in African Literatures* 29.4 (Winter 1998): 107–21.
Richards, Phillip M. "*Sula* and the Discourse of the Folk in African American Literature." *Cultural Studies* 9.2 (1995): 270–92.

Riley, Jeannette, Kathleen Torrens, and Susan Krumholz. "Contemporary Feminist Writers: Envisioning a Just World." *Contemporary Justice Review* 8.1 (Mar. 2005): 91–106.

Rimmen-Kenan, Schlomith, and Ruth Ginsberg. "Is There a Life after Death? Theorizing Authors and Reading Jazz." In *Narratologies: New Perspectives on Narrative Analysis*, edited by David Herman, 66–87. Columbus: Ohio State University Press, 1999.

Roark, Chris. "'My Mother's Fussing Soliloquies': Toni Morrison's *The Bluest Eye* and Shakespeare." *Borrowers and Lenders* 7.2 (Fall–Winter 2012): 1–29.

Robbins, Sarah. "Gendering the History of the Antislavery Narrative: Juxtaposing *Uncle Tom's Cabin* and *Benito Cereno*, *Beloved* and *Middle Passage*." *American Quarterly* 49.3 (Sept. 1997): 531–73.

Robinson, Timothy Mark. "Teaching the Ancestor Figure in African American Literature." *Teaching American Literature* 1.1 (Winter 2007): 41–66.

Robolin, Stéphane. "Loose Memory in Toni Morrison's *Paradise* and Zoë Wicomb's *David's Story*." *Modern Fiction Studies* 52.2 (Summer 2006): 297–320.

Rodgers, Norma. "A Mockery of Afro-American Life." *Freedomways* 18 (Second Quarter 1978): 107–9.

Rodriguez, Denise. "'Where the Self That Had No Self Made Its Home': The Reinscription of Domestic Discourse in Toni Morrison's *Beloved*." *Griot* 20.1 (Spring 2001): 40–51.

Rody, Caroline. "Toni Morrison's *Beloved*: History, 'Rememory,' and a 'Clamor for a Kiss.'" *American Literary History* 7.1 (Spring 1995): 92–119.

Rogin, Michael Paul. *Subversive Genealogy: The Politics and Art of Herman Melville*. Berkeley: University of California Press, 1983.

Rokonitz, Naomi. "Constructing Cognitive Scaffolding through Embodied Receptiveness: Toni Morrison's *The Bluest Eye*." *Style* 41.4 (Winter 2007): 385–408.

Romagnolo, Catherine. *Opening Acts: Narrative Beginnings in Twentieth-Century Feminist Fiction*. Lincoln: University of Nebraska Press, 2015.

Romero, Channette. "Creating the Beloved Community: Religion, Race and Nation in Toni Morrison's *Paradise*." *African American Review* 39.3 (Fall 2005): 415–30.

Rosenberg, Ruth. "'And the Children May Know Their Names': Toni Morrison's *Song of Solomon*." *Literary Onomastics Studies* 8.20 (1981): 195–219.

———. "Seeds in Hard Ground: Black Girlhood in *The Bluest Eye*." *Black American Literature Forum* 21.4 (Winter 1987): 435–45.

Rothberg, Michael. "Dead Letter Office: Conspiracy, Trauma, and *Song of Solomon*'s Posthumous Communication." *African American Review* 37.4 (Winter 2003): 501–16.

Roye, Susmita. "Toni Morrison's Disrupted Girls and Their Disturbed Girlhoods: *The Bluest Eye* and *A Mercy*." *Callaloo* 35.1 (Winter 2012): 212–27.

Roynon, Tessa. "Her Dark Materials: John Milton, Toni Morison, and Concepts of 'Dominion' in *A Mercy*." *African American Review* 44.4 (Winter 2011): 593–606.

———. "Lobbying the Reader: Toni Morrison's Recent Forewords to Her Novels." *European Journal of American Culture* 33.2 (2014): 85–96.

———. "A New 'Romen' Empire: Toni Morrison's *Love* and the Classics." *Journal of American Studies* 41.1 (Apr. 2007): 31–47.

———. "Sabotaging the Language of Pride: Toni Morrison's Representations of Rape." In *Feminism, Literature and Rape Narratives: Violence and Violation*, edited by Sorcha Gunne and Zoë Brigley Thompson, 38–53. London: Routledge, 2010.

———. *Toni Morrison and the Classical Tradition: Transforming American Culture*. Oxford: Oxford University Press, 2013.

Royster, Philip M. "Milkman's Flying: The Scapegoat Transcended in Toni Morrison's *Song of Solomon*." *CLA Journal* 24.4 (June 1981): 419–40.

———. "A Priest and a Witch against the Spiders and the Snakes: Scapegoating in Toni Morrison's *Sula*." *Umoja* 2.2 (1978): 149–68.

Rubenstein, Roberta. "History and Story, Sign and Design: Faulknerian and Postmodern Voices in *Jazz*." In *Unflinching Gaze: Morrison and Faulkner Re-Envisioned*, edited by Carol Kolmerten, Stephen Ross, and Judith Wittenberg, 152–64. Jackson: University Press of Mississippi, 1997.

Ruetenik, Tadd. "Animal Liberation or Human Redemption: Racism and Speciesism in Toni Morrison's *Beloved*." *Isle* 17.2 (Spring 2010): 317–26.

Rummell, Kathryn. "Toni Morrison's *Beloved*: Transforming the African Heroic Epic." *Griot* 21.2 (Spring 2002): 1–15.

Ruprecht, Louis, Jr. "Genres of Resistance, Tones of Intimacy, and Subtle Notes of Mercy." *Journal of the American Academy of Religion* 82.3 (Sept. 2014): 666–94.

Rushdy, Ashraf. "Daughters Signifyin(g) History: The Example of Toni Morrison's *Beloved*." *American Literature* 64.3 (Sept. 1992): 567–97.

Sairsingh, Marie. "Diasporic Connections: Erna Brodber and Toni Morrison's Literary Explorations of Black Existentiality." *CLA Journal* 56.4 (Jun. 2013): 315–28.

Sale, Maggie. "Call and Response as Critical Method: African-American Oral Traditions and *Beloved*." *African American Review* 26.1 (Spring 1992): 41–50.

Salvatore, Anne T. "Toni Morrison's New Bildungsromane: Paired Characters and Antithetical Form in *The Bluest Eye*, *Sula*, and *Beloved*." *Journal of Narrative Theory* 32.2 (Summer 2002): 154–78.

Salve, J. "The Theme of Marginality in Toni Morrison's *The Bluest Eye*." In *Literature of Marginality: Dalit Literature and African-American Literature*, edited by N. M. Aston, 127–43. Prestige Books, 2001.

Samantaray, Swati. "Non-Verbal Communication: The Use of Chromatics in Toni Morrison's Novels." *Language in India* 13.12 (Dec. 2013): 286–95.

"Same Old Story." *Times Literary Supplement*, Oct. 4, 1974, 1062.

Samuels, Wilfred D. "Liminality and the Search for Self in Toni Morrison's *Song of Solomon*." *Minority Voices* 5 (Fall 1981): 59–68.

Sandy, Mark. "'Cut by Rainbow': Tales, Tellers, and Reimagining Wordsworth's Pastoral Poetics in Toni Morrison's *Beloved* and *A Mercy*." *MELUS* 36.2 (Summer 2011): 35–51.

Sargent, Robert. "A Way of Ordering Experience: A Study of Toni Morrison's *The Bluest Eye* and *Sula*." In *Faith of a (Woman) Writer*, edited by Alice Kessler-Harris and William McBrien, 229–36. New York: Greenwood, 1988.

Satz, Martha. "Mothering Oneself in *Sula*." In Baxter and Satz, *Toni Morrison: Mothers and Motherhood*, 201–13.

Saunders, James Robert. "Why Losing a Tooth Matters: Shirley Jackson's 'The Tooth' and Toni Morrison's *The Bluest Eye*." *Midwest Quarterly* 53.2 (Winter 2012): 193–204.

Scarpa, Giulia. "Milkman and Ti Jean: The Mythical Journey in Toni Morrison and Simone Schwarz-Bart." *Caribana* 3 (1992–93): 111–22.

Schapiro, Barbara. "The Bonds of Love and the Boundaries of Self in Toni Morrison's *Beloved*." *Contemporary Literature* 32.2 (Summer 1991): 194–210.

Schappell, Elissa. "Toni Morrison: The Art of Fiction." 1992. In *Toni Morrison: Conversations*, edited by Carolyn C. Denard, 62–90. Jackson: University Press of Mississippi, 2008.

Scheiber, Andrew. "*Jazz* and the Future Blues: Toni Morrison's Urban Folk Zone." *Modern Fiction Studies* 52.2 (Summer 2006): 470–94.
Schell, David. "Engaging Foundational Narratives in Morrison's *Paradise* and Pynchon's *Mason & Dixon*." *College Literature* 41.3 (Summer 2014): 69–94.
Schiavonne, Michelle. "Images of Marginalized Cultures: Intertextuality in Marshall, Morrison, and Erdrich." *Bulletin of the West Virginia Association of College English Teachers* 17 (Fall 1995): 41–49.
Schindler, Melissa. "Home, or the Limits of the Black Atlantic." *Research in African Literatures* 45.3 (Fall 2014): 72–90.
Schmudde, Carol E. "The Haunting of 124." *African American Review* 26.3 (Fall 1992): 409–16.
Schreiber, Evelyn Jaffe. *Race, Trauma, and Home in the Novels of Toni Morrison*. Baton Rouge: Louisiana State University Press, 2010.
———. "Reader, Text, and Subjectivity: Toni Morrison's *Beloved* as Lacan's Gaze Qua Object." *Style* 30.3 (Fall 1996): 445–61.
———. *Subversive Voices: Eroticizing the Other in William Faulkner and Toni Morrison*. Knoxville: University of Tennessee Press, 2001.
Schroeder, Aribert. "Toni Morrison's Variations on Chester Himes." In *The Critical Response to Chester Himes*, edited by Charles L. P. Silet, 181–86. New York: Greenwood, 1999.
Schueller, Malini Johar. "Articulations of African-Americanism in South Asian Postcolonial Theory: Globalism, Localism, and the Question of Race." *Cultural Critique* 55 (Fall 2003): 35–62.
Schur, Richard L. "Locating *Paradise* in the Post-Civil Rights Era: Toni Morrison and Critical Race Theory." *Contemporary Literature* 45.2 (Summer 2004): 276–99.
Schuster, Donna Decker. "Teaching *Beloved*: Interrupting Cultural Logics and Defining Rememories as Elegaic Strategies." *Journal of the Midwest Modern Language Association* 39.1 (Spring 2006): 123–33.
Scott, Lynn. "Beauty, Virtue and Disciplinary Power: A Foucauldian Reading of Toni Morrison's *The Bluest Eye*." *Midwestern Miscellany* 24 (1996): 9–23.
———. "Revising the Incest Story: Toni Morrison's *The Bluest Eye* and James Baldwin's *Just above My Head*." In King and Scott, *James Baldwin and Toni Morrison*, 83–102.
Scruggs, Charles. "The Invisible City in Toni Morrison's *Beloved*." *Arizona Quarterly* 48.3 (Autumn 1992): 95–132.
———. "The Nature of Desire in Toni Morrison's *Song of Solomon*." *Arizona Quarterly* 38.4 (Winter 1982): 311–35.
Sempruch, Justyna. "The Sacred Mothers, the Evil Witches and the Politics of Household in Toni Morrison's *Paradise*." *Journal of the Association for Research on Mothering* 7.1 (Spring–Summer 2005): 98–109.
Sethi, Anita. "A Legacy of Hate." *Observer*, Nov. 16, 2003. https://www.theguardian.com/books/2003/nov/16/fiction.tonimorrison.
Seward, Adrienne Lanier, and Justine Tally, eds. *Toni Morrison: Memory and Meaning*. Jackson: University Press of Mississippi, 2014.
Sheed, Wilfred. "Improbable Assignment." *Atlantic Monthly* 247 (Apr. 1, 1981): 119–20.
Sheppard, R. Z. "Black Diamond." *Time*, Mar. 16, 1981, 90–93.
Sherard, Tracey. "Women's Classic Blues in Toni Morrison's *Jazz*: Cultural Artifact as Narrator." *Genders*, Mar. 2000. https://www.colorado.edu/gendersarchive1998-2013.

Sherman, Sarah Way. "Religion, the Body, and Consumer Culture in Toni Morrison's *The Bluest Eye*." In *Religion in America: European and American Perspectives*, edited by Hans Krabbendam and Derek Rubin, 143–56. Amsterdam: VU University Press, 2004.

Showalter, Elaine. "A Tangled Web." *Guardian*, Nov. 28, 2003. https://www.theguardian.com/books/2003/nov/29/fiction.tonimorrison.

Simon, Libby Bagno. "A Home on the Threshold: Family, Community and Identity in the Liminal Landscape of Toni Morrison's *A Mercy*." *Interactions* 23.1–2 (Spring-Fall): 243–50.

Simpson, Ritashona. *Black Looks and Black Acts: The Language of Toni Morrison in The Bluest Eye and Beloved*. New York: Peter Lang, 2007.

Singh, Monika. "Maternal Images: Reading Toni Morrison's *The Bluest Eye*." *Language in India* 1.1 (Jan. 2012): n.p.

Sissman, L. E. "Books: Beginner's Luck." *New Yorker*, Jan. 23, 1971, 92.

Sitter, Deborah Ayer. "The Making of a Man: Dialogic Meaning in *Beloved*." *African American Review* 26.1 (Spring 1992): 17–29.

Skeeter, Sharyn J. "*The Bluest Eye*." *Essence*, Jan. 1971: 59.

Sklar, Howard. "'What the Hell Happened to Maggie?': Stereotype, Sympathy, and Disability in Toni Morrison's 'Recitatif.'" *Journal of Literary and Cultural Disability Studies* 5.2 (2011): 137–54.

Smith, Abraham. "Toni Morrison's *Song of Solomon*: The Blues and the Bible." In *The Recovery of Black Presence: An Interdisciplinary Exploration*, edited by Charles B. Copher, Randall C. Bailey, and Jacquelyn Grant, 107–15. Nashville, TN: Abingdon, 1995.

Smith, Barbara. "Beautiful, Needed, Mysterious." *Freedomways* 14.1 (1974): 69–72.

———, ed. *Home Girls: A Black Feminist Anthology*. New Brunswick, NJ: Rutgers University Press, 2000.

———. "Toward a Black Feminist Criticism." *Radical Teacher* 7 (Mar. 1978): 20–27.

Smith, Cynthia J. "Black Fiction by Black Females." *Cross Currents* 14 (Fall 1976): 340–43.

———. "Intertextuality as Agent of Representation in Toni Morrison's *Tar Baby*." *Genre* 27.3 (1994): 165–81.

Smith, Dinitia. "Toni Morrison's Mix of Tragedy, Domesticity and Folklore." *New York Times*, Jan. 8, 1998. https://www.nytimes.com/1998/01/08/books/toni-morrison-s-mix-of-tragedy-domesticity-and-folklore.html.

Smith, Valerie. "The Quest for and Discovery of Identity in Toni Morrison's *Song of Solomon*." *Southern Review* 21.3 (Summer 1985): 721–32.

Smith, Victoria L. "Generative Melancholy: Women's Loss and Literary Representation." *Mosaic* 41.4 (Dec. 2008): 95–110.

Smith-Rosenberg, Carroll. *Disorderly Conduct: Visions of Gender in Victorian America*. New York: Knopf, 1985.

Sobat, Gail Sidonie. "If the Ghost Be There, Then Am I Crazy? An Examination of Ghosts in Virginia Hamilton's *Sweet Whispers, Brother Rush* and Toni Morrison's *Beloved*." *Children's Literature Association Quarterly* 20.4 (Winter 1995–96): 168–74.

Søfting, Inger-Anne. "Carnival and Black American Music as Counterculture in Toni Morrison's *The Bluest Eye* and *Jazz*." *American Studies in Scandinavia* 27.2 (1995): 81–102.

Sokolov, Raymond A. "Rev. of *The Bluest Eye*." *Newsweek*, Nov. 30, 1970, 96.

Somerville, Jane. "Idealized Beauty and the Denial of Love in Toni Morrison's *The Bluest Eye*." *Bulletin of the West Virginia Association of College English Teachers* 9.1 (Spring 1986): 18–23.
Spacks, Patricia Meyer. *Hudson Review* 27 (Summer 1974): 283–95.
Spain, Susan. "In Depth with Toni Morrison." C-Span, Feb. 4, 2001.
Spallino, Chiara. "*Song of Solomon*: An Adventure in Structure." *Callaloo* 25 (Autumn 1985): 510–24.
Spargo, R. Clifton. "Trauma and the Specters of Enslavement in Morrison's *Beloved*." *Mosaic* 35.1 (Mar. 2002): 113–31.
Spigner, Nieda. "A 'Best' Seller." *Freedomways* (Fourth Quarter 1981): 267–69.
Spillers, Hortense. "A Hateful Passion, A Lost Love." *Feminist Studies* 9.2 (Summer 1983): 293–323.
Staggers, Leroy. "The Critical Reception of Toni Morrison: 1970 to 1988." PhD diss., Clark Atlanta University, 1989. http://citeseerx.ist.psu.edu/viewdoc/download?doi=10.1.1.671.5533&rep=rep1&type=pdf.
Stanley, Sandra Kumamoto. "Maggie in Toni Morrison's 'Recitatif': The Africanist Presence and Disability Studies." *MELUS* 36.2 (Summer 2011): 71–88.
Stave, Shirley A. "Growing Up to Be a Man: Son Revisited." *Mosaic* 50.4 (Dec. 2017): 17–32.
———. "In a Mirror Dimly: The Limitations of Love in Toni Morrison's *Love*." In *Reading Texts, Reading Lives*, edited by Helen Maxson and Daniel Morris, 183–99. Newark: University of Delaware Press, 2012.
———, ed. *Toni Morrison and the Bible: Contested Intertextualities*. New York: Peter Lang, 2006.
———. "Toni Morrison's *Beloved* and the Vindication of Lilith." *South Atlantic Review* 58.1 (Jan. 1993): 49–66.
Stave, Shirley A., and Justine Tally, eds. *Toni Morrison's A Mercy: Critical Approaches*. Newcastle upon Tyne: Cambridge Scholars, 2011.
Stein, Jean. "William Faulkner, The Art of Fiction XII." *Paris Review* 12 (Spring 1956): 28–52.
Stein, Karen. "'I Didn't Even Know his Name': Name and Naming in Toni Morrison's *Sula*." *Names: A Journal of Onomastics* 28.3 (1980): 226–29.
———. "Note." *Names: A Journal of the American Name Society* 28 (Sept. 1980): 226–29.
Steinberg, Sybil, ed. *Writing for Your Life*. Wainscott, NY: Pushcart, 1992.
Steiner, Wendy. "The Clearest Eye." *New York Times Book Review*, Apr. 5, 1992. https://www.nytimes.com/1992/04/05/books/the-clearest-eye.html.
Stepto, Robert. "'Intimate Things in Place': A Conversation with Toni Morrison." In *Chant of Saints: A Gathering of Afro-American Literature, Art, and Scholarship*," edited by Michael S. Harper and Robert Stepto, 213–39. Urbana: University of Illinois Press, 1979. Rpt. in Gates and Appiah, *Toni Morrison: Critical Perspectives Past and Present*, 378–95.
Steward, Garrett. "The Deed of Reading: Toni Morrison and the Sculpted Book." *English Literary History* 80.2 (Summer 2013): 427–53.
Stewart, Jacqueline. "Negroes Laughing at Themselves? Black Spectatorship and the Performance of Urban Modernity." *Critical Inquiry* 29.4 (Summer 2003): 650–77.
Stockton, Kathryn Bond. "Heaven's Bottom: Anal Economics and the Critical Debasement of Freud in Toni Morrison's *Sula*." *Cultural Critique* 24 (Spring 1993): 81–118.
———. "Prophylactics and Brains: *Beloved* in the Cybernetic Age of Aids." *Studies in the Novel* 28.3 (Fall 1996): 434–65.

Storhoff, Gary. "'Anaconda Love': Parental Enmeshment in Toni Morrison's *Song of Solomon*." *Style* 31.2 (Summer 1997): 290–309.

Story, Ralph. "An Excursion into the Black World: The 'Seven Days' in Toni Morrison's *Song of Solomon*." *Black American Literature Forum* 23.1 (Spring 1989): 149–58.

———. "Sacrifice and Surrender: Sethe in Toni Morrison's *Beloved*." *CLA Journal* 46.1 (Sept. 2002): 21–47.

Strehle, Susan. "'I Am a Thing Apart': Toni Morrison, *A Mercy*, and American Exceptionalism." *Critique* 54.2 (Mar. 2013): 109–23.

Strouse, Jean. "Toni Morrison's Black Magic." *Newsweek*, Mar. 30, 1981, 52–57.

Stryz, Jan. "Inscribing an Origin in *Song of Solomon*." *Studies in American Fiction* 19.1 (Spring 1991): 31–40.

———. "The Other Ghost in *Beloved*: The Specter of *The Scarlet Letter*." *Genre* 24.4 (Winter 1991): 417–34.

Stuart, Andrea. "*A Mercy*, by Toni Morrison." *Independent*, Nov. 7, 2008. Retrieved from https://www.independent.co.uk/arts-entertainment/books/reviews/a-mercy-by-toni-morrison-997070.html.

Subryan, Carmen. "Circles: Mother and Daughter Relationships in Toni Morrison's *Song of Solomon*." *SAGE* 5.1 (Summer 1988): 34–36.

Sullivan, Mecca Jamilah. "'Put My Thang Down, Flip It and Reverse It': Black Women's Interstitial Languages of Body and Desire." *American Literary History* 29.4 (Winter 2017): 704–25.

Sulter, Maud. "Response to 'Feathered Wombs.'" *London Review of Books* 20.11, June 4, 1998.

Surányim, Ágnes. "*The Bluest Eye* and *Sula*: Black Female Experience from Childhood to Womanhood." In *The Cambridge Companion to Toni Morrison*, edited by Justine Tally, 11–15. Cambridge: Cambridge University Press, 2007.

Sweeney, Megan. "Racial House, Big House, Home: Contemporary Abolitionism in Toni Morrison's *Paradise*." *Meridians* 4.2 (2004): 40–67.

———. "'Something Rogue': Commensurability, Commodification, Crime, and Justice in Toni Morrison's Later Fiction." *Modern Fiction Studies* 52.2 (Summer 2006): 440–69.

Tabone, Mark. "Rethinking *Paradise*: Toni Morrison and Utopia at the Millenium." *African American Review* 49.2 (Summer 2016): 129–77.

Tabur, Şemsettin. *Contested Spaces in Contemporary North American Novels: Reading for Space*. Newcastle upon Tyne: Cambridge Scholars, 2014.

Tafreshi, Leila, and Wan Roselezam Wan Yahya. "Migration, Trauma, PTSD: A Gender Study of Morrison's *Jazz*." *Advances in Language and Literary Studies* 5.3 (June 2014): 120–25.

Tait, Althea. "The Harm in Beauty: Toni Morrison's Revisions of Racialized Traditional Theories of Aesthetics in *The Bluest Eye*." In *Globalizing Beauty: Consumerism and Body Aesthetics in the Twentieth Century*, edited by Harmut Berghoff and Thomas Kühne, 75–89. London: Palgrave Macmillan, 2013.

Tally, Justine, ed. *The Cambridge Companion to Toni Morrison*. Cambridge: Cambridge University Press, 2007.

———. *Paradise Reconsidered: Toni Morrison's (Hi)stories and Truths*. Piscataway, NJ: Transaction Press, 1999.

———. *Toni Morrison's Beloved Origins*. New York: Routledge, 2009.

Tanaka, Hisao. "Fōkunā to Morrison no kokujin hyoushō." *Rising Generation* 147.2 (May 2001): 94–96.

Tate, Claudia C. "*Song of Solomon*." *College Language Association Journal* 21.2 (Dec. 1977): 327–28.

Taylor, Paul C. "Malcolm's Conk and Danto's Colors: or, Four Logical Petitions concerning, Race, Beauty, and Aesthetics." In *African American Literary Theory: A Reader*, edited by Winston Napier, 665–71. New York: New York University Press, 2000.

Taylor-Guthrie, Danille Kathleen, ed. *Conversations with Toni Morrison*. Jackson: University Press of Mississippi, 1994.

———. "And She Was Loved: The Novels of Toni Morrison, A Black Woman's Worldview." PhD. diss. Brown University, 1984.

———. "Who Are the Beloved? Old and New Testaments, Old and New Communities of Faith." *Religion and Literature* 27.1 (Spring 1995): 119–29.

Temple, Joanne. "Review of *Sula*, by Toni Morrison." *Village Voice* 19, Mar. 7, 1974, 21.

Terrell, Lyne. "Storytelling and Moral Agency." *Journal of Aesthetics and Art Criticism*. 48.2 (Spring 1990): 115–26.

Terry, Jennifer. "'Breathing the Air of a World So New': Rewriting the Landscape of America in Toni Morrison's *A Mercy*." *Journal of American Studies* 48.1 (Feb. 2014): 127–45.

———. "Buried Perspectives: Narratives of Landscape in Toni Morrison's *Song of Solomon*." *Narrative Inquiry* 17.1 (2007): 93–118.

Terzieva-Artemis, Rossitsa. "Toni Morrison's *Beloved*: Feminine Mystique." *AnaChronisT* 10 (2004): 125–42.

Thomas, H. Nigel. "Further Reflections on the Seven Days in Toni Morrison's *Song of Solomon*." *Literary Griot* 13.1–2 (Spring–Fall 2001): 147–59.

Thomas, Jackie. "The Symbolic Black Male Ancestor in *Song of Solomon*." *Literary Griot* 5.2 (Fall 1993): 51–57.

Thomas, Leester. "When Home Fails to Nurture the Self: Tragedy of Being Homeless at Home." *Western Journal of Black Studies* 21.1 (Spring 1997): 51–58.

Thomas, Valorie D. "'1 1 3' and Other Dilemmas: Reading Vertigo in *Invisible Man, My Life in the Bush of Ghosts*, and *Song of Solomon*." *African American Review* 37.1 (Spring 2003): 81–94.

Thorsson, Courtney. "James Baldwin and Black Women's Fiction." *African American Review* 46.4 (Winter 2013): 615–31.

Thorsteinson, Katherine. "From Escape to Ascension: The Effects of Aviation Technology on the Flying African Myth." *Criticism* 57.2 (Spring 2015): 259–81.

Thurman, Judith. "A House Divided." *New Yorker*, Nov. 2, 1987, 175–80.

Tibbetts, John C. "Oprah's Belabored *Beloved*." *Literature/Film Quarterly* 27.1 (1999): 74–76.

Tidey, Ashley. "Limping or Flying? Psychoanalysis, Afrocentrism, and *Song of Solomon*." *College English* 63.1 (Sept. 2000): 48–70.

Travis, Molly Abel. "*Beloved* and *Middle Passage*: Race, Narrative, and the Critic's Essentialism." *Narrative* 2.3 (Oct. 1994): 179–200.

———. "Speaking from the Silence of the Slave Narrative: *Beloved* and African-American Women's History." *Texas Review* 13.1–2 (Spring–Summer 1992): 69–81.

Traylor, Eleanor. "The Fabulous World of Toni Morrison: *Tar Baby*." 1983. Rpt. in *Critical Essays on Toni Morrison*, edited by Nellie Y. McKay, 135–50. Boston: G. K. Hall, 1988.

Treherne, Matthew. "Figuring In, Figuring Out: Narration and Negotiation in Toni Morrison's *Jazz*." *Narrative* 11.2 (2003): 199–212.

Tyler, Anne. "Chocolates in the Afternoon and Other Temptations of a Novelist." *Washington Post Book World*, Dec. 11, 1977, E-1.
Ulin, David L. "*Home* by Toni Morrison Feels Distant." *Los Angeles Times*, May 6, 2012. Retrieved from http://articles.latimes.com/2012/may/06/entertainment/la-ca-toni-morrison-20120506.
———. "The Magic Is Missing in Toni Morrison's *God Help the Child*." *Los Angeles Times*, Apr. 23, 2015. Retrieved from https://www.latimes.com/books/jacketcopy/la-ca-jc-toni-morrison-20150426-story.html.
Umeh, Marie A. "A Comparative Study of the Idea of Motherhood in Two Third World Novels." *CLA Journal* 31.1 (Sept. 1987): 31–43.
Updike, John. "Dreamy Wilderness: Unmastered Women in Colonial Virginia." *New Yorker*, Nov. 3, 2008. Retrieved from https://www.newyorker.com/magazine/2008/11/03/dreamy-wilderness.
Valkeakari, Tuire. "Toni Morrison Writes B(l)ack: *Beloved* and Slavery's Dehumanizing Discourse of Animality." *Atlantic Literary Review* 3.2 (Apr.–June 2002): 165–87.
Van Der Zee, James, Owen Dodson, and Camille Bishops, eds. *The Harlem Book of the Dead*. Foreword by Toni Morrison. New York: Morgan & Morgan, 1978.
Vasques, Shalene. "In Her Own Image: Literary and Visual Representations of Girlhood in Toni Morrison's *The Bluest Eye* and Jamaica Kincaid's *Annie John*." *Griot* 31.2 (Fall 2012): 24–40.
Vega-González, Susana. "From Emotional Orphanhood to Cultural Orphanhood: Spiritual Death and Re-birth in Two Novels by Toni Morrison." *Revista Alicantina de Estudios Ingleses* 9 (1996): 143–51.
———. "Memory and the Quest for Family History in *One Hundred Years of Solitude* and *Song of Solomon*." *CLCWeb* 3.1 (Mar. 2001): 13 paragraphs.
———. "Remembering the Ancient Properties: Visions of Death and Re-Birth in *Sula* and *Tar Baby*." In *Proceedings of the 20th International AEDEAN Conference*. Barcelona: Universitat de Barcelona, 1997.
———. "Toni Morrison's *Love* and the Trickster Paradigm." *Revista Alicantina de Estudios Ingleses* 18 (Nov. 2005): 275–89.
———. "Toni Morrison's Water World: Watertime Writing in *Love*." *Grove: Working Papers on English Studies* 11 (2004): 209–20.
Vickroy, Laurie. "*Beloved* and *Shoah*: Witnessing the Unspeakable." *Comparatist* 22 (May 1998): 123–44.
———. "The Force Outside/The Force Inside: Mother-Love and Regenerative Spaces in *Sula* and *Beloved*." *Obsidian II* 8.2 (1993): 28–45.
———. "The Politics of Abuse: The Traumatized Child in Toni Morrison and Marguerite Duras." *Mosaic* 29.2 (June 1996): 91–109.
———. *Reading Trauma Narratives: The Contemporary Novel and the Psychology of Oppression*. Charlottesville: University of Virginia Press, 2015.
Vint, Sherryl. "'Only by Experience': Embodiment and the Limitations of Realism in Neo-Slave Narratives." *Science Fiction Studies* 34.2 (July 2007): 241–61.
Visser, Irene. "Fairy Tale and Trauma in Toni Morrison's *Home*." *MELUS* 41.1 (Spring 2016): 148–64.
Visvis, Vikki. "Alternatives to the 'Talking Cure': Black Music as Traumatic Testimony in Toni Morrison's *Song of Solomon*." *African American Review* 42.2 (Summer 2008): 255–68.

Wade-Gayles, Gloria. "The Truths of Our Mothers' Lives: Mother-Daughter Relationships in Black Women's Fiction." *SAGE* 1.2 (Fall 1984): 8–12.

Waegner, Cathy Covell. "Ruthless Epic Footsteps: Shoes, Migrants, and the Settlement of the Americas in Toni Morrison's *A Mercy*." In *Post-National Enquiries: Essays on Ethnic and Racial Border Crossings*, edited by Jopi Nyman, 91–112. Newcastle upon Tyne: Cambridge Scholars, 2009.

Wagner, Linda W. "Teaching *The Bluest Eye*." *ADE Bulletin* 83 (Spring 1986): 28–31.

Walker, Alice. *In Search of our Mothers' Gardens: Womanist Prose*. New York: Harcourt Brace, 1983.

Walker, Kara. "Toni Morrison's God Help the Child." *New York Times*, Apr. 13, 2015. Retrieved from https://www.nytimes.com/2015/04/19/books/review/toni-morrisons-god-help-the-child.html.

Wall, Cheryl A. "1970: 'You Love What Happens to the Air': Maya Angelou, Toni Morrison, Alice Walker." In *A New Literary History of America*, edited by Greil Marcus and Werner Sollors, 968–72. Cambridge: Harvard University Press, 2009.

———. "Resounding Souls: Du Bois and the African American Literary Tradition." *Public Culture* 17.2 (Spring 2005): 217–34.

Wallace, Cynthia R. "In the Beginning: *Beloved* and the Religious Word of Psychoanalysis." *Literature & Theology* 25.3 (Sept. 2011): 268–82.

———. "L as Language: *Love* and Ethics." *African American Review* 47.2–3 (Summer–Fall 2014): 375–90.

Wallace, Maurice. "Print, Prosthesis, (Im)personation: Morrison's *Jazz* and the Limits of Literary History." *American Literary History* 20.4 (Winter 2008): 794–806.

Walters, Wendy W. "'One of Dese Mornings, Bright and Fair,/Take My Wings and Cleave De Air': The Legend of the Flying Africans and Diasporic Consciousness." *MELUS* 22.3 (Fall 1997): 3–29.

Walther, Malin LaVon. "Out of Sight: Toni Morrison's Revision of Beauty." *Black American Literature Forum* 24.4 (Winter 1990): 775–89.

———. "Toni Morrison's *Tar Baby*: Re-Figuring the Colonizer's Aesthetics." In *Cross-Cultural Performances: Differences in Women's Re-Visions of Shakespeare*, edited by Marianne Novy, 137–49. Urbana: University of Illinois Press, 1993.

Wang, Elaine. "Art as Meaning-Making in a Secondary School English Classroom: A 'Secret Compartment' Book Project on Toni Morrison's *Beloved*." *English Journal* 104.5 (May 2015): 79–87.

Wang, Quan. "The Lack of Lack: The Lacanian Androgyny in Pilate." *Women's Studies* 42.1 (Jan.–Feb. 2013): 1–31.

Wardi, Anissa J. "Breaking the Back of Words: The Language of the Body in *Beloved*." *Griot* 17.1 (Spring 1998): 44–52.

———. "Freak Shows, Spectacles, and Carnivals: Reading Jonathan Demme's *Beloved*." *African American Review* 39.4 (Winter 2005): 513–26.

———. "Inscriptions in the Dust: *A Gathering of Old Men* and *Beloved* as Ancestral Requiems." *African American Review* 36.1 (Spring 2002): 35–53.

———. "Jazz Funerals and Mourning Songs: Toni Morrison's Call to the Ancestors in *Sula*." In *Toni Morrison and the Bible: Contested Intertextualities*, edited by Shirley A. Stave, 175–91. New York: Peter Lang, 2006.

———. "A Laying on of Hands: Toni Morrison and the Materiality of *Love*." *MELUS* 30.3 (Fall 2005): 201–18.

———. *Water and African American Memory: An Ecocritical Perspective*. Gainesville: University Press of Florida, 2011.
Warhol, Robyn, and Amy Shuman. "The Unspeakable, the Unnarratable, and the Repudiation of Epiphany in 'Recitatif': A Collaboration between Linguistic and Literary Feminist Narratologies." *Textual Practice* 32.6 (Aug. 2018): 1007–25.
Warnes, Andrew. *Hunger Overcome? Food and Resistance in Twentieth-Century African American Literature*. Athens: University of Georgia Press, 2004.
Washington, Mary Helen, ed. *Black-Eyed Susans: Classic Stories by and about Black Women*. New York: Anchor, 1975.
Washington, Teresa N. "The Mother-Daughter Ajé Relationship in Toni Morrison's *Beloved*." *African American Review* 39.1–2 (Spring–Summer 2005): 171–88.
Watson, Reginald. "Derogatory Images of Sex: The Black Woman and Her Plight in Toni Morrison's *Beloved*." *CLA Journal* 49.3 (Mar. 2006): 313–35.
———. "The Power of the 'Milk' and Motherhood: Images of Deconstruction in Toni Morrison's *Beloved* and Alice Walker's *The Third Life of Grange Copeland*." *CLA Journal* 48.2 (Dec. 2004): 156–82.
Waxman, Barbara Frey. "Girls into Women: Culture, Nature, and Self-Loathing in Toni Morrison's *The Bluest Eye* (1970)." In *Women in Literature: Reading through the Lens of Gender*, edited by Jerilyn Fisher and Ellen S. Silber, 47–49. Westport, CT: Greenwood, 2003.
Weathers, Glenda B. "Biblical Trees, Biblical Deliverance: Literary Landscapes of Zora Hurston and Toni Morrison." *African American Review* 39.1–2 (Spring–Summer 2005): 201–12.
Weems, Renita. "'Artists without Art Form': A Look at One Black Woman's World of Unrevered Black Women." In *Home Girls: A Black Feminist Anthology*, edited by Barbara Smith, 94–105. New Brunswick, NJ: Rutgers University Press, 2000.
Wegs, Joyce. "Toni Morrison's *Song of Solomon*: A Blues Song." *Essays in Literature* 9.2 (Fall 1982): 211–23.
Weinstock, Jeffrey Andrew. "Ten Minutes for Seven Letters: Reading *Beloved*'s Epitaph." *Arizona Quarterly* 61.3 (Autumn 2005): 129–52.
Weixlmann, Joe. "Culture Clash, Survival, and Trans-Formation: A Study of Some Innovative Afro-American Novels of Detection." *Mississippi Quarterly* 38.1 (Winter 1984–85): 21–32.
Werner, Craig Hansen. "The Briar Patch as Modernist Myth: Morrison, Barthes and *Tar Baby* As-Is." In *Critical Essays on Toni Morrison*, edited by Nellie Y. McKay, 150–67. Boston: G. K. Hall, 1988.
———. *Paradoxical Resolutions: American Fiction since James Joyce*. Urbana: University of Illinois Press, 1982.
Werrlein, Debra T. "Not So Fast, Dick and Jane: Reimagining Childhood and Nation in *The Bluest Eye*." *MELUS* 30.4 (Winter 2005): 53–72.
White, Artress Bethany. "From Africa to America by Way of the Caribbean: Fictionalized Histories of the African Diasporic Slave Woman's Presence in America in *I, Tituba, Black Witch of Salem* and *A Mercy*." In *Literary Expressions of African Spirituality*, edited by Elizabeth J. West and Carol P. Marsh-Lockett, 145–60. Lanham, MD: Lexington Press, 2013.
White, Jeanne Fuston. "Ocean Passage and the Presence of Absence: The Problem of Place in Four Contemporary Slave Narratives." *Griot* 26.2 (Fall 2007): 89–98.

Widdowson, Peter. "The American Dream Refashioned: History, Politics and Gender in Toni Morrison's *Paradise*." *Journal of American Studies* 35.2 (Aug. 2001): 313–35.

Wierzbinski, Jessica. "Biblical References in Toni Morrison's *Song of Solomon*." *Onoma* 40 (2005): 125–43.

Wigan, Angela. "Native Daughter." *Time* 110, Sept. 12, 1977, 76.

Wilentz, Gay. "An African-Based Reading of *Sula*." In *Approaches to Teaching the Novels of Toni Morrison*, edited by Nellie Y. McKay and Kathryn Earle, 127–34. New York: Modern Language Association of America, 1997.

———. "Civilizations Underneath: African Heritage as Cultural Discourse in Toni Morrison's *Song of Solomon*." *African American Review* 26.1 (Spring 1992): 61–76.

Willard, Mara. "Interrogating *A Mercy*: Faith, Fiction and the Postsecular." *Christianity and Literature* 63.4 (Summer 2014): 467–87.

Williams, Dana A. "Playing on the 'Darky': Blackface Minstrelsy, Identity Construction, and the Deconstruction of Race in Toni Morrison's *Paradise*." *Studies in American Fiction* 35.2 (Autumn 2007): 181–200.

Willis, Susan. "I Shop Therefore I Am: Is There a Place for Afro-American Culture in Commodity Culture?" In *Changing Our Own Words: Essays on Criticism, Theory, and Writing by Black Women*, edited by Cheryl A. Wall, 173–95. New Brunswick, NJ: Rutgers University Press, 1989.

———. *Specifying: Black Women Writing the American Experience*. Madison: University of Wisconsin Press, 1987.

Wilson, Elizabeth. "Not in This House: Incest, Denial, and Doubt in the White Middle Class Family." *Yale Journal of Criticism* 8 (1995): 35–58.

Wilson, Michael. "Affirming Characters, Communities, and Change: Dialogism in Toni Morrison's *Sula*." *Midwestern Miscellany* 24 (1996): 24–36.

Winchell, Donna Haisty. "Cries of Outrage: Three Novelists' Use of History." *Mississippi Quarterly* 49.4 (Fall 1996): 727–42.

Woff, Alice E., ed. *Kirkus Reviews* 38.16 (Aug. 15, 1970): 902.

Woidat, Caroline M. "Talking Back to Schoolteacher: Morrison's Confrontation with Hawthorne in *Beloved*." *Modern Fiction Studies* 39.3–4 (Fall–Winter 1993): 527–46.

Wolfe, Joanna. "'Ten Minutes for Seven Letters': Song as Key to Narrative Revision in Toni Morrison's *Beloved*." *Narrative* 12.3 (Oct. 2004): 263–80.

Wolter, Jürgen. "Southern Hesters: Hawthorne's Influence on Kate Chopin, Toni Morrison, William Faulkner, and Tennessee Williams." *Southern Quarterly* 50.1 (Fall 2012): 24–41.

Womack, Craig S. "Tribal Paradise Lost but Where Did It Go? Native Absence in Toni Morrison's *Paradise*" *Studies in American Indian Literature* 21.4 (Winter 2009): 20–52.

Wong, Shelley. "Transgression as Poesis in *The Bluest Eye*." *Callaloo* 13.3 (Summer 1990): 471–81.

Woodward, Kathleen. "Traumatic Shame: Toni Morrison, Televisual Culture, and the Cultural Politics of the Emotions." *Cultural Critique* 46 (Fall 2000): 210–40.

Wu, Yung-Hsing. "Doing Things with Ethics: *Beloved*, *Sula*, and the Reading of Judgment." *Modern Fiction Studies* 49.4 (Winter 2003): 780–805.

Wyatt, Jean. "The Economic Grotesque and the Critique of Capitalism in Toni Morrison's *Tar Baby*." *MELUS* 39.1 (2014): 30–55.

———. "Failed Messages, Maternal Loss, and Narrative Form in Toni Morrison's *A Mercy*." *Modern Fiction Studies* 58.1 (Spring 2012): 128–51.

———. "Giving Body to the Word: The Maternal Symbolic in Toni Morrison's *Beloved*." *PMLA* 108.3 (May 1993): 474–88.

———. "*Love*'s Time and the Reader: Ethical Effects of *Nachträglichkeit* in Toni Morrison's *Love*." *Narrative* 16.2 (May 2008): 192–221.

Wyman, Sarah. "Imaging Separation in Tom Feelings' *The Middle Passage: White Ships/Black Cargo* and Toni Morrison's *Beloved*." *Comparative American Studies* 7.4 (Dec. 2009): 298–318.

Yancy, George. "The Black Self within a Semiotic Space of Whiteness: Reflections on the Racial Deformation of Pecola Breedlove in Toni Morrison's *The Bluest Eye*." *CLA Journal* 43.3 (Mar. 2000): 299–319.

Yanyan, Zhu, and Quan Wang. "A Lacanian Reading of Milkman." *Consciousness, Literature and the Arts* 8.3 (Dec. 2007): n.p.

Yardley, Jonathan. "The Naughty Lady." *Washington Post Book World*, Feb. 3, 1974, 3.

Yates-Richard, Meina. "'WHAT IS YOUR MOTHER'S NAME?': Maternal Disavowal and the Reverberating Aesthetic of Black Women's Pain in Black Nationalist Literature." *American Literature* 88.3 (Sept. 2016): 477–507.

Yeates, Robert. "'The Unshriven Dead, Zombies on the Loose': African and Caribbean Religious Heritage in Toni Morrison's *Beloved*." *Modern Fiction Studies* 61.3 (Fall 2015): 515–37.

Yoo, Jae Eun. "Remembering the 'Forgotten War' after 9/11: *Indignation* and *Home*." *Orbis Litterarum* 73.3 (June 2018): 213–24.

———. "The Site of Murder: Textual Space and Ghost Narrator in Toni Morrison's *Love*." In *Space, Haunting, Discourse*, edited by Maria Holmgren Troy and Elisabeth Wennö, 153–67. Newcastle upon Tyne: Cambridge Scholars, 2008.

Young, Harvey, and Jocelyn Prince. "Adapting *The Bluest Eye* for the Stage." *African American Review* 45.1–2 (Spring–Summer 2012): 143–55.

Young, John. "Toni Morrison, Oprah Winfrey, and Postmodern Popular Audiences." *African American Review* 35.2 (Summer 2001): 181–204.

Young, Robert. "Invisibility and Blue Eyes: African-American Subjectivity." *Revisita Canaria de Estudios Ingleses* 39 (Nov. 1999): 169–90.

Zauditu-Selassie, Kokahvah. *African Spiritual Traditions in the Novels of Toni Morrison*. Gainesville: University Press of Florida, 2009.

INDEX

Abel, Elizabeth, 62, 177n6, 179
Acker, Kathy, 24
Adams, Tim, 204
Adorno, Theodor, 171–72
African American Review, 20n7, 99, 122, 125, 149, 167, 189, 206, 222. *See also Black American Literature Forum*
African American writers, shifting views of, 1, 28, 39, 49, 57, 105
African culture, 15–16; in *Beloved*, 132–33, 142; in *God Save the Child*, 235; in *Home*, 224, 227; in *Love*, 189; in *Song of Solomon*, 14, 85, 86; in *Sula*, 69; in *Tar Baby*, 94, 110–11
Aguiar, Sarah, 155, 173, 174
Ahmad, Soophia, 87
Aidoo, Ama Ata, 125
Aithal, Krishnamoorthy, 107
Akhtar, Jaleel, 66, 211, 224
Akoma, Chiji, 168
Alexander, Allen, 35
Alexandre, Sandy, 132, 213
Allende, Isabel, 90
Als, Hilton, 55
Alwes, Karla, 28
American Dream, 36, 85, 161, 169, 194, 212
American Literature (journal), 99–100, 101, 122, 124
Anderson, Elliot, 53
Anderson, Melanie, 176
Andrès, Emmanuelle, 223

Andrews, Jennifer, 156
Andrews, William, 131
Androne, Helane Adams, 178n7
Angelo, Bonnie, 121
Angelou, Maya, 26, 116
Anolik, Ruth, 213
Appel, Sara, 36–37
Appiah, Kwame Anthony, 238
Aristodemou, Maria, 127
Arizona Quarterly, 122
Armengol, Josep, 213
Armstrong, Nancy, 124
Armstrong, Piers, 38
Ashe, Bertram, 88
Askeland, Lori, 123–24
Asmat, Uzma, 31
Atieh, Majda, 173, 174
Atkinson, Yvonne, 35, 110, 111
Atlantic Monthly, 96, 98, 232
Atlas, Marilyn, 23, 117, 118, 119, 120–21, 154
Atwood, Margaret, 58–60, 116, 119
Aubry, Timothy, 141, 166
Awkward, Michael, 28, 87
Azouz, Samy, 42
Azumurana, Solomon Omatsola, 125, 141

Babaee, Rusbeh, 132
Babb, Valerie, 215
Babbitt, Susan, 127–28
Backes, Nancy, 26
Backus, Margo, 107

Bacon's Rebellion, 202, 207
Badode, R. M., 35
Baillie, Justine, 39–40, 86
Baker, Houston A., 65, 69, 116, 190
Bakerman, Jane, 27, 79, 87
Bakhtin, Mikhail, 24, 31, 38, 29, 67
Baldwin, James, 24, 25, 57, 120, 151, 192, 195n6
Balestra, Alisa, 40
Bambara, Toni Cade, 116
Banyiwa-Horne, Naana, 64–65
Baraka, Amiri, 116, 177n6
Barksdale, Richard, 65
Barnes, Deborah, 157
Barnett, Pamela, 130
Barr, Jason, 173
Barthes, Roland, 34, 69, 109
Barthold, Bonnie, 81
Bartley, Aryn, 217
Bassard, Katherine, 176, 214
Bast, Florian, 139
Basu, Biman, 67, 132
Baum, Rosalie, 22
Bawer, Bruce, 146–47
Baxter, Lee, 193
Beaulieu, Elizabeth, 45, 88
Beaver, Harold, 77
Beavers, Herman, 128–29, 196–97
Bechdel, Alison, 208
Being Mary Jane (TV series), 235
Beliveau, Laura, 141
Bell, Bernard, 15–16, 127
Bell, Pearl, 98
Beloved, 81, 112, 113–42, 168; African American/postcolonial criticism on, 117, 119–21, 122, 129–33, 206; awards for, 4, 116, 117, 143; book reviews of, 115–21, 163–64; critical studies of, 20nn5–6, 121–42; feminist/womanist/masculinist criticism on, 117, 127–29; film version of, 135–36, 167; foreword to, 113–15; intertextuality in, 123–26, 128; *Jazz* and, 152; *Love* and, 187, 189, 191; *A Mercy* and, 203–4; myth and archetypes in, 117, 127–28; new historical/cultural criticism on, 133–37, 216; psychoanalytic criticism on, 137–40; reader-response/pedagogical criticism on, 140–42; sentimentalism and, 120, 124, 127, 136; supernaturalism in, 119, 123, 125–26, 130, 133; Updike and, 205n4. *See also under* slavery
Benjamin, Shanna, 179, 181
Bennett, Michael, 63
Bennett, Paula, 23
Benston, Kimberly, 151
Berben-Masi, Jacqueline, 192
Bergenholtz, Rita, 66
Berger, James, 135
Bergthaller, Hannes, 131, 138–39
Berlant, Lauren, 124
Berret, Anthony, 39, 84, 150
Best, Stephen, 216
Bhabha, Homi, 153, 175
Bible: in *BE*, 25; in *Beloved*, 110, 123, 124, 126, 135; in *Love*, 191, 197; in *A Mercy*, 207–8, 212, 214; in *Paradise*, 160; in *Song of Solomon*, 80, 82, 91
Bidney, Martin, 125
bildungsroman genre, 20n6, 126; *BE* and, 37; *Beloved* and, 142; *Home* and, 226; *Song of Solomon* and, 75n5, 86
Billingslea, Alma Jean, 110–11
Bisla, Sundeep, 141
"Black," capitalization of, 238
Black American Literature Forum, 20, 61, 81, 99, 104
Black Arts Movement, 25, 78n9
Black Book, The (anthology), 114, 143, 160, 183, 184
Black Book Bulletin, 77n8
Blackburn, Sara, 19–20, 53, 54, 55
Black Enterprise, 98
"Black is Beautiful" slogan, 8, 12, 18, 111, 180
Black Nationalism, 89–90, 112, 171, 176
Black Power movement, 40, 78, 89, 110–11, 133, 135
Black Scholar, 104, 105
black subjectivity: in *BE*, 23, 29; in *Beloved*, 133, 137–38, 140; in *Song of Solomon*, 138
Black World, 18, 54
Blake, Susan, 82
Blake, William, 125, 186–87

INDEX

Bloom, Harold, 91, 105
Bluest Eye, The (*BE*), 7–45, 93, 126, 181, 219; African American criticism on, 35–37; afterword to, 4, 7n1, 8–12, 18; archetypal criticism on, 7–8, 12–15, 21–22; banning of, 1, 16n3, 40; book reviews of, 9, 12, 15–20, 48, 93; critical studies of, 20–45, 74; Dick and Jane primers in, 10, 35–36, 28, 40; ecocriticism on, 33–34; feminist/womanist criticism on, 26–31, 79n11, 207; *God Help the Child* and, 228–33; intertextual criticism on, 22–26; miscategorization of, 1, 3, 16; narratology/structuralist criticism on, 34; new historical/cultural criticism on, 38–43; Persephone myth in, 7–8, 12–15, 21–22; postcolonial criticism on, 36–38; reader-response/pedagogical criticism on, 43–45; psychoanalytic criticism on, 32–33; stage production of, 42–43; *Sula* and, 19, 47, 50
Blyn, Robin, 130
Bollen, Christopher, 219n7
Bonnet, Michèle, 131–32
Booklist, 53, 96, 116
Boston Globe, 220
Boswell, Mai, 65
Bredella, Lothar, 36
Boudreau, Kristin, 138
Bouson, Brooks, 32, 192
Boutry, Katherine, 156
Bowers, Ann, 85
Bowers, Maggie, 130
Bowman, Diane, 84
Bradley, David, 125
Branch, Eleanor, 89
Brenkman, John, 89
Brenner, Gerry, 87
Brickhouse, Anna, 216
Britton, Wesley, 125
Broad, Robert, 126
Brodber, Erna, 207
Brontë, Charlotte, 58
Bross, Kristina, 217–18
Brown, Bill, 38–39
Brown, Caroline, 157

Brown, Cecil, 14
Brown, Joseph, 91
Brown, Rosellen, 118, 119
Browning, Robert, 123, 125
Broyard, Anatole, 97
Bryan, Eugenia, 216
Bryant, Cedric, 67, 83, 125–26
Bryant, Ceron L., 68
Bryant, Jerry H., 55–56
Buchanan, Jeffrey, 44
Budick, Emily, 134
Buehrer, David, 88
Buisson, Françoise, 24
Bulsterbaum, Allison, 84
Bump, Jerome, 32, 44
Burgess, Françoise, 28
Burke, Solomon, 89
Burkhalter, Cindy, 85
Burr, Benjamin, 191
Burrell, Vernita, 25
Burton, Angela, 151–52
Busby, Margaret, 148
Butler, Octavia E., 124
Butler, Robert, 86–87
Byerman, Keith, 22, 23, 56
Byrne, Dara, 126n8

Callaloo, 20, 61, 81, 104, 116, 122, 149, 206
Campbell, Jan, 137
Campbell, Joseph, 72
Campbell, Josie, 90
Campion, Jane, 24
Candel Bormann, Daniel, 24
Cannon, Elizabeth, 155
Cantiello, Jessica, 215
Capuano, Peter, 131
Carden, Mary Paniccia, 129–30, 193
Carlacio, Jami, 213
Carpenter, Chatard, 42–43
Carruth, Alison, 109
Carter, Angela, 24
Caruth, Cathy, 210
Casler, Jeanine, 23
Cather, Willa, 41, 114
Chadwick-Joshua, Jocelyn, 157
Chang, Jeff, 235
Chang, Shu-li, 124
Charles, Ron, 165–66, 167, 220, 227

Chen, Chang-fang, 23
Cheng, Anne, 28–29
Chicago Tribune, 53, 75, 76, 119, 231
Chodorow, Nancy, 65
Choice, 53, 116, 119
Christian, Barbara, 33–34, 56, 79, 102, 103, 118, 121, 129, 197
Christian Science Monitor, 76, 77, 165
Churchwell, Sarah, 221–22
Cillerai, Chiara, 217
Civil Rights Movement, 89, 186, 190, 194
Clark, Norris, 21, 69, 80, 82
Clark, Petula, 59
Clary, Françoise, 35
Clément, Catherine, 173
Clemons, Walter, 116
Cliff, Michelle, 26
Coates, Ta-Nehisi, 237
Cohen, Leah Hager, 220–21
Coleman, James, 83, 99
College Language Association Journal, 18, 20, 61, 77, 78, 79, 81, 99, 101, 104–5, 122, 124, 149, 167, 206
College Literature, 122
Collins, Patricia Hill, 227
Commentary, 98, 116
Comparative Literature Studies, 99
Condé, Maryse, 207
Conner, Mark C., 36, 105, 152, 211–12
Coonradt, Nicole M., 127
Cooper, Brittney, 156, 193–94
Cornell, Drucilla, 127–28, 154–55
Cosby, Bill, 183–84, 186, 193, 197
Cosca, David, 135
Coughlan, David, 224
Cowart, David, 91
Crabtree, Claire, 123
Crane, Stephen, 22
Crisis, The, 77n8
critical race theory, 68, 175, 186, 190
Critique, 99
Croisille, Valérie, 194
Cross Currents, 57n2
Crouch, Stanley, 119–20, 124, 127
Cullinan, Colleen, 127
Cultural Critique, 122
Curtis, Susan, 218
Cutter, Martha, 126, 130, 152

Dahill-Baue, William, 23, 123
Dalsgård, Katrine, 169
Daly, Brenda, 44
Daniel, Janice, 131
Daniels, Jean, 131
Dante Alighieri, 48, 149
Danticat, Edwidge, 26
Danto, Arthur, 38
Darda, Joseph, 225
Darling, Marsha Jean, 121
Dauterich, Edward, 131
Davidson, Rob, 169
Davis, Arthur P., 78
Davis, Christina, 129–30, 131
Davis, Kimberly, 136
Dead Milkmen, the (band), 80
De Angelis, Rose, 69
De Arman, Charles, 75, 82
Dee, Ruby, 18
Degler, Rebecca, 25
Delancey, Dayle, 64
Delashmit, Margaret, 36
Delazari, Ivan, 179–80
Deleuze, Gilles, 133, 168
Demetrakapoulos, Stephanie, 81, 88, 105, 127
Demme, Jonathan, 136
Denard, Carolyn, 101, 189
Depci, Aytemis, 31
Derrida, Jacques, 154, 191
Desdemona, 61, 101
Deusner, Stephen, 188
DeVita, Alexis, 131
de Weever, Jacqueline, 82
Diamond, Lydia, 42
Dickerson, Vanessa, 28, 29, 63–64
Dickinson, Emily, 3
Dickson-Carr, Darryl, 153
Diedrich, Maria, 120–21
Ding, Yang, 33
Distel, Kristin, 173
Dittmar, Linda, 34
Diu, Nishia Lilia, 221
Dobbs, Cynthia, 128, 175
Dodman, Trevor, 65–66
Doughty, Peter, 35
Douglas, Christopher, 41
Douglas, Mary, 139

INDEX

Douglass, Frederick, 109, 213
Dowling, Collette, 76
Doyle, Laura, 29
Doyle, Mary Ann, 141
Drake, Kimberly, 23
Dreifus, Claudia, 197
Dubek, Laura, 89
Dubey, Madhu, 62, 63, 131, 157
Du Bois, Shirley Graham, 56, 99
Du Bois, W. E. B., 56, 66, 91, 99; "double consciousness" concept of, 88, 106, 156
Dudar, Helen, 119
Du Plooy, Belinda, 139
Duras, Marguerite, 24
Durkin, Anita, 122n6
Durrans, Stéphanie, 194
Duvall, John, 23, 85–86, 107–8, 123, 125, 152, 191–92, 214

Earle, Kathryn, 43, 105
Earle, Monalesia, 208
Early American Literature, 217
Eaton, Alice, 235
Ebony, 221
Eckard, Paula, 151
Eckstein, Lars, 131
ecocriticism: on *BE*, 33–34; on *Beloved*, 123n6, 131–32; on *A Mercy*, 211–12
Edelberg, Cynthia, 99–100, 101
Edmunds, Susan, 110–11
Edwards, Thomas, 118
Elia, Nada, 81, 86
Eliot, T. S., 23
Elkin, Stanley, 93
Elkin, Susan, 232–33
Elliot, Mary Jane, 133
Elliott, Mary Grace, 24
Ellis, Kate, 91
Ellison, Ralph, 23, 25, 57, 75, 83, 91, 119n3, 121, 125, 156, 200
Emberley, Julia, 29–30
Emecheta, Buchi, 23, 24
Emerson, Cheryl, 207–8
Emerson, Ralph Waldo, 202, 214
Enlightenment, 138, 171–72, 214
Eppert, Claudia, 142
Erdrich, Louise, 24, 123

Erickson, Peter, 101
Escoda Agusti, Clara, 124–25
Essence, 18, 78, 111
Euro-American vs. Afro-American criticism, 15–16, 54–56, 76–77, 98; Morrison on, 114
Evans, Mari, 102
Evans, Sheri, 170

fairy tales, 123; *God Help the Child* and, 230; *Home* and, 219n7, 221, 226; *Song of Solomon* and, 82, 89
Fanon, Frantz, 210
Farrell, Susan, 87
Faulkner, William, 3, 20nn5–6, 59, 113, 123n7, 147, 152, 163, 167, 200, 205, 226; *Absalom, Absalom!*, 91, 123, 172, 191, 214; *As I Lay Dying*, 23, 24; *The Bear*, 123; *Go Down, Moses*, 85, 86, 172, 214–15; *The Sound and the Fury*, 123
Feelings, Tom, 125
female friendship, 52, 55, 56, 58–61, 62, 64, 189
Feng, Pin-chia, 20n6
Ferrier, Carole, 45
Fick, Thomas, 22–23, 43
Fils-Aimé, Holly, 91
Fish, Stanley, 69
Fisher, Ann H., 116
Fishman, Charles, 100
Fitzgerald, F. Scott, 41, 59
FitzGerald, Jennifer, 157
Flanagan, Joseph, 139
Fletcher, Judith, 82–83
flight imagery: in *BE*, 14, 21; in *Song of Solomon*, 14, 72, 73–74, 82, 83–84, 86, 91; in *Sula*, 69
Flint, Holly, 175
folk traditions: in *BE*, 17, 35; in *Beloved*, 116, 120, 121; in *Home*, 224; in *Jazz*, 152–53; in *Song of Solomon*, 75, 82, 84, 99; in *Sula*, 69; in *Tar Baby*, 94–95, 99, 110–11
Forbes, Malcolm, 222
Foreman, Gabrielle, 90
Foucault, Michel, 39, 67, 126, 170, 196
Fowler, Doreen, 129, 214n5

Fraile-Marcos, Ana Maria, 175
Frampton, Edith, 88, 128
Franco, Dean, 140
Frankel, Haskel, 16–17, 19
Fraser, Rhone, 235
Freedomways, 18, 55, 56, 77n8, 78, 99
Freeman, John, 220
Freud, Sigmund, 65, 88–89, 137, 139, 196, 210
Frever, Trinna, 40
Friedman, Gabriella, 218
Fulton, Lorie, 91, 132
Fultz, Lucille, 64, 68, 85, 106, 168n3, 189–90, 191n4
Fulweiler, Howard, 138
Furman, Jan, 81, 223
Fuston-White, Jeanna, 138

Gaines, Ernest J., 125
Gallego-Durán, Mar, 189, 209–10
Gant, Liz, 18
Garabedian, Deanna, 84
Garbus, Lisa, 134
García Márquez, Gabriel, 76, 90
Gardner, John, 238–39
Gardner, Renee, 127–28
Garner, Margaret, 114–15, 136–37, 143
Gates, David, 203–4
Gates, Henry Louis, Jr., 49, 97n1, 101, 157, 238
Gauthier, Marni, 169
Gay, Roxanne, 232
George, Sheldon, 137
Géricault, Théodore, 216
Gerster, Carol, 39
Gibson, Donald, 34
Gilbert, Katherine, 32
Gillan, Jennifer, 37
Gillespie, Carmen, 42, 105
Gillespie, Diane, 65
Gillespie, Marcia, 118n2
Gilligan, Carol, 65
Gilroy, Paul, 226
Giovanni, Nikki, 77, 78
Girshin, Thomas, 128
Gladys, P. V. Annie, 31
Glover, Toni, 69
Gnosticism, 145n1, 152

Gobineau, Arthur de, 34
God, Morrison on, 35
God Help the Child, 20n5, 61, 181, 199, 228–35; book reviews of, 230–33; critical studies of, 233–35
Gold, Eva, 43
Goldman, Anne, 124
Goldstein, Philip, 25, 123
Goldstein-Shirley, David, 179
Goodburn, Amy, 43
Goodman, Walter, 116
Goodreads, 148–49, 233
Gornick, Vivian, 76
Gothic mode, 77, 119, 123, 125, 131, 196, 208, 213, 220
Gottlieb, Robert, 47n1
Gourdine, Angeletta, 44, 121, 141
Gowda, H. H., 27
Goyal, Yogita, 111–12
Grandt, Jürgen, 151
Grant, Robert, 66, 126
Grausam, Daniel, 171
Gravett, Sharon, 23
Gray, Paul, 116, 119
Greenbaum, Vicky, 141
Greenway, Gina, 132
Grewal, Gurleen, 30, 43, 112, 157, 174
Griesinger, Emily, 126
Griffith, Johnny, 171
Griffith, Paul, 81
Griot, 20, 81, 122
Grobman, Laurie, 141–42
Groover, Kristina, 24
Gruber, Elizabeth, 112
Guardian, 187, 204, 221, 232
Guattari, Félix, 133
Guess Who's Coming for Dinner? (film), 109
Guth, Deborah, 85, 126
Gwin, Minrose, 40

Haley, Alex, 75
Hall, Cheryl, 131
Hall, James, 83
Hamilton, Cynthia, 131
Hamilton, Virginia, 90, 125
Handley, William, 132
Hansberry, Lorraine, 26
Hansen, Morten, 206

INDEX

Harack, Katrina, 195–96
Hardack, Richard, 156
Hardin, Tayana, 142
Harding, Wendy, 131
Harlem Renaissance, 78, 144, 155
Harris, Jessica, 77–78
Harris, Leslie, 80, 82
Harris, Trudier, 35, 117–18, 177–78
Härting, Heike, 132
Hassan Khan, Reza, 33
Hastings, Phyllis, 36
Hausknecht, Gina, 24
Hawthorne, Evelyn, 111
Hawthorne, Nathaniel, 123, 125, 212, 216
Hayat, Mazhar, 31
Hayes, Elizabeth T., 7n1, 15n2, 21, 124, 180n8
Hébert, Kimberly, 43
Heffernan, Teresa, 140
Heller, Dana, 130
Heller, Zoë, 164–65, 166
Hellman, Lillian, 59
Hemingway, Ernest, 59, 114
Henderson, Mae, 69
Henke, Suzette, 210
Henton, Jennifer, 65
Herman, Judith, 210
Heyman, Richard, 83
Hichri, Asma, 139–40
Hilfrich, Carola, 173–74
Himes, Chester, 24
Hindman, Jane, 131
Ho, Wen-ching, 23, 206
Hobby, Blake, 105
Hogue, Bev, 90
Holden-Kirwan, Jennifer, 138
Holland, Sharon, 132
Holloway, Karla, 21–22, 81, 131
Holmes, Kristine, 124
Holton, Robert, 85
Homans, Margaret, 62, 63
Home, 199, 218–28; African American/postcolonial criticism on, 225–26; book reviews of, 220–22; critical studies of, 222–28; intertextuality in, 226–27; new historical/cultural criticism on, 224–25; psychoanalytic criticism on, 223–24

Homer, 75, 82, 152
hooks, bell, 34, 138
Hooper, Lita, 24
Hopkinson, Nalo, 212
Horkheimer, Max, 171–72
Horn, Miriam, 121
Horvitz, Deborah, 130
Höttges, Bärbel, 131
House, Elizabeth, 101, 130
Hovet, Grace Ann, 21, 68, 83
Hsieh, Yi-jo, 210
Huang, Hsin-ya, 88
Hubbard, Dolan, 85
Hudson Review, 116
Humann, Heather, 193–94
Hunt, Michelle, 26
Hurston, Zora Neale, 26, 49, 57, 75, 124
Hutchinson, Earle Ofari, 231
hybridity, 31, 109, 206

Iannone, Carol, 119
Ibarrola, Aitor, 223
Ikuenobe, Polycarp, 86
Imbrie, Ann, 90
Imitation of Life (film), 39, 40
incest, 25, 38, 75, 107
Independent (London), 148, 204, 232
In Process, 104, 105
Insko, Jeffrey, 136
Insoo, Lee, 31
Internet, reviews on, 148–49, 167, 188, 222, 233
intersectionality, 22, 36–37, 87, 124–25, 172, 194, 212, 227
Iqbal, Razia, 233
Irigaray, Luce, 28
Irving, John, 98
Izgjarjan, Aleksandra, 24, 30

Jablon, Madelyn, 101, 105, 124
Jackson, Chuck, 69
Jackson, Shirley, 25
Jacobs, Harriet, 124
Jaffrey, Zia, 57, 61, 164
Janowitz, Hans, 151
jazz. *See under* music
Jazz, 81, 121, 126, 143–58, 185; African American/postcolonial criticism on,

Jazz (continued): 156–58; book reviews of, 146–48; critical studies of, 149–58; feminist/womanist criticism on, 154–56; foreword to, 143–46; Internet reviews of, 148–49; intertextuality in, 151–53; reader-response criticism on, 150–51; structuralist and deconstructive criticism on, 153–54. *See also under* music
Jefferson, Margo, 53, 54, 75
Jenkins, Candice, 176
Jennings, La Vinia Delois, 110, 137
Jessee, Sharon, 170
Jesser, Nancy, 130–31
Jewett, Chad, 151
Jewett, Sarah Orne, 24
Jeyachandra, Edwinsingh, 31
John, Eileen, 43–44
Johnson, Charles, 124, 140
Johnson, James Weldon, 90
Joiner, Jennie, 172
Jones, Bessie W., 103–4, 113
Jones, Carolyn, 85, 126, 138, 154
Jones, Gayle, 22, 124–25
Jones, Jill, 172
Jordan, June, 116
Jordan, Margaret, 81
Jordan, Shirley, 101
Journal of Blacks in Higher Education, 81
Journal of Ethnic Studies, 20, 81
Jovović, Tamara, 37, 234–35
Joyce, James, 91, 113, 147
Joyce, Joyce Ann, 82
Jung, Carl G., 109
Jurecic, Ann, 105, 141

Kakutani, Michiko, 117, 163–64, 190, 203, 221, 227
Kang, Nancy, 129
Kaplan, Sarah, 157–58
Karavanta, Mina, 206
Katawal, Ubaraj, 171–72
Kawash, Samira, 132
Kearly, Peter, 167–68
Keizer, Arlene, 138
Kennedy, Rosanne, 228
Kérchy, Anna, 151

Khaleghi, Mahboobeh, 153
Khawaja, Mabel, 135
Khayati, Abdellatif, 34
Khushu-Lahiri, Rajyashree, 27
Kim, Aeju, 32, 88, 109
Kim, Kwangsoon, 64
Kim, Miehyeon, 177
Kim, Myung Ja, 44–45
Kim, Sun-ok, 206
King, Martin Luther, Jr., 90
King, Nicole, 135
King-Pedroso, Natalie, 235
Kingston, Maxine Hong, 20n6, 23
Kincaid, Jamaica, 26, 124
Kirkus Reviews, 16, 53, 75, 96, 116, 146, 163, 164, 186
Klotman, Phyllis, 38
Knadler, Stephen, 155
Knoflíčková, Marie, 177
Kodat, Catherine, 136–37
Kong, Xiangguo, 33
Koo, Eunsook, 210
Koolish, Lynda, 132
Koopman, Emy, 38
Kreyling, Michael, 139
Kristeva, Julia, 31, 173, 193, 195
Krumholz, Linda, 86, 111, 138, 167, 168
Krumholz, Susan, 30
Kubitschek, Missy, 65
Kübler-Ross, Elisabeth, 140
Kuehl, Linda, 76
Kuenz, Jane, 29
Kulkarni, Harihar, 32

Lacan, Jacques: *BE* and, 32, 33, 42; *Beloved* and, 128, 137; *Love* and, 194–95; *A Mercy* and, 209; *Paradise* and, 174–75; *Song of Solomon* and, 89; *Sula* and, 65
La Capra, Dominick, 174
Ladner, Joyce A., 27
Lady Esther Company, 180, 181
Lake, Christina, 126
Lange, Bonnie, 100
Langer, Adam, 163
Laplanche, Jean, 210
Larson, Charles, 75–76
Lawrence, David, 128
Lawson, Charles, 119

LeClair, Thomas, 35, 79n10
Ledbetter, Mark, 32
Lee, Catherine, 85
Lee, Dorothy, 83, 103
Lee, Hsiu-chuan, 216
Lee, Kun Jong, 62
Lee, Rachel, 66, 126
Lee, Soo-Hyun, 37
Lee, Spike, 38
Lee, Suk-Hee, 36
Lehmann-Haupt, Christopher, 54–55
Lei, Lily Wang, 189
Leonard, John, 17, 76
Lepow, Lauren, 109–10
lesbianism, 32, 58–59, 192
Lesoinne, Veronique, 157
Lesseur, Geta, 101
Levy, Andrew, 122n6
Lewis, Barbara, 150
Lewis, Charles, 125
Lewis, Miles Marshall, 221
Lewis, Sinclair, 41
Lewis, Vashti, 69
Li, Stephanie, 195
Library Journal, 16, 53, 75, 96, 116
Lilienfeld, Jane, 151–52
Lillvis, Kristen, 133
Lineham, Thomas, 138
Liscio, Lorraine, 127
Listener, 116
literacy and illiteracy, 23, 25, 43, 108, 131, 157; in *A Mercy*, 211; in *Paradise*, 159–60
Literature Interpretation Theory, 122
Littlest Rebel, The (film), 38, 39, 40
Łobodziec, Agniesz, 216
Lock, Helen, 125
Löffler, Philipp, 216
Logan, Lisa, 218
Loichot, Valérie, 81
London Review of Books, 164–65
Long, Lisa, 41
López Ramírez, Manuela, 33, 65–66, 84, 208, 210, 223, 226, 233–34
Los Angeles Times, 76, 222, 231
Lounsberry, Barbara, 21, 68, 83
Love, 5, 183–97, 232; African American/postcolonial criticism on, 189–91; book (and online) reviews of, 186–88; critical studies of, 188–97; feminist/womanist criticism on, 193–94; foreword to, 60n5, 183–86; humanistic poetics in, 197; intertextuality in, 191–92; as lesbian novel, 192; new historical/cultural criticism on, 192–93; patriarchy in, 185, 190, 193, 194, 195; psychoanalytic criticism on, 194–96
Luckhurst, Roger, 140
Lucky, Crystal, 36
Lutz, John, 108
Lyles, Lois, 134

MacKethan, Lucinda, 83
Magness, Patricia, 109, 110
Magras, Lydia, 135–36
Mahaffey, Paul, 106
Maher, Rob, 149
Major, Clarence, 19
Makino, Rie, 123
Malcolm, Cheryl, 24
Malcolm X, 38, 90
male gaze, 15, 28, 87
Malmgren, Carl D., 34, 131
Mandel, Naomi, 134
Mantel, Hilary, 204
Margaret Garner (opera), 136–37
Margaronis, Maria, 133–34
Marks, Kathleen, 33
Marshall, Paule, 23, 24, 26, 91, 116
Martin, Jacky, 131
Martin, José, 26
Martindale, Kym, 165
Martín-Salván, Paula, 234
Mason, Theodore, 84
Mathieson, Barbara, 127
Mayberry, Susan Neal: on *BE*, 31; on *Beloved*, 129; on color television, 171n4; on *Home*, 227–28; on *Jazz*, 153, 154; on *Love*, 183n1, 184, 193, 194–95; on *A Mercy*, 209; on Morrison's feminism, 57n3, 64; on *Paradise*, 170, 172; on *Song of Solomon*, 72n1, 81, 86; on *Sula*, 64; on *Tar Baby*, 109
Mbalia, Doreatha, 108, 154–55

McCarthy, Mary, 59
McClain, Ruth Rambo, 54
McClaren, James, 78–79
McDowell, Deborah, 62, 63, 64
McKay, Nellie, 43, 75n5, 81, 87n17, 105, 113, 205n3
McKee, Patricia, 67, 68, 169–70
McKible, Adam, 124
McMillan, Terry, 72, 116–17
McNamara, Marygai, 132
McWilliams, Mark, 124
Medoro, Dana, 89
Mellard, James, 174, 196
MELUS, 20, 44, 61, 81, 104, 122, 149, 167, 188–89, 206, 213, 215, 222
Melville, Herman, 49, 114, 124, 125, 216
Menand, Louis, 163
Mendelsohn, Jane, 146–47
Mercy, A, 199, 201–18, 220; African American/postcolonial criticism on, 206–7, 212; book reviews of, 203–5, 215, 221; critical studies of, 205–18; ecocriticism on, 211–12; feminist criticism on, 207–9; intertextuality in, 212–15; new historical/cultural criticism on, 215–17; pedagogical criticism on, 217–18; psychoanalytic criticism on, 209–11
Mermann-Jozwiak, Elisabeth, 29
Merrick, John, 73
Metting, Fred, 91
Michael, Magali, 173
Michlin, Monica, 25
Mickelson, Anne, 79n12
Middleton, Joyce, 43, 84–85
Midwestern Miscellany, 39, 107
Mikkelsen, Nina, 85, 125
Millar, Neil, 77
Miller, Adam, 79
Miller, Arthur, 212
Miller, Laura, 186–87, 190
Milne, Leah, 127
Milton, John, 101, 104, 161, 212, 214
Miner, Madonne, 21, 22
Minority Voices, 20, 81
Mississippi Quarterly, 99
Mitchell, Angelyn, 154–55
Mitchell, Carolyn, 126

Mitchell, Koritha, 42
Mitchell, Margaret, 123
Mix, Deborah, 173, 174
MLA International Bibliography, 1, 3, 20, 33, 38, 61, 62, 80n14, 81, 104, 117, 121–22, 149, 167, 188–89, 205–6, 222–23, 233
Mobley, Marilyn, 84, 105, 110
Mocha Moms, 185
Mock, Michele, 127
Modern Fiction Studies, 61, 104–5, 113n1, 122, 149–50, 166, 167, 174, 189, 206
modernism, 25, 41, 84, 109, 128, 134, 152, 157, 159, 218, 226; slave trade and, 190–91
modernity, 50, 69, 128, 133, 144, 146, 170
Moglene, Helene, 137
Mohanty, Satya P., 132, 141–42
Mohomet, Belali, 86
Montgomery, Maxine, 215, 224, 235
Monzón, Javier, 178n7
Moon, Set Byul, 64
Moore, Caroline, 204–5
Moore, Geneva, 214
Mootry, Maria, 75
Moqbel Al Areqi, Rashad Mohammed, 207
Moraru, Christian, 82
Moreland, Richard, 125
Morgan, Kathleen, 152
Morgenstern, Naomi, 139, 142, 208
Mori, Aoi, 155
Morris, Susana, 178, 190
Morrison, Slade, 73n4, 162, 218–19
Morrison, Toni: awards and honors for, 3, 4, 62, 78, 80, 81, 116, 117, 143, 180; classics background of, 8, 79n10, 101, 191; on conflict vs. crisis, 72n3, 238–39; editing career of, 1, 47n1, 80n12, 114; on feminism, 57–58; on literary canonization, 48–51; Louvre curatorship by, 62, 216, 218; on motives for writing, 1, 2–5, 30–31, 71, 79n10; parents and forebears of, 94, 195n5, 235n10; on politics in literature, 48–49, 78n9, 108, 237; on reader relationship, 200–201, 218; reputation of, 1–3, 62, 74–75, 78, 96,

116, 165; on role of universities, 4; teaching career of, 7, 81
Morrison, Toni, children's books by, 73n4, 162, 218
Morrison, Toni, essays, lectures, and nonfiction books by: *The Dancing Mind*, 200–201; "Grendel and His Mother," 72, 238; "Home," 3, 170, 219; Nobel Prize acceptance speech, 3, 11, 197, 201; *The Origin of Others*, 237; *Playing in the Dark*, 1, 3, 49, 86, 114, 164, 177, 201–3, 204; "Rootedness: The Ancestor as Foundation," 3, 108, 114, 176; *The Source of Self-Regard*, 2; "Unspeakable Things Unspoken," 9–10, 12, 48, 49–50, 52, 94, 114; *What Moves at the Margin*, 4
Morrison, Toni, interviews with: Als, 57; Angelo, 121; Bollen, 219n7; book collections of, 101–2; Brown, 14; Darling, 121; Davis, 129; Dowling, 76; Dreifus, 197; Horn, 121; Jaffrey, 57–58, 61, 164; LeClair, 1, 35, 69, 79n10, 93; McKay, 75n5, 87n17, 113, 145, 205n3; Moyers, 5, 50–51; Schappell, 61; Smith, 160–61
Morrison, Toni, novels by. See individual titles
Morrison, Toni, short stories by, 1, 4; "Recitatif," 61, 159, 177–81; "Sweetness," 61, 228n9
Moses, Cat, 35
motherhood (and mother–daughter relationships), 23, 27–28, 62, 64, 88, 106; in *Beloved*, 117, 127–29, 132–33, 210, 228; *Home* and "othermothering," 227–28; in *Jazz*, 155; in *Love*, 193; in *A Mercy*, 208, 210
Moya, Paula, 218
Moyers, Bill, 5, 50
Moynihan Report, 135, 140, 171, 194
Ms., 53, 116, 118n2
Mueller, Stefanie, 234
multiculturalism, 44, 129, 140–42, 187, 215
Munafo, Giavanna, 38
Murline, Anna, 163, 166
Murray, Robin, 44

Murray, Rolland, 85
music: in *BE*, 39; in *Beloved*, 131; the blues, 119n3, 156; jazz (and in *Jazz*), 39, 112, 131, 143, 144–48, 150–52, 154, 156, 174, 193; hip-hop and rap, 156, 193; in *Song of Solomon*, 84, 89; in *Sula*, 54, 67, 69; in *Tar Baby*, 95, 112
Muyumba, Walton, 232

Nag Hammadi Library, 145, 146
Nama, Charles, 101
Names: Journal of the American Name Society, 99, 100
naming: in *BE*, 23, 29; in *Song of Solomon*, 82–83; in *Sula*, 69; in *Tar Baby*, 100
Nation, The, 55, 98, 116, 119
National Book Award, 47n1, 115–16
National Review, 98
Naylor, Carolyn, 86
Naylor, Gloria, 91, 124, 125
Nedaee, Naeem, 133
Neelakantan, Gurumurthy, 30, 190
Nevins, Jake, 164
New Criterion, 146–47
New Criticism, 47, 48
New Republic, 53, 98
New Statesman, 98
Newsweek, 17, 53, 75, 76, 96, 97, 116
New Yorker, 17, 55, 57, 116, 163, 205
New York Review of Books, 75, 97, 165, 187
New York Times, 17, 57, 76, 97–98, 116, 147, 163, 186, 203–4, 220–21, 230, 238
New York Times Book Review, 16, 19, 53, 54, 76, 78, 97, 116
Ng, Andrew, 139
Ng, Lay Sion, 132
Nicholson, David, 147–48
Nicol, Kathryn, 177n5
9/11 attacks, 212, 215, 225
Nodelman, Perry, 90
Novak, Phillip, 67
Nowlin, Michael, 156
Nussbaum, Martha, 43

Oates, Joyce Carol, 172
Obama, Barack, 80, 204, 215
O'Brien, Edna, 147, 148, 153
Observer (London), 187

Obsidian: Black Literature in Review, 61, 75, 77n8, 81
Ochoa, Peggy, 135
O'Connor, Douglas, 54, 55
O'Connor, Flannery, 23
Oforlea, Aaron, 81
Ogunyemi, Chikwenye Okonjo, 69, 133
O'Keefe, Vincent, 124, 152
Oliver, Kelly, 38
Omry, Keren, 151, 174, 212
O'Neill, Caitlin, 124
oral traditions: in *BE*, 25, 39; in *Beloved*, 125, 131; in *Jazz*, 153, 157–58; in *Paradise*, 174; in *Song of Solomon*, 77, 84–85; in *Sula*, 68; in *Tar Baby*, 111
O'Reilly, Andrea, 27–28, 62, 81, 106, 155
Orr, Elaine, 81
Ortega, Gema, 31
Osagie, Iyunolu, 137
Osucha, Eden, 171
Otten, Terry, 101

Page, Philip, 50, 122n6, 154, 167, 168
Painter, Nell Irvin, 238
Pal, Payel, 30
Palladino, Mariangela, 197
Paquet, Sandra, 110
Paquet-Deyris, Anne-Marie, 136, 157
Paradise, 81, 149, 159–81, 184, 185; African American/postcolonial criticism of, 175–77; banning of, 170; book reviews of, 163–66; critical studies of, 166–77; feminist criticism on, 173–74, 175; foreword to, 113, 159–63, 164; intertextuality in, 172–73; men in, 162–64, 170–71, 176; Native Americans in, 172–73; new historical/cultural criticism on, 168–72; psychoanalytic criticism on, 174–75; reader-response criticism on, 167–68; "Recitatif" and, 177–81; westerns and, 170–71
Parker, Emma, 139
Parrish, Timothy, 124
Pass, Olivia, 140
pastoral mode, 90, 203–4, 214, 223
Pattison, Dale, 153
Paul, Saint, 197

Peach, Linden, 29, 64
Pearce, Richard, 155–56
Peirce, Charles S., 139
Penner, Erin, 226
Peoples, Tim, 26
Pereira, Malin, 37–38
Pérez-Torres, Rafael, 43
Perry, Imani, 81
Pessoni, Michele, 21–22
Peterson, Christopher, 140
Peterson, James, 211
Peterson, Nancy J., 2, 61, 105, 113, 138n11, 149–50, 156, 216
Pettis, Joyce, 27
Phelan, James, 141, 150, 178n7
Phipps, Keith, 166, 188
Phylon, 61
Pici, Nicholas, 150
Pickney, Darryl, 187–88
Pieces I Am, The (documentary), 2, 19
Pipes, Candice, 224–25
Plato, 23
PMLA, 122
Pocock, Judy, 91
Podolsky, Marjorie, 88
Poe, Edgar Allan, 114
Portales, Marco, 43
postmodernism, 2, 33, 41, 108; *Beloved* and, 126, 134, 138; *Jazz* and, 154; *Love* and, 189; *A Mercy* and, 216; *Paradise* and, 159; *Tar Baby* and, 110, 112
Potter, George, 24
Powell, Betty, 138
Powell, Timothy, 35–36, 68–69, 82
"presence of absence," 66, 115, 134, 148, 154, 219
Previn, André, 219
Price, Reynolds, 76
Prince, Jocelyn, 42
Pringle, Mary Beth, 107
Pryse, Marjorie, 157
Progressive, 98
Publishers Weekly, 53, 75, 96, 148
Pynchon, Thomas, 173

Qasim, Khamsa, 31
queer studies, 64, 65, 122n6, 209. *See also* lesbianism

race and racism: in films, 39–40, 42; Morrison on, 2–3, 50–51, 66, 230; US Army and, 224–25
Ragaišienė, Irena, 37
Rahman, Shafiqur, 33
Ramadanovic, Petar, 133
Ramey, Deanna, 88
Ramos, Peter, 123
Rampersad, Arnold, 105
Ramsey, William, 91, 126
Rand, Lizabeth A., 20n6, 27
Randle, Gloria, 138
Rank, Otto, 87
Ransom, John Crowe, 237
rape: in *BE*, 11, 16, 21, 23, 28, 29, 30, 38, 40, 185, 228n9, 229; in *Love*, 185, 191; in *A Mercy*, 207
Rashad, Phylicia, 184n2
Ravell-Pinto, Thelma, 24
Rayson, Ann, 106, 179
Read, Andrew, 175
Reagan administration, 89, 135, 140
Reed, Harry, 89–90
Reed, Ishmael, 91
Reed, Roxanne, 131
Reneau, Ingrid, 142
Reyes, Angelita, 101, 108, 109, 110
Rice, Alan, 36, 112, 132, 151
Richards, Phillip, 68
Riley, Jeannette, 30
Rimmon-Kenan, Shlomith, 153
Roark, Chris, 25–26
Robbins, Sarah, 124
Robinson, Timothy, 176
Robolin, Stéphane, 173, 174
Rodgers, Norma, 78
Rodrigues, Eusebio, 150
Rodriguez, Denise, 127
Rody, Caroline, 134
Roe, Frances, 199–200
Rogin, Michael, 48–49
Rokonitz, Naomi, 33
Romagnolo, Catherine, 20n6, 31
Romantic movement, 125, 213
Romero, Channette, 169
Roselezam Wan Yahya, Wan, 155
Rosenberg, Ruth, 27, 82
Roth, Philip, 20n6

Rothberg, Michael, 91
Roye, Susmita, 30–31, 207
Roynon, Tessa, 30, 191, 199–200, 201, 207, 212, 214, 219
Royster, Phillip, 69, 83
Rubenstein, Roberta, 152, 156
Rumens, Carol, 119
Rummell, Kathryn, 133
Ruprecht, Louis, Jr., 217
Rushdy, Ashraf, 127
Ryan, Judylyn, 106, 157
Ryan, Katy, 126

SAGE, 20, 61, 81, 99
Sairsingh, Marie, 207
Saldinar, José David, 101
Sale, Maggie, 131
Salvatore, Anne, 37, 126
Salve, J., 37
Samantary, Swati, 40
Sampson-Choma, Tosha, 227
Samuels, Wilfrid, 80
Sanchez-Scott, Milcha, 24
Sandy, Mark, 213–14
Sapphire, 25, 156, 193–94
Sargent, Robert, 27
Saturday Review, 76
Satz, Martha, 64
Saunders, James, 25
Scarpa, Giulia, 90
Schapiro, Barbara, 138
Schappell, Elissa, 61
Scheiber, Andrew, 157
Schell, David, 173
Schiavoone, Michelle, 24
Schindler, Melissa, 225–26
Schmudde, Carol, 130
Schreiber, Evelyn Jaffee, 20n6, 24, 66, 81, 137, 195–96, 210
Schroeder, Aribert, 23–24
Schueller, Malini, 133
Schultz, Elizabeth, 103
Schur, Richard, 175
Schuster, Donna, 141
Schwartz-Bart, Simone, 90
Scott, Lynn, 25, 39
Scruggs, Charles, 82, 130
Sempruch, Justyna, 173

Sethi, Anita, 187
Sewanee Review, 98
Shakespeare, William, 48, 149; *Hamlet*, 25–26; *The Tempest*, 112; *The Winter's Tale*, 152
Shange, Ntozake, 109
Sheed, Wilfrid, 96
Sheppard, R. Z., 96
Sherard, Tracey, 156
Sherman, Sarah, 29
Shoah (documentary), 134
Showalter, Elaine, 187, 188, 190
Shuman, Amy, 178n7
Silko, Leslie Marmon, 20n6, 123
Simms, Maria, 132
Simon, Libby, 215
Simpson, Ritashona, 20n6
Singh, Monika, 31
Sissman, L. E., 17–18
Sitter, Deborah, 128
Skeeter, Sharyn, 18
Skinner, Pat, 132
Sklar, Howard, 178n7
slave narratives, 23, 109, 124, 131, 134, 213; neo-slave narratives, 25, 127, 131, 139, 214
slavery, 65, 86, 89, 110–11, 126n8, 156, 190–91; in *Beloved*, 114–17, 120–25, 127–28, 131–32, 137–38, 142; in *A Mercy*, 202–10, 213, 216–17
Smith, Abraham, 84
Smith, Barbara, 55, 56, 62–63, 64, 192
Smith, Bessie, 136
Smith, Cynthia J., 56, 57, 110
Smith, Valerie, 139
Smith, Victoria, 140
Smith-Rosenberg, Carroll, 59
Snitow, Anita, 119
Sobat, Gail, 125
Søfting, Inger-Anne, 39
Sokolov, Raymond, 17
Somerville, Jane, 28
Song of Solomon, 14, 71–92, 126; African American/postcolonial criticism on, 74–75, 77–78, 84–86; awards for, 4, 96; banning of, 80; book reviews of, 74–78; conundrums in, 71, 72, 72n1, 73, 74, 78, 92; critical studies of, 20n5, 21, 78–92; feminist/womanist criticism on, 86–88; foreword to, 71–74, 78, 94; intertextuality in, 90–92; men in, 71–72, 77–78, 85–87; myths and archetypes in, 71, 75, 80, 82–84, 87, 89, 213; new historical/cultural criticism on, 89–90; psychoanalytic criticism on, 88–89
Sophocles, 89
Southern Review, 116
Spacks, Patricia Meyer, 56
Spallino, Chiaro, 82
Spargo, Christian, 139
Spectator, 98
Spielberg, Steven, 216
Spigner, Nieda, 99
Spillers, Hortense, 62, 103
Staggers, Leroy, 15, 18, 53–55, 56, 74, 76–77, 95–98, 99–100, 104, 117, 119, 120
Stampfl, Barry, 139
Stanley, Sandra, 178n7
Stave, Shirley, 25, 126, 197, 209–10, 227, 235
Stein, Jean, 200
Stein, Karen, 69, 80
Stewart, Garrett, 216–17
Stewart, Jacqueline, 42
Stillman-Webb, Natalie, 155
Stockton, Kathryn, 65, 134
Storhoff, Gary, 89
Story, Ralph, 90, 127
Stowe, Harriet Beecher, 43, 123–24, 128–29
Strehle, Susan, 215n6
Strouse, Jean, 96
Stryz, Jan, 91–92, 125
Stuart, Andrea, 204
Studies in American Fiction, 99, 101, 122, 167
Styron, William, 125
Subryan, Carmen, 88
Suggs, Jon-Christian, 135
suicide, 51, 72, 73, 126
Sula, 1, 47–69, 93, 126; book reviews of, 19, 53–56; critical studies of, 21, 27, 56–69, 74; feminist/womanist criticism on, 56–61, 62–64, 69, 79n11, 192; foreword to, 47–53, 93–94, 113,

115; as "nigger joke," 65, 69; other critical approaches to, 66–69, 80; psychoanalytic criticism on, 64–66, 223; queer studies and, 64, 65
Sullivan, Mecca, 194
Sulter, Maud, 165
Surányi, Ágnes, 31
Sweeny, Megan, 170, 192
Sydney, Philip, 74

Tabone, Mark, 171
Tabur, Şemsettin, 212
Tafreshi, Leila, 155
Tait, Althea, 30
Tally, Justine, 174, 212
Tanaka, Hisae, 24
Tanritanir, Bülent, 31
Tar Baby, 93–112, 194; African American/postcolonial criticism on, 110–12; book reviews of, 95–100; color imagery in, 100; critical studies of, 28, 101–12; feminist/womanist criticism on, 101, 106; foreword to, 93–95; *Home* and, 227; Marxist criticism on, 107, 108–9; myths and archetypes in, 100, 103, 109–10; psychoanalytic criticism on, 107–8
Tate, Claudia, 79
Taylor, Paul, 38
Taylor-Guthrie, Danille K., 101, 126
Telegraph (London), 164, 204, 221
Temple, Joanne, 54
Temple, Shirley, 38, 40, 43
Terrell, Lyne, 35
Terry, Jennifer, 85, 212
Terzieva-Artemis, Rossitsa, 139
Thomas, Jackie, 85
Thomas, Leester, 32
Thomas, Nigel, 90
Thomas, Valorie, 91, 225
Thoreau, Henry David, 23, 214
Thorsson, Courtney, 192
Thorsteinson, Katherine, 86
Thurman, Judith, 119
Tibbetts, John, 136
Tidey, Ashley, 88
Time, 76, 96, 97, 116, 119, 165
Times Literary Supplement, 54, 77, 119

Toni Morrison Society, 180, 184, 218–19
Toomer, Jean, 49
Torrens, Kathleen, 30
Towner, Theresa, 23, 214–15
Travis, Molly, 131, 140–41
Traylor, Eleanor, 108
Treherne, Matthew, 153
trickster figures, 156, 189
Truman, Harry S., 225
Trump, Donald, 237
Turner, Darwin T., 102–3
Tutuola, Amos, 91
Twain, Mark, 114, 123, 125
Tyler, Anne, 77

Ulin, David, 222, 231, 232
Umeh, Marie, 23
Umoja, 77n8
United Nations Food and Agriculture Organization, 109
Updike, John, 205, 221–22
U.S. News & World Report, 116, 163

Van Der Zee, James, 143–44
Vasquez, Shalene, 26
Vaughan, Sarah, 147
Vega-González, Susana, 69, 90, 107, 189, 209
Vendrame, Alessandra, 91
Venkatesan, Sathyaraj, 190
Vickroy, Laurie, 24, 64, 134, 211
Village Voice, 54, 75, 76, 97, 119, 146
Vinson, Audrey L., 113
Vint, Sherryl, 131
Visser, Irene, 226
Visvis, Vikki, 84

Wade-Gayles, Gloria, 23
Waegner, Cathy, 206
Wagner, Linda, 43, 103
Walker, Alice, 19, 49, 116, 120; *The Color Purple*, 7n1, 24, 25, 26, 59–60, 121, 136; *Meridian*, 57; *The Temple of My Familiar*, 124; *The Third Life of Grange Copeland*, 124; and "womanist" term, 22n9, 57, 128n9
Walker, Kara, 230–31
Walker, Madam C. J., 181, 229–30, 234

Wall, Cheryl, 26, 91
Wallace, Cynthia, 138, 197
Wallace, Maurice, 157–58
Wall Street Journal, 119
Walters, Wendy, 86
Walther, Malin, 28, 87–88, 112
Wang, Elaine, 141
Wang, Quan, 89
Wardi, Anissa, 69, 109, 125, 128, 136, 191, 211
Warhol, Robyn, 178n7
Warnes, Andrew, 108–9
Washington, Mary Helen, 63
Washington, Theresa, 133
Washington Post, 53–54, 75, 147–48, 220
Watson, Reginal, 124
Waxman, Barbara, 44
Weathers, Glenda, 124
Weems, Renita, 27
Wegs, Joyce, 84
Weinstock, Jeffrey Andrew, 140
Weixlmann, Joe, 90
Welles, Orson, 181
Werner, Craig Hansen, 109–10, 157
Werrlein, Debra, 40
West, Dorothy, 23
Whatever Happened to Baby Jane? (film), 59
Wheatley, Phillis, 49
White, Artress, 207
White, Jeanne, 134
white characters, 9, 11, 19, 28, 76n7; in *Beloved*, 129; in *Paradise*, 162; in "Recitatif," 177–81; in *Tar Baby*, 97, 104, 108
white gaze, 8, 14–15, 17, 19–20, 51, 228–29
white guilt, 77
Whitehead, Colson, 91, 125–26
whiteness, 1, 17–18, 32, 44
white privilege, 42–43
white supremacy, 135, 206
white universalism, 162
Wicomb, Zoë, 174
Widdowson, Peter, 163

Wideman, John Edgar, 116
Wierzbinski, Jessica, 91
Wigan, Angela, 76
Wilentz, Gay, 69, 83
Willard, Mara, 217
Williams, Dana, 176–77
Williams, Sherley Anne, 124, 125
Williams, William Carlos, 173
Willis, Ardelia, 94, 194, 195n5
Willis, Susan, 36, 38, 112
Wilson, Elizabeth, 25
Wilson, Harriet, 49
Wilson, Michael, 67–68
Winchell, Donna, 125
Winfrey, Oprah (and Book Club), 2, 41–42, 80, 89, 90, 136, 166, 167, 200
Winnicott, D. W., 208
Winthrop, John, 161, 215
Woff, Alice, 16
Woidat, Caroline, 125
Wolfe, Joanna, 131
Wolter, Jürgen, 125
Womack, Craig, 172–73
Wong, Shelley, 36
Woodward, Kathleen, 39
Woolf, Virginia, 23, 123, 152, 226
Wordsworth, William, 125, 200, 213–14
Wright, Richard, 23, 57, 75n6, 83, 125–26
Wu, Yung-Hsing, 141
Wyatt, Jean, 108, 128, 195–96, 210
Wyman, Sarah, 125

Yale Review, 98
Yancy, George, 32
Yanyan, Zhu, 89
Yardley, Jonathan, 53–54
Yates-Richard, Meina, 90
Yeates, Robert, 133
Yoo, Jae Eun, 193, 225
Young, Harvey, 42
Young, John, 41–42, 90
Young, Robert, 23

Zauditu-Selassie, Kokahvah, 110
Žižek, Slavoj, 174–75, 196

www.ingramcontent.com/pod-product-compliance
Lightning Source LLC
Chambersburg PA
CBHW051601230426
43668CB00013B/1935